Churchill's Dilemma

Churchill's Dilemma

The Real Story Behind the Origins of the 1915 Dardanelles Campaign

GRAHAM T. CLEWS

AN IMPRINT OF ABC-CLIO, LLC
Santa Barbara, California • Denver, Colorado • Oxford, England

Library of Congress Cataloging-in-Publication Data

Clews, Graham T.
Churchill's dilemma : the real story behind the origins of the 1915 Dardanelles Campaign / Graham T. Clews.
p. cm.
Includes bibliographical references and index.
ISBN 978-0-313-38474-5 (hardcopy : alk. paper) — ISBN 978-0-313-38475-2 (ebook) 1. World War, 1914–1918—Campaigns—Turkey—Gallipoli Peninsula. 2. Churchill, Winston, 1874–1965—Military leadership. I. Title.
D568.3.C54 2010
940.4'26—dc22 2010015942

ISBN: 978-0-313-38474-5
EISBN: 978-0-313-38475-2

14 13 12 11 10 1 2 3 4 5

This book is also available on the World Wide Web as an eBook. Visit www.abc-clio.com for details.

Praeger
An Imprint of ABC-CLIO, LLC

ABC-CLIO, LLC
130 Cremona Drive, P.O. Box 1911
Santa Barbara, California 93116-1911

This book is printed on acid-free paper ∞

Manufactured in the United States of America

To Juliet,
Amery, and Imogen

Contents

Acknowledgments

The completion of this work has been a long, albeit stimulating and enjoyable experience. It has undoubtedly tested the forbearance and patience of my supervisor, Professor Robin Prior, and my wife, Juliet, and to them I give my special thanks.

Robin has guided me through this study over a number of years and I have considered myself blessed to have had access to his wisdom and advice during this time.

Juliet has given me the support that only a spouse can. She has shared all the ups and downs of this project. It would probably not have been completed without her.

My thanks must also go to Geoffrey Miller and Edward Erikson. Each has completed works cited in this project. In the early stages of my research, I was fortunate to establish a much-valued correspondence with Geoffrey and Edward. In particular, Geoffrey provided me with access to documents that otherwise might only have been gained through a trip to England.

I would also like to thank Bernadette McDermott. In her position as school administrator, Bernadette has assisted me in innumerable ways over a number of years and has generally been a real lifesaver. Thank you, Bernadette.

In more recent times, as this work has progressed from thesis to book, the list of those I must acknowledge has grown. At the top of this list is Michael Millman of Praeger (ABC-CLIO). His faith in this work has been the foundation of all that has followed. Additionally, I offer a general "thank you" to all of the staff of ABC-CLIO who contributed to bringing this work through to publication. It is clearly a substantial team effort.

I also express my appreciation to the Trustees of the Liddell Hart Centre for Military Archives at King's College London for their permission to cite from the Robertson Papers.

Thanks, also, must go to the staff of the Imperial War Museum, the Australian War Museum, the Library of Congress, and the Ulster Folk and Transport Museum (with particular thanks to Mr. Alan McCartney) for their assistance in securing the images used in this book.

Finally, I would like to thank my good friend, John Gilbert. It was his efforts, some considerable time ago now, that started me along this most interesting journey.

Introduction

In August 1911, Winston Churchill became First Lord of the Admiralty and, thereby, inherited one of the most powerful military weapons on the face of the earth. This extraordinary inheritance came at a time when Britain was resigning herself to the probability she would soon become embroiled in a war with Germany on the European continent alongside the French Army. This book is a study of Churchill's search for the ways and means to bring to bear, in a decisive manner, the immense offensive power of the British Navy upon this continental conflict.

Although other schemes will be considered, two offensive thrusts—each intimately linked to the other—take center stage in this work. The first is Churchill's advocacy, from the earliest days of the war, of full-scale amphibious operations along the northern coastline of Europe. The second is Churchill's promotion of a naval-only attempt to force the Dardanelles in January 1915.

Churchill's northern schemes, best exemplified by his Borkum/Baltic plans, were borrowed from ideas for close blockade and military descents conceived by Lord Fisher and Sir Arthur Wilson between 1905 and 1908. Churchill believed that Borkum, the westernmost of Germany's East Frisian islands, could be successfully occupied to blockade the Ems Estuary and facilitate mighty amphibious assaults on Schleswig-Holstein and Germany's Baltic coastline.

His first sea lords' enthusiasm for such adventures diminished in the reality of war, but Churchill developed and retained an extraordinary preoccupation with them.

Almost as soon as he became first lord, Churchill endeavored to instill an offensive spirit into his navy. Although he would commit himself to ensuring that his navy facilitated the rapid movement of a British Expeditionary Force to France in the event of war with Germany, Churchill dreamt of amphibious operations based on the old Admiralty plans that would engender a lively offensive vigor in the fleet, possibly open new fronts and bring in new allies and, ultimately, contribute to Germany's rapid defeat.

Churchill, however, would find it almost impossible to overcome the reservations of his naval planners, who were unable to find a solution to the sea mine, the submarine, and the large-caliber shore batteries, which could be used against any amphibious assault force operating near Germany. Then, in the opening months of the war, Churchill would discover his own solution—the big-gunned monitor. Although these vessels would never fulfill his expectations, they became the centerpiece of Churchill's plans for decisive amphibious assaults upon Europe and his ongoing hopes for a quick war. His belief in these vessels was no mere whimsy. It developed as a real, deep-seated conviction, which ultimately would have an enormous influence on his role as first lord.

Churchill's second major offensive thrust, the Dardanelles operation, is the much more publicly well known and manifest example of Churchill's offensive spirit. This campaign has acquired notoriety inconsistent with either the military commitment involved in it or the casualties it generated. The interest it engenders perhaps stems primarily from the involvement of Churchill in its conception and flawed execution and the fact that it led to his dismissal as first lord in May 1915.

Despite much historical argument to the contrary and despite the central position the Dardanelles operation holds in most studies of Churchill in World War I, it will be a central contention of the present work that this operation was, as far as Churchill was concerned, always of *secondary* importance to his northern aspirations. Moreover, it will be further contended that his ongoing pursuit of his northern schemes seriously compromised the planning for, and outcomes of, the assault on the Dardanelles in 1915.

The historical view of Churchill's involvement in the Dardanelles operation has continued to evolve. Although there are numerous exceptions of his involvement, early scholarship tended to accept the brilliance of the conception and its potential consequences—the removal of Turkey from the war and the opening of a Balkan Front. This scholarship also readily accepted the idea that, from the earliest moments of the war, Churchill's eyes were focused on a southern front as a means of avoiding the bloody deadlock in the West. Additionally, these scholars were inclined to accept the arguments presented by Churchill himself in *The World Crisis* that reasons for the failure of the Dardanelles plan were to be found in faulty execution—not of his making—and not in a flawed conception.

Rarely, if ever, did these early studies of the Dardanelles campaign mention, even in passing, Churchill's interest in Borkum or the Baltic. Despite Churchill acknowledging his interest in the Baltic in *The World Crisis*, it was not until the works of the 1960s and 1970s that historians began to realize that an accurate perspective on the origins of the Dardanelles must provide a consideration of these northern ambitions.

By the 1990s, scholarship had established with growing clarity that Churchill's commitment to the Dardanelles and a southern front was much less than Churchill would have had us believe. This work demonstrated that, as late as January 1915, the idea of an attack on the Dardanelles was only one of a number of offensive schemes being considered by Churchill and that his preference for an offensive lay, first and foremost, in the northern theater.

Even these studies, however, were uniform in their conviction that, by the end of January 1915, Churchill had lost interest in the north and, thereafter, was consumed by the promise offered by the Dardanelles operation. Two recent assessments have described the origins of the Dardanelles campaign in the following manner. The first acknowledged Churchill's interest in Borkum and noted his rather telling declaration of January 4, 1915, in response to proposals for operations in the Mediterranean, that "Germany is the foe, and it is bad war to seek cheaper victories and easier antagonists." This assessment went on to assert that, soon after receiving the telegram from Vice Adm. Sackville Carden (commander, Anglo-French Squadrons Eastern Mediterranean) regarding the forcing of the Dardanelles, Churchill's strategic views underwent an extraordinary and absolute transformation: "Borkum was forgotten. All his energies were focused, laser like, on this new enterprise, with all the opportunities it seemed to offer for breaking the deadlock of the war."[1]

The second work argued that Churchill reluctantly adopted the "naval-only" Dardanelles project in January 1915, after he realized that land forces were not available for operations in either northern or southern Europe and that, even when forces became available, the War Council would not support his northern schemes. Additionally, it was argued that Churchill's decision was influenced by a growing conviction that the decisive naval engagement against the German fleet, viewed as a necessary preliminary to the execution of any northern amphibious offensive operations, was no longer likely to occur. Only then did he "seize" upon Carden's Dardanelles plan and "once the opportunity had presented itself and the basic decision had been taken, he obstinately clung to the plan."[2]

These assessments are important because they recognize Churchill's considerable northern offensive ambitions, and they establish a close link between the origins of the two peripheral strategies.

At their core, however, these assessments are incorrect. Although they recognize a link between the Borkum/Baltic plans and Churchill's Dardanelles operation, they fundamentally misunderstand the nature of that link. The error in argument lies in the belief that Churchill adopted and promoted the "naval-only" assault on the Dardanelles only after he had discarded, reluctantly or otherwise, his northern aspirations. This work will argue that Churchill's promotion of the naval-only attempt to force the Dardanelles is best explained by the fact that, from the conception to conclusion of this operation, his strategic priorities remained firmly in Northern Europe.

This perspective rejects any description of Churchill as a *Southerner (or Easterner)* and Fisher as a *Northerner* in the sense of Grand Strategy. In January 1915, while steadily promoting the Dardanelles operation, Churchill remained a committed *Northerner*, while it is arguable that such labels are entirely inappropriate for Fisher at all. Indeed, such labels are not helpful in unraveling what took place throughout January 1915. This is because both Churchill and Fisher viewed the various operations mooted at this time, not in terms of north and south or east, but as short-, medium-, and long-term operations, and major versus subsidiary. Historians err when assuming that the adoption of one operation necessarily excluded another. The adoption of Carden's naval-only operation did not, in Churchill's eyes, exclude any of his major schemes including the Borkum/Baltic operation or his hopes to invade Schleswig-Holstein and bring Holland into the war. On this point, one might let Churchill speak for himself from an early draft of *The World Crisis*:

> Up till the end of 1914 I was working at the Borkum-Baltic plan, encountering some opposition, much apathy, but also enjoying a

> great deal of support, especially from Fisher. . . . Anyhow it had been clear from the beginning that many months would be required before any decision other than preparation and study need be taken as far as the Northern Borkum movement was concerned. Meanwhile the naval operation at the Dardanelles, which was a far smaller and less formidable business, would either fail or succeed. If it failed, then very likely I should be made the scapegoat and the responsibility for further events would be passed to others. If it succeeded, we should gain the prestige, which alone would enable so terrific and deadly a business as the storming of Borkum . . . to be carried out. . . . even while the Dardanelles was on I always regarded it as [long] as I was in office only as an interim operation, and all the plans for the Borkum-Baltic project going forward.[3]

It has been suggested that Churchill rejected this draft and others like it because he "was concerned that the Dardanelles plan should be viewed as the great strategic conception of the war, not merely as the preliminary to another enterprise which had been almost universally condemned as being too hazardous and not likely to achieve any lasting results."[4] Although I will not agree with everything Churchill had to say in this quotation, I will argue that it reflects with reasonable accuracy the real status of the Dardanelles scheme in the early months of 1915. The Dardanelles operation was an interim plan, the success of which would help overcome the resistance Churchill was then experiencing toward his Northern operations.

I accept the fact that Churchill was at all times more keen on the Borkum/Baltic plans than Fisher, whose ambivalence has been noted in Ruddock Mackay's detailed biography. This perspective is in fundamental disagreement with one of the most recent books on the subject, Geoffrey Penn's *Fisher, Churchill and the Dardanelles*. Penn's book takes the view that Fisher's inspired Baltic schemes were stymied by Churchill's ambitions in the Dardanelles and, he generally appears to believe that this was a great misfortune. The various plans for the northern theater were, indeed, overtaken by the Dardanelles, but Churchill never wanted this. As to the merit of amphibious operations over a continental commitment, despite the great tragedy of the Western Front, no supporter of maritime peripheral strategy has yet satisfactorily explained how this strategy might have prevented the defeat of the French Army in the opening weeks of the war or might have prevented or reduced the conflagration that followed without giving Germany hegemony in Europe.

In light of the quotations above, an important question arises: To what extent did Churchill's ongoing commitment to a northern peripheral strategy affect the conception and execution of the Dardanelles operation? As intimated, this study will argue that the effect was significant—and negative.

Central to my thesis will be the issue of troops. One of the more cherished assumptions surrounding the origins of the Dardanelles is an acceptance of Churchill's assertion in *The World Crisis* and elsewhere that he would have preferred a "joint" operation, but he did not believe troops were available or would be made available away from the Western Front. In a preamble to the Dardanelles Commission in 1916, Churchill unequivocally declared that

> Had the decision of affairs rested with me throughout, I should undoubtedly have attacked the Gallipoli Peninsula with an army and a fleet at the first opportunity when joint forces were available, and I should never have put my question of the 3rd January to Admiral Carden, which resulted in the production of the purely naval plan.[5]

I do not seek to dispute Churchill's awareness of the advantages of a joint operation nor, in a world of unlimited troops, that he would have preferred military assistance. January 1915, however, was a time of troop shortages and competing schemes for offensive operations. Among these schemes—always in competition with the essential need to feed the Western Front—were Churchill's and Fisher's northern plans and the proposals from within the War Council for major operations in the Mediterranean. Churchill was reluctant to support military operations in a southern theater because they would have spread the available troops too thinly and compromised his northern ambitions. In short, Churchill did not seek the use of troops in the Mediterranean because he did not want them.

Churchill conceived and viewed his naval-only scheme as an experiment—a mere interlude—preceding what he hoped would be the beginning of major operations in the North in the spring or early summer. He saw the Dardanelles operation as a low-risk opportunity to unite the Balkan States, create a Balkan Front, and knock Turkey out of the war. It involved old, redundant battleships, the loss of which would not affect the balance of naval power in the North Sea. It was an operation that could be terminated quickly if it failed to prosper and, most important, it offered success with minimal commitment of British troops.

Churchill undoubtedly always recognized that the likelihood of achieving his two objectives, the forcing of the Dardanelles and, subsequently, the creation of a Balkan Front, was just as limited as the resources he originally had been prepared to commit to it.

Churchill's hopes of limiting the military commitment to the southern theater began to come unstuck in late January 1915. By this time, the expectations for the Dardanelles operation began to move beyond what was ever likely to be delivered by a naval-only operation. Moreover, the secretary of state for war, Lord Kitchener, began viewing success at the Dardanelles as a possible precursor to a great southern offensive through Hungary with 400,000 men. This was entirely incompatible with Churchill's own hopes of using the New Armies in a great northern offensive in May or June.

Churchill failed to respond appropriately to these burgeoning expectations of the War Council. At the heart of these high hopes was his failure to adequately address the limitations of a naval-only operation. In particular, he obfuscated over the ability of the fleet to put the guns protecting the Straits *permanently* out of action and refused to address the near impossibility of the fleet securing its own lines of communications once inside the Marmora. Without secure lines of communications, however, the fleet was unlikely to achieve much lasting value.

As the naval-only operation progressed, the issue of "communications" became even more important because the War Council developed the expectation that Churchill's naval operation would secure the entrance into the Marmora of a force of 60,000 to 85,000 men.

This expectation is a matter of critical importance in any analysis of the Dardanelles operation yet it is entirely neglected by historians. Those who have studied the merit or otherwise of the naval-only operation have failed to grasp that, from late February onward, the Dardanelles operation was no longer naval-only in concept. Although it continued to be expected that the navy would force the Straits with little or no military assistance, by this time everyone within the War Council, including Churchill, assumed that a military force would be needed to gain and secure any advantage from the navy's success and that this force would be required to enter the Marmora. The question was how this was to be achieved by a naval operation designed to admit fully armored ships only through the Straits? The reality was that troops were likely to enter the Marmora only if at least one side and probably both sides of the Straits had first been occupied.

The issue of the fleet's lines of "communications" into the Marmora and the manner in which Churchill dealt with or failed to deal with this issue will be a consistent thread throughout this study, and in the final analysis, it will be argued that it was this matter, along with the belated appreciation that a large body of troops would be needed at Constantinople to secure success, that terminated Churchill's naval-only operation at the Dardanelles. With this failure, so too ended his northern dreams.

Churchill waited far too long before he sought, in any emphatic way, a military force with which to support his naval operations. He did so despite a full awareness that, without troops, the fleet alone would have great difficulty in achieving the political and military successes expected of it—most particularly, as time went on, the provision of the conditions under which a military force could enter the Marmora. He allowed the War Council to believe the fleet could achieve much more by itself than it was ever reasonable to expect. He hoped the success of the fleet might be sufficient to draw in the Balkan States and, thereby, limit the commitment of British troops to the theater. When he did call for troops from mid-February onward he did so to bolster this strategy, not to replace it.

Despite the growing availability of troops, and the expectation they would be used in the Marmora, Churchill never relented on his naval-only timetable and, for as long as possible, attempted to maintain the naval-only orientation of the Dardanelles operation.

He could take no other course because he continued to hope his northern schemes might begin in May or June 1915. A full-scale amphibious operation to secure the Peninsula—the only probable way success would be achieved at Constantinople and certainly the only way troops ever would enter the Marmora—would ensure substantial delay and seriously compromise his northern plans.

An important part of this study will be a consideration of the mystery surrounding the 29th Division. It is known to students of this period that, after planning a naval-only operation and clinging to this idea long after everyone else had lost confidence in it, Churchill had an apparent change of heart and became vociferously insistent that the 29th Division be sent *immediately* to the Mediterranean. He found it difficult to justify his insistence on these troops because he simultaneously maintained they were not required to support the initial naval operations and already more than 60,000 troops were available for other contingencies. Not surprisingly, this situation led one or two of his War Council colleagues—and subsequently a number of historians as well—to suggest that he had lost confidence in the naval-only operation and that he intended, and fully expected, to use the troops to help force the Dardanelles in a full-scale amphibious assault.

An alternative perspective can explain Churchill's insistence on the 29th Division and one that more reasonably reflects the circumstances of the time and the actions of Churchill. Additionally, this study will explicate Churchill's apparent surrender to a full-scale southern offensive in late February 1915. Once again, the source of these answers will be found in his ongoing determination to fulfill his northern plans.

Finally, in presenting my case, I will challenge much of the accepted lore surrounding Churchill and the Dardanelles. I contend that Churchill was well aware of the prevailing Admiralty opinion surrounding the issue of ships versus forts—especially that of Lord Fisher—and that, had he heeded such opinion, he would not have gone forward with the operation. At the same time, I will argue that all such opinion was largely immaterial to Churchill's decision to proceed with the operation. Indeed, I will suggest that a prime motivating force for the operation, again in the nature of experimentation, was to prove a case for ships over forts. This, he hoped, would advance his ongoing plans to attack Borkum and gain the credibility and moral advantage that a successful operation of this nature could offer.

The role of Lord Fisher will be considered in detail. Claims of ambivalence, inconsistency, and silence at vital junctures on the behalf of his first sea lord are often used by Churchill and, subsequently, by many historians to support the argument that the emergence of Fisher's violent opposition in late January 1915 represented a surprising *volte face* in his opinion of the project. It is possible that Churchill gained succor from some elements within the Admiralty, but it is more likely than generally considered that little support came from Fisher. It will be shown that Fisher consistently maintained an entirely negative attitude toward naval-only operations and such an opinion was well known to Churchill. The mystery surrounding his offer of the *Queen Elizabeth,* and the consternation surrounding his relative silence on the Dardanelles operation before January 13, and his subsequent outspoken opposition to the enterprise soon thereafter will be explored.

Lord Kitchener's role in the Dardanelles will be reassessed. Kitchener generally has come off too lightly for his part in the Dardanelles debacle. Glib explanations of Kitchener being captivated by Churchill's glowing description of the mighty guns of the fleet—especially those of the *Queen Elizabeth*—will not do. I will show that

Kitchener had already formed his own opinion on the ships versus forts issue months before the Dardanelles operation.

Additionally, although Kitchener's expectations for the Dardanelles were premised on the conviction the fleet could and would make inoperable the fortifications protecting the Straits, it was his own disdain for his Turkish enemy as much as Churchill's enthusiasm for the operation that sustained the naval-only concept. At the very least, Kitchener must share equal responsibility for the Dardanelles debacle. It was surely the least impressive performance of his career.

I also will address other issues. I will argue that the Russian call for a diversion on January 1 had almost nothing to do with the decision to force the Dardanelles operations on January 13. Finally, I will address the hitherto largely unexplored matter of Churchill's attitude to the neutral states of Europe in World War I. I will show that his attitude was hard and uncompromising. He frequently viewed the needs and interests of the various neutrals as incompatible with Britain's own. Of particular concern was his long-held apprehension that the actions of neutrals would compromise the value of the economic blockade of Germany. On the other hand, the occupation of neutral ports or islands would not only tighten the economic noose around Germany's neck to the point where the High Seas Fleet would be forced to battle, but also would provide the springboard for a variety of offensive schemes. His views were rarely, if ever, supported by anyone in either political or military spheres, and they became particularly problematic and unwelcome when Britain finally entered the war as a defender of Belgian neutrality. Nevertheless, in the early months of the war, Churchill continued to anticipate that Britain would press one or other of the neutral states in a manner that would be advantageous for blockade and his own offensive aspirations.

NOTES

1. Michael Howard, "Churchill and the First World War," Chapter 8, in *Churchill*, ed. Robert Blake and William Roger Louis (Oxford: Oxford University Press, 1994), 137.

2. Tuvia Ben-Moshe, *Churchill: Strategy and History* (Boulder, CO: Lynne Rienner, 1992), 44.

3. Cited in Robin Prior, "Churchill's 'World Crisis' as History" (bound thesis, University of Adelaide, 1979), 200–201.

4. Ibid., 264.

5. Public Record Office, CAB 19/28 (hereafter CAB).

CHAPTER 1

Britain's Defense Policy, 1900–1911

The first decade of the 20th century was a period of momentous change in the British Army and Navy. During these 10 years, the size of Britain's standing army and the organization of its reserves changed substantially. The navy viewed all these developments as a serious threat to its preeminent status as defender of King, Country, and Empire. It also viewed with growing disquiet the influence these changes would have on its role in future wars. This chapter will not provide an exhaustive analysis of these changes. Rather, an overview will be given with a particular emphasis on the role played by and attitudes to these changes of the two main protagonists in this study, Winston Churchill and his future First Sea Lord, Sir John Fisher, up to Churchill's appointment as First Lord of the Admiralty in 1911.

Britain ended the 19th century with the largest navy in the world and a modestly sized standing army. This was as it had been for centuries, with the size of the army periodically inflating to deal with overseas threats to her Imperial power. The 20th century began with Britain embroiled in one of these periodic threats in South Africa. In the aftermath of this conflict, for which Britain was militarily ill prepared, the British government appointed a Royal Commission to find out what had gone wrong and why.[1] The stage was set, in a time when the threat from continental Europe would steadily grow, for a decade-long reassessment of defense policy and the respective roles of the army and navy.

One of the earliest and most significant consequences of the commission's investigations was the establishment of the Committee of Imperial Defence (CID) in May 1904. Supplied with a permanent secretariat, and with the prime minister as president and permanent member, the committee was given the task of considering "from the broadest possible viewpoint all questions of Imperial defence" and ensuring cooperation in planning between the Royal Navy and the British Army.[2]

Lord Esher, Liberal Member of Parliament and a key figure behind the CID, hoped the committee would act as a "Great General Staff." Not surprisingly, there was immediate resistance to this from both services, each of which was understandably reluctant to see the role of their respective staffs usurped by a committee. However, a more significant barrier to the progress of the CID was the immense rivalry between the army and navy and the degree to which this was fueled by one of its foundation members, Lord Fisher. He viewed his role within the CID as one that would ensure, in any planning for war, that the navy would be recognized as the senior service and the army as clearly subservient to it.

The army, of course, had a different agenda and thus would be played out through the first decade of the new century—for much of the time in competition with the Liberal Party's platform of social reform—a partisan battle for the finite resources of the Exchequer.

As a protector of an island nation with a great empire, the Royal Navy would seem to have had the advantage in any race for funding. The army attempted to undermine the navy's case by periodically contriving threats of invasion, which, it argued, demanded a large and ready army to combat. The navy usually was able to demonstrate that the power of the Royal Navy made such an event impossible. Among other things, Fisher argued that "the development of the submarine boat had absolutely precluded the idea of a mass of transports approaching any position where the landing of troops is feasible."[3]

Argument such as this, however, was problematic for the navy. The threat posed by the submarine and the mine, combined with the improvements in coastal ordnance, could work against the Royal Navy as much as it could work for it. In the event of war with a continental power, would the navy be able to enforce its traditional policy of the close blockade? In the face of such threats, could the navy continue to retain the power to land an army when and where it chose? Moreover, would this policy alone be sufficient to protect Britain's national interest and that of her empire?

As the decade progressed and Germany emerged as an ever more likely threat, the answer to this last question became increasingly urgent. Close blockade had been effective against Britain's traditional enemy, France, but it was much more difficult against Germany, whose ports were considerably more distant. Moreover, Germany's position as Europe's greatest military power posed a new and critical question. Could Great Britain remain the predominant imperial power if it allowed German hegemony in Europe? Would a naval policy that precluded a continental commitment prevent this happening? These last questions neither Fisher nor his successor seemed able to satisfactorily address.

In 1905, amid the Moroccan crisis, it was suggested the CID establish a Subcommittee on Overseas Expeditions. The navy prepared a variety of plans for close blockade and sudden amphibious descents. Recognizing that the navy would never have the number of destroyer flotilla and cruisers necessary to blockade German ports successfully, a variety of plans were proposed to capture an island closer to Germany to act as a base.

Much to the annoyance of Fisher, the Army began to take a different tack. Anticipating future German aggression and an attack on France through Belgium, they sought Admiralty cooperation to affect a rapid delivery of a British Army to Belgium.[4] At the same time they began secret and informal discussions with the French.

Fisher remained violently opposed to any schemes that hinted at a formal military commitment to a continental ally and spoke only of "the occupation of isolated colonial possessions of the enemy, or the assistance of an ally by threatening descents on the hostile coast, or otherwise effecting a diversion on his behalf."[5]

The army did, at least, consider the navy's ideas, including the possibility of amphibious operations in Schleswig-Holstein and a plan to land 200,000 British and French soldiers in the Baltic at the outbreak of war. The CID concluded these were impracticable and the French confirmed that they preferred British troops to support the French Army.[6]

Throughout the second half of the decade, Fisher continued his resistance to any form of continental commitment, but he must have done so with a declining confidence in the alternatives he offered. His pronouncements regarding the power of the submarine alone must have caused him to consider plans for close blockade and military descents as increasingly impracticable. War plans drawn up in 1907 continued to promote close blockade and raids along the

German coast and elsewhere. Fisher would continue to speak of occupying the Baltic, but there were grave warnings of the serious dangers offered by mines and submarines in such operations.

In light of this, it seems probable that his continued resistance to a continental commitment was driven by short-term expediency rather than a genuine conviction that such plans were a real substitute for continental commitment. So long as there was a fiduciary conflict of interest between the army and navy, a political climate promoting the restriction of funding, and a conviction that Germany did not yet pose the threat some held it to be, Fisher seemed prepared to ignore the reality of these serious challenges to traditional naval policy if, thereby, he could maintain the paramountcy of the navy. Even as late as August 1911, he characterized the army's plan to send troops to France as designed to secure "compulsory service and an increase of the Army Estimates and military influence."[7]

In an ongoing effort to keep the Continentalists at bay, Fisher adopted a new tactic in 1907–1908. Choosing no longer to denigrate the value of an enlarged army, he began to link it directly to his own amphibious plans. A "seagoing army" became his new mantra. In an effort to requisition the army for the purposes of the navy, he declared to the Invasion Committee in February 1908 that "the success of the Navy cannot be carried to its proper conclusion unless you have got a military force able to land and take advantage of it."[8] A force of 60,000 British troops gathered at a secret rendezvous in the North Sea would force a considerable portion of the German Army to await a landing at an unknown point by this substantial force.[9]

In late 1908, the CID formed another subcommittee to consider the "Military Needs of the Empire" in the context of events on the continent. During these discussions, Fisher continued his vehement opposition to placing a British force alongside the French and instead Fisher returned to a plan to land a British Army on the Pomeranian Coast, 90 miles from Berlin. His ongoing support for this operation leaves one somewhat confused over his attitude to a continental war. Such a plan surely represented a serious commitment to a war on the continent. It might be concluded, therefore, that it was the nature of the commitment—British forces fighting alongside and subservient to the French—that bothered him more than the commitment itself.

Fisher's Baltic strategy failed to persuade anyone outside the navy that this was the way to deal with a German threat. Further joint studies generally attested to the impracticability of intervention in the Baltic, and by March, Fisher seemed no longer prepared to challenge this. Instead a hybrid solution to the ongoing debate appears to have developed in which four divisions of infantry and one of cavalry would be dispatched to France—with a guarantee from the First Lord that this could be done—while another one or two divisions would be free for coastal operations. Despite this apparent concession, no effort was made to prepare for the landing of troops in France. The navy remained reluctant to accede to the inevitability of a continental intervention and stubbornly continued to support naval blockade as their chosen strategy to a continental problem.

This situation failed to improve when Sir Arthur Wilson replaced Fisher as first sea lord in 1910. The author of many of the plans for naval blockade and amphibious operations, and convinced of the importance of total secrecy, Wilson was even more reluctant than Fisher to cooperate with the army in any joint planning for war. He refused to work with the CID, which, like Fisher, he believed usurped the roles of the first sea lord. It would take another major political crisis in 1911 to force his hand. Among those who finally brought the Admiralty to heel was Winston Churchill.

The young Churchill was, at most times, only on the periphery of these issues, but he did have opinions. His earliest recorded views can be traced back to his maiden speech in 1901 in which he criticized a proposal to expand the regular army to three corps.[10] This, he believed, could only occur at the expense of the navy, upon which the honor and security of the Empire depended. Moreover, he was wary this might lead to intervention in a European war.

During the middle years of the first decade—and now a Liberal alongside the future wartime prime minister, David Lloyd George—Churchill championed social reform and saw the limiting of army and naval estimates as one way to pay for it. This zeal for reform left Churchill slower than most to pick up on the growing threat Germany posed to peace in Europe. By 1909, Churchill was fully supporting Lord Haldane's intentions to expand the regular army and expressed the belief that the regular army, together with the militia units, would provide for "massive and swift expansion of the army once war broke out." Most of his statements, however, suggest he continued to view the role of the army in the context of imperial rather than continental solutions.[11]

During the Agadir crisis in 1911, Churchill's opinions changed dramatically. Agadir was a cathartic moment in which Germany crystallized as a bellicose new enemy and France a new ally. Amid this tension, the CID met on August 23 to once again establish a clear policy in the event of war. Over the previous several months, Churchill had come into regular contact with the chief of the general staff, Maj. Gen. (later Field Marshal) William Nicholson, and director of military operations, Brig. Gen. (later Lt. Gen.) Henry Wilson, and had become convinced that Britain should be ready to send four divisions immediately to the continent at the outbreak of war. Ten days before the meeting, he circulated a memorandum, remarkable for its anticipation of the events of 1914, to members of the CID. At the meeting, he was among the most aggressive in demolishing the navy's resistance to the rapid dispatch of an expeditionary force to Europe.

The army was first to put its case. Emphasizing the importance of time in any attack by Germany on France, Sir Henry Wilson presented a well-prepared and measured case for the immediate dispatch an expeditionary force of, not four, but all six regular divisions to the left flank of the French Army. If the force was not sent quickly, he argued, France might otherwise suffer a rapid defeat at the hands of an invading German army. Detailed plans had been prepared for this eventuality.

Not surprisingly, the representatives of the navy proceeded to disagree with any policy that could be viewed as committing Britain to war on the continent alongside France. They considered it would weaken Britain, embolden France, and provoke Germany. Moreover, the army's policy would prevent the execution of the navy's own plans. Speaking only from notes—for concerns over secrecy continued to preclude preparations of detailed plans—the First Sea Lord, Sir Arthur Wilson, put his case for independent action. He deprecated the idea of an expeditionary force, arguing that the effect of the dispatch of the entire regular army might be an outbreak of panic and result in the "movements of the Fleet being circumscribed with serious effect upon . . . naval operations."[12]

Wilson intended to implement two interlocking strategies that would fully occupy the navy and involve a number of the soldiers the army intended to send overseas. The first was to immediately institute the navy's traditional policy of close blockade by the capture of several islands.

Once the blockade of Germany's North Sea ports and debouches were secured, Wilson argued, the navy would implement a second class of operation. Britain would aid France by keeping Germany's North Sea coast in a "state of constant alarm" by threatening to land troops at any point on Germany's North Sea coastline and require the Germans to maintain a force of 10 divisions on constant alert.[13] Should operations in the North Sea lead to a successful fleet action, an effort might then be made to enter the Baltic and blockade the Prussian coast.

Wilson's failure to explain how such plans were to be implemented in face of submarines, mines, improved long-range coastal ordnance, and "modern" methods of surveillance ensured that he was challenged from all quarters. Field Marshal Sir William Nicholson disparaged Wilson's plan to keep the Germans in a "state of constant alarm," arguing that the Germans could easily concentrate a superior force wherever the navy threatened to land. As to the fire of the guns of the fleet, he thought its effects were "overrated."[14]

Among the most incisive critics was Churchill, who concentrated on the possible threat to the fleet of such an operation. He considered that Wilson's plans "would appear to involve keeping the Fleet very close to the shore and would expose the ships to the fire of shore guns and torpedo attacks." The capture of Cuxhaven would, he thought, offer some advantage but "he did not imagine that we could do so." The besieging of Wilhelmshaven was surely out of the question. Would not the attack on Heligoland prove a very difficult and costly operation?

The meeting was a resounding failure for the First Sea Lord. In a subsequent letter to the British foreign secretary, Sir Edward Grey, Churchill wrote, "I am not at all convinced about the wisdom of a close blockade, and I did not like the Admiralty statement."[15] Several weeks later, he wrote to Prime Minister Herbert Asquith, "[a]fter his revelations the other day I cannot feel implicit confidence in (Sir Arthur) Wilson. No man of real power could have answered so foolishly."[16]

Wilson's poor showing almost guaranteed the army would carry the day. Soon thereafter it was determined that, in the event of war, the navy must be ready to convey to France the divisions of the British Expeditionary Forces, should it be finally decided to send them. Within weeks, Churchill, whose paper for the CID of August 13 supported such a proposal, was sent to the Admiralty as First Lord to ensure that, should such a decision be made, an expeditionary force could be dispensed quickly to the continent.[17]

NOTES

1. The terms of reference were to "inquire into the military preparedness for the war in South Africa and into the supply of men, ammunition,

equipment, and transport by sea and land in connection with the campaign, and into military operations up to the occupation of Pretoria." Cited in John Gooch, *The Plans of War: The General Staff and British Military Strategy c. 1900–1916* (London: Routledge and Kegan Paul, 1974), 52.

2. Maurice Hankey, *The Supreme Command 1914–1918* (London: Allen and Unwin, 1961), 46.

3. Ruddock F. Mackay, *Fisher of Kilverstone* (Oxford: Clarendon Press, 1973).

4. Ibid., 331.

5. Ibid., 332. Excerpt from Fisher Memorandum, *The Elaboration of Combined Naval and Military Preparation for War.*

6. Ibid., 352.

7. These sentiments were conveyed to A. K. Wilson in a letter written on August 20, 1911, just before the decisive CID meeting of August 23. It is therefore not surprising Wilson acted the way he did at the meeting. Mackay, *Fisher of Kilverstone*, 429.

8. Mackay, *Fisher of Kilverston*, 396–397.

9. Ibid.

10. Tuvia Ben-Moshe, *Churchill: Strategy and History*, 9.

11. Ibid., 13.

12. CAB 2.2, Meeting of CID, August 23, 1911.

13. Ibid.

14. Ibid.

15. Randolph S. Churchill, *Winston S. Churchill: Volume II Young Statesman 1901–1914* (London: Heinemann, 1967), 530.

16. Ibid., 532.

17. Another important task given Churchill was to put into place a naval war staff. Having completed a similar task at the War Office, Lord Haldane tried to persuade Asquith that he was the best man for Admiralty. It is probable, however, that this ultimately worked against him. Asquith feared that Haldane's close links with the War Office would have represented a concentration of too much influence and authority in a single man. For a detailed perspective on the machinations behind Asquith's selection of Churchill as first lord—and the factors that influenced his decision, see Geoffrey Miller, *The Millstone: British Naval Policy in the Mediterranean, 1900–1914* (Hull, UK: The University of Hull Press, 1999), chapter 8.

CHAPTER 2

First Lord Churchill

Churchill's performance at the CID meeting was an impressive one. He had displayed a clear appreciation that the navy's position was untenable. He evidently was persuaded by Sir Henry Wilson's conviction that the military support offered by Britain could make the difference between survival and defeat for the French Army in its opening battles with Germany. The First Sea Lord's policy of military descents—or merely the threat of them—was no substitute for this decisive action.

Churchill's appreciation of the difficulties of close blockade also demonstrated a certain perspicuity regarding naval matters. In the face of the modern realities of war, close blockade seemed hardly possible. His criticisms were informed, measured, and incisive and appeared to have struck a cord with his prime minister's reservations regarding naval policy. Here was the man to replace the First Lord who had so loyally and so disastrously supported his First Sea Lord.

It soon became evident that his performance on August 11 had not been designed to neuter offensive action by the fleet but to ensure the rapid passage of a force sufficient to save France from defeat in the early weeks of war. "One cause alone," he declared a month later to Lloyd George, "would justify our participation [in war with Germany]—to prevent France from being trampled down and looted by the Prussian junkers—a disaster ruinous to the world, and swiftly fatal to our country."[1]

Once this task was accomplished and lines of supply to Britain and the continent secured, it was never likely the pugnacious and combative Churchill would be content to patiently and passively await any aggressive action by the German Fleet. He would not sit idly while the war was won by continental armies and the slow working measures of a distant blockade designed to protect the blockading ships from the threat of German submarines.

Although he recognized that the transports of a British Expeditionary Force (BEF) might prove a morsel irresistible to the High Seas Fleet in the opening weeks of war, Churchill also saw beyond this to the possibility that no decisive battle might ever be fought. He was not oblivious to the fact that his insistence as First Lord on a 60 percent preponderance over the High Seas Fleet in the North Sea would discourage the Germans from seeking battle.[2] In 1913, Churchill wrote that a decisive naval battle might be "indefinitely delayed and may perhaps never be obtained in the whole course of the war."[3] The German command of the Baltic, he argued, made a decisive naval battle even less likely. Efficiency and training and therefore morale could be maintained within the Baltic without ever fearing an encounter with a superior force.[4] The Germans need only fight when and if they chose.

Opportunities for great offensive naval actions, therefore, were likely to be few and far between. It was perhaps not surprising that not long after he became First Lord, Churchill dusted off some of the old Admiralty war plans and began to agitate for offensive action that bore a remarkable resemblance to that which he had played a direct role in undermining. Paramount among such plans was a scheme to capture an island to act as base for an advanced naval flotilla.

His doubts over a decisive battle and his natural pugnacity aside, Churchill's interest in a return to close blockade appears to have been influenced by his concern over the capacity of neutral countries to erode the effectiveness of a commercial blockade against Germany. In 1908, Churchill had dissented from an Admiralty report that minimized the effect Holland and Belgium would have on a naval blockade of Germany.[5]

On August 31, 1911, at the time of Agadir, he had expressed to Sir Edward Grey his concern that, in the event of war with Germany, aid to Belgium might be hindered by strict Dutch neutrality. In the circumstances, he considered that Britain "should be prepared at the proper moment to put pressure on the Dutch to keep the Scheldt open for *all* purposes. If the Dutch close the Scheldt, we retaliate by a blockade of the Rhine."[6]

In early December 1912, the CID discussed the issue of Belgian and Dutch neutrality in the event of war with Germany. At this meeting, Churchill declared that "[i]f these countries were neutral, the efficacy of our blockade would be halved . . . neutrality was out of the question. They must be friends or foes." The meeting itself concluded that "it is essential that the Netherlands and Belgium should be compelled to declare at the outset to which side in the struggle they will adhere."[7]

An apprehension that action might be taken against countries whose neutrality compromised Britain's ability to wage war presented Churchill with opportunities for the resumption of a close blockade and the subsequent decisive naval battle of the war that few others saw. He believed a successful blockade would force the High Seas Fleet to fight.

The following month (January 31, 1913), the Admiralty, at Churchill's direction, asked Vice Adm. (later Rear Adm.) Lewis Bayly to investigate the possibility of capturing and holding a base on the "Dutch, German, Danish or Scandinavian coasts for operations of Flotilla on the outbreak of war with Germany, the other countries *named being either unfriendly neutrals or enemies*" (emphasis added).[8]

These investigations coincided with a push by Churchill to revert to a traditional but temporary policy of close blockade in the opening weeks of war. He argued it would be possible, with the use of all destroyer flotilla, to blockade the Heligoland Bight for an entire week. This would be the best means by which to protect the movement of the BEF to France and would instill the "moral superiority" he considered essential for the effective functioning of distant blockade thereafter.[9]

None of his advisers considered the idea practicable. The director of the operations divisions (D.O.D. Naval Staff), Capt. George Alexander Ballard, considered it impossible to establish an overwhelming flotilla superiority "if the enemy chooses to concentrate his own."[10]

Having failed in his effort to use concerns over the BEF to secure a more aggressive role for his navy, Churchill returned to the theme of an island base and the manner in which such an acquisition would protect Britain from invasion. In a March memorandum, he laid bare the difficulties the navy would have in preventing the movement of the High Seas Fleet. Mines and torpedoes prevented the close watch of the Heligoland Bight and of the skaw or the belts providing egress from the Baltic. The enemy could therefore strike "with their whole force on either line" unless German, Dutch, Danish, or Norwegian territory was occupied as a forward base.[11] This line of argument, as had his contentions regarding the BEF, drew little enthusiasm from his naval staff.

One other line of argument—and always the most hopeful—remained open to Churchill, and it continued to succor his hopes for aggressive naval action into the early months of the war. This was Britain's policy toward Holland in the event of war. In 1912, he had nominated the maintenance of strict neutrality by Holland in a war with Germany as grounds for acting against her. Now, in May 1913, more subtly and more reasonably, he contended that "land" pressure from Germany "would be irresistible in a war and would compel her either to join Germany as an ally or to remain neutral in form while helping Germany by every means to carry on her trade."[12] This, he imagined, would allow Britain to react to Holland in a way that would not only tighten the economic noose around Germany's neck but also provide opportunities for close blockade. He did not believe there was any practicable means of making Holland join Britain in a war. He contended, "[w]hatever her views, she would be compelled to go with Germany openly or covertly."[13]

Unfortunately for Churchill, his Admiralty advisers did not share his view that a forceful reaction to minor breeches of neutrality by Holland would be worth pushing her whole-heartedly into the German camp. In any event, the capture of Dutch islands would not make close blockade desirable or practicable. Throughout 1913, he made no more headway with Bayly's plans to occupy other islands. In July, the DOD, Ballard, assessed the various reports as "in the nature of a gamble at best. . . . Gambles in war are justified if an adequate advantage may be forthcoming, but here that does not appear to be the case."[14]

Nevertheless, although in abeyance, such plans were not forgotten by Churchill. On the eve of war in June 1914, he directed the chief of the war staff to prepare plans for "a close blockade of the Heligoland Bight by strongly supported flotilla for four or five days at least, closing the Elbe absolutely during that period without an overseas base and with an overseas base."[15]

Churchill's request led to the resurrection of Bayly's 1913 investigations. He sent copies of these to Prime Minister Asquith on July 31, suggesting it was now necessary that the "War Office shd study these plans so that military and naval action can be coordinated and concerted in harmony."[16] He believed that

> the following shd be the order in wh the work shd be undertaken
>
> 1. Ameland or Born Deep
> 2. Ekersund
> 3. Laeso Channel
> 4. Kungsbacka Fjord
> 5. Esbjerg
> 6. Sylt
> 7. Borkum
> 8. Heligoland
>
> These last 4 are less urgent on account of the forces required being probably not available.[17]

The study of operations against these places was to be undertaken "without regard either to (a) questions of violation of neutrality (b) questions of whether the troops could be better employed elsewhere. These are matters of policy which must be decided later by higher authorities."[18]

We have in these closing lines the clear indications that Churchill's offensive strategies did not exclude the possibility that Britain might consider challenging the neutrality of one or other of the North Sea states. It ought to be noticed that the Dutch island of Ameland is first on Churchill's list.

Any intention, however, to threaten countries that might be either too exacting or too selective in their neutrality became particularly problematical when Britain entered the war as a champion of Belgium. Having taken the moral ground against Germany, it was impossible for Britain to contemplate any action akin to this. This was readily understood by Sir Edward Grey and most other members of the government, but filled with the responsibility of seeing the BEF safely to France, convinced of the inevitability of Dutch complicity with the Germans, and determined to press aggressive offensive operations at the earliest opportunity, Churchill continued to view Dutch territory as a potential target for some weeks after the war had begun.

Churchill recognized only belatedly that Holland did not likely prove the key to his offensive operations, but this did not deflect him from their pursuit. His determination to see his navy play a more central and decisive role in the defeat of Germany, and an undisciplined conviction that solutions could be found to the intractable problems that so curtailed the offensive powers of his superior fleet ensured that he would continue to press vigorously a number of offensive schemes throughout his remaining time as First Lord.

NOTES

1. Miller, *The Millstone,* 531.

2. A decision concomitant with committing an expeditionary force to the European continent was the decision to move much of Britain's Mediterranean Fleet and concentrate it in the North Sea against Germany. This void was filled by France, which denuded its Atlantic coastline of ships and stationed them in the Mediterranean to protect French and British interests. Britain, it was understood, would protect the French North Sea coastline and Atlantic interests. While such informal cooperation smacked of something very close to an alliance, Churchill went to extraordinary lengths to establish that such cooperation represented no such thing. It was merely both countries independently acting in self-interest. Churchill was determined Britain maintain a "free hand" in its relationship with France, while simultaneously preparing for a war with Germany. His determination to maintain this "free hand" should not be interpreted as Churchill baulking at assisting France in a continental commitment. Rather, it should be seen as an effort by Churchill to ensure that nothing other than an aggressive full-scale invasion of France by Germany entangled Britain in a continental war alongside France.

3. Undated memorandum estimated to have been written in April 1913. See Martin Gilbert, *Winston S. Churchill Companion Volume II,* Part 3 (London: Heinemann, 1972), 1737.

4. Ibid.

5. In 1908, Churchill dissented from an Admiralty report minimizing the impact Holland and Belgium would have on a naval blockade of Germany. His concern over the capacity of neutrals to undermine the blockade can be traced back at least to this point. See Foreign Office, *Official History of the War: The Blockade of the Central Empires 1914–1918* (London: H. M. Stationery Office, 1961), 29.

6. R. Churchill, *Winston S. Churchill Vol. II,* 530.

7. CAB 2.3, CID Meeting, December 6, 1912. Asquith, however, altered the conclusion the next day to the following, believing the other conclusion went "rather farther than he thought the Committee meant to go." See CAB 2.3, CID Meeting, January 7, 1913. "In order to bring the greatest possible economic pressure upon Germany, it is essential that the Netherlands and Belgium should be either entirely friendly to this country, in which case we should limit their overseas trade, or that they should be definitely hostile, in which case we should extend the blockade to their ports." In July 1912

when the CID was discussing the "*Attitude of Great Britain towards Belgium In the Event of a Violation of Belgian Territory by Germany in Time of War,*" Churchill expressed his belief that should Belgium be a cobelligerent with Great Britain, Germany would most likely "be compelled to violate the neutrality of Holland." He considered this "from the naval strategical point of view was important as it would give us an excuse to blockade Dutch ports also, and add to the efficiency of the sea pressure upon Germany. Similar action might perhaps be taken if the Dutch obstructed the transport of troops or supplies to Antwerp." CAB 2.2, CID Meeting, July 4, 1912.

8. Arthur J. Marder, *Portrait of an Admiral: The Life and Papers of Sir Herbert Richmond*, Vol. 2 (London: Jonathon Cape, 1952), 178.

9. Arthur J. Marder, *From the Dreadnought to Scapa Flow: The Royal Navy in the Fisher Era 1904–1919*, Vol. 1 (London: Oxford University Press, 1961), 373.

10. Ibid., 375.

11. Winston S. Churchill, *The World Crisis: 1911–1914,* Vol. 1 (London: Odhams Press Ltd., 1923), 156–157.

12. Gilbert, *Winston S. Churchill CVII*, Part 3, 1750.

13. Ibid.

14. Marder, "Memorandum Ballard to Jackson," *Portrait of an Admiral*, Vol. 2, 179.

15. Churchill also passed on to Jellicoe a copy of Bayly's report on Borkum and Sylt for comment. After returning from a holiday, Jellicoe expressed his opinion to the Chief of Staff that he was not "of the opinion that the advantages to be derived from the use of such a base are worth the cost in men and ships of capture." See A. Temple Patterson, ed., *The Jellicoe Papers*, Vol. 1 (Cheltenham, UK: Navy Records Society, 1966), 40–41.

16. Martin Gilbert, *Winston S. Churchill Companion Volume III*, Part 1 (London: Heinemann, 1972), 7 (hereafter Gilbert, *CVIII*).

17. Ibid.

18. Ibid.

CHAPTER 3

At War!

If Churchill's years as First Lord before the outbreak of war reflected a growing inclination toward a more proactive and less reactive naval policy, his nine months as First Lord after the outbreak of war represented a compulsion. Having recognized early the stultifying effect on naval policy of any decision by the High Seas Fleet not to seek battle—and frustrated by the unromantic and unsatisfactorily slow hand of naval blockade—Churchill sought any and every means to bring the German Fleet to battle or neutralize it within its own harbors so the full amphibious power of the British Navy could effectively and rapidly be brought to bear in the defeat of Germany.

While his objective remained clear, the means by which to achieve it were not. Always in the way were the objections of his naval staff, which saw much more clearly than Churchill the impractical nature of many of his suggestions. Churchill was not interested in criticism. He wanted solutions, and it is certain he viewed his own unremitting agitation as a way to inspire the ingenuity required to find them. It was not uncommon for Churchill to counter objections to his plans with amendments that would be found in the next outline for the capture of an island or other strategic initiatives. Churchill's sudden and considerable interest in monitors—not at all present before the war—represented a typical reaction to his naval staff's inability to address the problems of the mine and submarine. These vessels, along with such things as "chicken coops" and "bulging," would be woven into each new initiative to provide the means by which to end the war in 1915.

Unfortunately Churchill's enthusiasm was no substitute for common sense in such complicated business. In the opening days of August, in response to his request of July 31, his naval staff once again passed dour judgment on Bayly's schemes, including plans to take the Ameland.

Churchill ignored the criticism and wrote to the First Sea Lord, Prince Louis of Battenburg, and Chief of the Admiralty War Staff, Adm. Doveton Sturdee on August 9 recommending preparations be made to establish a base at Born Deep by taking possession of the Dutch island of Ameland. He clearly remained expectant that the government might react against any breech of neutrality by Holland—a prospect Churchill continued to view as almost inevitable.

Immediately before the outbreak of war, with the likelihood of a German breech of Belgian neutrality not yet in full view, Churchill had reminded Grey of the critical importance of "the three small states bordering on the North Sea . . . Norway, Holland, and Belgium." The advantage of an alliance with these countries in blockading Germany and controlling her naval movements "cannot be overestimated," and he recommended strongly they be approached to join an Anglo-French-Russian alliance.[1]

When war broke out, this appeal was replaced by a more threatening tone and a reversion to his traditional Dutch theme. On August 5, he wrote again to Grey:

> If Holland: a. condones the violation of her territory by Germany b. closes the Scheldt to the supplies for Antwerp, c. allows free importation of supplies to Germany through Rotterdam we shall be at a grave disadvantage if we are forced to respect her neutrality. She ought to accept our alliance. Failing this we must insist on absolute equality with Germany in the use made by either belligerent on Dutch territory or ports.[2]

Churchill's letter to Prince Louis and Sturdee four days later was written in anticipation of imminent conflict with Holland.[3] The plan he outlined in this letter attempted to address the various criticisms of his staff over capturing and holding Ameland. The island could be protected easily by "the sweeping fire of machine guns, . . . and could only be attacked by a division of troops over 4 miles of bare sand."[4]

He went on to point out that the island was 60 miles from the German frontier and, thus, was not exposed to serious bombardment from the shore. The Germans could not attack because to do so they would have to invade the Dutch territory and their mainland. This, he argued, would be "a more tangible violation" of Dutch territory than any British occupation of the Dutch island.[5] Therefore, the Germans would be forced to leave the island alone or invade Holland. In such circumstances, Churchill argued with considerable dexterity, Britain's violation of Dutch territory would see the Dutch go to war with Germany for their subsequent but serious breech of neutrality, rather than Britain's initial but minor breech. Thus, he undoubtedly foresaw, by such a bold act Britain might soon have access to the great harbors of Holland.

Once the base was secured, it was to be used to maintain surveillance and control of the southern approaches to the Elbe and "above all to maintain in lively vigour the spirit of enterprise and attack."[6]

As for the threat of the German Fleet, Churchill believed an attack on Born Deep from the sea by heavy ships could only "be the best thing for us: . . . If modern ships are sent we may inflict losses, one of which would compensate for the whole risk of the enterprise."[7]

Although all Churchill's proposals had, as their foundations, the prewar naval policies of Fisher and A. K. Wilson, strikingly absent from his plans at this time was any mention of large amphibious operations in the North Sea or operation in the Baltic. Therefore, while it is reasonable to deduce these were his ultimate objectives, it is not possible to conclude that the operations enumerated in the foregoing were precursory to the major amphibious plans Churchill unfolded from the middle of August onward.

The first hint to Churchill's naval policy after command of the North Sea was achieved can be found in a letter to Grey on August 3.[8] Churchill was responding to an inquiry from the Foreign Office regarding his appeal to the neutral states outlined in his letter to Grey discussed above: "How would Norway be protected from Sweden?" they had asked. Churchill responded: "the Triple Entente possess substantial preponderance of the Sea. Therefore the invasion of Sweden by Russia is a practicable operation *from the moment it becomes convenient to establish the naval control of the Baltic*" (emphasis added).[9]

The idea of a British-facilitated invasion of Sweden and the suggestion that Churchill intended the navy at some point to enter the Baltic preceded his memorandum of August 19 by 16 days. In it, he outlined his desire to gain command of the Baltic to facilitate a Russian invasion of Germany's Baltic coastline.[10]

It is surely more than coincidence that three days earlier, on August 16, Sir John Fisher had come up from Richmond to London for a tête-à-tête with Churchill, the first time they had met since the outbreak of war.[11] It would be extremely surprising, therefore, if Churchill's actions at this time were not being influenced by Fisher.

The day after he spoke with Fisher, Churchill began a letter seeking the organization of two Naval Brigades, as one author has put it, "to form, with the Marine Brigade, a complete Naval Division for the occupation of advanced naval bases."[12]

Churchill's memorandum of August 19 argued that command of the Baltic required first a decisive naval battle at sea or that the Kiel Canal be effectively blocked—either by aerial or destroyer attack, or by both.[13] He considered it "important that plans should be prepared *now* to make the best use of our getting the command of the Baltic" through either of these circumstances.[14] He requested that the Russian general staff be asked "what military use they would think it worthwhile to make of that command assuming we were to get it." Churchill then enumerated plans, which included the landing of a Russian army, to achieve the following:

1. [To] turn the flank and rear of German armies holding the Dantzig-thorn line, or which were elsewhere resisting the main Russian attack;
2. To attack Berlin from the North, only 90 miles in the direct line;
3. To attack Kiel and the Canal in force and to drive the German Fleet to sea.

Although his schemes would evolve appreciably and have added to them a plan to land a huge British army in Schlewig-Holstein, from this point forward until his dismissal as First Lord in May 1915, these northern offensive operations would be the central pillar of Churchill's naval policy and would have an overarching influence on all else, including the Dardanelles.

A further indication of the extent to which Churchill's mind was now fully preoccupied with his various northern schemes was a secret letter written to Sir Edward Grey on August 21. He informed Grey he intended to travel the following day to France to discuss with the French Minister of Marine the "general policy of the naval war, and more particularly to open up the possibility of ultimate action in the Baltic."[15] At Grey's request, Churchill postponed his project for another day, and it appears it never took place.

So restless was he at this time for action in this quarter that when the Cabinet was informed of a Greek offer of military and naval assistance to the Allies, Churchill "propounded a Napoleonic plan for forcing the Danish passage with the help of the Greeks and convoying Russian troops to the coast of Berlin and making a 'coup de theatre'."[16]

Three days later, on August 24, Churchill received a qualified reply from the Russian commander in chief, Grand Duke Nicholas, regarding his Baltic plans. The duke considered the command of the Baltic would "prove a most valuable and desirable factor towards the development of our offensive operations against Germany." Furthermore, he believed it would "under favourable circumstances . . . be quite feasible and fully expedient," but he also believed it an offer that "we could avail ourselves thereof, only should the general military situation lend itself to its application."[17]

Churchill apparently viewed this as a favorable response because he continued to pursue the ways and means of making such an operation a reality. On August 19, Austria declared war on Britain and France. In a letter of August 25 to Prime Minister Asquith, Grey, and Kitchener, Churchill pointed out that the destruction of the Austrian Navy or the accession to the Allied cause of the Italians and Greeks—or of the Italian Navy alone—would "allow two Fleets each superior to Germany to be maintained" and, therefore, one of these could be placed in the Baltic. He viewed "this phase of naval operations . . . as an event to be sought for during October or later."[18]

These were novel suggestions. Should either of these events transpire, an entrance could be made into the Baltic without the need for a decisive naval battle in the North Sea or an operation to block the Kiel Canal. Thereafter might follow the landing of a vast Russian force within 90 miles of Berlin. Such, at least, appeared to be Churchill's wishful thinking.

Four days later, he viewed Austria's declaration of war on Japan in a similar light. The possibility of Japanese naval assistance—perhaps of a battle-squadron in the Mediterranean or elsewhere—"could not be over-rated." He declared: "It would steady and encourage Italy, & would *bring nearer the situation so greatly desired of our being able to obtain command of the Baltic*" (emphasis added).[19]

Sadly for Churchill, the Japanese, just as the Greeks and the Italians, were to prove a disappointment.

During late August and early September, Churchill was distracted by events in Turkey—to which we shall subsequently turn—and later by the German threat to Antwerp. The imminent threat to Antwerp saw Churchill's animosity toward Holland once more emerge in a letter to Asquith, Grey, and Kitchener. He considered two things were essential to save Antwerp, the first being an effective defense of Belgium's fortress line. The second was "free and uninterrupted communications with the sea," which he believed "involved our whole relations with the Dutch." Harping on an old theme, he argued that:

> *from a purely naval point of view, war with Holland would be better for us than neutrality . . .*
>
> Their reinforcement of German naval forces would be puny, and the closing of the Rhine which we could accomplish without the slightest additional effort, is almost vital to the efficiency of the naval blockade. (emphasis added)[20]

Churchill went on to rather reluctantly acknowledge that Britain had to consider the "proper treatment of small nations who are neutrals: and I agree that for our own purposes and our own interests we cannot deal roughly with the Dutch, however unfairly their neutrality is interpreted."[21] However, he continued: "When Belgium, a small people fighting for its last breath of life, is considered, a different set of standards come into force."[22]

He wanted to:

> tell the Dutch now bluntly that we insist upon the Schledt being kept open permanently for supplies and reinforcements of all kinds for Antwerp under siege, and that any attempt to close or obstruct those waters must be regarded as a disloyal act to a small neighbour, and as an unfriendly act to Great Britain. . . . For the sake of keeping at peace with Holland, we are giving up all the advantages of blockading the Rhine, all the facilities by seizing Dutch islands of controlling the Elbe; and if on top of this we are to allow Antwerp to be choked and murdered and fall into German hands, we shall find it difficult to prove that we have taken the necessary measures to secure the success of the war.[23]

Churchill was undoubtedly angry that strict Dutch neutrality would restrict British assistance to Belgium and make blockade ineffectual, but clearly evident also was frustration over the lost opportunity to blockade the Elbe and to set into motion his great offensive plans.

Meanwhile in early September, he broached the subject of close blockade with his old friend Fisher. Fisher's attitude had hardened considerably since his days as First Sea Lord and his comments were not encouraging for any of Churchill's offensive plans: "I know of course A. K. Wilson's ideas of attacking Cuxhaven, etc., but even if desirable for ships to attack forts (and Nelson was dead against it always!) It must be done before the declaration of war and as a surprise."[24] The comments were a portent of future conflict between the two.

Uppermost in Churchill's mind during the second half of September and October was the siege of Antwerp, which culminated in his decision to take command of the naval marines in Belgium in October. Despite the enormous stresses surrounding the operations in Belgium, he returned to his northern schemes on September 24 when he attended a meeting aboard commander of the home fleet, Adm. John Rushworth Jellicoe's flagship, the *Iron Duke*, at Loch Ewe.[25]

Discussion took place on a plan for attacking the island of Heligoland as another means by which to blockade Germany's North Sea debouches. This proposal had been resurrected by A. K. Wilson with whom Churchill had recently made informal contact. Wilson feared greatly the impact of submarines and believed strongly that this operation ought to be attempted. Those aboard the *Iron Duke* were dead against the idea. It was the unanimous opinion of those gathered that a successful bombardment would be difficult and the loss of ships would not be compensated by any advantage gained. It was decided that "in the present phase of the war, no enterprise of this nature should be attempted."

Discussion then moved to the Baltic Problem and the ways and means by which it might be successfully entered. Once again, the general opinion (based largely on the danger from minefields) was that any risks to achieve this were not then advisable. Nevertheless, Churchill's persistence shone through in the final paragraph of the minutes where it was declared that "the question of policy to be adopted when it becomes possible to form two strong fleets, one in the North Sea and one in the Baltic to be thoroughly investigated."[26]

Churchill had been fobbed off yet again and he reluctantly had accepted that such schemes were not desirable "in the present phase of the war," but the respite for his war staff would be brief. Churchill understood "the present phase of the war" applied to the period during which Britain would be busy hunting down and destroying German raiders. This he anticipated would be comparatively brief. Thereafter, large numbers of craft would be freed for other duties, among which, Churchill hoped, would be one or other of his own offensive plans.

Apparently concerned at his First Lord's relentless pursuit of the offensive, Lord Jellicoe wrote to Churchill six days after this meeting and developed elements of the discussion that had taken place aboard the *Iron Duke*. Jellicoe counseled patience: "It is suicidal to forego our advantageous position in the big ships by risking them in waters infested by submarines."[27]

Not as yet anticipating the potentially devastating impact of the future submarine offensive on trade, he declared: "They can't hurt our over-sea commerce, nor can they help theirs to get in. So long as we retain our superior Sea-going Fleet they are powerless."

Jellicoe suggested the idea that southerly Battle Fleet movements be given up until "the submarine threat had been minimised."

Churchill claimed to be in full agreement with Jellicoe in a letter of October 8.[28] He agreed it was essential to secure the safety of the Battle Fleet during the long and indefinite period of waiting for a general action. He could not see any reason to "force the Battle Fleet to keep a station of danger during the winter months."[29]

This acknowledgment made, he began to build his case for an offensive in the Baltic. He argued that the Germans pursued a "wise policy in declining battle" because "by remaining in harbour he secures for Germany the command of the Baltic with all that that implies both in threatening the Russian flank and protecting the German coast and in drawing supplies from Sweden and Norway." To deny such advantage to the Germans, he believed that all future naval operations must tend to "the eventual command of the Baltic." He had, he wrote, already pointed out in papers given to Jellicoe the "three alternative conditions under which this would be possible" and hoped he would study the "method by which the entrance to the Baltic could be effected when the time arrived."

The three conditions of which Churchill had written were a decisive sea battle against the High Seas Fleet, a successful operation to destroy or block the Kiel Canal by aerial or destroyer attack, or the development of circumstances that would allow the formation of two fleets, each superior to that of the Germans. As we have seen, Churchill apparently hoped this third alternative might be achieved through an alliance with Italy and Greece or Japan. The destruction of the Austrian Fleet might also render this possible by freeing British and French forces in the Mediterranean.

These were all slim prospects and the meeting aboard the *Iron Duke* had made it clear that Churchill would get little support from his Admiralty advisers. Nevertheless, his reply to Jellicoe reflected a determination to press on and find a way through all obstacles, and he did so with a restless vigor. On October 24, Asquith wrote of Churchill's numerous schemes for cheating and baffling the submarine, including huge networks of wire and net—hencoops—in which "our big ships can refuge and nestle, without any fear of torpedo attack."[30]

Unfortunately, while earning the admiration of the prime minister, who thought such ideas as "inventive and resourceful" and showing "originality and dash,"[31] Churchill was unable to move the men who counted. Capt. Herbert Richmond, assistant D.O.D., recalled a meeting with Churchill of that evening:

> He was in low spirits . . . oppressed with the impossibility of *doing* anything . . . He wanted to send battleships—old ones—up the Elbe, but for what purpose except to be sunk I did not understand, and as I did not wish to oppose & be counted among the do-nothings, I let it alone.[32]

In his role as naval adviser, it was soon to be Richmond's destiny to be considered by Churchill among the worst spoilers and "do-nothings" at the Admiralty, for he was required repeatedly to pour cold water on a variety of Churchill's proposals.

From the depth of despondency, which was further deepened by the sinking of the *Audacious* on October 27, was born a new resolve. Fed up with the inertia of naval policy, Churchill focused on fundamental changes at the Admiralty. Asquith confided to socialite and love interest, Venetia Stanley, this same day:

> He has quite made up his mind that the time has come for a drastic change in his Board; our blue-eyed German [First Sea Lord Battenberg] will have to go, and (as W says) he will be reinforced by two "well-plucked chickens" of 74 and 72. We both enlarged on the want of initiative and constructive thought of the present naval advisors.[33]

The two "well-plucked" chickens were former First Sea Lords, Fisher and A. K. Wilson. Churchill was selecting a team he dearly hoped would breathe life into his offensive aspirations. Within days, Wilson was sent to work developing "all sorts of plans for Belgian and German coast attack."

On November 2, Churchill pressed on with his plans to recruit Japanese naval assistance to allow operation in the Baltic. He informed the Japanese minister of marine that after the defeat of the

German cruisers he hoped "to be strong enough to enter the Baltic and greatly increase the severity of the naval pressure upon the Germans."[34] He hoped the Japanese would "look forward to this situation in order to consider how the powerful naval aid they are giving in this early stage of the war may be made to play a decisive part in its conclusion."[35]

Meanwhile, opportunities for new initiatives occurred almost immediately. On November 3, Churchill and Fisher met Charles Schwab of the American Bethlehem Steel Works regarding the "sale of ships to the British Admiralty and the construction of new ships especially torpedo boat destroyers and submarines."[36] It was here the *British* monitor was born and with it the rebirth of Churchill's dreams for an aggressive naval offensive.

Churchill recorded that during conversations, Schwab made it known to him and to Fisher that he had available four 14-inch twin turrets. At this point, Churchill suggested to Fisher that these be bought and monitors built to carry them. According to Churchill, Fisher "took up the idea with avidity and thereafter we embarked in the closest agreement upon a very large policy of monitor building."[37] At the close of this meeting, the third Sea Lord, Adm. Frederick C. T. Tudor, minuted the director of naval construction, Eustace d'Eyncourt, "to design . . . armoured Monitors to be built in four months—each to carry 2-14 guns or equivalent. Draft 10 feet. Speed 10 knots. To have crinolenes. An armoured conning tower. Armoured deck."[38]

Here was the ultimate bombardment vessel: big-gunned, armored, and, with its shallow draft and enormous crinolenes (bulges), unsinkable by mines and torpedoes. All to be built in four months. It would be with these vessels that Churchill would soon invest the means by which to overcome his staff's reluctance to take on his offensive plans.

With Fisher and Wilson now members of the Admiralty war staff, the various plans for an offensive in the North Sea were again dusted off and placed under review. Wilson pressed his plans for an attack on Heligoland, but the commander of the channel fleet, Vice Adm. Burney, whose ships would have undertaken the project, refused flatly to support it. He informed Churchill on November 8 that "[t]he scheme if carried out would result in a national disaster."[39]

On December 1, Churchill began promoting his island schemes through an "invasion scare" strategy he had last used in 1913. Amid ongoing fears over the threat of German invasion, he argued at the first meeting of the newly formed War Council that the best way to ensure home defense was to capture an island near the enemy's coast. This would allow the navy to "maintain large numbers of submarines and destroyers constantly off German ports" and "make it very difficult for the Germans to prepare for invasion without our knowledge."[40]

While not commenting directly on Churchill's island schemes, Lord Fisher lent his support for a more aggressive policy by declaring his belief that the "present defensive attitude (of) the fleet was bad for morale and did not really protect from submarines."[41] The War Council agreed the Admiralty should examine the question in more detail. Arthur Balfour, former prime minister and current influential member of the War Council, subsequently supported the proposal strongly, although a paper he wrote set out four conditions he believed had to be fulfilled before such an operation could take place.[42]

Thus inspired, Churchill composed a three-page memorandum the following day for the benefit of his colleagues in which he outlined an operation to capture the island of Sylt. The bombardment force would not include modern vessels but four pre-dreadnought Majestic or Royal Sovereign (dreadnought) battleships lightened to 20 feet by caissons to protect them from torpedoes, three monitors, and 20 torpedo boat destroyers. His memorandum again attempted to address former criticisms as to how such an island might be capture and then held. As to German naval attack, he repeated his conviction that "[t]he more the enemy employs his naval forces in the attack on Sylt, the greater the advantage to us, the provocation of such an attack being an essential in itself."[43]

Rather calculatedly, his plan, like his discussion at the War Council, scrupulously and probably wisely omitted any mention of invasions against the mainland or the Baltic and focused instead on the maintenance of "a regular observation and control upon the debouches of the Heligoland Bight, thus preventing any raid or invasion from putting to sea unperceived & without full warning."[44] As always, his naval advisers were unmoved. They could see many difficulties and few advantages in this operation.

By December 15, Chief of the Naval Staff Henry Oliver had produced a reassessment on Borkum that was far from encouraging. He pointed out that Borkum, if captured, could be held more easily than any other German island because of its distance from the mainland, but it would be very difficult to capture. It had a well-dispersed and substantial heavy armament; the guns would have to be hit to be disabled because the soil was sand and shells bursting into sand produced little effect. The bombarding ships would be kept 12,000 to 14,000 yards offshore by off-lying shoals, and the approaches to the island would be mined. Finally, Oliver doubted the troops required were available.[45]

Churchill was unperturbed by these concerns. His decision to build his unsinkable 14-inch monitors would, to his mind, overcome most of the concerns expressed by Oliver. Oliver's assertion that Borkum was the most easily held of the German island appears to have caused Churchill to discontinue any further investigations into Sylt. Henceforward, all attention would be on Borkum.

In the meantime, Churchill was still exploring the other means by which a naval force might enter the Baltic. He evidently continued to hope that Italian intervention in the Mediterranean would provide the two fleets "each superior to the Germans" he had written of several months earlier. His hopes were dashed by A. K. Wilson on December 10 when he informed Churchill that he did not think that, even with ships drawn from the Mediterranean, any combination of French and British forces could enter the Baltic while leaving the North Sea secure "until we have found some means of greatly reducing the danger from submarines, or else of completely blocking the [Kiel] canal."[46]

This disappointing news, undoubtedly reinforced by a growing conviction that no decisive clash of fleets was likely, led Churchill to write to Fisher the following day suggesting they order "without delay" more monitors (codenamed Styx)—immune to mine and torpedo—for heavy inshore work. He drew attention to four reserve 13.5-inch guns of *Audacious* and reserve 15-inch guns that might be used. He wanted ships that could be built within six or seven months that could attack the German Fleet in its harbor:

> We must look to them in default of a general action for giving us the power of forcing a naval decision at the latest in the autumn of 1915. . . . The root principle is to build vessels to be ready in June or July capable of going in to fetch them.[47]

Despite the continued resistance of his naval staff toward his northern schemes, Churchill refused to be distracted. At the beginning of November, he had begun a monitor force to take and defend an island off the German coast. He had now decided a force also must be built to attack the German fleet in its harbor or to compel it to remain there. When, on December 20 and 21, Lord Fisher lobbied him for new, superfast battle cruisers, the request was initially and emphatically declined by Churchill because he believed that "long before they can be finished, we shall have smashed up the German Navy in harbour with our monitors, or they will have fought their battle on blue water, or peace will have been signed."[48] He went on:

> I could never undertake to attempt to persuade the cabinet to such a measure, after the immense program of monitors and submarines that I have asked them for on the opposite policy—viz everything that can be finished in 1915 and nothing that you can't.
>
> You will have to beat and destroy them with what you've got in 1915: and God knows there is enough—if handled.
>
> The key to the naval situation is an overseas base, taken by force and held by force . . . and for which a series of desperate fights will take place by sea and land, to the utter ruin of the enemy.[49]

Churchill wanted a short war and intended to win it in 1915. On August 8, he had instructed Rear Adm. Horace Lambert Alexander Hood, who was then Churchill's naval secretary, that "all departments should proceed on the general assumption that the war will last one year of which the greatest effort should be concentrated on the first six months."[50] Churchill did not review this arrangement until May 1915.

Perhaps as a sweetener to secure his new battle cruisers, around this time Fisher discussed with or showed to Churchill a memorandum being prepared for him by naval Historian Julian Corbett. The memorandum promoted a possible incursion into the Baltic to "enable an adequate Russian army to land in the spring on the coast of Pomerania within striking distance of Berlin so as to threaten the German communications eastward."[51]

Sweeten, it did not. The memorandum recognized the importance of first blocking German access to the North Sea through the Kiel Canal before any force could enter the Baltic. Rather than promoting the capture of an island to achieve this, the paper argued one must "sow the North Sea with mines on such a scale that naval operations in it would become impossible."[52]

This represented a significant difference in opinion between Fisher and Churchill. Each was frustrated by the slow hand of blockade and sought a more aggressive policy. Each supported an incursion in the Baltic as an alternative to continued conflagration in

France and the continuation of the relatively supine role of the fleet. The one thing on which they could not agree was how best to fulfill this vision. Fisher, driven to a more aggressive policy but uncertain in the face of the realities of war, was unsure how this was to be done. Churchill, however, was emphatic:

> I am wholly with you about the Baltic. But you must close up on this side first. You must take an island and block them in a la Wilson; or you must break the canal or the locks, or you must cripple their fleet in a general action.
>
> No scattering of mines will be any substitute for these alternatives.
>
> The Baltic is the only theatre in which naval action can appreciably shorten the war. Denmark must come in, and the Russians let loose on Berlin.
>
> There are 4 good Russian dreadnoughts.[53]

Churchill was careful not to alienate his strongest supporter, however. Whether from caution or conversion, his next attempt to win over his War Council colleagues for his island scheme wisely recommended that the effort be accompanied by an intense mining program. In the end, Fisher also got his battle cruisers, but only after emphasizing the rapidity of their construction—to meet Churchill's time frame—and demonstrating the degree to which their limited draft made them eminently suited to operations in the Baltic. It is probable Churchill was persuaded to support the battle cruiser plan because the eight-gunned battleships were converted to six-gunned battle cruisers freeing up a number of 15-inch turrets that were subsequently used in the new 15-inch monitors laid down in January 1915.

With the dawn of a new year rapidly approaching, and the war in France in stalemate, Churchill wrote a letter to Prime Minister Asquith on December 30 outlining his proposal for offensive action in 1915. He followed this with a more detailed memorandum on December 31. This time he made a direct appeal for a Baltic strategy. His memorandum again emphasized the value of such an operation to the "security of Great Britain. . . . Surprise, raid or invasion would be prevented. The military forces in England would be liberated for oversea service in any direction required."[54]

Churchill argued that it was unlikely that either side had the strength to penetrate the other's lines in either the west or east. He wanted the War Council to consider alternative strategies to sending

Britain's growing military power to "chew barbed wire in Flanders."[55] He asked, "Ought we not engage him on new frontiers, and enable the Russians to do so too?"[56]

In his memorandum distributed to the members of the War Council, he elaborated:

> The British must capture a German island for an oversea base as soon as possible; It must mine on the most extensive scale the channels and rivers of the German coast; and from their advanced base must prevent the mines from being removed. . . . The German fleet having been effectually excluded from the North Sea by the blocking of the Heligoland Bight. . . . Schleswig-Holstein could be invaded in force, and an advance made upon the Kiel Canal. . . . As soon as a British army has established itself in Schleswig-Holstein, Denmark should be invited to join the Allies. . . . On the accession of Denmark to the alliances, Funes Island can be occupied by British troops and the passage of the Great Belt secured. . . . A British fleet strong enough to fight a decisive battle should then enter the Baltic and establish command of the sea. . . . It would then be possible to land a Russian army at various points on the Baltic shore.[57]

In his penultimate paragraph to Asquith, Churchill wrote:

> There are three phases of the naval war, first the clearance of the seas and the recall of the foreign squadrons, that is nearly completed; second, the closing of the Elbe—that we have now to do; and third, the domination of the Baltic—that would be decisive. . . . Plans could be made now for April and May which would offer good prospects of bringing the war to its decisive stage by land and sea. We ought not to drift.[58]

These proposals were not unlike those mooted with Jellicoe some months before, except in one essential way. His former proposals had mentioned the use of Russian troops on Germany's northern coast. Now Churchill was also proposing a use for the Kitchener's New Armies—the invasion of Schleswig-Holstein. Thus protected from the threat of German invasion, the Danes could join the allies. This, in turn, would give a British Fleet the opportunity to sweep the entrances to the Baltic clear of mines and overcome one of the more obvious impediments to the Baltic operation.

Thus at the end of 1914, despite years of resistance from his key naval advisers and equally unsympathetic hearings from the army, Churchill remained convinced that the quickest way to end the war was through amphibious operations in the northern theater. His Chief Naval Advisors, Oliver, Admiral, Sir Henry Jackson, and Richmond, and his Naval Secretary, Charles de Bartolome, all were against such operations, but Churchill always had just enough support from Fisher, Wilson, and Bayly to sustain him. Never once did he surrender to the obstacles placed before him by his advisers. Instead, he countered with ideas of his own, whether they be at the tactical level with his "hen-coops" and "bulging" and unsinkable monitor fleet or at a strategic level with his plan to use Kitchener's New Armies in Schleswig-Holstein to open the Baltic to the British Fleet.

It is probable Churchill sometimes agitated for agitations sake, but it would be a gross underestimation of his commitment to his offensive schemes to suggest that he promoted them merely to provoke some kind of offensive outcome from his naval advisers. Churchill's actions—especially toward the Borkum Baltic—were too earnest, too prolonged, and too consistent to be marked merely as "kite-flying."

Churchill was convinced that his navy must be allowed to act more decisively on the outcome of the war and was equally certain that he knew the best means by which it could do so. Moreover, for much of his time as First Lord, he was driven by a time frame probably not shared by anyone else. He retained a determination to see the war ended—or at least decided—in 1915.

This, he believed, could be achieved only in the north and he would remain determined, whatever distractions might occur, to persuade his colleagues and his naval staff that he knew the best way forward. Before proceeding to consider the developments of the new year and the manner in which Churchill continued to nurture his northern aspirations, one must first address two of the "distractions" to which he gave his attention during 1914: Zeebrugge and the Dardanelles.

NOTES

1. Gilbert, *CVIII*, part 1, 12–13. Letter, Churchill to Grey.
2. Ibid., 19.
3. On August 20, when Churchill learned that the Dutch were allowing large importations of food-stuffs to Germany via Rotterdam but were

refusing admission to Belgium via Antwerp, he wrote to Grey, "I have always felt that if Holland were to strangle her small neighbour who is fighting for her life, she would commit an offence which would deprive her of all claims to our sympathy." Ibid., 46–47.

4. Gilbert, *CVIII*, 24–26. Letter Churchill to Prince Louis and Sturdee, August 9, 1914.

5. Ibid.

6. Ibid.

7. Ibid.

8. Ibid., 14–15. Letter, Churchill to Grey, August 3, 1914.

9. Ibid.

10. Ibid., 45–46. Churchill Memorandum, August 19, 1914.

11. Fisher to Lady Jellicoe, August 16, 1914, *Fear God and Dreadnought: The Correspondence of Admiral of the Fleet Lord Fisher of Kilverstone*, ed. Arthur J. Marder (London: Jonathon Cape, 1959), 51.

12. Marder, *Fear God and Dreadnought*, footnote 2, 57.

13. He does not mention that the establishment of an island would precede any attempt to block the Kiel Canal. However, the idea of using an island as an air base for such attacks is mentioned in his August 9 proposal so this can be reasonably assumed.

14. Gilbert, *CVIII*, 45–46. Churchill Memorandum, August 19, 1914.

15. Gilbert, *CVIII*, 48.

16. David Edwards, *Inside Asquith's Cabinet: From the Diaries of Charles Hobhouse* (London: John Murray, 1977), 183.

17. Gilbert, *CVIII*, 53. Telegram, Grand Duke Nicholas to Winston S. Churchill, August 24, 1914.

18. Ibid., 53.

19. Churchill to Grey, August 29, Gilbert, *CVIII*, 65. Such issues may have been part of cabinet discussions on September 2 and September 4.

20. Gilbert, *CVIII*, 97–98. Letter, Churchill to Asquith, Grey, and Kitchener,. Churchill attached a letter "written three years ago when these problems were considered in cold blood." Gilbert does not identify the letter mentioned.

21. Ibid.

22. Ibid.

23. Ibid.

24. CHAR 13/28/27-28. Letter, Fisher to Churchill, September 9, 1914.

25. Notes of meeting are from Patterson, *The Jellicoe Papers*, 69.

26. Ibid., 69.

27. Ibid., 71–73. Letter, Jellicoe to Churchill, September 30, 1914.

28. Ibid., 73–75. Letter, Churchill to Jellicoe, October 8, 1914.

29. Ibid.

30. Gilbert, *CVIII*, 217. Letter, Asquith to Venetia Stanley, October 24, 1914.

31. Ibid.

32. Richmond's diary entry, October 24, 1914, Marder, *Portrait of an Admiral*, 121.

33. Gilbert, *CVIII*, 220.

34. CHAR 13/27a. Telegram, Churchill to Japanese Minister of Marine, November 2, 1914.

35. Ibid.

36. Gilbert, *CVIII*, Part 2, 967.

37. Ibid.

38. Ian Buxton, *Big Gun Monitors: Design, Construction, and Operation 1914–1951* (World Ship Society and Trident Books, 1978), 12.

39. Marder, *From Dreadnought to Scapa Flow*, vol. 2, 184.

40. Gilbert, *CVIII*, 290. Minutes of War Council Meeting, December 1, 1914. (Also 42.1.5)

41. Ibid.

42. I have not been able to find a copy of this document.

43. Gilbert, *CVIII*, 292–294. Churchill Memorandum, December 2, 1914.

44. Ibid., 292.

45. Marder, *From Dreadnought to Scapa Flow*, vol. 2, 188–189.

46. Gilbert, *CVIII*, 304. A.K. Wilson to First Lord, December 10, 1914.

47. Ibid., 305. Churchill to Fisher, December 11, 1914.

48. Gilbert, *CVIII*, 324. Letter, Churchill to Fisher, December 21, 1915.

49. Ibid.

50. Ibid., 21–22. Letter, Churchill to Rear Adm. Horace Lambert Alexander Hood, August 8, 1915.

51. Ibid., 286. Fisher's Memorandum: "On the possibility of using our Command of the Sea to influence more drastically the Military Situation on the Continent." This probably had been discussed at a luncheon engagement with Corbett on December 14. See Marder, *From Dreadnought to Scapa Flow*, vol. 2, 93. For more on the origins of this document, see Mackay, *Fisher*, 472.

52. Ibid.

53. Gilbert, *CVIII*, 325–326. Letter, Churchill to Fisher, December 22, 1914.

54. Gilbert, *CVIII*, 347–348. Churchill Memorandum, December 31, 1914.

55. Gilbert, *CVIII, 343–345.* Letter, Churchill to Asquith, December 30, 1914. Churchill (*The World Crisis*, 484) says that he wrote this letter on December 29.

56. Ibid., 343–345.

57. Gilbert, *CVIII*, 347–348. Churchill Memorandum, December 31, 1914.

58. Gilbert, *CVIII*, 345. Letter, Churchill to Asquith, December 30, 1914.

CHAPTER 4

Churchill, French, and Zeebrugge

One of the more significant operations to occupy Churchill's mind during the opening months of the war was a joint assault along the Belgian coast that would include an amphibious operation to liberate Zeebrugge from the Germans. Although the complete operation would have involved a considerable number of troops and a substantial bombardment force, it was not of the grand strategic scale of Churchill's northern plans. It was driven more by necessity than grand design. Initially, it was viewed as an outflanking maneuver; then it was considered desirable to prevent German use of Zeebrugge and Ostende as submarine bases. Finally, Churchill viewed a creep ever closer to the Dutch frontier as a means by which to stiffen the Dutch backbone for an accession to the Allied side.

The origin of a joint military-naval operation along the Belgian coast was probably a trip to France by Churchill on September 17. Lord Kitchener had suggested Churchill propose to Sir John French that the BEF——then separated from the coast by French troops——take over the extreme left of the line in France.[1] French initially resisted the proposal but, on September 27, Churchill visited French again and they agreed that, should they be unable to turn the German Army, it might be possible "to snatch from the enemy's possession the Belgian coastline as far as, at any rate, Zeebrugge."[2]

Churchill left France undertaking to prepare a fleet to support a flanking operation on the Belgian coastline.[3]

As military action drew ever more closely to the Belgian coast, Churchill's bombardment squadron of old cruisers, sloops, gunboats, and the three recently acquired monitors, HMS *Severn*, HMS *Humber*, and HMS *Mersey*, began operations on October 18. The fighting on the Western Front had indeed developed into a series of outflanking maneuvers that became known as the "Race to the Sea." The bombarding vessels were charged with "breaking up . . . German troop movements, particularly along the coastal road from Ostende to Nieuport and the prevention of any German movements by sea."

As the prospect of German control of parts of the Belgian and French coastline loomed ever larger, Churchill wrote to French on October 26, again proposing a serious attempt to outflank the Germans with the assistance of his naval firepower. "We must have them off the Belgian coast even if we cannot recover Antwerp," he insisted. "I could give you overwhelming support from the sea, and there you will have a flank which certainly they cannot turn."[4] Churchill was quite enamored with the performance of his bombardment squadron and, on October 29, he requested Rear Admiral Hood, no longer Churchill's Naval Secretary but commander of the Dover Patrol, to signal his ships the following message: "The inshore flotilla and squadron have played an appreciable part in the great battle now proceeding. You have shown the Germans that there is one flank they cannot turn."[5]

Of course, apart from some minor disruption, naval operations had little to do with the German failure to outflank the Allies. This laurel must go to the natural barrier of the Yser River, the Belgian decision to flood their countryside, and, subsequently, the First Battle of Ypres.

Hood's correspondence with Churchill did not overflow with optimism either. On November 5, he informed Churchill he could see little from his ships and that it was "impossible to tell friend from foe." As to naval-only operations, "ships cannot win battles onshore, though they can exert effect (chiefly moral) by [dumping] heavy fire over a certain area."[6]

Churchill's convictions were otherwise and, as a result, he maintained an unbridled confidence in the efficacy of naval bombardment on land targets.

During November, with the ports of Zeebrugge and Ostende firmly in the hands of the Germans, Churchill grew ever more anxious over the threat that would soon be posed by German submarines operating from these bases. On November 19, he instructed

Fisher, Wilson, and Oliver to prepare plans to "bombard Zeebrugge and Ostende as soon as possible in the most effective manner."[7] Three days later, he again encouraged French to undertake a major operation "along the sand-dunes of the shore to Ostende and Zeebrugge," seductively describing the "absolutely devastating support" his bombardment fleet could offer. He proposed, "[f]or four or five miles inshore we could make you perfectly safe and superior. Here at least, you have their flank, if you care to use it."[8]

Despite this profoundly optimistic assessment of naval bombardment, Sir John French had begun to doubt the viability of a flanking operation. Among his concerns was the belief an advance to Ostende would be met by more deliberate flooding of the lowlands and this might arrest progress and cut off support by the fleet. In any circumstance, he wished to await events in Poland, where Germans surrounded Russian forces at Lodz.[9]

Churchill persisted. He informed French that "the idea of the lines congealing for the winter with those people in Ostende and Zeebrugge" was "very unpleasant to the Admiralty. Mining is no use against submarines and bombardment only gives temporary relief."[10]

Churchill organized a visit to French on December 7, and they discussed the projected coastal operation and naval cooperation. He returned to England the same day and put his views and those of French—now apparently more enthusiastic for the operation—to Kitchener, Asquith, and Grey.[11] A decision was reached to support a flanking operation and, on December 9, Grey instructed Sir Francis Bertie, Britain's ambassador in Paris, to make the French government aware of "the strong opinion held by His Majesty's Government that British troops should be so placed in the line as to advance along the coast in immediate co-operation with our Fleet."[12]

The same day Churchill beseeched French to "find every means to press the policy on Joffre." The "Admirals here are red hot for it," he declared and promised to send details of the naval preparations the next day.[13]

Whether all his Admirals were truly "red hot" for the operation is unclear, but his First Sea Lord certainly was. Indeed, Fisher's own testimony suggests that he was the primary driving force behind the operation. It is probable it was Fisher who had proposed the idea, first mentioned in Churchill's letter of November 22, of landing a military force at Zeebrugge in conjunction with French's advance. He had written to Fitzgerald, Kitchener's secretary, on December 8: "[W]e must as I said the first day I came here get . . . the British

Army on the Sea Flank . . . and shove along and sweep the whole Belgian Coast clear of Germany and get Antwerp."[14]

Fisher had written to Jellicoe on December 9: "I'm fighting to get the British Army on the sea flank. It's so obvious, yet it's not done. Our coast bombardments are futile now, as no military advantage taken of them. 10,000 British soldiers at Zeebrugge after the bombardment would have turned the German flank. *All admit this!*"[15]

The same day he wrote in a similar vein to Adm. David Beatty: "I've staked my billet on getting the British Army on the sea flank next week with the British Fleet bombarding. If so, we ought to be in Antwerp in 10 days and recover all the Belgian coast to the Dutch frontier."[16]

Fisher's letter to Jellicoe illustrates an early resistance to bombardment operations not supported by the army. This would become manifest in January when the Dardanelles operation came to the fore. The Zeebrugge bombardment referred to in Fisher's letter to Jellicoe occurred on November 21 when a fleet of two "Duncans" and supporting vessels sent 400 shells into the port. Subsequent anecdotal evidence suggests considerable damage was achieved, but Fisher evidently placed little store in this. In any event, any damage done could be quickly repaired.[17]

Churchill was not happy with Fisher's proposal to land a force at Zeebrugge and he wrote to Fisher on December 10: "I am shy of landing under fire—unless there is no other way."[18] Nevertheless, he went along with the proposal. The same day Churchill offered French two battleships, three monitors, two gunboats, six destroyers, and 20 armor-plated trawlers for the operation, which he considered "should be sufficient to support the advance of the Army to Ostende." He also proposed a force of 10,000 men be used to take and hold Zeebrugge until the army "came up."[19] Once Zeebrugge was captured, he hoped the submarines would be destroyed or driven off and the ships could then "keep abreast" of French's advance along the coast.

While Churchill and French planned for the operation, the French government referred any decision on a coastal operation to Gen. Joseph Joffre. French feared Joffre and Foch would make difficulties, and this they proceeded to do. He was informed that Foch was planning an attack on Wytschaete and Messines, and the British army would be required to lend support.[20]

In the meantime, the French requested British naval support along the Belgian coast for another minor operation. Churchill was angered by France's insistence to attempt "their feeble secondary 'dog-in-the-manger' attack on the left flank,"[21] but he offered nevertheless to support it with a reduced force. He expressed, however, his extreme reluctance to risk his ships "unless to support a real movement in which case every risk will be run and ample support provided"[22]

By December 19, Churchill's reluctance to support minor French operations along the coast had grown further: "small vessels by themselves cannot free the new shore batteries and it is not justifiable to expose battleships to submarine perils unless to support a land attack of primary importance."[23]

While Churchill brooded over France's refusal to fall in behind his coastal offensive, the French attack against Wytschaete and Messines concluded with indifferent results. Churchill wrote to Sir John French on December 28, expressing his sorrow over the British losses but hoping he now would "get to the sea flank." The same day, French wrote to Kitchener informing him that General Joffre, chief of the French general staff, finally had agreed to allow the British Army to move to the sea flank, but he had refused to accede to a coastal advance.

By this time, and in face of practical difficulties and his own efforts to energize his Borkum/Baltic aspirations, it was Churchill who was beginning to cool toward the Zeebrugge operation. In his Borkum/Baltic letter to Asquith on December 29, he assumed two more corps would be required to relieve the French and take up a position on the coast and that these could not be supplied before March. Delay had already given the Germans time to build defenses and, in his judgment, the flank move was a "very different move from what it was when we first talked it over six weeks ago."[24]

Two days later, however, Churchill's interest was rekindled when French informed him of his intention to enter negotiations with the Belgian king regarding a scheme that "should enable me to take over the line within the next two or three weeks and find a sufficient reserve to enter energetically upon a land advance."

The following morning, events conspired to provide even greater impetus to the Zeebrugge operation while temporarily foiling Churchill's Borkum plans. Vice Admiral Bayly, since 1913 Churchill's strongest advocate of amphibious operations and newly appointed to command of the 5th Battle Squadron at Nore, was exercising his squadron when HMS *Formidable* was struck and sunk by a torpedo. *Formidable* was one of the vessels Churchill hoped would become the nucleus of his specially trained bombarding fleet through which he intended to "develop the means of a naval offensive."[25] It was rumored at the time that Bayly was coming down to prepare for an attack on Borkum.[26]

Bayly was considered culpable and was removed from command. Now, under serious pressure from Fisher and the Admiralty staff,[27] Churchill drafted a letter to Kitchener recommending in the strongest terms that Zeebrugge be taken as part of major joint operation along the Belgian coast. Citing the sinking of the *Formidable* and the threat posed by the submarines at Zeebrugge as grounds for a serious offensive, he asked Kitchener to place before the French commanders his admirals' conviction that it would be "possible, under cover of warships, to land a large force at Zeebrugge in conjunction with any genuine movement along the seashore to Ostende."[28]

Churchill followed this with a letter of his own to French:

> The coast game is I think more difficult now; and if we do it we must concert the naval measures with you to a nicety. Zeebrugge I feel sure shd at the critical moment—and as the thong of your attack—be assailed from the sea; and then kick back towards Ostende.[29]

Churchill told French that "[w]e shall be ready to run great risks in your support," but there was a hint his mind was already elsewhere:

> Here—within my own ramparts—I have a very strong line whether for defence or offence. Yet it would be a great relief to me to talk over with you the ideas which are now coming to the fore, and which will determine the scope and character of the war in the summer. Well perhaps a chance will come.[30]

The "ideas" to which Churchill referred were his own Baltic scheme and papers prepared in the last days of December by Hankey and Lloyd George. These latter papers will be discussed when this book moves to the events of the new year.

Thus, at the end of 1914, in addition to his Borkum/Baltic scheme, Churchill was supporting a subsidiary but complementary operation that would see the Navy contributing a vital role in divesting the Germans of the Belgian coastline. The operation would have the practical advantage not only of significantly reducing the German submarine threat, but also in drawing the Allied armies closer to Holland and, therefore, in Churchill's mind, increasing the likelihood of Dutch accession to the Allied side. This in turn increased the likelihood of his much larger amphibious operations taking place.[31]

Yet within weeks, all Churchill's northern aspirations were to be subsumed by operations in the Dardanelles in such a manner it has caused historians to assert Churchill had discarded the impossible for the possible and turned his back on his northern dreams. Before looking more closely at the events of 1915 and the extent to which this assessment is inaccurate, we must return to August 1914 to consider the evolution of Churchill's interest in Turkey and the Mediterranean.

NOTES

1. George H. Cassar, *The Tragedy of Sir John French* (Cranbury, NJ: Associated University Presses, 1985), 154.

2. Field Marshal Viscount of Ypres (John) French, *1914* (London: Constable, 1919).

3. Ibid., 303.

4. Ibid., 304.

5. Gilbert, *CVIII*, part 1, 229. In Prior, "Churchill's 'World Crisis,'" 166–167, it is pointed out that Churchill was possibly entitled to enthusiasm in October, but subsequent reports were far more doubtful as to the efficacy and value of the bombardment. By the end of December, "Hood was convinced the ships could not silence the land batteries and he strongly hinted his squadron should be withdrawn."

6. CHAR 13/44, 89–96. Hood to Churchill, November 5, 1914. Winston S. Churchill, Chartwell Papers, Churchill College, Cambridge.

7. Gilbert, *CVIII*, part 1, 269. Churchill to Fisher, Oliver and Wilson, November 19, 1914.

8. Letter, Churchill to French, November 22, 1914.

9. See Gilbert, *CVIII*, footnote 282. Gilbert notes that Lodz fell to the Germans on December 6, and as a result, all hope of a Russia advance into German Silesia ended.

10. Ibid., 282.

11. Ibid., 298. Letter, Churchill to Asquith, Grey and Kitchener, December 7, 1915.

12. French, *1914*, 306. Telegram, Grey to Bertie, December 9, 1914.

13. CHAR 13/27a/45-49, Telegram, Churchill to French, December 10, 1914. Also Admiralty memorandum sketching out naval support for army.

14. Prior, "Churchill's 'World Crisis,'" 190.

15. Marder, *Fear God and Dreadnought*, 90.

16. Ibid., 92.

17. For a brief description of the operation see: Julian S. Corbett, *History of the Great War: Naval Operations*, vol. 2 (London: Longmans, Green & Co., 1921), 12–13.

18. Marder, *Fear God and Dreadnought*, 91.

19. Gilbert, *CVIII*, part 1, 302–303.

20. French, *1914*, 52.

21. Gilbert, *CVIII*, part 1, 312. Telegram, Churchill to French.

22. Ibid.

23. Ibid., 317. Churchill to French, December 19, 1914. (Also, CHAR 13/27b/133) This was, in fact, based on a recommendation from Hood made on December 17. See Prior, "Churchill's 'World Crisis,'" 167.

24. Churchill, *The World Crisis*, 55–56.

25. Ibid., 56–57.

26. Admiral of the Fleet (Rosslyn Erskine) Wester-Wemyss, *The Navy in the Dardanelles Campaign* (London: Hodder and Stoughton, 1924).

27. This is strongly suggested in Churchill, *The World Crisis*, 57.

28. Ibid., 58.

29. Gilbert, *CVIII*, part 1, 358. Letter, Churchill to French.

30. Ibid.

31. Such motivations are revealed in a letter from Churchill to French written on January 11, 1915, Gilbert, *CVIII*, 402–403.

CHAPTER 5

Churchill and Turkey, August–December 1914

While Churchill's strategic focus remained in Northern Europe during 1914, his attention was inevitably drawn to the possibilities and responsibilities of the Mediterranean in the opening days of the war. The belated Austrian declaration of war, Britain's decision to withhold Turkey's new battleship, *Oman I*, and the escape of *Goeben* and *Breslau* into the Sea of Marmora were just three events that placed Turkey at the center of Cabinet and Admiralty discussion during the early months of the war. The combined additional threat of Austria and a Turko-German fleet quickly drew two more British battle cruisers and sundry other craft to the Mediterranean. As indicated, these were unwelcomed developments for Churchill who saw this new threat as a constraint on his northern strategies.

Almost from the outbreak of war, Churchill and Lloyd George displayed a desire to establish a Balkan Federation of Greece, Bulgaria, and Romania against the Central powers. They were encourage by the representation of Greek Prime Minister Eleutherios Venizelos in early August, who suggested that this force of united Balkan States could go to the aid of Serbia and together they would destroy Austria.[1] Venizelos proposed that they could be rewarded for unity and cooperation by slices of Austrian territory.[2] Churchill and Lloyd George were inclined to agree.

Churchill quickly went one step further. Acutely chaffed by the actions of Turkey and the escape of the *Goeben* and *Breslau* into

Turkish waters, he quickly concluded that it would only be a matter of time before Turkey was lost to the enemy. He would soon begin to argue that Turkish territory also might be offered as a reward for a Balkan Federation and with much better results.

From the beginning of the war, Churchill took an aggressive stance against the Turks. On August 15, he urged Enver Pasha, the Turkish Minister for War, to maintain strict and honest neutrality, warning that superior naval power rendered it possible for England, France, Russia, and Japan to transport unlimited troops to strike a blow at the heart of Turkey.[3] Two days later, he spoke hotly of sending a torpedo flotilla through the Dardanelles to sink the two offending German vessels.

Neither threats nor more diplomatic measures saw any satisfactory movement from the Turks and served only to harden Churchill's conviction that Turkey already had been lost to the enemy.

In the meantime, with tension between Turkey and Greece escalating, Venizelos informed the British government on August 19 that Greece was willing to place her military and naval forces at the disposal of the entente if required. Here, suddenly, was an army with which Churchill might fulfill his bold threat to Enver Pasha made four days earlier.[4]

At the end of August, with Anglo-Turkish relations in a serious state and an offer of Greek naval and military support still standing, Churchill requested Kitchener organize a group of naval and military officers to "work out a plan for the seizure by means of a Greek Army of adequate strength . . . the Gallipoli Peninsula, with a view to admitting a British Fleet to the Sea of Marmora."[5]

The following day, September 1, a meeting was held at the Admiralty between members of the War Office and the Admiralty, where it was concluded that an attack on the peninsula was not a feasible military operation.[6]

While these discussions were taking place, the prospect of war between Greece and Turkey became even more serious. Turkish and Bulgarian demands for Greek territory, and assertions by Ottoman ambassadors in Paris and Petrograd that the acquisition of the *Goeben* and *Breslau* was directed against Greece, had prompted Prime Minister Venizelos to ask whether Greece might expect support from the British government in the event of aggression by the new Turkish Fleet.

Grey responded that in such an event the British government, which continued to view the *Goeben* and *Breslau* as German warships, would not permit them or Turkish ships to leave the Dardanelles.

The imminent prospect of war with Turkey prompted Churchill to organize another meeting to discuss plans for the forcing of the Dardanelles.[7]

At the end of the meeting, the Director of Military Operations, Major Gen. Charles Edward Callwell, put his point of view on paper. He argued that an attack upon the Gallipoli Peninsula was "likely to prove an extremely difficult operation of war."[8] Despite offering a number of serious reservations, Callwell was drawn to suggest that the operation—always in the context of a surprise attack—might be attempted with an army of not less than 60,000 men, which would be moved onto the peninsula in two echelons.

This concession was enough for Churchill to direct Rear Adm. Mark Kerr, the commander in chief of the Greek Navy, to begin discussions with the Greek armed forces over a policy to be followed if Britain and Greece became allies in a war against Turkey.[9] Churchill informed Kerr of his wish to have a Greek Army seize the Gallipoli Peninsula to open the Dardanelles, to allow an Anglo-Greek Fleet to enter the Marmora, and to destroy the Turko-German ships. He offered to reinforce the Greek Fleet "to give decisive and unquestionable superiority over the Turkish and German vessels."[10] Once the Straits had been forced, this fleet, "in combination with the Russian Black Sea Fleet and Russian military force could dominate the whole situation."[11] Repeating the words of his warning to Enver Pasha in August, he expressed his belief that the right and obvious method of attacking Turkey was to strike immediately at the heart.

Churchill's preparations for war were most unwelcomed by his Russian allies. The Russian ambassador at Constantinople was desperate to avoid conflict with Turkey, and he was angry that a dispute between Turkey and Greece over Greek possession of Turkish islands might end this way. Far from being prepared to support Churchill's notion of a naval breakthrough into the Marmora intended to destroy the Turko-German Fleet and unleash Russian forces "to dominate the situation," Russia wanted Greece to make the necessary territorial concessions to avoid war.

The Russians had further apprehensions. Should war occur, they believed it would compromise any hope Serbia might attack Austria and thereby take the pressure off Russian forces. Furthermore, the German threat meant that Russia would be unable to support Greece in any conflict with Turkey and neither, he believed, would France or England if the war, "as seems probable be restricted to land."[12]

This final observation suggested the Russians believed one of two things. The first is they feared that, should the Turks confine their attacks on Greece to land, they would avoid direct conflict with Britain and her naval forces and thus avoid giving Britain a *casus belli* for war. The second possibility was that the Russians believed that neither Britain nor France had troops available to help Greece if the conflict was restricted to land.

Churchill assumed the latter was the cause of their anxiety and was completely dismissive of Russian concerns that they would not be able to support the Greeks against Turkey. Once again taking a great liberty with Russia's armed forces, he told Grey that, even if the Greek Army Corps were paralyzed by Bulgarian and Turkish attack, a Russian Army Corp could be brought from Archangel, Vladivostock, or Port Arthur. He noted, "[a] good army of 50,000 men and sea-power—that is the end of the Turkish menace."[13]

Churchill's desire to strike a rapid and decisive blow at the heart of Turkey received another blow two days later when he received his reply from Kerr. Kerr informed him on September 8 that the Greek general staff would not contemplate attacking the Gallipoli Peninsula unless Bulgaria also attacked Turkey with all her force.[14] This particular impediment to Greece's involvement in the war would continue to hamstring Churchill's Balkan aspirations for some time to come.

Despite Churchill's anger over the *Goeben* and *Breslau*, his primary interest in Turkey, like that of Lloyd George, was as a means to achieve a Balkan Federation that would unite against Austria and go to the aid of Serbia. Churchill's aggressive and at times bellicose attitude toward Turkey did not signify a keenness to go to war with her for war's sake. There was a rational basis to his aggressive stand. He was fully aware that war with Turkey risked compounding the Allies' responsibilities in the Mediterranean. He also just had been made clearly aware that war with Turkey would be unwelcomed by his Russian ally.

Nevertheless, Churchill saw no point in trying to supplicate the Turks when all the evidence suggested they would soon throw in their lot with the Germans. Moreover, if war were still to be avoided, he believed a forceful policy would best achieve Britain's aims. He wrote to Grey on September 11: "If Mallet thinks he is dealing with a Govt. amenable to argument, persuasion & proof of good faith, he is dreaming. . . . Nothing appeals to the Turkish Government but force; and they will continue to kick those who they think are unable or unwilling to use it against them."[15]

Churchill was reluctant to miss any opportunity to secure Greek involvement in a war with Turkey when subsequent events might see Britain at war with Turkey without Greek assistance. A failure to deal decisively with Turkey also meant an opportunity was being lost to offer Turkish rather than Austrian territory to unite and draw in the Balkan States in a war against Austria. Bulgaria, for one, might be bought with Turkish territory and, if the Greeks were true to their word, their participation on the Allied side would be assured.

Grey's diplomatic measures were designed to keep Turkey out of the war. He had been against taking up the Greek offer of military aid, fearing this would bring immediate war with Turkey and would foster Russian apprehensions over Constantinople.[16] Grey considered the wisest course was to guarantee the integrity of the Turkish Empire in return for her neutrality. He had offered as much to Turkey on August 19 when he had added a final paragraph to Churchill's letter to Enver Pasha.

Churchill reluctantly accepted this course, but as his certainty over Turkish perfidy grew, he became frustrated and angry. On September 15, he wrote to Grey that "[w]e ought to have absolute freedom to deal with her at the peace as the general convenience & interests of the allies require. I earnestly trust that freedom will not be compromised."[17]

A note exchanged between Kitchener and Churchill during the following day's Cabinet meeting illustrates the points in question:

> LORD KITCHENER:
> I agree that Turkey is behaving so disgracefully that she ought to be informed we shall not forget it after the war is over—I am doubtful whether we should tell Bulgaria that she shall have Adrianople after the war—This would definitely tie us down to action tht might be unpleasant to carry out I quite agree Turkey should be punished but I would not say definitely how this is to be done—
>
> CHURCHILL:
> I don't want vengeance after the show is over—but aid of a Balkan confedn. now—
>
> LORD KITCHENER:
> I do not think that Adrianople offer would be very tempting, they want Servian land & Greek.
>
> CHURCHILL:
> Well—all I ask for is no more consideration for Turkish interests if we can get any advantage with Bulgaria.

KITCHENER:
I agree.[18]

On September 23, Churchill, who was more than ever convinced that Turkey's interests should be freely bartered to secure the support of the Balkan States, continued to press Grey for a change of policy:

> We are suffering very seriously from Turkish hostility. Our whole Mediterranean Fleet is tied to the Dardanelles. We are daily trying to buy Turkish neutrality by promises and concessions. Meanwhile the German grip on Turkey tightens and all preparations for war go steadily forward. *But all this would in itself be of minor consequence but for the fact that in our attempt to placate Turkey we are crippling our policy in the Balkans. I am not suggesting that we should take aggressive action against Turkey or declare war on her ourselves, but we ought from now to make our arrangements with the Balkan States, particularly Bulgaria, without regard to the interests or integrity of Turkey.* (emphasis added)[19]

Grey would not budge and continued to resist any effort to negotiate Turkish territory for the intercession of other Balkan States into the war.

Nevertheless, relations with Turkey were in a downward spiral. On September 27, after one of her destroyers was stopped from putting to sea by an Allied squadron, Turkey closed the Straits and began laying mines and setting nets.

By October 20, even the Cabinet had concluded that Britain "ought to take a vigorous offensive against Turkey and to make every effort to bring in Bulgaria, Greece and, above all, Roumania."[20]

The murky waters of Balkan diplomacy were muddied further on October 21, when Charles Buxton, former Liberal Member of Parliament and now self-appointed Balkan negotiator, telegraphed both Grey and Churchill to fill in the details of his Balkan visit. Pro-Bulgarian, Buxton suggested that Bulgaria's immediate friendly neutrality toward Romania and Serbia could be achieved if the entente powers guaranteed her claim to parts of Macedonia. He suggested, "[f]or her 'support' (corrupted text) in the event of war between Turkey and the Entente powers. Bulgaria ought to be offered the region to the Enos Media line."[21]

To Churchill, Buxton indicated that the only remaining difficulties to bringing in the Balkan States on the side of the Allies were "fear of Bulgaria and uncertainty of European military situation." He sought from Churchill public assurances, which he believed would increase the likelihood of Bulgarian intervention.[22]

It was at this time that Churchill learned of Turkish plans to make an advance on Egypt. Churchill was extremely angry with Grey. Britain now appeared on the verge of war with Turkey—an event Churchill had long considered inevitable—while his hope of a Balkan Federation remained unresolved. He made his feelings known to Grey on October 23 when forwarding a copy of his own telegram: "I should like to talk to you about this. I am very unhappy about our getting into war with Turkey without having Greece as an ally. This was the least to be hoped for. Surely it is not too late."[23]

This had been the crux of his attitude toward Turkey since the earliest days of the war. The Turks, he had long been convinced, were in the German camp. Better act preemptively or in a manner that might best secure Balkan allies, rather than await the inevitable and thereby forego the element of surprise. Grey agreed to meet but continued to argue against making "open statements of support for Balkan ambitions."

In the event, Churchill was right and Grey wrong. On October 29, the *Goeben* and *Breslau*, commanded by Admiral Wilhelm Souchon but flying the Turkish flag, bombarded the Russia Black Sea ports of Odessa, Niolaev, and Sevastapol. Grey wrote to Sir Louis Mallet, the British ambassador to Turkey, insisting on immediate reparations to Russia to avoid war but also expressed the opinion he did not see how it could be avoided. The Cabinet still wished to avoid war, but Churchill sought an immediate demonstration of British sea power and on November 2 with Britain's ultimatum to Turkey now expired, he ordered Vice Adm. Sackville Carden to commence a demonstration against the outer forts of the Dardanelles. War was officially declared between Britain and Turkey on November 5.

It was during this final descent toward war that Churchill sought a third discussion with Callwell on possible operations against the Dardanelles. It is not clear what the source of troops for this operation would be. Callwell once again told Churchill that it was a difficult operation requiring a large force.[24] He apparently added that, in any event, such a force could not be landed until the spring.[25] Churchill also sought information from the Fourth Sea Lord, Capt. Cecil Lambert, and asked him to collaborate with him on "an appreciation of the Dardanelle's problem." Lambert prepared a short paper in which he stated the fleet could transport the army without difficulty, possibly cover a landing but that "the future proceedings of the Fleet would depend on what success the armies met with."[26]

The subject of an attack on the Dardanelles would emerge twice more in events between this time and the end of 1914, but it would seem that late October was the last time Churchill really pressed a joint operation against the Dardanelles as a viable operation. Instead, from November onward—perhaps as a result of Callwell's warning that troops could not be landed until spring (and despite Lambert's advice)—he appeared more interested in forcing the Dardanelles by ships alone.

In contradiction to accepted understanding that Churchill's January 3 telegram represented the genesis of a navy-only attempt to force the Dardanelles, Churchill's Naval Secretary Charles Martin de Bartolome and Chief of Staff Henry Oliver both claimed that Churchill began discussing naval-only operations against the Dardanelles in early November 1914. Bartolome claimed he discussed such an idea informally and frequently "almost from the first occasion of me working with him."[27] Oliver confirmed frequent discussions on the subject from November or December onward.[28] It can reasonably be assumed from their comments that these inquiries failed to succor Churchill's hopes in this regard.

Meanwhile, on November 25, the War Council gathered to discuss Turkey in the context of a CID investigation undertaken during peacetime, which had recommended that a Turkish threat against Egypt could be dealt with by a "counter-offensive at certain points on the coast of Asiatic Turkey." As an extension of this discussion, the minutes record Churchill suggesting "that the ideal method of defending Egypt was by an attack on the Gallipoli Peninsula. This, if successful, would give us control of the Dardanelles, and we could dictate terms at Constantinople. This, however, was a very difficult operation requiring a large force."[29]

The subsequent discussions suggest he did not press the proposition or really consider it viable and, indeed, he seemed to accept that such an operation was undesirable (certainly there was no subsequent discussion over whether it was practicable). His closing statement indicated that he knew that, whatever his preference might have been, his view was not shared by the military:

> If it was considered impracticable, it appeared worthwhile to assemble transports and horse boats at Malta or Alexandria, and to make a feint at Gallipoli, conveying the impression that we intended to land there. Our real point of attack might be Haifa, or some point on the Syrian coast. The Committee of

Imperial Defence in 1909 had recommended that a serious invasion of Egypt could best be met by a landing at Haifa.[30]

It would appear that while still hankering after a more emphatic and decisive operation against the Dardanelles, Churchill was now reluctantly bowing to military and political realities and to recommendations of his naval staff. Churchill's proposals for an attack against Haifa and a feint against Gallipoli were not his own but those of Secretary to the War Council Maurice Hankey and Assistant Director of Operations (ADOD) William Herbert Richmond.[31]

Churchill was in fact typically impatient and premature in recommending any action at all against the Turks. Kitchener agreed that it would be desirable to make diversions on Turkish communications but that the time for this had not yet arrived. It was important at this time to organize the considerable military forces in Egypt. Kitchener "felt no anxiety about Egypt and Suez Canal."[32]

Churchill suggested that "at any rate tonnage should now be collected."

Grey was not enamored of the idea, pointing out that there were already shortages of tonnage for mercantile purposes and it was not desirable to aggravate this.

At this point, the new First Sea Lord, who obviously was not intimate with the preceding months' efforts to draw Greece to the aid of Serbia, asked whether Greece might not undertake an attack on Gallipoli on behalf of the Allies. Grey explained that neither Greece nor Romania were likely to cooperate with the Allies for fear of Bulgaria.

Despite Grey's pessimism on this question, efforts to form a Balkan block were continuing and, indeed, became even more earnest on December 1 when Serbia, then in a desperate fighting withdrawal against Austro-German forces, made a simultaneous appeal to Greece and Romania for immediate assistance. Romania declined to become involved, while Greece returned to its fear of Bulgaria. Venizelos again made it plain that Greece would assist Serbia only provided the entente "guaranteed that Bulgaria would not attack Greece." This might be achieved by Bulgarian intervention in the war or, failing this, a commitment from Romania to protect her from Bulgaria.

Unable to secure anything more than a Bulgarian commitment to neutrality, on December 5, the entente powers finally took the significant step of formally guaranteeing Greece against Bulgaria, provided the latter went immediately to Serbia's aid. At the same time, they asked Romania to join them and guarantee Greece against Bulgaria. This, Romania again declined to do.

With neither Romania nor Bulgaria prepared to play the entente's game, the question then arose of how Britain, France, and Russia were to fulfill their commitment to protect Greece against Bulgaria—and Turkey—if the Greeks went to the aid of Serbia. Venizelos, not surprisingly, was unimpressed by the commitment, informing Elliot on December 7 that he did not see how the entente powers could enforce their promise.

Nor, apparently, did anyone else—except Churchill. On December 5, Asquith wrote to Venetia Stanley that "Churchill's "volatile mind is at present set on Turkey & Bulgaria, and he wants to organise a heroic adventure against Gallipoli and the Dardanelles: to which I am altogether opposed."[33]

A note written by Churchill in the Kitchener Papers entitled "A Vision" sheds some light on the plans that so horrified Asquith:

December 14th	Baghdad captured
December 15th	Concerted advance in the Near East
December 25th	Dardanelles forced. Turkish Army surrenders (Your Christmas present to the Allies)
January 1st	Greece and Roumania come in
January 17th	Occupation of C'ple by British
January 30th	Conference at C'ple of all the Allies to make the plans for a general attack in the summer on all fronts and to fix the quotas of each in men and resources.[34]

This is a rather fanciful document and its title suggests that it was rather whimsical as well. However, it is to be taken seriously as a further indication of Churchill's thinking at the time. Among other things, Churchill's solution to the problem of guaranteeing Greece and Romania against Bulgaria was a naval-only attempt to force the Dardanelles. If this is in fact the plan written of by Asquith on December 5, it is not surprising that he was wholly opposed to it.

After canvassing the use of a Greek army to force the Dardanelles, it appears that Churchill did, for a time, consider a joint operation using British troops—presumably those troops in Egypt. It is evident that the great attraction of an attack against the Dardanelles was that it offered an opportunity to influence the Balkan States at the same time. For this reason, he probably was less than enthusiastic about the smaller and more practicable alternatives—specifically, Alexandretta and Haifa—suggested and supported by his naval advisors and by the military at this time. These alternatives were unlikely to sufficiently impress or inspire Bulgaria, Greece, or Romania. By November 25, however, Churchill already had conceded the impracticability of the attack on the Dardanelles and had begun to explore a naval-only alternative with his advisers.

Churchill's interest in the Dardanelles in 1914–1915 is indisputable. What is much more open to contention is the price Churchill was prepared to pay for the Dardanelles. No evidence suggests Churchill was willing to undertake a full-scale military assault on the Dardanelles with British troops and accept all the risks and commitment such an attempt would entail.

It is important to juxtapose all discussion surrounding the Mediterranean with Churchill's ongoing efforts to initiate serious war-winning amphibious operations in the northern theater.

Writers on the Dardanelles campaign who have not done this—and there are many—have too easily drawn a direct line between Churchill's interest in the Dardanelles up to the end of 1914 and his promotion of a naval-only operation to force the Straits in January 1915. This has led them to accept readily the idea that Churchill's naval-only operation was, at once, a continuation of his preoccupation with the Dardanelles, and a choice reluctantly made at a time when troops were in short supply.

Historians who recognize the paramountcy of Churchill's northern schemes are open to a different and more compelling explanation for the naval-only operation in February and March 1915. They might recognize that Churchill's intense interest in his various northern schemes and his purported desire to have the Dardanelles at all costs—including the prospect of opening a large southern front in which to pour thousands of British troops—were fundamentally incompatible. As the northern winter turned to spring and the War Council searched desperately for an alternative to fighting in France, these two strategies might even be in competition with one another. Churchill could not hold to both strategies—one must subsume the other.

As 1914 drew to a close, with little doubt, Churchill remained particularly enthusiastic for joint operations in a northern theater: Zeebrugge as a near-term possibility and, more distant, Borkum/Baltic. In tandem with Fisher, he still held great hopes for operations in the Baltic. Many of the vessels approved in the last months of 1914 had been authorized with such amphibious operations in mind and even more of these vessels would be ordered in January.

On the cusp of a new year, however, two other members of the War Council, David Lloyd George and Maurice Hankey, sat down and prepared memoranda that promoted the idea of using some of the growing forces in Britain to defeat Turkey, draw in the Balkan States, and begin a southern front. Rather than enthusiastically falling in behind such ideas—surely the most likely response from a man regarded as a great "Easterner" by so many historians—Churchill would resist such operations, especially those propounded by Lloyd George. Instead, in early January, he would continue to press his various northern schemes while conceiving a naval-only operation against the Dardanelles. This plan had the immediate—and this book will argue—deliberate effect of compromising his colleagues' plans to turn the Mediterranean into a major theater of war.

NOTES

1. Churchill to Grey, August 11, 1914, Gilbert, *CVIII*, 30. Also see footnote 3 same page.

2. Asquith to Venetia Stanley, Gilbert, *CVIII*, 32.

3. Ibid., 38–39.

4. Prior, "Churchill's 'World Crisis,'" 181. It appears this was a unilateral decision taken by Venizelos without consultation with the king. Venizelos had just returned from Europe where he had failed to resolve problems surrounding certain Aegean Islands held by Greece but claimed by Turkey and must have feared eminent attack by Turkey and Bulgaria.

5. Gilbert, *CVIII*, 72.

6. Ibid., 91.

7. This meeting took place on September 2 or 3.

8. Gilbert, *CVIII*, 81–82. Paper by Charles Edward Callwell regarding an assault on the Gallipoli Peninsula. Composed September 2 or 3, 1914.

9. Ibid., 83–84. Letter, Churchill to Rear Adm. Mark Kerr.

10. Ibid.

11. Ibid.

12. Buchanan to Grey, September 6, 1914, Gilbert, *CVIII*, 94. This final statement appears to have been based on an assurance conveyed to Grey by Mallet on September 5 that "the Turkish Ministers had assured him that the Turkish Fleet would not try to enter the Aegean" but that "unless Turkish Government could get some real satisfaction about (Aegean) islands . . . they would go to war on land." See Ibid., 93, footnote 2.

13. Gilbert, *CVIII*, 95. Letter, Churchill to Grey.

14. Ibid., 104–105. Telegram, Rear-Admiral Kerr to Churchill, September 8, 1914.

15. Ibid., 108.

16. There were other good reasons for preventing or delaying Turkish entry into the war, not the least of which was to secure the movement of Indian forces through the canal to Europe and to avoid inciting Muslim opinion on Egypt and India by doing anything at all that could be interpreted as "taking the initiative against Turkey." See W. W. Gottlieb, *Studies in Secret Diplomacy During the First World War* (London: Allen and Unwin, 1957), 53.

17. Gilbert, *CVIII*, 118.

18. Ibid., 119–120.

19. Ibid., 131–132.

20. Trumball Higgins, *Winston Churchill and the Dardanelles* (London: Heinemann, 1963), 66.

21. Gilbert, *CVIII*, 208–209.

22. Ibid., 209–210. Correspondence, Buxton to Churchill.

23. Ibid., 214.

24. CAB 19/33, Callwell, Dardanelles Commission, Question 3752–3759.

25. CAB 19/28, Callwell's Statement to Dardanelles Commission.

26. CAB 19/33, Question 4100. In his statement, Lambert suggested this meeting took place in early October.

27. CAB 19/33, Dardanelles Commission, October 5, 1916, Question 1575.

28. CAB 19/33, Dardanelles Commission, Question 1756–1758.

29. CAB 42/1/5, Secretary's Notes of Meeting of War Council, November 25, 1914.

30. Ibid.

31. See letter from Hankey to Crease, May 19, 1915, CAB 42; and Richmond's diary entry, January 16, 1915, in Marder, *Portrait of an Admiral.*

32. CAB 42/1/5, Secretary's Notes of Meeting of War Council, November 25, 1914.

33. Gilbert, *CVIII*, 327. Letter, Asquith to Venetia Stanley, December 5, 1915.

34. Kitchener Papers, PRO, 30/57/74, cited by Sara Reguer, "Churchill's Role in the Dardanelles Campaign," *The British Army Review* 108 (December 1994): 71.

CHAPTER 6

The War Council's Dilemma: North or South?

In the opening weeks of 1915, the War Council began to search in earnest for an alternative to the stalemate on the Western Front. Casualties in the first months of the war had astounded and appalled everyone. All were convinced that the probable result of renewed fighting in France in the spring would be further heavy losses and continued deadlock. To Hankey, Lloyd George, and even Kitchener, the idea of holding the line in France while undertaking operations in a southern theater that might bring in the various Balkan and Mediterranean States appeared an attractive option. Churchill, too, saw merit in operations of this nature. Such an idea had been at the center of his arguments with Grey over Turkey in the preceding four months. Without doubt, however, his heart remained more firmly set on an amphibious strategy in Northern Europe that would seize the advantage against the Germans. There were precious few resources available for one, let alone two, additional theaters of war, and Churchill must have known one must give way to the other. Here were the makings of a true strategic dilemma. In the opening days of 1915, the challenge for Churchill would be to reconcile the arguments for these two offensive thrusts and keep his northern dreams alive.

* * * * *

The day before Churchill presented his letter to Prime Minister Asquith on December 29, in which he proposed his Borkum/Baltic operations as the decisive strategy for 1915, another memorandum was circulated to the War Council by Colonel Hankey.[1] The memorandum was Hankey's own strategic plan for 1915.

Like Churchill, Hankey had been inspired by the eve of the new year to set to paper his thoughts on the strategies best adopted in 1915. Also, like Churchill, he had as a central theme a belief that further action in the West would be not only bloody but unproductive, and he sought to break the deadlock through action in another theater of war.[2]

Hankey wanted to bring in the united Balkan states of Bulgaria, Greece, and Romania to attack Turkey and Austria. This was not an original idea. What was novel was the suggestion—hitherto avoided by the Allies—that, instead of merely inciting these countries to attack Turkey and Austria, the Allies should commit three Allied corps, including one first-line army corps to a campaign in Turkey. This force, he believed, in conjunction with Greece and Bulgaria, ought to be sufficient to capture Constantinople. Once this was achieved, "Russia could hold an entrenched line against Germany, while combining with Serbia and Roumania in an advance into Hungary. The complete downfall of Austria-Hungary could then be secured."[3]

Not surprisingly, Churchill had some sympathy for Hankey's ideas regarding Turkey. Churchill forwarded a copy of Hankey's memorandum to Asquith on December 31, writing, "I have talked to Hankey. We are substantially in agreement and our conclusions are not incompatible. I wanted Gallipoli attacked on the Turkish declaration of war. But Kitchener does not work far afield or far ahead, *vide* Antwerp. Meanwhile the difficulties have increased."[4]

It is notable that his Borkum/Baltic memorandum distributed to the War Council that day now included the assertion that if the Baltic offensive "were accompanied by the entry into the war of Italy and Roumania, the end would not be long deferred."[5] This appeared to be a concession to Hankey's proposals. Churchill recommended the War Council meet daily for a few days the following week to discuss the proposals.

Two proposals now were before the War Council. A third soon followed. Lloyd George circulated a paper on January 1 recommending two independent operations designed to destroy Germany's allies and force Germany to "attenuate her line of defence."[6] In making his proposals, he took the opportunity to take a swipe at Churchill and Fisher's Borkum/Baltic aspirations, describing them as "very hazardous, and by no means certain to fulfil the purpose which its originators have in view."[7]

The first operation proposed by Lloyd George involved using 600,000 of the vast number of men that would be available in England by April to attack Austria "in conjunction with the Serbians, the Roumanians and the Greeks." Like Hankey, he believed the assistance of "the two latter countries would be assured if they knew that a great English force would be there to support them."[8]

Lloyd George's second plan proposed an attack on Turkey. However, one of his conditions for such an action—quite the opposite of Churchill's idea of "striking at the heart"—was that it should force "Turkey to fight at a long distance from her base of supplies and in country which would be disadvantageous to her."[9] He hoped that some 80,000 Turkish troops might be trapped and destroyed in Syria, one advantage of which would be the relief of pressure on the Russians in the Caucasus.

The impact of stalemate on the Western Front and the advent of a new year, therefore, had precipitated an intense search for an alternative theater of war. Churchill, for long a lone voice within the War Cabinet in proposing alternative offensive action, was alone no longer. Rather than uniting behind his northern schemes, however, Churchill's Cabinet colleagues were looking southward to the Mediterranean as an alternative theater for serious naval and military operations.[10] Fortunately for Churchill, Asquith thought all three plans worth reviewing and instructed him to prepare his proposals for a War Council meeting of the following week.[11]

Churchill took immediate advantage of this directive and on January 3 wrote to Lord Fisher, Sir Arthur Wilson, and Vice Admiral Oliver requesting that all preparations should be made for the capture of Sylt (Churchill's codename for Borkum), which, he hoped, would begin either on March 1 or April 15. To this end, he demanded "[a]ll necessary appliances, and any likely to be useful should be ordered *now.*"[12]

Clearly sensitive to earlier criticisms of such an operation, but clearly undeterred, Churchill nominated a number of appliances and materiel he believed would make a decisive difference, including monitors, unsinkable transports for 12,000 infantry, and flat-bottomed landing craft. He believed his bombarding vessels would be able to subdue the fire from batteries to allow the transports, protected by darkness and smoke and sheltered by older cruisers, to land 8,000 to 12,000 infantry who would locate the guns. Thereafter, the ships could quickly silence them.

Into this scene now crowded with a variety of offensive plans came events that would, seven weeks later, culminate in an attempt to force the Dardanelles Straits with a number of old battleships. Lloyd George's and Hankey's ideas of using a large British or Allied army to draw in the Balkan States had failed to bear fruit, while Churchill's Borkum/Baltic dreams had been forgotten by all but Churchill himself.

On January 1, Sir Edward Grey received a Russian request for a demonstration against the Turks—either naval or military—to ease the pressure on the Russian Army in the Caucasus.[13] He had it circulated to Churchill and Kitchener the same day.

This request for aid has acquired greater historical importance than it deserves because most historians and Churchill himself contend that the obligation this request imposed on Britain, combined with Kitchener's subsequent assertion that no troops were available for military operations, led directly to the naval-only attempt to force the Dardanelles. There is, however, only a slim link between the Russian call for aid on January 1 and Churchill's decision to promote a naval-only operation against the Dardanelles on January 13—and it is by no means direct. There *is* a more direct link between Churchill's naval-only operation and the shortage of troops in January 1915, but it is not that which Churchill or the countless histories on this subject would have us believe.

As will be seen in the analysis below, the grand duke's request for a demonstration was of passing importance to the War Council (indeed it was never discussed at this forum) and to the Russians themselves. Within days, the Turkish thrust into the Caucasus had been crushed and with it went any "moral" commitment for action in the Mediterranean. It is here that any plan to force the Dardanelles by either a naval "rush," as conceived by Churchill, or a more "gradual" naval assault, as subsequently recommended by Carden, ought to have died a fairly quick death.

This was particularly so given the imminence of discussions within the War Council regarding serious full-scale military and naval operations in the Mediterranean as proposed by Hankey, Lloyd George, and then, on January 3, by Fisher. Nothing was more likely to undermine the potential of such operations than the promotion of a proposal to force the Dardanelles by naval forces alone. Yet, this is precisely what Churchill did. Why? Because in Carden's proposal for a gradual naval assault, Churchill began to see a germ of an idea by which he could neutralize supporters of a large-scale southern offensive, confirm the efficacy of naval bombardment, retain the growing military forces in Europe, and thereby keep his various northern schemes on the strategic agenda. It is in these matters, rather than any claimed commitment to Russia or supposed discussions over troops, that one will find the origins of the Dardanelles operation.

On January 2, the day after he and Kitchener had become aware of the Russian request for a demonstration, Churchill received a note from Kitchener that read, "You have no doubt seen Buchanan's telegram about the Russians and Turks; if not Fitzgerald is taking it over. Do you think any naval action would be possible to prevent Turks sending more men into the Caucasus and thus denuding Constantinople?"[14] Later in the day, presumably after discussing military action with his staff, he informed Churchill no troops were available to land anywhere and that "the only place that a demonstration might have some effect in stopping reinforcements going east would be the Dardanelles."[15]

Writing with even less optimism, Kitchener telegraphed the grand duke through the Foreign Office that "steps will be taken to make a demonstration against the Turks. It is, however, feared that any action we can devise and carry out will be unlikely to seriously affect numbers of enemy in the Caucasus, or cause their withdrawal."[16]

Unable or unwilling to use troops at early notice, Kitchener was leaving it to the navy to undertake a demonstration against the Turks to satisfy the Russian request.

Despite his inability or unwillingness to do anything at this time, this episode and the various proposals of his War Council colleagues for alternative offensives, had prodded Kitchener to think in the longer term regarding operations in the Mediterranean. In the evening of January 2, he wrote to Sir John French:

> [T]he feeling here is gaining ground that although it is essential to defend the line, troops over and above what is necessary for that service could be better employed elsewhere. . . . The question *where* anything effective can be accomplished, opens a large field and requires a good deal of study. What are the views of your staff? Russia is hard pressed in the Caucasus and can only just hold her own in Poland. Fresh forces are necessary to change the deadlock. Italy and Roumania seem the most likely providers; therefore some action that would help bring these out seems attractive, though full of difficulties.[17]

If we are to believe *The World Crisis,* until January 3, Churchill did little regarding the Russian appeal beyond his written communications and purported direct discussions with Kitchener and Fisher. Then, on January 3, Churchill received Fisher's Turkey Plan. This proposed the immediate dispatch of 100,000 men from Europe to land at Besika Bay while the Greeks attacked Gallipoli, the Bulgarians attacked Constantinople, and the Russians, Serbians, and Romanians attacked Austria. This was to be accompanied by an attempt to force the Dardanelles by a fleet of old battleships.

Early in the afternoon (again, according to Churchill's timetable of events), after more purported discussions with Fisher and Jackson, during the latter of which he requested the preparation of a paper on a naval assault on the Dardanelles, Churchill finally acted on Kitchener's promise to the Russians and telegraphed the commander of British Naval Forces, Mediterranean, Vice Admiral Carden:

> Do you consider the forcing of the Dardanelles by ships alone a practicable operation?
>
> It is assumed older Battleships fitted with minebumpers would be used preceded by Colliers or other merchant craft as bumpers and sweepers.
>
> Importance of results would justify severe losses. Let me know your views.[18]

In the context of the time, this was a curious telegram for Churchill to send. The nature of the operation proposed was well beyond that promised by Kitchener to the Russians and presumably well beyond anything discussed with Kitchener by Churchill.[19] Given Fisher's plan and the great differences between it and Churchill's proposal, it would seem highly unlikely that he discussed his telegram with Fisher before he sent it.

In *The World Crisis*, Churchill identified the various catalysts for his decision to send this telegram to Carden: the urgent Russian call for a diversion; Kitchener's repeated declarations that no troops were available for any operations; the arrival of the Fisher plan on his desk, including the idea of using old battleships at the Dardanelles; his conviction that he "saw a great convergence of opinion in the direction of that attack upon the Dardanelles which I had always so greatly desired";[20] and, finally, his desire to not waste an assault on the Dardanelles on a mere diversion of temporary effect.

In *The World Crisis*, Churchill addressed these various catalysts. He spent some time addressing the influence of Fisher's plan on his thinking. He began by inaccurately, and perhaps mischievously, representing Fisher's plan as a response to the Russian call for aid, when it was primarily written to promote Hankey's Mediterranean proposal.[21] Having representing it thus, Churchill went on to explain why it would not have worked. He argued that there was never any chance of "the whole of the Fisher plan being carried into effect."[22] He contended that the withdrawal of the Indian Corps and 75,000 seasoned troops from Sir John French's command and their replacement by Territorial Divisions would have been "resisted to the point of resignation by the Commander-in-Chief."[23] However, he *was* taken by Fisher's idea of using old battleships against the Dardanelles. Prompted by the novelty of this proposal, he sent his telegram to Carden and asked Admiral Jackson (then employed on special duties at the Admiralty), to write an appreciation for an attempt to force the Straits by a naval force alone.[24]

There are reasons to doubt this version of events and, indeed, a great deal of what Churchill has written on the first week of January 1915. First, Churchill's effort to legitimize his own naval-only concept by describing the Fisher plan as "unrealistic" is disingenuous and insincere. As a response to Russia's call for aid, Fisher's plan was certainly not practicable; but as we have seen, this was not what it had intended to be. It had an eye to the imminent discussions over future operations in the Mediterranean. To this extent, it was no more foolhardy than anything else up for consideration within the War Council in forthcoming days.

Churchill's retrospective and rather dismissive criticism of the Fisher plan ignored the fact that, in the opening days of January, he had not only sought to have the Indian divisions sent to the Mediterranean but also discussed with the prime minister the idea of progressively trading French's experienced troops in France with the growing forces of Kitchener's New Armies. He believed this was "the only way to attain a large homogenous army capable of acting together against the enemy in April and May."[25] Unlike Fisher, who was proposing this system be used to provide forces for the Mediterranean, Churchill nominated dates that suggest he saw such a proposal as the best means by which to provide a large, experienced army for his grand operations in Northern Europe. Here we find a clue for Churchill's resistance to the Fisher plan for a Mediterranean offensive.

Another reason to doubt Churchill's version of events was that Fisher's suggestion to use old ships to force the Straits really had no novelty. We have seen in the previous chapter that Churchill had been discussing naval operations—including naval-only operations—for some time before this suggestion, and these operations always would have included elements of his inshore bombardment squadron of old ships and monitors. Fisher did not need to plant the seed of a naval assault using old battleships. It was already present.

A third reason to question Churchill's attempt to link the Fisher plan with the genesis of his own was that the two operations shared virtually nothing—save the use of old ships—in common. Fisher's memorandum spoke of a Greek army attacking the Gallipoli Peninsula while his fleet forced the Narrows. There was no suggestion here that a fleet—regardless of its composition—would force the Straits by itself. Indeed, his memorandum was gravely concerned that the War Council would "decide on a futile bombardment of the Dardanelles." Yet, despite this, the title of the paper completed by Jackson on January 5 made clear that Jackson's brief from Churchill had been to explore a naval-only operation: "Notes on Forcing the Passage of the Dardanelles and Bosphorus By the Allied Fleets, In Order to Destroy the Turco-German Squadron and Threaten Constantinople Without Military Co-operation." In short, Churchill was proposing an operation diametrically opposed to the spirit of the Fisher plan. It would appear, under the circumstances, hard to believe that Fisher's plan in any way prompted Churchill's telegram to Carden or that discussion with Fisher (if any had taken place) had in any way supported such an idea.

Doubt also must be cast over the one catalyst that could explain Churchill's naval-only plan—that is, his discussion with Kitchener on January 2, in which Kitchener declared no troops were available for alternative operations against Turkey. The difficulty for Churchill was that Jackson claimed he was asked about a naval-only operation to force the Straits on January 1, the date on which Churchill almost certainly became aware of the grand duke's request for assistance and the day before Churchill had any discussions with Kitchener.[26] The possibility exists, therefore, that Churchill had conceived a naval-only operation *before* Kitchener had declared no troops were available. It had been his first and immediate response to the Russian call for aid and was simply an extension of the discussions he had had and enquiries he had made in previous months. It certainly seems difficult to imagine that the pugnacious Churchill would allow two full days to elapse from the time he became aware of the Russian request to the point at which he instructed Jackson to investigate a naval assault. Such, however, is what *The World Crisis* would have us believe.

Whether or not Churchill began investigating a naval-only assault on January 1 or January 3, Kitchener's declaration that no troops were available never could justify Churchill's subsequent explanation—typically accepted by historians—that had troops been available in January 1915, he would have pressed for an amphibious assault on the Dardanelles. The reality was that, even had 100,000 troops been available in January, no amphibious assault ever would have taken place at the Dardanelles at this time. Operations, perhaps, might have occurred elsewhere but not at the Dardanelles. The prevailing weather would have prohibited such an operation, and Churchill would have known this.

When Churchill began considering a naval response to the Russian call for aid and Kitchener's suggestion that this occur at the Dardanelles, he really had only three choices: a naval demonstration at the Dardanelles as per the Russian request, a serious attempt to force the Straits with old ships, and a demonstration other than at the Dardanelles while preparing to support Hankey's and Lloyd George's plans for major operation in the Mediterranean in the spring. Whether or not troops were available, an amphibious assault was not an option in January 1915, yet in none of his writing does he acknowledge this. To this extent, the issue of the unavailability of troops has always been something of a red herring for anyone trying to understand the origins of the Dardanelles operation.

Churchill, of course, chose to explore a plan to force the Dardanelles. His justification was the *urgent* need to do something and his belief that it would be improvident to stir up the Turks for a "mere demonstration if there was any prospect of a serious attempt to force the Straits of the Dardanelles at a later stage."[27] The problem with this latter explanation was that, as has been noted, the War Council was set to explore a variety of southern offensives, including a serious amphibious assault on the Dardanelles.

As for *urgency*, this argument cannot be used to explain his pursuit of his naval-only operation beyond January 4 or 5. By this time, Russia's emphatic success in the Caucasus was becoming known and the Russian call for aid was very soon a dead issue.[28]

From around this time, had Churchill been genuinely committed to the southern theater and to the prospects of serious operations at the Dardanelles, he would have pulled back from the contemplation of any sort of naval-only proposal. He surely must have recognized that to continue promoting the virtues of a naval-only operation against the Dardanelles would necessarily diminish the likelihood of the larger scale operations proposed by Hankey, Lloyd George, and Fisher from taking place at some point in the near future. Churchill, however, showed no such discretion. Instead, as will be seen, he continued to pursue the seed of an idea that was to be planted by

Carden's suggestion that the Dardanelles might be forced by a gradual assault.

That Churchill was generally unsympathetic to the idea of major military operations in the Mediterranean at this time is indicated by his ongoing preparations for his northern schemes. It is indicated further by his real response to the Fisher plan, which was written the same day he telegraphed Carden. He did not counsel Fisher over the impossibility of his plan as *The World Crisis* suggested he might, but wrote only that they should both "hear what others have to say about the Turkish plans"[29] before taking a decided line. He continued, "I would not grudge 100,000 men [the approximate number proposed by Fisher] because of the great political effects in the Balkan Peninsula; *but Germany is the foe and it is bad war to seek cheaper victories & easier antagonists.* This is however a very general question" (emphasis added).[30]

The contention that fighting foe other than Germans was "bad war" was not among the arguments nominated in *The World Crisis* as reasons for rejecting Fisher's plan. This communication to Fisher suggests strongly that, whatever Kitchener had said about troops, Churchill was not interested in large-scale operations against the Dardanelles because this would necessarily have drawn forces from Europe or from the New Armies, which, in turn, would compromise his own offensive plans.

Churchill displayed considerable sensitivity over his response to the Fisher plan at the Dardanelles Commission Inquiry. Of these comments, he declared:

> That was the only inconsistent argument I have used. I do not think that that is a good argument. I think it was not the general view that I held that it would not be worthwhile to make a diversion of that kind, but I find I did put that in at that date.[31]

He showed similar sensitivity in *The World Crisis,* omitting entirely the italicized portion of the response.

Despite Churchill's assertion, without doubt, at this critical juncture, he still was focused strongly on his northern schemes and there is good reason to believe he would have viewed with some anxiety the sudden avalanche of interest in the Mediterranean.

The objective of the letter to Fisher from which his response is taken was to find common purpose with his First Sea Lord before the next War Council meeting. In this letter, Churchill's mind remained firmly in the north. He declared his intention to "ask that a Regular division of Infantry be assigned to the capture of Borkum, and that plans be made on that basis for action at the earliest moment." He believed that "Borkum is the key to all Northern possibilities whether defensive against raids or invasion, or offensive to block the enemy in or to invade either Oldenburg or Schleswig-Holstein."[32] Supporting an operation that would draw 100,000 or more men from Europe was hardly compatible with his desire to extract a division of the best troops from Kitchener's grasp sometime in the early spring. Moreover, such an operation might lend support to Lloyd George's proposal to use a huge army in the Mediterranean.

Churchill's letter to Fisher also addressed Sir John French's coastal operation, in which he still held some interest. Fisher evidently had continued to press this operation with Churchill and, in particular, his personal wish to take Zeebrugge with troops. Churchill was prepared to support Fisher's idea to land troops at Zeebrugge but only "as an incident in a general British advance and at the desire of Sir John French." Failing this, he proposed to adopt Sir Arthur Wilson's scheme to bombard Zeebrugge and block the canal. This, along with schemes such as Borkum/Baltic, had been one of a number of projects on which Wilson had been working since returning to the Admiralty late in 1914.

Churchill's final comments in the letter reflected his conviction that a deadlock now existed in France. He informed Fisher he was not prepared to send further reinforcements to France unless they were used to support French's coastal operation. It was a campaign in which French and he believed the navy could offer a unique and decisive advantage.

The clear import of the entire letter was that Churchill wanted British troops to fight and kill Germans in Europe, not Turks—or even Austrians—in the Mediterranean. Despite his assertion to the contrary to the Dardanelles Commission, it was neither the first nor the last time he expressed sentiments deprecating a full-scale military commitment to the Mediterranean.

According to Fisher, the first instance had occurred on January 2 when Fisher and Churchill discussed Hankey's memorandum. While Fisher liked the idea very much—he had in fact previewed and contributed to the proposal several days earlier—Churchill declared himself "against it" because it was "too far from the main theatre of war."[33] In a letter to Hankey, Fisher said that this was all "rot" and he offered advice on how he might win the day. He included an outline of his Turkey Plan. He told Hankey he should do some vigorous "spade work" with Balfour, Grey, and the prime minister while he would tackle Kitchener and Churchill.[34] True to his word, Fisher sent Churchill his Turkey Plan the following day.[35]

Churchill's assertion that Turkey was "too far from the main theatre of war" for a major military operation provides further evidence that, whatever Kitchener had said about troops on January 2, he did not consider, and would not have seriously considered, a joint operation against the Dardanelles at this time because he did not want a large number of troops from France or Britain drawn to this theater. If this were to happen, all his northern aspirations would be put at serious risk.

Churchill's commitment to his northern schemes at this time is further illustrated by his ongoing correspondence with Sir John Jellicoe. Jellicoe's support was critical if the plan for Borkum were to proceed. On January 4, he wrote to Jellicoe that:

> everything convinces me that we must take Borkum as soon as full and careful preparations can be made . . . *It is the key not only to satisfactory naval policy but to future military action whether by the invasion of Schleswig-Holstein or (better perhaps) Oldenburg.* Troops for Borkum will be available; and although the capture is a difficult operation I am sure we ought to make the attempt (emphasis added).[36]

Churchill's determination to push on with Borkum was undoubtedly increased by a memorandum he received this day from Roger Keyes, Commodore in Charge, Submarine Service, in which Keyes asserted that he did not "think the defence of Borkum from seaward would be a difficult matter provided a sufficient number of submarines, destroyers, trawlers and aircraft can be maintained there in an efficient condition."[37] Earlier appreciations of this problem had been much less sanguine. Here, at last, had he gained a reputable opinion that such a thing was possible.

Also on January 4, Churchill received Fisher's reply to his January 3 letter in which he had sought a common purpose over future naval policy. Consensus was not forthcoming. First, Fisher expressed his belief that British naval policy should "conserve our naval superiority over the Germans and in no wise jeopardise it by minor operations whose cumulative effect is to wear out our vessels and incur losses in ships and men. We can't afford any more losses or any further deterioration except for absolutely imperative operations."[38] He then dismissed the idea of a landing anywhere on the North Sea coast during the winter but suggested that preparations should be made for such expeditions in the spring. Unlike Churchill, Fisher could see no advantage in "futile" bombardment of Zeebrugge if a military advance along the coast did not happen. He agreed Borkum offered "great possibilities" but considered it "a purely military question" as to whether it could be held. As for the Dardanelles, he considered that the "Naval advantages of the possession of Constantinople and the getting of wheat from the Black Sea are so overwhelming that I consider Colonel Hankey's plan for Turkish operations vital and imperative and very pressing."[39]

Fisher also forwarded Churchill a copy of his Baltic paper completed the previous month and a memorandum recommending a more intensive mining campaign.[40]

Despite the impression conveyed in *The World Crisis,* Churchill and Fisher were struggling to find much common ground. Churchill clearly was interested in dealing with Zeebrugge, one way or another, and securing a large-scale amphibious assault in the North. As he waited for Carden's reply to his soon-to-be-redundant telegram,[41] it is difficult to fathom Churchill's attitude to this plan beyond what his overwhelming preoccupation with Northern Europe tells us.

The tone of Fisher's reply to Churchill indicated that he was generally supportive, if uncertain, toward the various northern schemes. Fisher still hoped that the Baltic operation might take place in the summer, but it is questionable whether he was quite as wedded to it as he would later claim. At the top of a letter written to Hankey the following day, he wrote, "Can you kindly suggest any alternatives to the Baltic paper I gave you which would come into operation at end of May when ice all gone in Gulf of Finland?"[42] This search for an alternative very probably reflected a growing insecurity with such a bold project and fears over the probable impact of mines and submarines on the operation.[43]

One thing was clear in all Fisher's writing at this time: he was unwilling to support any form of naval bombardment operation that was not accompanied by military operations. This had been evident in his January 4 memorandum. On January 5, Fisher wrote to Churchill of "futile bombardments . . . that result in nothing as the Army does not take advantage of them."[44] The following day he again wrote to Churchill, this time seeking to have plans to bombard Zeebrugge postponed until the likely cost of the capture of Borkum, the attack on the Dardanelles, and the Baltic operations—which he hoped would include a landing of a British Army in the Spring in Schleswig-Holstein—be assessed. He noted that whatever damage was inflicted on Zeebrugge could be quickly repaired and he asked, "Are we going to bombard every 3 weeks?"[45]

Churchill was not impressed by Fisher's pleas. He replied, "I do not agree that the bombardments which have taken place have been *futile*. On the contrary the results have fully justified the expenditure of ammunition."[46]

Fisher's keenness to support a southern offensive at this time was influenced by a profound fear and frustration over the "stagnation" he anticipated would occur during the winter months in Europe. In a letter to Hankey on January 5, he wrote that the next three months were likely to be "a very ugly time for us as the Germans have a free hand to do what they like with an unmolested capability of doing a great deal in any direction they like."[47] He considered it "especially bad for the navy" because the Zeebrugge operation had "fizzled out" thereby giving the German submarines a "free cruise" over subsequent months and providing "fresh impetus" to the German's mining activities. Altogether he considered "the lookout from the navy point of view has never been so gloomy but there seems no help for us."[48]

Thus were Churchill and Fisher at loggerheads. In the short term, Churchill was continuing to explore a plan to force the Dardanelles to assist the Russians, although the Russian victory would soon make this issue irrelevant if it were not already. In the medium term, he was intent on securing military and naval forces—and political support—for his major offensives in the spring. Meanwhile, if Zeebrugge could not be attempted as a joint amphibious operation, he proposed dealing with the problem by the navy alone. As for southern offensives, he was prepared to listen, but generally he thought they were too far from the main theater of war and he did not support the idea of seeking easier antagonists.

Fisher continued to support—albeit ambivalently—Churchill's northern schemes planned for the spring, but he wanted immediate operations in the south to counter the stagnation of a cold, dark, northern winter and thus he also remained an ardent supporter of the Hankey plan. He saw no virtue at all in naval bombardment operations that were not supported by the army and, therefore, was strongly against a naval bombardment of Zeebrugge. If Fisher was concerned about or interested in Churchill's telegram to Carden, we do not know. His attitude to the naval bombardment of Zeebrugge, however, suggests that he would likely find little to commend in a naval-only assault against the Dardanelles.

Fortunately for Fisher, and for his relationship with Churchill, his concerns over Zeebrugge were about to be temporarily eased. On January 4, Sir John French had replied to Churchill's letter of January 1, enclosing two memoranda written by the chief of the Imperial general staff, James Wolfe Murray, expressing French's views on the "general situation," his ideas for the employment of the New Army, and plans for action in conjunction with the French. The "Coast Game" was "the most prominent feature" in the proposed operations.[49]

These assessments of the "general situation" had been written in response to Kitchener's letter of January 2. It is possible that Kitchener may have sent a copy of the three proposals—Churchill's, Hankey's, and Lloyd George's—to French because the criticism in the documents appeared to mark its target well. If French or Murray had read Churchill's proposal, they did not let on. Not surprisingly given its source, the memoranda deprecated all operations outside the western theater. These included operations in the Baltic, Denmark, Holland, and the German North Sea coast, while various operations in the south were criticized as being politically problematic, exposed to problems of mines and submarines, or devoid of decisive result.[50]

The receipt of this material on January 5 caused Churchill to decide against sending another letter to French in which he had summarized the emerging inclinations of his War Council colleagues and, of course, his own. The general feeling, he had explained, was that a condition of stalemate had been reached in France and Flanders and that it now was time to look for other theaters of war for the employment of the New Armies. Without identifying himself as the author of the proposal, he had nominated plans to "invade Emden and Wilhemshaven and attack Germany from there, and the invasion of Schleswig-Holstein with the consequent opening of the Baltic and the exposure of the Baltic shore to Russian oversea attack."[51] In competition with these plans, he had identified "the capture of Constantinople and an advance on Belgrade and a scheme to invade Austria from the Adriatic shore."[52] Despite this summary he had concluded in a mollifying tone that

> Of course if there were good prospects of a fruitful offensive in Flanders or on the French front, that would hold the field. . . . But I fear that the losses would not be repaid by gains, except perhaps along the coast; & that is not the job it was.

> The need of clearing the coast is however a very real one, and if you are in a position to effect this with naval aid, the operation wd have paramount claims.[53]

Clearly Churchill had a strong ally in French against any proposal to send troops to a southern theater. His challenge would be to persuade French that the Royal Navy could provide the ways and means to attack in the north.

Meanwhile, still brewing in the background was the matter of Churchill's naval-only assault against the Dardanelles. On January 5, Carden replied to Churchill that he did not think the Dardanelles could be rushed but "they might be forced by extended operations with a large number of ships."[54] Churchill claimed he read Carden's telegram at a War Council meeting that day where it was heard with "extreme interest" as a way of "influencing the Eastern situation in a decisive manner without opening a new military commitment on a large scale while also affording an effective means of helping the Grand Duke without wasting the Dardanelles possibility upon nothing more than a demonstration."[55]

There was, however, no War Council meeting on the January 5, so one must take all this with a grain of salt. What did take place was an informal dinner at the Admiralty, which included the prime minister. Asquith's comments at the dinner indicate that Turkey was under discussions, but Carden's telegram was not mentioned. At the end of a letter to Venetia Stanley, Asquith wrote:

> We now have a lot of alternative objectives: (1) Schleswig (Winston) (2) Salonika or Dalmatia (Ll. George—curiously enough, French in his letter to me suggests that we might send a diversion to help the Montenegrians) (3) Gallipoli & Constantinople (Kitchener) (4) Smyrna & Ephesus (F.E. & others—I like this).[56]

So, despite supposedly presenting his colleagues with the idea of a naval attack on the Dardanelles, it had not made a sufficient impact for Asquith to nominate it as one of Churchill's "alternative objectives." If the telegram was indeed read to the guests, and it was concluded such an operation could act in a "decisive way" without opening a new military commitment on a large scale, it was a barrow being pushed by Churchill to ensure that his northern schemes remained a viable strategic option.

It is interesting to note Asquith's comment on Kitchener's interest in Gallipoli and Constantinople. Given his subsequent comments regarding the Dardanelles at the War Council of the January 7 (to be discussed in Chapter 7) it is fair to assume this referred to a joint operation against these objectives. It is Kitchener here, and not Churchill, who is identified as the promoter of amphibious operations in the south.

Earlier on January 5, Admiral Jackson completed his memorandum addressing Churchill's plans to force the Dardanelles. The title of Jackson's memorandum also indicated an intention to consider the forcing of the Bosporus, but this part of the operation was not analyzed.

Jackson's memorandum contended that the minimum force needed to break through the Dardanelles, destroy the enemy squadron in the Marmora, and dominate Constantinople would be at least two battle squadrons and two cruiser squadrons. He anticipated that six out of eight battleships of the first squadron likely would be lost in forcing the Straits, and it would be the second accompanied by cruisers and torpedo craft in proportion closely following on from the first that would enter the Marmora. He warned that even assuming the enemy squadron destroyed and the batteries rushed, the fleet still would be open to the fire of field artillery and infantry, and to torpedo attack at night, and would be without store ships with ammunition. The fleet would not have a safe retreat unless the shore batteries had been destroyed when forcing the passage. Although the ships might dominate the city and inflict enormous damage, "their position would not be an enviable one, unless there were a large military force to occupy the town."[57]

As to the strategic value of such an operation, he declared: "such a diversion would only be carried out when the object to be gained was commensurate with the loss the fleet would sustain in forcing the passage."[58] He believed the capture of Constantinople would be worth a considerable loss; but its bombardment alone would not greatly affect the distant military operations in the Caucasus it was hoped to influence, and "even if it surrendered, it could not be occupied and held without troops, and would probably result in indiscriminate massacres."[59]

The rest of the paper focused on the execution of the operation. Among Jackson's recommendations was a proposal to undertake a methodical bombardment of the outer forts and, perhaps, some of the inner forts as well to reduce the volume of fire to be faced in the approach to the Narrows and, thereby, leave the fleet better prepared to face the enemy fleet in the Marmora.

It was, we are told by Churchill, the convergence of Jackson's and Carden's proposal for methodical bombardment, coupled with the purported support from his political colleagues, that prompted Churchill to telegraph Carden on January 6 that "[y]our view is agreed with by high authorities here. Please telegraph in detail what you think could be done by extended operations, what force would be needed and how you consider it should be used."[60]

In *The World Crisis*, Churchill failed to mention another, much more significant convergence. On the morning of January 6, British newspapers were trumpeting a great Russian victory in the Caucasus with such headings as "Crushing Blow to Turkey" and "Remnants of Army in Flight."[61] The immediate threat to Russia was over. Yet, Churchill continued to investigate a naval-only assault on the Dardanelles.

Were the possibilities offered by a methodical bombardment truly worthy of Churchill's confidence? Did the possibilities of a gradual naval assault justify Churchill putting at risk the imminent discussion over southern offensives, including potential full-scale amphibious operations sometime in the spring?

The reality was that there was less difference than Churchill would have us believe between the gradual bombardment being suggested by Carden and Jackson and the naval rush Churchill originally had proposed. A rush meant the big guns in the forts would still be intact after the fleet had forced a passage. The Carden proposal implied the possibility the forts would be put out of action before the fleet had broken through. Carden's proposal also offered a more methodical sweeping of the minefields. This would mean that more battleships might enter the Marmora safely and risk would be lower should they have to return.

However, because neither concept secured the lines of communications, the probability that any ships that broke through into the Marmora would have to return due to lack of supplies, coal, and ammunition remained about the same. Securing the lines of communication could be achieved only by the capture of the peninsula—and more likely both sides of the Straits—and the destruction of all mobile guns in the vicinity. Moreover, troops could not enter the Marmora to take advantage of any gains.

The first Admiralty response to Carden's plan recognized this inherent flaw immediately. Entitled "Considerations Affecting the Passage of the Dardanelles," the response expressed the view that the effect of such an operation would be "almost exclusively limited to the moral effect produced by the operations since the material result would be small and of a very temporary nature in the absence of larger land forces to confirm success, and at present no troops are available for the enterprise."[62]

Jackson similarly questioned the value of a fleet of battleships inside the Marmora unsupported by an army. The most significant aspect of Jackson's notes was his insistence that troops would need to be landed to put any guns silenced by a gradual bombardment *permanently* out of action. This was in complete contradiction to the notion soon to be peddled by Churchill within the War Council that the forts could be made innocuous by the fleet alone. The clear implication of Jackson's memorandum was that whatever merit he saw in "gradual bombardment" it did not include the *permanent* destruction of the forts and their guns. A fleet inside the Marmora would have to deal not only with the certainty of a mobile gun threat but also a renewed threat from the forts when forced to return. This it would most surely have to do unless its presence precipitated revolution or Balkan intervention.

On the eve of the first War Council meeting of 1915—and the first since early December—it was evident that Churchill remained somewhat at odds with most members of the War Council—including his First Sea Lord—over the direction of future offensive action. He remained determined to attack Germany through Northern Europe, while his colleagues sought action in the south that might bring more allies to the cause. The Russian call for military aid briefly added a new dimension to these matters, but its importance rapidly disappeared. Churchill, however, continued to investigate the Carden proposal. The evidence suggests he continued to do so because, in the idea of a "gradual" naval-only assault, he foresaw the prospect of a viable alternative to major southern operations. If he could prevent the large-scale movement of troops to a southern theater as promoted by Hankey and, in particular, Lloyd George, and simultaneously achieve a significant naval success, he could keep his own northern schemes alive.

NOTES

1. Hankey began his memorandum on Christmas Day. A draft was shown to Oliver and Callwell, and "afterwards, amended to meet their criticisms, to Fisher and Wolfe Murray," then, a copy was sent to Churchill and Kitchener and afterward other members of the War Council. See Hankey, *The Supreme Command*, 244.

2. Hankey also proposed a number of mechanical devices that he hoped would make action in the west more profitable and less costly in lives.

3. Hankey Memorandum, *CVIII*, pp. 337–343.

4. Gilbert, *CVIII*, 346. Letter, Churchill to Asquith, December 31, 1914.

5. Ibid., 348.

6. Gilbert, *CVIII*, 352–356. Lloyd George Memorandum, "Suggestions as to the Military Situation," Hankey indicates Churchill had seen an advance copy of this on December 31, before he wrote his brief note to Asquith. See Hankey, *The Supreme Command*, 252. Churchill makes no mention of this in his note.

7. Ibid.

8. Ibid.

9. Ibid.

10. Hankey's memorandum did consider an attack on Schleswig-Holstein, but noted it could only be attacked through Denmark or Holland and, "There appears to be no reasonable probability that either of these nations will voluntarily enter the war, and it would be inconsistent with our attitude towards the German violation of Belgium for us to force them to do so." Gilbert, *CVIII*, 340.

11. Ibid., 357.

12. Ibid., 365–366.

13. Buchanan to Grey, telegram, January 1, 1915. Gilbert, *CVIII*, 359–360.

14. Ibid., 361. Most texts assume it was this communication from Kitchener that alerted Churchill to the telegram. It is much more likely he received his own copy the day before. Churchill is vague on the sequence of events. At the Dardanelles Inquiry, Churchill claimed he spoke to Kitchener on January 1, CAB 19/33, Question 6210. This clearly is not the case.

15. Gilbert, *CVIII*, 360–361. Although there is no evidence to support the assertion, Churchill claimed in *The World Crisis* that prior to this second communication Kitchener had come to the Admiralty and told him repeatedly that there were no troops to spare. Churchill, *The World Crisis*, vol. 2, 528–529.

16. Ibid., 94–95.

17. Philip Magnus, *Kitchener: Portrait of an Imperialist* (London: John Murray, 1958), 310–311.

18. Gilbert, *CVIII*, 367.

19. Kitchener's rather conservative commitment to the Russians suggests he had no awareness of the plan Churchill was considering on January 3.

20. Churchill, *The World Crisis*, vol. 2, 531.

21. There is only a small suggestion that the plan was partly a response to the Russian call for aid. In criticizing the futility of naval only bombardments in the letter Fisher remarked, "What good resulted from the last bombardment? Did it move a single Turk from the Caucasus?" However, most of the letter and Fisher's subsequent communications with Hankey indicate that it was a response to Hankey's memorandum.

22. Churchill, *The World Crisis*, Vol. 2, 531.

23. Churchill, *The World Crisis*, Vol. 2, 531.

24. Jackson asserts this request was made on January 1. CAB 19/33, Question 2046.

25. Churchill to Asquith, January 6, 1915; Gilbert, *CVIII*, 382–384.

26. See also CAB 19/33, Question 2287–2288.

27. Churchill, *The World Crisis*, Vol. 2, p.528.

28. In Ward Rutherford, *The Tsar's War 1914–1917* (Cambridge: Ian Faulkner, 1992), 105. Rutherford recorded, "As the invaders pulled back, the Grand Duke sent immediate word to London that the help he sought from them was now unnecessary."

29. One can note here Churchill refers to "plans" (plural). This suggests he was referring to the plans of Hankey, Lloyd George, and Fisher.

30. CAB 19/33, Dardanelles Inquiry, Question 1127.

31. Ibid.

32. Ibid.

33. Fisher to Hankey, CAB 63/4.

34. Fisher to Hankey, CAB 63/4.

35. Gilbert, *CVIII*, 367–368.

36. Ibid., 369.

37. Paul G. Halpern, ed., *The Keyes Papers*, vol. 1, 1914–1918 (Cheltenham, UK: Navy Records Society, 1972), 69.

38. Gilbert, *CVIII*, 371–372.

39. Ibid.

40. For a copy of the paper on minelaying, see Ibid., 373–374.

41. *The London Times* of January 5, published reports from its correspondents sent on January 4, which already included the heading, "A Turkish Rout." The following day, headlines included "Remnants of Army in Flight" and references were made of the "annihilation" and "complete defeat" of Turkish forces. The same article referred to Joffre receiving news of victory on January 5. Sir John French recorded in his diary that he had received news from the grand duke about the great Russian victory on the evening of January 5. It is inconceivable in the circumstances that the British government did not know of the Russian victory any later than January 5. The myth of the importance of the January 1 call for aid continues to live on in recent scholarship, as does the notion that Kitchener's promise of action represented a commitment that had to be met. See Dan Van der Vat, *The Dardanelles Disaster: Winston Churchill's Greatest Defeat* (London/New York: Duckworth Overlook, 2009), 81–85, including the observation, "Nicholas neglected to tell his British allies of this favourable turn of events [the Turkish rout in the Caucasus], and they went on believing that their Dardanelles intervention, whatever form it took, was for the immediate relief of Russia, as well as for her and the Entente's longer term benefit."

42. Fisher to Hankey, January 5, 1915, CAB 63/4.

43. As was noted in chapter 5, much of this paper was the work of Corbett who wrote to Fisher on December 19, 1914: "There is one—unfortunately rather obvious—objection which I have not mentioned because I don't see

how to meet it. It is this—if it is possible for us to make the North Sea untenable with mines, is it not even more possible for the Germans to play the same game in the Baltic?" Mackay, *Fisher of Kilverstone*, 473.

44. Gilbert, *CVIII*, 380.

45. Around this time (the date is unclear on the handwritten letter), Fisher wrote to Bartolome expressing concern about the growing number of vessels Wilson was committing to an attack on Zeebrugge. He feared the "absolutely unseaworthy" monitors might founder but was prepared to risk this if "we were going to hold Zeebrugge permanently" with the support of the Army. Chartwell Papers 13/56.

46. Gilbert, *CVIII*, 380.

47. Fisher to Hankey, CAB 63/4.

48. Ibid.

49. Ibid., 375.

50. The above is drawn from French, *1914*, 315–316.

51. Gilbert, *CVIII*, 379. Letter, Churchill to French (not sent), January 5, 1915.

52. Ibid.

53. Ibid.

54. Quoted in Churchill, *The World Crisis*, Vol. 2, 533 (Odhams Press).

55. Ibid.

56. Michael Brock and Eleanor Brock, eds., *H.H. Asquith's Letters to Venetia Stanley* (London: Oxford University Press, 1982), 360.

57. Memorandum by Sir H. Jackson: *Notes on forcing the Passage of the Dardanelles and the Bosphorus By the Allied Fleet To Destroy the Turko-German Squadron and Threaten Constantinople Without Military Co-operation*, CAB 19/29, also Churchill Papers 2/82.

58. Ibid.

59. Ibid.

60. *The World Crisis*, Vol. 2, 533.

61. *The London Times*, January 6, 1915.

62. Quoted in Geoffrey Miller, *Straits: British Policy towards the Ottoman Empire and the Origins of the Dardanelles Campaign* (Hull, UK: University of Hull Press, 1997), 368. In a note to this writer, Miller explained that this minute is to be found after Carden's telegram but before a copy of Jackson's memorandum, PRO, Adm. 137/96.

CHAPTER 7

Selling Borkum

It must have been clear to everyone in attendance at the War Council of January 7 that it would be a meeting of great moment. Nothing short of the future policy of the war was open for discussion. Would a decision be made to proceed with French's coastal operation? Was there a viable or desirable alternative to the Western Front? Was there virtue in opening a third front and diverting precious resources to it? Could this be achieved without compromising the fighting in France? Given the various alternatives on offer, could common ground be found?

After some preliminary discussion on the defense on London against German airships, Lord Kitchener moved the discussion to the Zeebrugge coastal operation and, in particular, French's request for 50 territorial battalions. It became quickly apparent that Kitchener did not support the operation. He was unwilling to compromise the preparation of his New Armies and there was the issue of home defense.

Despite general surprise that there was a need to retain in Britain such a large force for home defense (some 500,000 men) and despite Churchill's assurance that the Navy was prepared to protect the country against invasion, Kitchener was not pressed unduly to give ground on the matter.

At the end of this discussion, the prime minister concluded that Kitchener considered that the military reinforcements required by

Sir John French for the capture of Zeebrugge could not be supplied without dislocating the organization not only of the existing territorial force but also the future armies.

Nevertheless, Churchill made a last effort to support French when he warned that the abandonment of the Zeebrugge operation would put in jeopardy the lines of communication across the channel. If the navy attempted it alone, he added, it would involve great risk and probable losses and the results would be only temporary.[1]

Kitchener remained unmoved. He explained his reluctance to proceed with a new offensive was not only a matter of troops but ammunition as well.[2]

The meeting finally concluded that "the offensive against Zeebrugge is not approved, as the advantages would not be commensurate with the heavy losses involved."[3] As will be seen, it was a conclusion with which Churchill was not entirely happy. However, it is enough to say that his concern over the Zeebrugge operation was probably assuaged by the fact that it did not appear to be Kitchener's intention to precipitate alternative offensives in France in the near future, or to support those of the French beyond helping to free up French troops for General Joffre's next proposed attack.[4] It was for this reason, although endeavoring to pass to the army the responsibility for subsequent losses to the fleet that might result from not taking Zeebrugge, that Churchill did not press the operation as strongly as his evident support of French suggested he would.

To this explanation can be added the fact that he was about to promote his pet Borkum/Baltic scheme. In response to the prime minister's question as to "whether the Navy could do anything to circumscribe the activities of the Germans at Zeebrugge,"[5] Churchill turned the discussion—just as he told Fisher he would on January 4—to his Borkum operation. He informed the council that he "attached much more importance to the seizure of an island on the German coast. Effective action by the Navy in limiting the operations of the German fleet depended to a great extent upon our being able to seize and hold an island possessing the requisite qualifications."[6]

Churchill briefly described the nature and virtues of the operation and observed with obvious reference to the number of troops then in England:

> It was anticipated that about a division of troops would be the largest force that could be employed in the enterprise, and, if it

> succeeded, the Army would be fully recouped by the greater security of, and the fewer troops required for, Home Defence. A large amount of detailed work would be required before the plans were ready and, if this expedition were approved in principle, the Navy would desist from risking heavy ships at Zeebrugge.[7]

Fisher added that "two or three months would be required before the Navy was ready to carry out the proposed operation."[8]

The meeting approved the Borkum attack in principle, "subject to the feasibility of the plans when worked out in detail. The Admiralty to proceed with the making out of plans."[9]

Possibly dissatisfied with aspects of the meeting or perhaps seeking clarification, Churchill sought a further meeting with Asquith later that day. The conclusions he drew from that meeting are illuminating. He accepted that future policy in France would be to await a new German offensive, and that "anything aggressive must be on the coast. That or nothing." Further to this, he believed that "the intermingling of the Kitchener and Regular armies at any rate by brigades must be further considered."[10] As briefly mentioned, Churchill believed such a policy would provide a large and professional army for aggressive offensive action more quickly and effectively than Kitchener's policy. Also of great importance, he concluded that "Sylt (his codename for Borkum) was to be taken as soon as arrangements can be made. Admiralty may count on the necessary military aid, up to one division."[11]

Two points of particular importance can be noted from this meeting. The first is that Churchill had received tentative political support for his Borkum operation. This inevitably calls to question the argument contended by recent historical analysis that his pursuit of a naval-only operation on the Dardanelles was based on a belief his northern operations would not take place. The second point is Churchill's assumption that a division of troops would be made available within two or three months for Borkum. His confidence stands in contrast to his later claims that the Dardanelles operation went ahead because Kitchener had declared no troops were available. Historians might ask whether Churchill would have gained any sort of commitment of troops for his Borkum operation if he had simultaneously fought for an amphibious operation at the Dardanelles.

Despite lengthy discussions and an attempt by Lloyd George to broach the issue early in the meeting, the War Council had yet to focus on the three memoranda seeking a solution to the anticipated conflagration on the Western Front, although Churchill, at least, had managed to get a foot in the door over Borkum. Asquith wrote to Venetia Stanley on the night of January 7: "There remains for discussion the larger questions of theatres and objectives, in regard to the choice of which one must always keep in view the chances of bringing in Italy, Roumania, & and such minor but not negligible quantities as Greece and Bulgaria."[12]

With these matters as yet unresolved, the War Council took the unprecedented step of consecutive meetings and met again at noon on January 8. Lloyd George was finally able to develop the theme of his December memorandum: "Great losses," he argued, "would be entailed in any attempt to break through the German lines in France. Was there no alternative theatre in which we might employ our surplus armies to produce a decisive effect?"[13]

Kitchener's response was to quote Sir John French's reply to his letter of January 2 in which French had denied the impossibility of a breakthrough on the Western Front and had rejected the various alternative theaters of war.[14]

These opinions did not deter the War Council members who proceeded to discuss the various proposals before them. Kitchener informed the Council that preliminary War Office discussions had concluded that, as far as operations in the south were concerned, the Dardanelles was the most suitable objective "as an attack here could be made in co-operation with the Fleet. If successful, it would re-establish communication with Russia; settle the Near Eastern question, draw in Greece and, perhaps, Bulgaria and Roumania; and release wheat and shipping now locked up in the Black Sea."[15] He believed "that 150,000 men would be sufficient for the capture of the Dardanelles, but reserved his final opinion until a closer study had been made."[16] Lloyd George expressed surprise at the smallness of this number.

Kitchener also suggested an interim, subsidiary operation on Alexandretta requiring 30,000 to 50,000 men. This, he contended, would "strike an effective blow at the Turkish communications with Syria." However, all plans he commented later must wait until the "Germans had delivered another big attack on the west."[17]

Although Churchill expressed his full support for a study of operations in the Mediterranean, he made no comment at all on Kitchener's interest in an assault on the Dardanelles—quite an extraordinary fact given history's assumption that he was obsessed with the idea himself. Instead, he hoped that sight would not be lost of possible action in Northern Europe and then asked, "Was there was no possibility that Holland might enter the war on the side of the Allies?"[18] In an unveiled declaration of his real priorities, he concluded: "If Holland could be induced to enter the war *the advantages would far outweigh those of the Mediterranean*; we could then have an island as a naval base without fighting for it, and our armies, in conjunction with the Dutch, could attack to wards Essen" (emphasis added).[19]

Kitchener gave heartening support. He believed that the effect would be "decisive."

Sir Edward Grey said, "as soon as we were in a position to guarantee military assistance to Holland on a sufficient scale, he would be prepared to sound the Dutch Government. It would be necessary to satisfy Holland that there was no prospect that she would share the fate of Belgium."[20]

At the end of the meeting, Churchill addressed the ongoing issue over Zeebrugge. He asked whether the risk of a naval attack on Zeebrugge ought to be run to avoid the threat of submarines. The council declined to offer direction, noting only that this ought to be decided by the navy.

In a rare moment, Fisher spoke up and expressed the view that the results of a naval attack would not justify the danger involved. This was now the third occasion in recent days that Fisher had indicated his displeasure with a naval attack on Zeebrugge which was not supported by the military, and he undoubtedly was angry that Churchill continued to press such a proposal, particularly when Churchill himself had several times acknowledged the temporary effect of naval bombardment. The previous day Churchill had promised that the navy would not risk large vessels on such an operation should the War Council agree to Borkum. Having now secured conditional support for Borkum, he was provocatively attempting to gain War Council support for a bombardment of Zeebrugge. It was a point of conflict between Churchill and Fisher that was destined to fester.

The greatest significance of this War Council meeting was its focus on "alternative" theaters for the New Armies and the clear evidence of Churchill's ongoing reluctance to see anywhere other than the north become a major theater of war. Although Churchill supported investigations into operations in the south, for him, the northern theater and, in particular, the Borkum scheme remained of paramount importance. His declaration that military success in the north would far outweigh any advantages of operations in the

Mediterranean was a statement of profound significance in any attempt to understand the origins of the naval-only operations against the Dardanelles. Should Carden's plan for a naval-only attack prove viable, he could keep his northern schemes on the strategic agenda and simultaneously satisfy his colleagues' interest in a southern offensive.

With most members of War Council looking southward for future offensive operations and aware his immediate naval advisers harbored considerable doubts over his northern plans, Churchill recognized he must secure allies—and powerful ones—if he were to succeed with his ambitious projects. In addition to Fisher, whom he probably believed to be unpredictable but malleable, Churchill knew he must recruit admiral of the fleet, Sir John Jellicoe, and his friend, Sir John French.

Jellicoe had proven a hard nut to crack since Churchill had first broached his various amphibious operations with him in June 1914, but Jellicoe's letter of January 8 in reply to Churchill's January 4 letter outlining his Borkum plan was, for the first time, not without support for Churchill. The letter was by no means all good news. He expressed concern at the many vessels that "probably" would be lost in the process of capturing Borkum, and he worried that, once captured, it would be difficult to keep. However, Jellicoe also expressed his belief that, should Borkum be captured and kept, "the losses might well be worth the gain." Furthermore, he did not "for a moment wish to appear to be in opposition to the idea."[21] Rather than taking emphatic steps to discourage Churchill from such action, Jellicoe offered in a most positive manner an alternative to this operation: "Sylt seems to me more feasible and strikes at a flank, from the naval point of view, but from the military point is I suppose not so good."[22]

Jellicoe has been universally characterized as an ardent critic of Churchill's Borkum scheme. Marder and others quote Jellicoe's own postwar autobiographical notes in which Jellicoe asserted that he was unable to understand:

> how an attack on Borkum could possibly assist operations in the Baltic or lead to the German fleet being driven from the North Sea. . . . To suggest that we could mine them in their harbours as the result *of the capture of* Borkum is ludicrous, as is the idea that the capture of Borkum, even if it could be held, would have assisted us in a military attack on Schleswig-Holstein.[23]

However, while it is probable Jellicoe *was* against such operations, it is evident that he was much more critical in his postwar notes than he was in his correspondence with Churchill in January 1915. Always seeking support from whatever quarter for his operations, Churchill had much to glean that was positive from this correspondence.

Overall, despite some possible apprehension over the direction the War Council was taking, by the end of January 8, Churchill could feel more positively about his northern aspirations than at any time since the beginning of the war. He had received in-principle support for Borkum from the War Council; he had gained the advice from Roger Keyes that Borkum, once captured, was defensible from seaward; and Jellicoe had spoken highly of the prospect for the operation should such a capture be achieved. Furthermore, he appeared to have an understanding with Asquith that a division of troops would be forthcoming to capture Borkum, should the operation proceed. Finally, the War Council, and in particular Kitchener, had received with interest his long-standing wish to bring in Holland.

Although it remained by no means certain that the operation would, in the end, take place, there was real hope that it might. What put the operation at greatest risk was the obvious preference of the War Council for serious full-scale operations in the south and the prospect that whatever troops might eventually be spared from the Western Front would be consumed in a southern offensive.

Fisher had anticipated two to three months' preparations for Borkum, which, it must not be forgotten, was merely a progenitor to much bigger and greater things in Northern Europe. Kitchener anticipated serious operations in the south after the next German offensive. This would most probably occur in the spring. The large bodies of men needed to make either operation possible would begin to appear in April. The two alternative offensive thrusts, therefore, were destined to come to fruition around the same time. One must inevitably compromise the other.

Fortunately, Churchill still had a powerful ally and friend in Sir John French, although, based on his criticism of any theater of war outside France, he would not be an easy man to win over. Immediately after the War Council meeting on January 8, Churchill wrote to French summarizing the War Council discussions and, in particular, the current status of the Zeebrugge operation. He informed him the War Council had decided, in view of the arguments presented by Kitchener, that it was best to await a new German attack before Britain launched any offensive action of its own. Churchill suggested that, if it were true the Germans were going to attack, "then it would be much better to give them another good bleeding before clearing the coast, urgent though that be." He then added, "But is it true?"[24] He concluded by entreating French to come over and present his case if he could at the next War Council meeting.[25]

Churchill forwarded this letter with his secretary, Freddie Guest, along with a copy of his, Lloyd George's, and Hankey's memoranda, for French's consideration. Churchill would have been heartened by a note in French's diary after he had read them, "I agree partly with Winston's memo, but entirely disagree with the other two."[26]

Sometime during January 9, French received the official War Council perspective on his correspondence with Kitchener a few days earlier and a summary of the discussions that had occurred within the War Council over the previous two days. Written by Kitchener, the letter addressed the "Zeebrugge operation", "the organization of the New Armies" and "The Possibility of Employing British Forces In a Different Theatre Than That In Which They Are Now Used."[27] Kitchener informed him that the coastal operation had not been agreed to and that it had been decided "for the time being British troops should work alongside and in co-operation with French troops and operations."[28] The letter made clear that the decision had been influenced by French's request for 50 more battalions, his call for more artillery shell, and Kitchener's conviction that the German's would soon renew the offensive.

The final part of his letter addressed alternative theaters. Kitchener noted that, should deadlock set in after another German attack, it was "desirable to find some other theatre where obstruction to advance would be less pronounced and . . . lead to more decisive results."[29] With this view in mind, Kitchener continued, the War Council had decided that certain projects should be studied:

> so that, as soon as the new forces are fit for action, plans may be ready to meet any eventuality that may then be deemed expedient, either from a political point of view, or to enable our forces to act with the best advantage in concert with the troops of other nations.[30]

Although in the face of subsequent intransigence from France, this change of policy would prove something of a "paper tiger." Kitchener's letter demonstrated the strength of the movement for operations in alternative theaters of war that had emerged within the War Council during January 1915. This body accepted the inevitability of another German attack in France. Equally, they anticipated this would fail and that the apparent deadlock would continue. Thereafter, despite Sir John French's certain resistance, it was their determination to use some of the New Armies to fight in concert with "the troops of other nations throwing in their lot with the Allies."[31] Clearly the frontrunners for military support in such a scheme were the various Mediterranean and southern European states nominated by Hankey and Lloyd George in their respective memoranda. Only two men in positions of power stood out as clear opponents of such plans: Sir John French and Winston Churchill.

As soon as he received this news and Churchill's letter, an agitated French replied to Churchill declaring his determination to see through his coastal operation. He believed he had been misrepresented by Kitchener and told Churchill that the artillery and ammunition Kitchener had informed the War Council that French believed to be "physically impossible" to acquire was, in fact, to be supplied by the Belgians and French. He dismissed altogether the threat of an imminent German attack.[32] The coastal operation was thus planted firmly back on Churchill's agenda.

Upon the receipt of this reply, Churchill discussed the operation with General Murray and Asquith. He wrote to French on January 11 that the prime minister and he had concluded that the coast operation offered the prospect of a "definite success" and "relief from a grave danger which threatens our sea communications."

Churchill went on to express his "entire agreement" with the notes French had sent him with his previous letter. This almost certainly referred to French's summary of arguments for continued operations in Northern Europe. Churchill told French he had "argued strongly in the War Council against deserting the decisive theatre and the most formidable antagonists to win cheaper laurels in easier fields."[33] He considered that *"the only circumstances in which such a policy could be justified would be after every other fruitful alternative had been found impossible"* (emphasis added). He feared the New Armies would be consumed "in doing what the Germans have failed in, viz frontal attacks on successive lines of entrenchments" and declared his desire to remain in the northern theater, "but endeavouring, as our numbers increase, to lengthen the G. line and compel him to expose new surfaces to the waste of war." Here was the kernel of the Churchill strategy—to lengthen the German lines in Northern Europe and kill Germans.

Once again, Churchill was mounting a bid for his various northern schemes and he undoubtedly had in mind defusing French's concerns over mines and torpedo mentioned in his letter of January 2. He wrote of "4 possible lines of activity in this direction," as follows:

> 1. [I]f we could get command of the Baltic, the Russian armies cd threaten the whole Baltic shore, and Berlin at close quarters. 2. A landing in Schleswig wd directly threaten the Kiel Canal and bring Denmark out on our side. 3. A landing at Emden wd strike at Wilhemshaven & at the German heart. Yr headquarters are twice as far from Berlin as Emden is.

He acknowledged, however, that the three operations all depended on "a naval situation not yet realised"—the command of the sea. He then went on:

> But the capture of Borkum, (always to be referred to as 'Sylt') was approved in principle by the War Council and if this could be achieved in March or April, it may be found possible to establish a control on the German rivermouths vy different from that wh now exists. Therefore I do not exclude these possibilities, tho it is premature to build on them now.
>
> But after all the greatest hope in the North is 4. bringing Holland in. If in the summer we are in a position to offer Holland the protection of an army of 700,000 or 800,000 men, it is by no means impossible that she might join the Allies. Her fate is bound up in our victory. *One of the reasons why I favour the Coast open is that it is a step in the direction of Holland & that every yard of Belgian soil cleared shows the Dutch that England never deserts her friends.* (emphasis added)[34]

In 1913, Churchill had declared the "German land pressure on Holland" to be irresistible and believed it would "compel" her to join her as an ally or remain neutral in the event of war. Now, through the power of the navy and the might of the New Armies, he saw a way to bring in Holland, tighten the economic and military noose around Germany, and, ultimately, win the war.

Churchill concluded his letter to French by reiterating his clear preference for operations in the north: "It is not until all the Northern possibilities are exhausted that I would look to the S of Europe as a field for the profitable employment of our expanding military forces. But plans shd be worked out for every contingency."[35]

This is an important memorandum because it provides a clear summary of Churchill's strategic impulses three days before the decisive January 13 meeting. With the exception of a renewed emphasis on Holland, the priorities had changed little from those Churchill had held for some time.

* * * * *

While Churchill promoted Zeebrugge and Borkum, his First Sea Lord was taking an entirely different tack. Not unreasonably, Fisher had concluded from the War Council meetings on January 7 and 8 that French's coastal attack was stone dead and any joint attack against the Dardanelles along the lines of his and Hankey's plans was some distance in the future. He remained desperate for some kind of immediate action—as his letter to Hankey several days earlier had indicated—and he wrote Churchill a typically effusive note supporting Kitchener's suggestion for an operation against Alexandretta made at the previous day's War Council meeting: "*I suggest that not a single day be lost in pushing it* . . . if done quickly and suddenly a very small force will no doubt suffice, but *we ought to push on*."[36]

In the second half of the letter, he was equally enthusiastic for Churchill's plans—also addressed at the previous day's War Council meeting—to draw in Holland and use her as a base from whence to launch an attack against Germany:

> I don't think that you at all realise that your Dutch project will sweep the board on May 1st (when all chance of Holland being frozen is past!) All other schemes will be swallowed up by it & it will MEAN THE END OF THE WAR! provided we put our shoulders to the wheel and prepare our transport arrangements and their convoy for 750,000 men being landed at Antwerp, Rotterdam, Amsterdam, and all the other spots (however small) along the Dutch coast—LAND EVERYWHERE! AT ONCE! *sudden-secret-subtle*-our 3 watchwords![37]

Fisher is sometimes viewed as exhibiting erratic, almost unstable behavior at this time. He appears to be wildly inconsistent in his support for a variety of offensive operations: Borkum, Baltic, Zeebrugge, the Dardanelles, Alexandretta, and now Churchill's hopes to bring in Holland. However, all this behavior is readily explained.

Fisher is utterly consistent in his insistence that major naval operations be supported by serious military operations. On this point, his attitude never changes. At the same time, he was keen for some kind of operation that might draw the initiative from the Germans.

Kitchener had made it clear that serious operations against the Dardanelles or other southern objectives would only occur in the spring and after an anticipated offensive on the Western Front by the Germans. Troops would not be withdrawn from Europe to support an operation on the scale needed to take any of these objectives until then. Moreover, Zeebrugge, a firm favorite with Fisher, had just been rejected by the War Council. In such circumstances, it is not at all surprising that Fisher's attention turned to Alexandretta for the same reasons he had been keen to support Hankey's scheme as well as that of Sir John French.

His enthusiasm for Churchill's Holland scheme is no less explicable. He was interested because it represented a serious full-scale amphibious operation of war-winning dimensions (if not of any real war-winning possibilities). It probably appeared a much more viable and less threatening option than any Baltic scheme, about which, as we have seen, he appears to have had growing doubts.

Fisher's letter undoubtedly had another purpose. Unaware of Churchill's most recent communications with French and Asquith over the Zeebrugge operation, it was probable Fisher's letter was intended to distract Churchill from a renewed determination to proceed with the naval bombardment of Zeebrugge. He seems to have been almost oblivious to the "alternative" Dardanelles plan still being quietly pursued by Churchill and that soon would completely rewrite the War Council's strategic agenda and that of the navy.

NOTES

1. Gilbert, *CVIII*, Minutes of the War Council Meeting, January 7, 1915, 384–390.
2. Ibid., 388.
3. Ibid., 389.
4. This was to be achieved by taking over responsibility of part of the line to the left of the BEF then being held by the French.
5. Ibid., 389.
6. Ibid., 389.
7. Ibid., 389.
8. Ibid., 390.
9. Ibid.
10. Churchill intervened in the dispute between Kitchener, who wanted to send out his New Armies *en masse*, and French who wanted them to go to France as they became available. Churchill suggested swapping two brigades of every division of "the" New Army with two brigades from France. This issue had emerged even before the January 7 meeting. French obviously

saw his treatment of this matter as the best way to provide the 50 extra battalions needed for his coastal operation.

11. Ibid., 390.
12. Ibid.
13. Gilbert, *CVIII*, 391. Minutes of War Council Meeting, January 8, 1915.
14. Ibid., 392–393.
15. Ibid.
16. Ibid., 393.
17. Ibid.
18. Ibid., 395.
19. Ibid.
20. Ibid., 395–396.
21. Gilbert, *CVIII*, 398–99, Letter, Jellicoe to Churchill, January 8, 1915.
22. Ibid., 398.
23. Marder, *From Dreadnought to Scapa Flow*, vol. 2, 190.
24. Gilbert, *CVIII*, 396–397, Letter, Churchill to French, January 8, 1915.
25. Ibid.
26. Ibid., 398–399. See footnote page 398: these papers were sent to French on January 6. This is almost certainly not the case. See page 397, the second to last paragraph of Churchill's letter.
27. CAB 42/1/12. Also, George Arthur, *Life of Lord Kitchener*, vol. 3 (London: MacMillan, 1920), 90–92.
28. Ibid.
29. Ibid.
30. Ibid.
31. Ibid.
32. Gilbert, *CVIII*, 401–402, Letter, French to Churchill, January 11, 1915.
33. Ibid., 402.
34. Ibid.
35. Ibid.
36. Ibid., 399–400. Letter, Fisher to Churchill, January 11, 1915.
37. Ibid.

CHAPTER 8

The Carden Plan

During the morning of January 11, Churchill received Carden's plan for a naval attack on the Dardanelles. It has been argued by the few historians who seriously address Churchill's interest in the Baltic (and by Churchill himself) that he was transformed by this plan and that, from this point, his focus turned forever southward.[1] It is also argued that Fisher greeted the plan with interest and support. Before addressing the accuracy of such assertions, it is desirable to consider the Carden proposal in some detail.[2]

Carden's plan[3] outlined a four-stage reduction of the defenses of the Dardanelles:

A. The reduction of the defences at the entrance
B. Clearing of the defences insides the Straits including Kephez Point battery No. 8
C. Reduction of defences at the Narrows Chanak
D. Clearing of passage through minefield advancing through Narrows reducing forts above Narrows and final advance to Marmora[4]

Carden was careful to point out that the term "defenses" "includes *permanent, semi-permanent and field works also guns or howitzers whose positions are not yet known*" (emphasis added).[5]

While stages A and B were taking place, part of Carden's battleship force would be "employed in demonstrations and bombardment of Bulair line and coast and reduction of battery near Gaba Tepe."[6]

Carden requested a force of 12 battleships, three battle cruisers (two of which would be needed in the Marmora), three light cruisers, one flotilla leader and 16 destroyers, one depot repairing ship, six submarines, four seaplanes, and the "Foudre" 12 minesweepers, including perhaps four fleet sweepers, one hospital ship, six colliers, and two supply and ammunition ships. He estimated the time required for the operation would "depend greatly on morale of enemy under bombardment, garrison largely stiffened by the Germans, also on the weather conditions. Gales now frequent. Might do it all in a month about."[7]

Upon the completion of the operation, Carden anticipated that two battle cruisers, four battleships, three light cruisers, one flotilla leader, 12 torpedo boat destroyers, three submarines, one supply and ammunition ship, four minesweepers, and a collier would enter the Marmora. The remainder of his force would keep open the Straits and cover remaining minesweepers clearing the minefields.

Churchill took the proposal to the Admiralty War Group, although whether Fisher was anything more than briefly involved in these discussions is unclear. One of the important issues to be discussed immediately was the size and nature of the force available for such an operation. Once this was established, Churchill forwarded a paper on the subject to Fisher for comment noting at its head that "[t]he forcing of the Dardanelles as proposed, and the arrival of a squadron strong enough to defeat the Turkish Fleet in the Sea of Marmora, would be a victory of importance, and change to our advantage the whole situation of the war in the East."[8]

He listed the forces available, declaring that "no capital ship would be ordered from home water except four already ordered to be dismantled."[9] He pointed out that "the vessels nominated did not take account of four French battleships on the spot and six others reported available."[10]

Carden's plan had evident appeal for Churchill. Here was a means by which a fleet could enter the Marmora with limited loss. Should a squadron capable of destroying the *Goeben* and *Breslau* break through, he believed the moral impact of this success might change "the whole situation of the War . . . to the Allies advantage."[11] There seemed little doubt that the entire force for the operation could be provided without compromising margins in home waters, and it would not interfere with his Borkum project. Bombardment could begin on February 1 and, allowing four weeks for completion, two months would remain to prepare for Borkum.

What of the views of his First Sea Lord? At some point before the compilation of this memorandum a suggestion had been made to use the *Queen Elizabeth* for the bombardment of the outer forts. It is sometimes stated that it was Fisher who made this suggestion. This is by no means certain. Churchill, who would have had considerable interest vested in claiming so, simply states in *The World* Crisis that "the *staff* . . . proposed that she (*Queen Elizabeth*) should test her enormous guns against the Dardanelles and pointed out that she could fire at ranges far outside those of the Turkish forts" (emphasis added).[12]

Fisher did write a memo to Oliver that day, however, asking whether it were possible for the *Queen Elizabeth* to give off

> all her ammunition at the Dardanelles forts instead of uselessly into the ocean at Gibraltar.
>
> If this is practicable she could go straight there, hoist Carden's flag and go on with her gunnery exercises and free the *Indefatigable* to go to Malta to refit and allow *Inflexible* to come straight home from Gibraltar to join the Second Battle Cruiser Squadron.
>
> Perhaps you'll think over this.[13]

This minute often is used to show that Fisher fully supported Churchill's intention to set Carden's scheme before the War Council the next day. Surely, it is said, if Fisher had opposed the operation, he never would have offered the newest and most powerful capital ship in the British Fleet.

One must be careful when accepting such a claim at face value. Whether or not Fisher initiated the idea of a preliminary bombardment by the *Queen Elizabeth*, it is by no means clear that the offer reflected Fisher's enthusiasm for the operation or, indeed, enthusiasm for anything at all.

More likely, he was trying to make the best of a difficult situation. Fisher already had made clear to Churchill his grave concerns over the shortage of shells and also his apprehensions over the condition of guns of the battle cruiser, *Indefatigable*, one of the vessels nominated as available for the bombardment of the Dardanelles.[14] The proposal to use the *Queen Elizabeth* would provide her with an ideal gunnery trial, and it would save ammunition, allow *Indefatigable* to proceed to an urgently needed refit, and, most significant, allow the *Inflexible* to immediately join the Second Battle Fleet Squadron. Moreover, Fisher's offer should be viewed as a commitment limited to attacking the *outer* forts only at the Dardanelles, as the telegram below makes clear.

The prospect of an early return of his battle cruisers from the Mediterranean was of great importance to Fisher. In the previous months, he had exchanged considerable correspondence with Jellicoe and Beatty over the matter of battle cruisers and their employment in the North Sea. Ever since the Scarborough raid of early December, the battle cruisers and their superior speed had come to be viewed as the weapon most desirable in dealing with the hit-and-run raids of the German Fleet. Indeed, so preoccupied was he with the virtue of his battle cruisers, Fisher was pressing for the construction of four more battle cruisers during December and January.

It must have seemed a wise offer, therefore, to barter the immediate return of a fast battle cruiser and the rapid refit of another for the *temporary* use of the *Queen Elizabeth*—not yet ready for active service—for a long-range bombardment out of range of the enemy's shore batteries and in waters largely free from submarines.

Churchill's telegram to Carden on January 12 seeking clarification on one or two points hints that the use of relatively modern battle cruisers in the fleet was immediately a point of contention between Churchill and Fisher:

> *By battle-cruisers I take you mean Dreadnoughts with modern guns. High speed does not appear essential* (emphasis added). You should consider also the effect of utilising the 15 inch guns of *Queen Elizabeth* for 1, 2, and 3 power and accuracy of range of these guns far exceed any other weapon. Are any French battleships included in your estimate, or are they inferred to be additional?[15]

If Fisher was digging in his heels over the battle cruisers, his concern at their prospective use in Carden's plan could only have been exacerbated by Carden's telegram of January 13, confirming they were highly desirable: "High speed considered necessary in the two ships required for meeting GOEBEN in Marmora."[16] This meant the two battle cruisers would remain in the Mediterranean and that Churchill's effort to ameliorate this problem—if such had indeed been his purpose—would fail. Meanwhile, Carden's reply that "*Queen Elizabeth* very desirable should certainly shorten operations"[17] would ensure that Fisher would receive nothing from his generous offer of the *Queen Elizabeth*. All these vessels were soon to become central to Fisher's concerns over the operation.

It should be noted here that in *The World Crisis*, Churchill rather mischievously stated that Fisher subsequently added the *Agamemnon* and *Lord Nelson* (the two most modern pre-dreadnoughts sent) to the list of ships available for the Dardanelles.[18] He did so as evidence of Fisher's support for the operation at this time. However, Admiralty telegrams show quite clearly that the *Agamemnon* was added to facilitate the early return of the *Inflexible*. Similar evidence is not available to explain the addition of *Lord Nelson*, but one can reasonably assume that it was intended to be part of a two for one trade.

The above telegram from Churchill to Carden identifies another potential point of conflict or misunderstanding with Fisher—the contribution to be made by France. This would directly influence the level of commitment undertaken by Britain. It has been noted that when Churchill identified 12 battleships available for the operation in his minute to Fisher, he wrote that "[t]he above takes no account of four French battleships on the spot, and six others reported available."[19] Fisher had cause to expect that the French contribution to a Dardanelles might reduce the force committed by Britain. However, the number of British battleships and battle cruisers nominated never dropped below 13. Fisher became seriously alarmed when the number of supporting vessels—especially destroyers—became known, and when it became apparent that this burden would not be borne by France.

Yet another issue was to provide aggravation for Fisher. Churchill's minute suggested the operation might begin on February 1 with the bombardment from the *Queen Elizabeth*. Fisher's note to Oliver anticipated almost instant action. In the event, the commencement date for the operation quickly moved from February 1 to February 7 to February 15 and was actually begun on February 19. This marks a significant change in the commitment implied in the memorandum, especially of the *Queen Elizabeth*, which Fisher reasonably could have expected to be back in home waters by this time.

Finally, Churchill's minute made clear that the full commitment of ships and resources need not occur until "the effect of the first stage of the operation has become apparent."[20] Carden would soon recommend that *all* the vessels be gathered before the operation began.

All these issues were central to the level of commitment the navy would be required to make. Serious rumblings were heard from Fisher the moment the level of commitment became clear and it exceeded that which he was prepared to give to such a speculative operation.

If Fisher did briefly give *real* support to Churchill for his Dardanelles proposal and moderated his long-standing concerns over naval-only operations, it might also have been because he believed this operation, once begun, would quickly become a joint operation with the assistance of the Greek Army and, perhaps, other Balkan powers.

On January 7, Elliot, the British minister in Athens, informed the Foreign Office of a new development in Greek attitude to intervention in the war. Britain had been trying for months to get Greece to go to the aid of Serbia. In recent discussions with Elliot, Venizelos had again dismissed this prospect because public opinion would never approve of a war against Austria. However, he had added, "war against Turkey would be popular."[21] This was a new development, and Elliot quickly conveyed it to Grey. Venizelos had suggested that, in return for such intervention, the Allies could guarantee certain territorial gains in Asia Minor and alluded to the possible partition of the Ottoman Empire and to firm Allied control of the Straits.

Four days later on January 11, Fisher was approached by Lord Grey's private secretary, William Tyrrell, who wished to find out "what chance there was of Britain capturing Constantinople, as the diplomatic advantages of such a victory would be considerable, and Britain's bargaining position with Russia greatly enhanced."[22] The next day, January 12, the day *after* Carden's proposal for a naval attack on the Dardanelles was received, Fisher wrote to Tyrrell that if the Greeks attacked the Gallipoli Peninsula in concert with a British naval attack on the Dardanelles, "we could count on every success and [a] quick arrival at Constantinople." However,

> a naval approach to Constantinople: without any troops at all would occupy a month for the first shot fired at the mouth of the Dardanelles and would involve a <u>loss of ships</u>, and <u>expenditure of ammunition</u> and a <u>wearing out of the heavy guns of the fleet</u> beyond approval and when the remains of the Fleet got to Constantinople it could do nothing else but carry out a

futile bombardment with an accompanying massacre *a la* the bombardment of Alexandria.[23]

The same day, Grey telegraphed the British ambassador in Russia, George Buchanan, and informed him that "[a] Greek force landed at Gallipoli would be of great service."[24] On January 13, the day the War Council agreed to prepare for a naval-only operation, Grey went into negotiations with the Russian foreign minister, M. Sergei Dmitrievich Sazanov. Grey was willing to promise Greece a slice of Anatolian coast and Cyprus for her immediate intervention. Sazanov also agreed in principle to offer Smyrna to Greece but made it clear that "if for strategic reasons the Greek army should operate in the environs of the Straits and Gallipoli, Greece should be told that Russia would not agree to the future extension of Greek sovereignty in that area."[25]

All these negotiations fell by the wayside when Sazanov learned of Britain's plans to force the Dardanelles by ships. The issue for Fisher was that, at a critical moment, he was given the prospect of an army. It was to prove another serious disappointment. This prospect would diminish just as the full dimensions of the Dardanelles operation were becoming apparent. Conversely, Fisher's positive comments about a Greek army and his fears for the loss of ships, expenditure of ammunition, the wearing out of heavy guns "beyond approval," and reference to the "remains" of a fleet reaching Constantinople and thereafter achieving nothing hardly represented a ringing endorsement of the naval-only operation hatching that very day.[26]

It is difficult to find anything to suggest Fisher's strong support for what Churchill was proposing. At best he could count on Fisher's reluctant acquiescence in the project.

Did the Carden Plan truly have the cathartic influence on Churchill he described in *The World Crisis* and that is accepted in so many histories of the Dardanelles Campaign? Did Churchill now look forever southward and discard his northern aspirations? One must note the closing paragraph of his memorandum to Fisher in which Churchill nominated the vessels available for the Dardanelles: "The special operation under consideration in the Heligoland Bight could follow the Dardanelles in April or May, when the first batch of monitors is ready. Definite plans should be worked out accordingly."[27]

Moreover, amidst all these discussions surrounding the arrival of Carden's telegram on January 11, Churchill had taken the opportunity to reply to Jellicoe's letter of January 4 and wrote of Borkum:

"This is the only aggressive policy which gives the Navy its chance to apply its energy and daring, and in 6 weeks of fierce flotilla warfare we could beat the enemy out of the North Sea altogether."[28]

Churchill was not surrendering Borkum, he was merely postponing it. Instead of March or April—the dates mentioned in his letters to Fisher and Sir John French (and, subsequently, Jellicoe)—as the desirable starting times for Borkum, he now wrote of April or May. He was, in fact, giving away very little because his unsinkable fleet of monitors—the weapons he believed would mute the objections of his advisers to such an operation—would not be ready in March or April.[29] In the meantime, the Dardanelles would take place as a short-term intermediary operation that, Carden anticipated, might be completed in around a month.

Apart from the golden prospect of destroying the Turko-German Fleet and possibly bringing Turkey to its knees with the aid of its Balkan neighbors, the Dardanelles operation was important in one other respect. Should it succeed, it would confirm the efficacy of naval bombardment against land targets and secure for Churchill the prestige necessary to resist the critics and detractors of the Borkum project.

NOTES

1. Examples include: Michael Howard, "Churchill and the First World War," 137. Tuvia Ben-Moshe, "Churchill as Strategist and Historian," is another: see footnote 2. Prior, "Churchill's 'The World Crisis,'" recognizes Churchill's paramount interest in the Baltic but accepts that, from around this point, the Dardanelles became Churchill's priority. Ted Morgan, *Churchill: 1874–1915* (London: Jonathon Cape, 1983), 422–425, is another. Richard Hough, *Former Naval Person: Churchill and the Wars at Sea* (London: Weidenfeld and Nicolson, 1985), mentions the Baltic plan during his description of the early stages of the war but it receives no mention at all in the vital days of early January.

Typically, historians hardly address the Baltic at all and assume an overriding interest by Churchill in the Dardanelles. Alan Moorehead, *Gallipoli* (London: Hamish Hamilton, 1997), makes little reference to the Baltic—or Churchill's interest in it. Stephen Roskill, *Churchill and the Admirals* (London: Collins, 1977), is another book that barely touches on Churchill's attachment to the Baltic (except in World War II). The list could go on. Churchill's Baltic aspirations are not to be found in the index of the most recent work on the Dardanelles—Dan Van der Vat, *The Dardanelles Disaster*.

2. Virtually all sources, including most of the above, mention Fisher's offer of the *Queen Elizabeth* for the operation as evidence of Fisher's albeit unwise support for the scheme. This matter will be addressed subsequently.

3. Gilbert, *CVIII*, Telegram, Vice-Admiral Carden to First Lord, 405–406. Also, CAB 19/29.

4. Ibid.

5. Ibid.

6. Ibid.

7. Ibid.

8. *The World Crisis*, 541, Memorandum Churchill to Fisher. Churchill only provides an edited version of the memo in *The World Crisis*. For the complete version, see Churchill Papers 8/78.

9. Churchill Papers 8/78. These were *Victorious, Mars, Magnificent,* and *Hannibal*. These vessels were subsequently replaced by four others of a similar vintage and dismantling went ahead, their guns being used for the 12-inch monitors. It is not clear whether the decision to proceed with the dismantling of these vessels was a result of a decision by Fisher or Churchill (or a recommendation of a third party). However, the delay in these monitors would not affect Churchill's Borkum plans. His four 14-inch monitors had already been commissioned and the commissioning of two 15-inch monitors was imminent. These larger vessels were viewed as sufficient for his island schemes.

10. Ibid.

11. *The World Crisis*, 541, Memorandum Churchill to Fisher. Also see Churchill Papers 8/78.

12. *The World Crisis*, 536.

13. Gilbert, *CVIII*, 406–407. In his volume, The Challenge of War, Gilbert asserts that Churchill "wrote to Fisher of how glad he was that, as a result of the Admiral's suggestion, the *Queen Elizabeth* would be firing all her ammunition at the Dardanelles forts instead of uselessly into the Sea." Unfortunately, he does not provide details of this source.

14. Ibid., 367.

15. CAB 19. Telegram Churchill to Carden, January 12, 1915.

16. Telegram, Carden to Churchill, January 13, 1915, CAB 19.

17. Ibid.

18. *The World Crisis*, 542.

19. Churchill Papers, 8/78.

20. Ibid. A similar statement was made in a minute of January 13 to Lord Fisher and Vice-Admiral Oliver. See Gilbert, *CVIII*, 413.

21. George Leon, *Greece and the Great Powers 1914–1917* (Thessalonika: Institute for Balkan Studies, 1974), 103–104.

22. Gilbert, *CVIII*, 247.

23. Quoted in Miller, *Straits*, 378.

24. Leon, *Greece*, 90, footnote.

25. Ibid., 103–104.

26. The Foreign Office's inquiries do not necessarily indicate foreknowledge of Churchill's naval-only scheme. They appeared to have occurred coincidentally. However, the fact that the War Council gave "in-principle"

support to a naval-only operation while Grey was simultaneously attempting to secure Greek military assistance is a fact of importance that requires further investigation. While these events have been discussed in a number of Greek diplomatic histories, they have not been considered in any of the vast number of publications dealing primarily with the Dardanelles operation.

27. Churchill Papers 8/78.

28. Gilbert, *CVIII*, 402–404.

29. None was ready by May either, although it is certain Churchill hoped and expected they would be. The first 14-inch monitor commissioned was *Admiral Farragut* (soon to be *Abercrombie*), but this vessel, as did all the rest, had to undergo sea trials.

CHAPTER 9

Securing Borkum, Selling the Dardanelles

That Churchill's enthusiasm for Borkum or Sir John French's coastal operation remained unaltered despite the arrival of the Carden plan is further demonstrated by events of January 12. At the same time he was working through plans with his War Group for a naval-only operation against the Dardanelles, he was again expressing in the most unequivocal terms to Sir John French that he had no desire to see large-scale military operations in the south.

Sir John came to London on January 12, at Asquith's invitation, to sell his coastal offensive to the War Council the following day. At 5:00 P.M., French received a visit from Lloyd George, who tried to recruit French for his southern cause. One and a half hours later, Churchill visited him. French's diary record of this meeting is instructive: "He (Churchill) was bent upon the attempt to capture Ostende and Zeebrugge. *He thought the time was not yet ripe to consider a diversion of our troops to other more distant theatres*" (emphasis added).[1]

Churchill's assertion that the time was not yet ripe to consider a diversion to more distant theaters was a sentiment he had now expressed repeatedly, and it cannot be ignored as the primary motivation for him selling so forcefully his naval-only scheme to the War Council the following day. There were enough old vessels for this operation and his northern schemes at a later date. In any event, he must await his monitors.

The idea of a full-scale naval operation at the Dardanelles would be an attractive substitute for Lloyd George's and Hankey's plans to send a large army to the Mediterranean to influence the Balkan States. Thus, the growing forces of the New Army could stay in Europe and remain ready and available for one or other of his amphibious plans.

In addition to his communication with Jellicoe and French, some evidence shows that Churchill spoke to one other person vital to the decision-making process before the War Council meeting of January 13—Kitchener. His two-time biographer, George Cassar, recently revisited a theme developed in an earlier work.[2] He has focused his attention on Kitchener's comments at the War Council meeting of May 4, 1915, in which he declared that he had doubted "whether the attempt [to force the Straits] would succeed but was led to believe it possible by the First Lord's statements of the power of the *Queen Elizabeth* and the Admiralty staff paper showing how the operations were to be conducted." Cassar has argued that this assertion, along with the evidence of four staff members of the War Office: George Arthur, Herbert Creedy, Major-General Stanley von Donop, and General Sir John Cowans, indicate that Churchill had had a meeting with Kitchener before January 13, probably on January 12, and that it was here Churchill managed to secure Kitchener's reluctant support for the operation by emphasizing the enormous power of the *Queen Elizabeth.*

Churchill denied the meeting ever took place and, despite Cassar's analysis, there are a number of reasons to believe him. First, Kitchener's comments on May 4 might easily have referred to the January 13 War Council meeting itself. The *Queen Elizabeth* was spoken of in that meeting and, as per Kitchener's comments on May 4, both Fisher and Wilson were present and neither spoke out against the plan. Second, Kitchener's reference to an Admiralty staff paper on May 4 made it clear that his was a "composite" recollection. It was quite certain no relevant staff paper existed on January 12. He was almost certainly referring to the paper or papers prepared by Oliver and circulated in late January and early February outlining the naval operation. Third, and this is conceded by Cassar, none of the testimonies were able to provide a precise date of this meeting. The earliest date given was January 14 or 15, which approximates the date of the War Council meeting. Only Arthur leaves any strong impression that a meeting other than the War Council occurred before January 13 between Churchill and Kitchener, but this belief is based entirely on conversations with Kitchener at a time when he was disgruntled over the withdrawal of the *Queen Elizabeth* and clearly in need of a target on which to vent his spleen.

The point of Cassar's assessment of this meeting appears to have been to establish that Kitchener had to be *persuaded* to support Churchill's naval-only scheme and thereby to exculpate Kitchener or, at least, limit Kitchener's culpability in the original decision-making process. Even accepting that such a meeting did take place, a number of issues mitigate against this assessment. First, unequivocal evidence, hitherto overlooked by historians, shows that, by January 1915, Kitchener was predisposed to any arguments concerning the potential power of naval bombardment. On October 7, 1914, during a CID meeting on invasion, Kitchener countered the Admiralty's argument that the navy could secure Britain from a large-scale invasion by asserting that "modern artillery had rendered forts and fortifications no longer a serious obstruction, if vigorously attacked."[3] The import of this extraordinary statement was that forts would not prove to be an obstacle to a concerted German naval attack. It would seem from this that Kitchener, apparently content to draw naval lessons from experience gained in land battles on the Western Front, would not have needed to be persuaded that ships could fight forts—especially Turkish ones.

Second, at least one of Cassar's sources made clear that, whatever Churchill's pronouncement regarding the *Queen Elizabeth* may have been, Kitchener was at no time certain that his naval advisers shared these views. Despite this, he gave his support to the operation on January 13. When, as will be seen, Fisher's evident dissatisfaction with the naval-only scheme became abundantly clear in late January, Kitchener remained wedded to the scheme. Kitchener's acceptance of Churchill's advocacy of the naval scheme, while simultaneously harboring doubts as to its efficacy, would seem to be indefensible by any measure.

Although it is probable that, at one time or another, Churchill spoke highly of the impact of the *Queen Elizabeth* on the likely success of the operation, it ought not to be held a decisive component of the decision-making process. Two other factors would have been much more influential. The first factor was Kitchener's rather naïve view that there was nothing to be lost in the attempt. Moreover, he held the view that even an unsuccessful attempt would reap rewards because, while the attempt to force the Straits was taking place, Germany would be forced to hold troops in reserve. The second factor, as noted by Cassar, was his belief that the operation could be withdrawn from if unsuccessful.

For the purposes of this book, the most significant import of this meeting between Kitchener and Churchill, if it did indeed take place, was that Churchill was attempting to secure support for a naval-only attempt on the Dardanelles from the man within the War Council who appeared most willing to seriously contemplate an amphibious assault on the Dardanelles at some point in the future. Nothing could have compromised this prospect more successfully than the advocacy of a naval-only operation.

* * * * *

It is perhaps not surprising given Churchill's evening tête-à-tête with Sir John French on January 12 that it was the coastal operation and not the Dardanelles operation that Churchill first supported when the War Council met on January 13. His Dardanelles proposal was presented late in the afternoon and only after it was apparent that the War Council was still seriously considering a diversion of troops for southern operations in the spring.

After extensive discussions Churchill and French, were successful in gaining preliminary acceptance of the Zeebrugge operation, but Kitchener insisted that a final decision on the operation be postponed until February.[4] French was to be supported in the operation by the early departure of two additional Territorial Divisions.

Sir Edward Grey supported the decision. He also recommended, however, the Admiralty study operations in Cattaro—a major Austrian naval base—or elsewhere in the Adriatic to help draw in Italy. In the event of a complete stalemate, study should be made of cooperation with Serbia and an attack on the Gallipoli Peninsula.[5] His proposal led to a decision to prepare a subcommittee to investigate alternative theaters and objectives for British troops.[6]

It was only after French had been given the green light for Zeebrugge and only after the War Council, at Grey's behest, had resolved to prepare plans for serious operations in the South—including the prospect of amphibious operations against the Dardanelles—that Churchill introduced the naval-only scheme to his colleagues. It has been remarked elsewhere that, given the nature of discussions, this was hardly a discreet move if one truly sought full-scale amphibious operations in a southern theater.[7] The observation is a percipient one. It was an extraordinarily wise move, however, if one's intentions were to undermine plans for a large-scale southern front.

It was the idea presented by Grey of a serious naval operation in the Adriatic to help draw in Italy that gave Churchill a window of opportunity to present the Dardanelles proposition, and he seized it immediately. He gave a brief summary of Carden's plan to reduce the Dardanelles forts one by one and introduced the possibility that the new battle ship, *Queen Elizabeth*, could be made available for the task. He indicated that the Admiralty were studying the question and

> believed that a plan could be made for systematically reducing all the forts within a few weeks. Once the forts were reduced the minefields would be cleared, and the Fleet would proceed up to Constantinople and destroy the "*Goeben*." They would have nothing to fear from field guns or rifles, which would be merely an inconvenience.[8]

The response to the proposal was immediately positive. Lloyd George liked the plan while Kitchener "thought it was worth a try. We could leave off the bombardment if it did not prove effective."[9]

Significantly, however, even after mooting the operation and gaining considerable support for it, Churchill made clear that his eyes, like those of Sir John French, remained focused firmly in Northern Europe.

French was reluctant to look elsewhere until the Zeebrugge operation had been attempted, although he did concede that "[i]f we found it impossible to break through, . . . it would be desirable to seek new spheres of activity—in Austria, for example."[10]

At this point, Churchill reaffirmed his belief that no effort should be made to go south—and by this he clearly meant the movement of large numbers of troops away from Northern Europe for joint offensive operations—until he was satisfied that nothing could be done in the north, and he once again offered his Holland scheme.

Sir Edward Grey put forward two conditions that must apply before he could approach Holland: "that they should experience some successes during the next few weeks, (presumably on the Western Front) and that they should be able to offer Holland the assistance of 3–400,000 men."[11] These forces, Churchill hoped, might become available in the spring or early summer should a deadlock on the Western Front be confirmed—and a major diversion southward be avoided.

Thus, despite Grey's hesitation, the War Council arrived at the third of its conclusions: "That the Admiralty should also prepare for a naval expedition in February to bombard and take the Gallipoli peninsula, with Constantinople as its objective."[12]

Churchill's performance on January 13 represented a remarkable *coup*. In one brilliant presentation, he had offered Grey an adequate substitute to his Adriatic proposal, eased his own and French's apprehensions about a new southern theater of operations, overcome the difficulties Kitchener faced in finding sufficient troops to do this, and, most important, he had kept his northern operations alive.

However, what precisely had Churchill offered the War Council and what did the War Council believe had been offered to them? Had he adequately apprised them of the difficulties of the operation and its limitations?

It is probable that all members of the War Council recognized the experimental nature of Carden's proposal. All were undoubtedly attracted to the limited risk and commitment of the operation. Old and new ships bombarding out of range of the fortifications must have appealed. Kitchener had noted that it was an operation that could be "left off" if the early bombardment did not succeed. There seems to have been some hope that a successful entrance into the Marmora could precipitate revolution in Turkey and perhaps draw in wavering Balkan States such as Greece, Italy, and Romania. Our earlier discussions also suggest that some members at least considered that the operation might be helped on its way by Greek intervention.

Had Churchill reflected the true spirit of Carden's plan to the War Council? The answer is no. Hankey's summary of Churchill's presentation suggests its focus was the step-by-step destruction of the forts. The ships "would effect their object without coming into range." "The more modern works," he told the War Council, "could be reduced by the modern 12 inch guns of two battle-cruisers and the 15inch guns of the new battle-cruiser, '*Queen Elizabeth*', which all outranged them."[13]

By emphasizing the ability of modern ships to outrange the guns in the Dardanelles forts, Churchill left unmentioned several important issues, all of which would have undoubtedly given his naval advisors much greater cause for the thought than they did him. His first omission was the ability of the fleet to *destroy*, as opposed to *silence* these guns at such a range. Jackson's memorandum, which was not shown to the War Council, had emphasized the need to land troops to "destroy" guns, even after a gradual bombardment process. Churchill had led the War Council to believe that the fleet could do this by itself.

Even Carden's plan—and this represents Churchill's second serious omission—made clear that the forts would only be "silenced" at long-range but "destroyed" at decisive range. Decisive range meant ships must come within range of forts which, for all sorts of reasons, might temporarily fall silent but which, at any moment, could become deadly again. This, of course, was something that was experienced repeatedly by the fighting ships but never satisfactorily grasp by the War Council.

This issue is more problematic when one appreciates the fact that Churchill had given the War Council the understanding that the guns of the fleet would be able to effect the destruction of the forts *before* the protective minefields were swept. According to Hankey's minutes, the minefields would only be swept *after* all the forts had been reduced. This would have meant that the guns in the forts at the Narrows would have to be *destroyed* at a distance of seven kilometers or about four and a quarter miles—hardly a "range" compatible with safety and way too long to have fitted Carden's notion of "decisive" range.

A third critical omission was his failure to discuss the difficulties the fleet would have in dealing with concealed guns and howitzers and his failure to explain the potential impact these weapons would have on the efficacy of the entire operation, especially on the accuracy of the ships' firing and the fleet's ability to secure the Straits.

Indeed, Churchill did even worse at the War Council by dismissing field guns as "unimportant" and ignoring howitzers altogether. By ignoring the importance of mobile guns, however, Churchill was implicitly offering a plan to the War Council that could only ever facilitate the entrance into the Marmora of fully armored vessels. The critical implication of this plan was that any vessels that broke through into the Marmora could not be guaranteed coal or ammunition or other supplies. In the best of circumstances, therefore, the fleet could remain in the Marmora two or three weeks before it was forced to withdraw. This was not the Carden plan, which clearly had in view the permanent control of the Straits.

For Churchill's plan to have any significant level of success, the Turks had to be so intimidated by the sight of the British Fleet in the Marmora they would surrender almost immediately. Alternatively, it had to be hoped that Bulgaria, Greece, or Romania would be spurred into action by the example of the fleet and provide the military support needed for success. The chance that either of these events would occur must have been slim.

The Turks and their German leaders undoubtedly were aware that as long as they commanded the peninsula with their mobile guns and howitzers, the fleet's occupation of the Marmora must necessarily be temporary. Perhaps more important, as long as the peninsula was held, troops could never be brought up to threaten

Constantinople. In other words, a plan that did not provide secure lines of communication could not control its own destiny.

In its essentials, therefore, Churchill's plan (as opposed to the plan conceived by Carden) was little different to an attempt to "rush" the Straits analyzed by Jackson several days earlier. It is probable that a "gradual reduction" plan would reduce losses while the fortifications were destroyed. Furthermore, it would substantially reduce the risks involved in returning through the Straits, should this prove necessary. However, under Churchill's plan, the fleet would be in the same parlous condition once inside the Marmora as a fleet that had "rushed" the Straits because neither course secured lines of communication. Precious little evidence suggests that such limitations were conveyed to or understood by his non-military War Council colleagues.

In an attempt to understand what else was discussed at the War Council meeting but not conveyed clearly in Hankey's minutes, it is important to address the wording of Asquith's conclusion that initiated the attempt to force the Dardanelles. This was "[t]hat the Admiralty should also prepare for a naval expedition in February to bombard and ***take the Gallipoli peninsula,*** with Constantinople as its objective" (emphasis added). The inability of ships to take a peninsula has been noted in countless histories, but it begs the question as to why such a bizarre conclusion was made. It is possible the conclusion is carelessness and nothing more should be made of it. However, one must explore other possibilities.

In his book, *The Supreme Command 1914–1918,* Hankey provided a footnote to explain Asquith's conclusion: "I have no doubt that Asquith had in mind that, after the fall of the forts and the passage of the fleet into the Sea of Marmora, the Peninsula would be isolated and the garrison compelled to surrender."[14] This is a plausible explanation and nothing that will follow in this paper will disprove it. Conversely, there is nothing to be found to confirm it either. The idea of isolating the Gallipoli Peninsula by a naval breakthrough into the Marmora is a proposition that was argued by Kitchener and Hankey and, to a lesser extent, Churchill from late February 1915 onward, but no evidence suggests that this was being argued in early January. There is some concern, therefore, that Hankey has put words into Asquith's mouth *post facto*. If Churchill had given such an understanding in his discourse of January 13, it is rather surprising it is not to be found in the body of Hankey's minutes.

It is also possible, given our earlier discussions regarding Greece, that Asquith's conclusion anticipated the capture of the Gallipoli

Peninsula by a Greek army. Again, no evidence supports this in the minutes of the January 13 meeting. As has been noted, however, it is a mystery worthy of further investigation.

If we can anticipate discussions that took place during February, a third possibility is that the War Council was led to expect the Turks might evacuate the peninsula once the success of the fleet appeared imminent. Apart from the fact it is in contradiction to what Asquith was purported to believe would happen, it ought to be discounted immediately for three reasons. First, nothing indicates such a proposition was under discussion on January 13. Second, and perhaps most compellingly, this proposition must surely have been accompanied by the organization of a force—even a small one—to take immediate advantage of such an eventuality. No such plans were made or even suggested until after the operation had begun. Third, Churchill's plan—as was to become increasingly evident—was intended to admit an *armored* fleet only into the Marmora because this fleet alone would not be threatened by field guns and rifles. This seems to imply the peninsula would continue to be occupied, although it is possible it was assumed that, even if the peninsula were evacuated, such a threat still would be present from the southern shores of the Straits.

A fourth possibility, and this returns to the proposition that Asquith's wording is merely aberrant, is that neither Churchill, nor anyone else, addressed the taking of the peninsula at all at this time. The need to secure the peninsula with troops became an issue in Hankey's mind during February, but it is probable that it was not a critical issue for Churchill on January 13—if ever. No evidence suggests his plan to admit an armored fleet into the Marmora capable of destroying the *Goeben* and *Breslau* was dependent on maintaining secure lines of communication. Again, the minutes indicate that Churchill anticipated the lines of communications would be contested. He always knew that if the hoped-for moral or political objectives were not achieved within a couple of weeks, the fleet would have to return through the Marmora. This, however, did not stop him pressing on with the operation in the hope that the fleet's success would draw in one or other of the Balkan States. It was in this possibility rather than any suggestion the Turks on the peninsula would be cut off and surrender that Churchill placed his faith. Such would seem to be the implication of his subsequent criticism of Grey's Cattaro proposal to be discussed hereunder.

A final possibility is that, in agreeing to prepare for an attack on the Dardanelles on January 13, the War Council was content to look no further than the exciting possibility that once the fleet was through, the Turks would surrender, or Bulgaria, Greece, or Romania would rush in and save the show. With such a prospect before them, it is possible all failed to consider the importance or otherwise of controlling the peninsula and how this might be achieved by ships alone.

An extension of this argument is that the general discussion of the Dardanelles operation was far from thorough. A number of histories have pointed out that the War Council members viewed the decision as giving permission for preparations only and that no final decision had been made. Indeed, on January 13, it was impossible to make any definite decision on the efficacy of Dardanelles operation. Despite Hankey's description of the meeting in *The Supreme Command*, it is evident in the instructions Churchill gave his naval staff the same day that they were still only in the preliminary stages of their study of the viability of the operation. In other words, Churchill had jumped the gun on his naval advisors and had proposed the operation before many of the difficulties to be faced had been identified.

Did the War Council understand the nature and limitations of the plan as proposed by Churchill? It will be shown that at least one member of the War Council, Sir Arthur James Balfour, accepted and understood that Churchill's plan was designed to admit fully armored vessels *only* into the Marmora, although whether this was grasped on January 13 or in subsequent private discussions is unclear. The evidence suggests that Churchill did not shy away from making this known. However, it is much less likely Balfour or other nonmilitary members of the War Council understood that this was not the Carden plan. They appear to have been kept largely ignorant of the problems inherent in a plan that failed to accommodate unarmored supply vessels and smaller vessels such as minesweepers.

One thing is certain: the War Council had been given the slimmest of information on which to base their conditional support for the operation. Hankey lamented this fact in a letter to Asquith in May when he expressed his frustration at the dearth of information made available to the War Council by the Admiralty and War Office. He noted by way of example that "the War Council sanctioned the original attack with only such knowledge as they could glean from the statements made at the time by the First Lord, and without any opportunity for the mature examination of the problem in detail."[15]

Where did Churchill's staff stand in regard to the January 13 decision to prepare to force the Dardanelles? The evidence is that most, including Fisher, Bartolome, Wilson, and Oliver considered that a gradual bombardment might force the Dardanelles. None, however, with the probable exception of Oliver, saw any virtue in the fleet being inside the Marmora with unsecured lines of communication.

Churchill's naval advisers recognized, just as he must surely have done, that the full moral and political impact of the fleet's breakthrough would be achieved only if the Turks and their Balkan neighbors understood that the fleet, once in the Marmora, was there to stay. Churchill was prepared to overlook this rather fundamental detail and made no effort to address its implications within the War Council. The operation, should it succeed, just might be sufficient to bring in one other of the Balkan States, and it just might create unrest in Constantinople. At the very least, it would remove the thorn of the *Goeben* and *Breslau*—assuming they chose not to escape to the Black Sea. Most important of all, it would delay, and perhaps remove the need for, a large-scale southern offensive. His northern dreams could continue to live.

NOTES

1. Gilbert, *CVIII*, footnote 407. Gilbert indicates this was written in French's diary on January 12. The mention of the War Council in the footnote shows this was not the case. Without access to the diaries, however, I cannot establish when the entry was made. The full quote is in Gerald French, *The Life of Field Marshal John French First Earl of Ypres* (London: Cassell and Company, 1931), 273.
2. George Cassar, *Kitchener's War: British Strategy from 1914–1918.* (Washington, DC: Brassey's, 2004).
3. CAB 2/3, Committee of Imperial Defence Meeting, October 7, 1914.
4. Gilbert, *CVIII*, 411. Quotation from Hankey's Notes of War Council Meeting, January 13, 1915.
5. Ibid., 409.
6. Ibid., 411.
7. Prior, "Churchill's 'World Crisis,'" made such an observation in his thesis.
8. Gilbert, *CVIII*, 407–411, Minutes of the War Council Meeting, January 13, 1915.
9. Ibid., 410.
10. Ibid.
11. Ibid.
12. Ibid., 411.
13. Ibid., 409.
14. Hankey, *The Supreme Command*, vol. 1, 267.
15. Hankey to Asquith, May 17, 1915, CAB 63/5.

CHAPTER 10

Clearing the Decks

While most histories indicate there was some subsequent uncertainty within the War Council as to the extent to which the Admiralty had been given permission to "prepare" for an operation against the Dardanelles on January 13, Churchill took no half-measures. Immediately after the War Council meeting concluded, he ordered detailed preparations and acted as though the operation would definitely go ahead. At the very least, he must have reasoned that the more thorough and advanced the preparations, the more likely it was that the operation would be acceded to. In the meantime, he could continue with plans to support French's coastal operation and to win over Sir John Jellicoe to his Borkum/Baltic cause.

Immediately after the War Council meeting of January 13 finished, Churchill instructed Fisher and Oliver that:

> Admiral Carden's proposal should be carefully analysed . . . to show exactly what guns the ships will have to face at each point and stage of the operations, the character of the guns, and their range; but this officer is to assume that the principle is settled, and all that is necessary is to estimate the force required. . . . A telegram should be drafted to Admiral Carden approving his proposal and informing him of the forces which will be placed at his disposal.[1]

This was a rather emphatic minute from Churchill. Clearly, he intended to brook no challenge to the operation from his naval advisers. This is somewhat disturbing given that the rest of the minute suggests that many of the potential pitfalls and problems of the operation had yet to be established. The staff discussions regarding the operation before the War Council on January 13 would seem to have been rather rudimentary if all these presumably critical factors had yet to be worked out.

To clear the decks completely for his new initiative and to secure its paramountcy over other southern alternatives, Churchill wrote to Asquith, Grey, and Kitchener the following day, dismissing Grey's request for an operation against Cattaro, which, it was hoped, would bring in Italy. He informed them that the French, who had a large naval force in the area, had made no progress because of the absence of a friendly army and the presence of hostile submarines. He went on to argue that:

> the bombardment of the forts at Cattaro would be a sterile operation attended by great risk from submarines and some damage from gunfire. The entry of the harbour would lead to nothing by itself. Unless therefore adequate military force is forthcoming to storm and hold the forts after bombardment, there are no means of producing good results. . . . The attack on the Dardanelles will require practically our whole available margin. If that attack opens prosperously it will very soon attract to itself the whole attention of the Eastern theatre, and if it succeeds it will produce results which will undoubtedly influence every Mediterranean power.[2]

Churchill's criticisms of operations against Cattaro are valuable because they give us further insight into how he viewed the Dardanelles attack at this time. By implication, the Dardanelles was more desirable than Cattaro for two reasons. First, it was not threatened greatly by submarines. Second, while an entry to the harbor at Cattaro would lead to nothing, a breakthrough into the Marmora could have considerable results. Churchill is typically vague on these results, but the clear impression is that he anticipated that an entry into the Marmora might be the catalyst for revolt in Constantinople or Balkan intervention and assistance from a "friendly" army. One of the results he undoubtedly continued to think might inspire foreign assistance was the destruction of the *Goeben* and *Breslau*.[3] With these vessels out of the way, it might even have been possible for the Russians to sail an army across the Black Sea. Thus, although clearly being aware of the need for soldiers to secure success from a naval bombardment as a general rule, he appears to consider a naval-only operation against the Dardanelles worth pursuing.

Perhaps the most important element of this minute is Churchill's observation that "*unless therefore adequate military force is forthcoming to storm and hold the forts after bombardment, there are no means of producing good results*" (emphasis added).[4] The extraordinary import of this observation is that, whatever his declarations to the War Council might have been, Churchill understood that neither the guns nor the forts his ships were destined to attack at the Dardanelles would be put beyond repair without military assistance. In the case of the Dardanelles, he was prepared to ignore this critical issue because the political and moral results might be so immediate that the threat to his forces was justified.

While Churchill was busily setting down the foundations of his naval-only operation and undermining other southern possibilities, he continued to nurture his northern schemes. Churchill spent a considerable part of January 14 with Sir John French in conference with A. K. Wilson and Fisher planning the proposed joint operations against Zeebrugge and Ostende.[5] It is probable that the ongoing preparation for this operation—especially in the company of such an important figure as French—contributed to Fisher's relative quiescence over preparations for the Dardanelles at this time.

The following day, Churchill heard again from Jellicoe on the topic of Borkum. Again, in contrast to his biographical notes, Jellicoe was almost effusive in his support of Borkum. He told Churchill he was very much aware of "the immense advantages . . . such a base would confer on us."[6] He believed that the operation was "probably feasible so long as we are prepared to accept heavy losses, principally naval losses, and provided an adequate military force is used."[7] Although Jellicoe then set about listing a number of serious concerns, including fears for lines of communication and difficulties in retaining the island once captured, the tone of his letter was by no means the best way to discourage Churchill. He did not help his cause by emphasizing again at one point that "as I said earlier, if we *could* get established firmly the advantages are immense."[8]

Churchill responded three days later, dismissing entirely the problems of communications and declaring that the risk of recapture would be limited by his monitors: "I expect we shall have to wait till 4 or 5 heavy monitors are ready at the end of April. Proximity to the enemy's guns from shore water, probably only partially commanded, coupled with immunity from mines and S/M are decisive advantages."[9]

Meanwhile, on January 15, the Dardanelles naval-only operation took another step forward when Sir Henry Jackson submitted to Churchill an assessment of Carden's scheme entitled "Remarks on Vice-Admiral Carden's Proposals as to Operations in Dardanelles."[10] Jackson's appreciation provided considerable impetus to the Dardanelles operation, although it is not clear this was Jackson's intention.

In the opening sentence of his appreciation, Jackson pronounced that he concurred "generally" with the Carden plan, noting that "[o]ur previous appreciations of the situation differed only in small details."[11] At least one of the previous appreciations alluded to his January 5 memorandum criticizing any attempt to force the Dardanelles.

Curiously, however, Jackson proceeded to discuss only the first two stages of Carden's Plan ("*a. Total reduction of defences at the entrance and b. clearing of defences inside of Straits up to and including Kephes Point battery.*").[12] The document did not address points c and d of Carden's plan. These were as follows: "*c. Reduction of defences at the Narrows Chanak* and *d. Clearing of passage through minefield and advance through Narrows reducing forts above Narrows and final advance on Marmora.*"[13] To present an incomplete assessment of the operation would seem a very strange thing to do but might be explained by the fact Jackson was ill around this time.

If Jackson genuinely found the operation as unpalatable as he subsequently claimed at the Dardanelles Commission hearings, his concurrence in the opening paragraph was a serious indiscretion. Churchill subsequently used this memorandum to indicate the support of his advisors. It allowed him to write to Carden on January 25, "your plans are in principle agreed with by Jackson who examines for the board all naval questions connected with the East."[14]

Given the incomplete nature of the report, Churchill was, at best, only half right on this point. In defending his acquiescence in the plan, Jackson was on firmer ground when he argued at the Dardanelles Commission that his memorandum was a recommendation only to attempt to destroy the forts at the entrance "as the experience gained would be useful."[15]

When assessing the support or otherwise afforded Churchill, two other issues are more important. The first is his warning that "there were . . . at least 200 guns of 6-inch and above to be silenced, and many of these will be concealed and probably protected from direct gunfire."[16] Like Carden, Jackson was making it clear that *all* guns would need to be silenced (destroyed) for the operation to be successful. Twice he emphasized the importance of destroying every gun: "It will be essential to close them in latter stages to *ensure every gun being destroyed*" (emphasis added).[17] Elsewhere he wrote that the bombardment of the outer forts should continue "till all guns at the entrance *are permanently silenced*."[18] It is evident from our foregoing discussion that Churchill did not consider the destruction of all guns on the peninsula as imperative.

Although emphasizing the need to destroy "every gun" in his memorandum, Jackson unwisely gave considerable support to Churchill by implicitly appearing now to accept the idea that the fleet alone might achieve this. He would correct this impression a little under a month later in another, more thorough, memorandum on the operation. For the time being, Jackson had committed a major tactical error if he really did wish to curtail Churchill's Dardanelles plans.

Nevertheless, Jackson's careless failure to reinforce his earlier pronouncements that troops were needed to put guns permanently out of action should not and could not be used to explain Churchill's determination to press on with his naval-only operation. The Cattaro memorandum and Churchill's own pronouncements on the Carden plan suggest strongly that Jackson's requirement that "every gun be destroyed" was not a *sine qua non* of the Churchill plan and never would be. Jackson's concern to destroy all guns undoubtedly had an eye to the question of what the fleet might do inside the Marmora without secured lines of communication. Churchill simply viewed this as one of the uncertain elements of the operation. If the gradual bombardment did enough damage for long enough he would press on regardless. It was a gamble he was prepared to take because the alternative was a full-scale assault on the peninsula or an alternative southern offensive, and as long as hope remained for his northern schemes, he was determined to avoid such serious entanglements.

While the Admiralty staff forged ahead with their preparations, Churchill, Grey, and the Foreign Office had to pave the political path to such a delicate operation. This was by no means an easy task because, as Balfour had pointed out 11 days before, the control of the Dardanelles was a political minefield and it was all the more so because of Prime Minister Venizelos's recent overtures. Churchill drafted a letter to the French and passed it on to Grey for comment. Grey agreed with the letter but footnoted:

> [W]e must say something to Russia, not necessarily in detail, or she will think we are stealing a march to forestall her a

> Constantinople. *The peg to hang our communication on would be the Grand Duke's appeal to us some days ago to make a diversion to prevent Turkish pressure in the Caucasus.* (emphasis added)[19]

The reference to the grand duke's appeal is striking for its offhandedness and shows, in a decisive manner, that the grand duke's January 1 appeal for aid was little more than a distant memory as far as Grey and the Foreign Office were concerned.[20] In the circumstances, it is extremely difficult to imagine it had carried any more weight with Churchill or Kitchener since the earliest days of January. It surely undermines the long-held belief that the Russian request for aid was the decisive influence behind Churchill's naval-only operation.

Churchill took Grey's advice and it was for this reason only that his letter to the grand duke began with reference to the Russian call for assistance at the beginning of January:

> The Admiralty have considered with deep attention the request conveyed through Ld Kitchener from YIH [the Grand Duke Nicholas of Russia] for naval action against Turkey to relieve pressure in the Caucasus. They have decided that the general interests of the Allied cause require a serious effort to be made to break down Turkish opposition, in addition to the minor demonstration of which Ld Kitchener telegraphed to YIH.[21]

It is ironic in the circumstances that Churchill's closing paragraph sought not only Russian naval assistance at the mouth of the Bosporus but also troops "to seize any advantage that may be gained for the allied cause."[22] Rather than aiding Russia, Churchill's plan required Russian naval and military intervention to secure the "advantage" gained through a successful entrance into the Marmora. To this extent, it ought to be noted, Churchill's operation was never entirely *naval-only* in its concept and usually this is entirely lost in the debate over the Dardanelles. Churchill had promised only to force the Dardanelles without troops. He knew that whatever might happen thereafter was entirely speculative and that results could not be forced upon the Turks unless troops were found from some source. This had been made clear to him in two naval staff memoranda in early January, but it is unlikely he needed to be told this rather self-evident truth.

When the grand duke responded a week later, he made it clear that neither naval nor military assistance could be anticipated.

Nevertheless, he welcomed the operation, believing, somewhat optimistically, that a successful attack against Turkey would "infallibly be a deciding factor in determining the attitude of neutral states in the Balkans."[23]

Here was another who readily accepted the moral impact of a successful breakthrough into the Marmora. What is not clear, however, is whether the "successful attack on Turkey" presupposed "command" of the Marmora as per the Carden plan or the temporary visit of the fleet offered by Churchill's naval-only operation. It was concerns held by his First Sea Lord over this very issue that began to cause the first serious cracks in the preparations for the Dardanelles operation in mid-January 1915.

NOTES

1. Gilbert, *CVIII*, 412–413.
2. Gilbert, *CVIII*, 414–415. Churchill to Asquith, Grey and Kitchener.
3. Churchill confirmed with Carden the day before that two fast capital ships (battle cruisers) were required to destroy the *Goeben* and *Breslau*.
4. Ibid., 414.
5. French, *The Life of Field Marshal Sir John French*, 274.
6. Gilbert, *CVIII*, 417–418. Jellicoe to Churchill, January 15, 1915.
7. Ibid.
8. Ibid.
9. Gilbert, *CVIII*, 426; Churchill to Jellicoe, January 18, 1915.
10. Gilbert, *CVIII*, 419–421. Jackson to Oliver, *Remarks on Vice Admiral Carden's Proposals as to Operations in Dardanelles*, January 15, 1915. See also, CAB 19/29. It is not clear whether Jackson had produced this memorandum as a result of Churchill's January 13 instruction above or whether Jackson had produced this on his own initiative or because of a request on January 11. A number of factors make this issue uncertain. At the Dardanelles Inquiry, Churchill asserted the memorandum was unsolicited. Second, Churchill's January 13 memo to Fisher and Oliver indicated that Jackson was ill at this time. Churchill therefore instructed that the detailed proposal be worked out by the COS, that is, by Oliver. It is not clear how quickly Jackson returned to good health. Finally, Jackson had had four days to work on his appreciation, suggesting that he had been asked to investigate Carden's plan on the day it had arrived. See Churchill, *The World Crisis*, 547.
11. Gilbert, *CVIII*, 419–421. Jackson to Oliver in *Remarks on Vice Admiral Carden's Proposals as to Operations in Dardanelles*, January 15, 1915. See also, CAB 19/29.
12. Gilbert, *CVIII*, 405–406. Carden to Churchill, January 11, 1915. See also, CAB 19/29.
13. Gilbert, *CVIII*, 405–406. The copy of this telegram in CAB 19/29 varies in wording but not in substance. The wording here is from *CVIII*.

14. CAB 19/31. Telegram, Churchill to Carden, January 25, 1915.

15. Jackson's Evidence before Dardanelles Commission, CAB 19/33.

16. Gilbert, *CVIII*, 420. It is not entirely clear in his appreciation whether this is an estimate for the entire peninsula or merely up to the end of the second stage of the attack, that is, up to the Kephez battery.

17. Gilbert, *CVIII*, 419–421. Jackson to Oliver in *Remarks on Vice Admiral Carden's Proposals as to Operations in Dardanelles*, January 15, 1915. Also, CAB 19/29.

18. Ibid.

19. Gilbert, *CVIII*, 423. Note by Sir Edward Grey attached to draft Churchill's letter to Comte de Saint Seine written on January 16, 1915 (see *CVIII*, 421–422).

20. The tone of this quotation does not fit comfortably with Grey's testimony to the Dardanelles Commission. He, like Churchill, contended that the request demanded action. It would not be too strong to suggest Grey was not responding with total honesty.

21. Gilbert, *CVIII*, 430–431. Telegram, Churchill to Grand Duke Nicholas, January 19, 1915.

22. Ibid.

23. See Buchanan to Grey, telegram, Ibid., 455–456. The text of the telegram noted that "Russian Dreadnoughts were not finished; they had no submarines of modern type and only an insufficient number of swift Destroyers. Their Fleet was therefore not more than equal of Turkish Fleet and that only when all ships were together. Russian ships only carry four days coal and coaling at sea in the Black Sea was rendered impossible in the winter by bad weather. The nearest Russian base was moreover 24 hours from the entrance of the Bosphorus. Guns of the Bosphorus Batteries as compared both in number and power with those placed in Russian ships were such as to give little hope of a successful attack by the latter." None of this appears to have been conveyed to the War Council on January 28. Grey kept only one copy of the telegram and gave the other to Churchill telling him it was up to Churchill to inform Kitchener and Asquith of its contents if he wished. It is not apparent that he did.

CHAPTER 11

"I Just Abominate the Dardanelles"

—Lord Fisher to Sir John Jellicoe, January 19, 1915

In the middle of January, Lord Fisher's apprehensions over the Dardanelles preparations began to develop into a more serious form of dissent. His long-standing concerns over battle cruisers and ancillary craft committed to the Dardanelles—in particular destroyer flotilla—began to be fueled by his correspondence with Jellicoe, who wanted the battle cruisers and destroyers returned to the Home Fleet immediately. "BATTLE CRUISERS," Jellicoe declared, "ARE OUR LIFE BLOOD."[1]

Initially Fisher was diplomatic in his efforts to draw Churchill back from his ever-growing commitment to the Dardanelles. "I desire," he wrote:

> to emphasise the necessity of sticking to the enemy's vitals! I am not minimising the coming Dardanelles operation, but I wish to aggrandise the great big fact that 750,000 men landed in Holland, combined with intense activity of the British Fleet against, say, Cuxhaven, would finish the War by forcing out the German High Sea Fleet and getting in the rear of the German Armies.[2]

On January 20, in another letter to Churchill, he wrote of Jellicoe's apparent depression and suggested:

> If by any means the Admiralty can meet his wishes, without prejudicing other requirements, it is obviously desirable for them to do so (even if not convinced of the absolute necessity of the case) because such a state of mind is infectious and may easily spread throughout the Grand Fleet.[3]

Although he did not press for the immediate return of the battle cruisers—an argument he would have found difficult to sustain—he believed the 1st Destroyer Flotilla should be returned to the Home Fleet as soon as possible.

In his responses to Fisher, Churchill was conciliatory if unsympathetic. He thought Jellicoe's margin considerable, but nevertheless agreed the 1st Destroyer Flotilla would be soon returned. Aware of Jellicoe's concerns over the battle cruisers, he also recommended that "the refit of the *Invincible* should be accelerated to the utmost" and promised that the *Inflexible* could sail for home on February 12th.[4]

Fisher was not satisfied with Churchill's response and, although he left the issue of the battle cruisers alone, he again pressed for the immediate return of the destroyer depot ship *Blenheim* and the 1st Destroyer Flotilla from the Dardanelles and suggested they be replaced with French Destroyers.[5] Churchill refused the request because it would have "paralysed the Dardanelles Fleet and destroyed the plans which the staff was maturing."[6]

Having achieved little success with his first lord, Fisher attempted to mollify his commander in chief in a letter the next day. He pointed out that he had enormously increased the power of his individual ships since the beginning of the War, and Fisher defended the use of the vessels in dispute by noting that, should "the Government of the Country decide on a project as a subject of high policy, one can't put oneself up to govern the diplomatic attitude of the nation in its relation with foreign powers."[7] Whether or not he believed this or had been told by Churchill this was so, he also noted that "apparently the Grand Duke Nicholas has demanded this step, or (I suppose he would make peace with Germany)."[8]

Nevertheless, he could not hide his true feelings: "I just abominate the Dardanelles operation unless a great change is made and it is settled to be a military operation, with 200,000 men in conjunction with the Fleet."[9]

This final comment by Fisher identifies another reason why his support for Jellicoe had been somewhat more muted than might have been expected. He did not wish to condemn out-right the movement of ships away from the defense of the North Sea for other operations, save only they be used to support an operation in which he believed. He did not believe in a naval-only attempt to force the Dardanelles but continued to hope that it might yet be converted to an amphibious operation.

In an ongoing effort to counter the slide toward a naval-only assault on the Dardanelles, he sought the assistance of Julian Corbett,[10] and the secretary to the War Council, Maurice Hankey, to prepare a document setting forth his attitude to the Dardanelles and naval policy in general.[11] Hankey, who had been a regular confidant over the previous few weeks, did not wish to become embroiled in a conflict between the first lord and his first sea lord, and it is not clear what input he made. He had, however, informed Asquith of the tension between the two on January 20.[12]

In the meantime, Fisher's frustration found new depth when he learned that French's coastal operation might again be postponed. He wrote to Churchill on January 23,

> I hope you will make a big fight before surrendering over the military retreat from the Zeebrugge bombardment. . . . It's simple folly not to use the British Army to win back the Sea Frontier to the Dutch border instead of (*to use your own words*) playing the ignoble petty part of occupying a small sector of the French line in its most damnable part! Is there no Marlborough to be had anywhere?[13]

Sir John French's Zeebrugge operation was indeed under attack from a new direction. Concern over the German and Austrian threat to Serbia had caused members of the War Council to contemplate sending up a corps of Allied troops to her assistance.

Fisher was deeply disappointed at the suspension of Zeebrugge and angry at the fact that Churchill intended to go ahead with a naval bombardment. He wrote to Jellicoe that day that:

> A written decision was come to that the British Army should cooperate with the British Fleet and advance along the sea frontier to the Dutch border, bombarding Zeebrugge, on February 15th. *The day was fixed.* Now this is cancelled and no reason given! But they want to bombard all the same with futile results, as in the last three weeks they have made good again! And we risk the loss of six battleships![14]

Fisher was now faced with the demise—or at best—postponement of the Zeebrugge operation. In its place stood two substantial naval operations that had no military support. It was inevitable the ax would fall, and it did so on January 25. He wrote to Churchill that he had "no desire to continue a useless resistance in the War Council to plans I cannot concur in, and I would ask that the enclosed may be printed and circulated to its members before the next meeting."[15] The enclosed was a "Memorandum on the Position of the British Fleet and its Policy of Steady Pressure."[16] The postponement of Zeebrugge—and its probable replacement with a naval bombardment, along with Churchill's obduracy over the destroyers and other modern ships to be used in the Dardanelles—had brought events to a head.

Although there was novelty in the approach taken in Fisher's memorandum, the essentials of its criticism of naval bombardment not supported by the British Army were not new and could not have held any surprise for Churchill.[17] Fisher wanted joint operations or no operations at all. Only then, he believed, could something of value be achieved and only then could the risks to the British Fleet be justified. In perhaps what was a new emphasis, he declared that, unless an army supported the fleet, the enemy would not take the operation seriously and risk their own ships to prevent its success. He had first developed this novel approach to strategic thinking in his earlier letter to Jellicoe. In his memorandum he explained:

> the sole justification of coastal bombardments and attacks on fortified places, such as the contemplated prolonged bombardment of the Dardanelles forts by our fleet, is to force a decision at sea, and so far and no further can they be justified . . .
>
> It has been said that the first function of the British Army is to assist the fleet in obtaining command of the sea. This might be accomplished by military cooperation with the Navy in such operations as the attack of Zeebrugge, or the forcing of the Dardanelles, which might bring out the German and Turkish fleets respectively. Apparently, however, this is not to be. The English Army is apparently to continue to provide a small sector of the allied front in France, where it no more helps the Navy than if it were at Timbuctoo.[18]

Such elements of this letter bear the strong influence of Corbett and reflect a strong maritime philosophy. The emphasis is on how the army could assist the navy to draw out and defeat the German High Seas Fleet and not how the navy could assist the army in sustaining its continental commitment. This was hardly a point worth laboring, particularly given that Britain was irreversibly committed to a continental war by this time. It is unlikely Fisher had supported the Zeebrugge operation only because he anticipated it would prevent further damage to the British Fleet by destroying an efficient German submarine base. Nor would his interest in the Dardanelles have been focused solely on the destruction of the Turkish Fleet. He undoubtedly viewed plans to bring in Balkan States and assist Russia as valuable. Nevertheless, although these arguments were anachronistic and, by this time, largely irrelevant distractions, they did not obscure his fundamental point: naval bombardment without military support would have no lasting impact on the actions of the enemy.

Churchill remained unimpressed. The following day he wrote: "There is no difference in principle between us. But when all your special claims are met, you must let the surplus be used for the general cause."[19] He accompanied the note with a memorandum of his own and a suggestion that "I [will] show your Memo and my comments to the Prime Minister: instead of printing and circulating the documents. You and I are so much stronger together."[20]

Churchill's memorandum targeted a critical flaw in Fisher's paper—the notion that subsidiary operations, typically conducted by surplus ships—threatened Britain's naval superiority. In what might well have been a tactical ploy to avoid debating this issue in front of the prime minister, Churchill's paper ignored altogether the more important issue of what a bombardment by ships alone might achieve.

His memorandum demonstrated how the main functions of the British Fleet were taken care of. In addition to the forces required for these purposes, he argued a large force was available "to use for special services and for bombarding as may be necessary from time to time in furtherance of objects of great strategic and political importance."[21] These included:

1. The operations at the Dardanelles;
2. The support of the left flank of the army;
3. The bombardment of Zeebrugge; and later on
4. The seizure of Borkum.

The force included 21 old battleships and 14 monitors that would be completed between April and the end of July.

Churchill argued that it could not be said:

> the employment of ships which are (except the "Duncans") not needed and not suited to fight in the line of battle conflicts with any of the sound principles of naval policy set forth by the First

> Sea Lord. Not to use them where necessary because of some fear that there will be an outcry if a ship is lost would be wrong.[22]

Failing as it did to address his primary concern—namely the futility of naval-only bombardment—Fisher was far from satisfied with Churchill's arguments. He did not dispute the use of such craft for ancillary operations, so long as they were joint operations. Another point ignored by Churchill's paper was the fact that the Dardanelles would employ large modern craft that were not among the "ancillary" craft nominated, and sundry smaller craft—especially destroyers and submarines—which, he believed, were needed immediately in home waters. On January 28, Fisher wrote to Asquith:

> His reply to my memorandum does not meet my case. I say that the Zeebrugge and Dardanelles bombardments can only be justified on naval grounds by military co-operation, which would compensate for the loss in ships and irreplaceable officers and men. As purely naval operations they are unjustifiable, (because results not permanent)[23] as they both drain our naval margin.[24]

He wrote similarly to Churchill:

> My position is quite clear:
> *I make no objection to either Zeebrugge or Dardanelles if accompanied by military cooperation on such a scale as will permanently hold the Belgian coast to the Dutch Frontier and our permanent military occupation of the Dardanelles Forts pari passu with the Naval bombardment.* Simultaneous Military and Naval actions but no drain thereby on Grand Fleet Margin so therefore *no modern vessels at Dardanelles.* (emphasis added)[25]

Fisher's demand for the "permanent military occupation of the Dardanelles forts" is clear evidence he apprehended that, although the fleet might break into the Marmora unaided, it would remain grievously exposed unless and until the guns in the forts were put permanently out of action. This, he knew, demanded military support.

The tension between Churchill and Fisher resulted in a three-way conference in the prime minister's chambers with Asquith as chief conciliator and arbiter. Before considering the outcome of this meeting, it is instructive to compare Fisher's arguments with the perspective implicit in Churchill's Cattaro letter discussed in chapter 10. This letter showed Churchill clearly understood the importance of using troops to follow up bombardment operations to destroy guns and prevent their re-use. He had, one might add, pronounced similarly regarding Zeebrugge. Where he differed from Fisher was in his belief that this principle could be dispensed with at the Dardanelles because the potential military and political consequences of the operation might make the prior control of the peninsula unnecessary. A coup might take place at Constantinople, or one of the Balkan States (or Russia) might provide an army to assist the operation. Moreover, should no military assistance be forthcoming, the fleet could retreat through the Straits after destroying the Turko-German Fleet.

Fisher believed the risk to be too great. Like most of Churchill's advisers, he appreciated that, should the fleet be unable to secure its line of communications, the moral impact it might achieve in forcing the Straits would be diminished seriously and little of consequence would be achieved. Additionally, should the *Goeben* and *Breslau* retire to the Black Sea, the fleet would be denied even this victory.

In bringing down his decision, Asquith was unmoved by Fisher's pleas. He, like Churchill, appeared to have been convinced that forcing the Dardanelles by ships alone *was* a risk worth taking, although it is likely, in making this judgment, he was not in possession of the full facts. His inaction poses a fundamental historical question. If Fisher's concerns were received and understood by Asquith, was the idea that the fleet's guns could *destroy* the Dardanelles forts quite as important to the War Council's acceptance of the operation as is generally accepted? It seems possible that Asquith and his War Council colleagues may have been content to accept the temporary disablement of guns if this meant a substantial force could enter the Marmora to achieve the moral impact they all hoped would be sufficient to achieve victory. In other words, they were prepared to ignore the importance of secured lines of communication because of an excessively sanguine view of the martial qualities of the Turks at this time and the probable Balkan intervention following the successful entrance of the British Fleet into the Marmora.

Any judgment as to what was driving the War Council's continued interest in the Dardanelles operation at this time is blurred by the fact it remained an operation from which most members of the War Council believed they could safely withdraw. The idea that there was "nothing to lose" in such an operation might alone have provided reason enough to continue with it and to place in abeyance the question of what might reasonably be gained from an operation that did not secure a line of communication for the fleet once inside the Marmora.

This work will not subscribe to these propositions. Rather, it will argue that at the heart of the War Council's acceptance of the naval-only operations was Churchill's persistent unwillingness to identify and address its fundamental weaknesses. Nevertheless, it is a perspective not without merit, particularly when the events described above suggest that Asquith, at least, ought to have understood Fisher's concerns over the impermanence of bombardment.

Asquith's actions, however, suggest he did not accept Fisher's concerns, as he asserted at the Dardanelles hearings. Rather than taking steps to investigate more closely, Asquith merely patched over this serious rift between Fisher and Churchill with a bizarre quid pro quo solution. Churchill, he resolved, would surrender his plans to bombard Zeebrugge if Fisher would withdraw his opposition to the Dardanelles operation.[26]

Churchill subsequently would assert that he left the meeting convinced this had resolved the entire matter to Fisher's satisfaction and he confidently proceeded to the day's War Council meetings.[27] It would prove a naïve assumption.

NOTES

1. Marder, A.J. *Fear God and Dreadnought Vol. III*. Letter from Jellicoe to Fisher, Jan. 17, 1915.

2. Gilbert, *CVIII*, 428. Letter, Fisher to Churchill, January 18, 1915; also, Churchill Papers 29/1.

3. Marder, *Fear God and Dreadnought*, 134, Fisher to Churchill, January 20, 1915. (Also Churchill Papers, 13/56). Richmond shared a number of the concerns of Fisher and Jellicoe, especially the absence from the North Sea of the battle cruisers and destroyers. See the diary entry from Richmond quoted in Marder, *Portrait of an Admiral*, 137.

4. Gilbert, *CVIII*, Churchill to Fisher, 433–435.

5. Gilbert, *CVIII*, 435, Letter, Fisher to Churchill.

6. Churchill, *The World Crisis*, Volume 2, 581.

7. Marder, *Fear God and Dreadnought Vol. III*, 141. Letter, Fisher to Jellicoe, January 21, 1915.

8. Ibid.

9. Ibid.

10. See Mackay, *Fisher of Kilverstone*, footnote, 482.

11. The document, *"Memorandum By The First Sea Lord On The Position Of The British Fleet And Its Policy of Steady Pressure,"* is to be found in Gilbert

CVIII, 452–454. Hankey is imprecise as to whether his help was sought on this day or the next. Hankey, *The Supreme Command*, vol. 1, 269.

12. Hankey, *The Supreme Command*, vol. 1, 269.

13. Fisher to Churchill, Gilbert, *CVIII*, 443.

14. Marder, *Fear God and Dreadnought*, 144–145.

15. Churchill Papers 13/56, Letter, Fisher to Churchill, January 25, 1915. Also, *The World Crisis*, 581.

16. Gilbert, *CVIII*, 453–454. Also, Churchill Papers 13/56.

17. Ruddock Mackay quite rightly observes that Fisher's paper was not essentially different from the sentiments expressed to Churchill on January 5. See Mackay, *Fisher of Kilverston*, 483.

18. Gilbert, *CVIII*, 453–454.

19. Gilbert, *CVIII*, 458 and Fisher Papers. Letter, Churchill to Fisher, January 26, 1915.

20. Gilbert, *CVIII*, 458. Churchill to Fisher, January 26, 1915.

21. Churchill, *The World Crisis*, vol. 2, 161

22. Churchill, *The World Crisis*, vol. 2, 161.

23. This was added when Fisher had the letter printed.

24. Marder, *Fear God and Dreadnought*, 149. Also, Fisher Papers.

25. Gilbert, *CVIII*, 460.

26. Asquith to Stanley, ibid., 462.

27. Churchill, *The World Crisis*, 149.

CHAPTER 12

Decision Time: The War Council, January 28

PART I: PRELIMINARY DISCUSSIONS

In the history of the Dardanelles operation, January 28 represents a day of considerable importance. Despite Fisher's strong resistance, the War Council would postpone French's coastal operation and give the go-ahead to the naval-only operation against the Dardanelles. Discussions would also briefly see the reemergence of Lloyd George's Salonika plan—albeit a seriously diluted one, but this operation would succumb, as had all the rest, to the glowing prospects offered by Churchill's naval-only operation.

January 28, therefore, represented a giant step in the evolution of the Dardanelles operation from a minor, highly speculative operation to a central and essential platform of an entire southern strategy. Perhaps more ominously—for it was the very thing Churchill had hoped to avoid—the operation would begin to be viewed by Kitchener as the progenitor of a large-scale offensive through Hungary.

As this evolution progressed, Churchill's naval-only solution ought to have been found an inadequate platform for a southern offensive and the War Council ought to have become increasingly reconciled to a more substantial and more immediate military commitment in the Mediterranean. That neither situation developed would have little to do with conventional explanations such as the shortage of troops and French intransigence and everything to do with Churchill's insistence the fleet could break through without military assistance and with Kitchener's complicit conviction that, once through, Turkish resistance would collapse. Had each not clung to these convictions, it is probable that some kind of southern offensive operation—if not at the Dardanelles, then elsewhere—would have been agreed to. Alternatively, the theater would have been withdrawn from completely. From around this time forward, Churchill and Kitchener must share equal responsibility for the debacle that would follow.

* * * * *

The discussions of the War Council on January 28 occurred over three sessions. A preliminary meeting began at 11:30 A.M. After an adjournment for lunch, members of War Council, consisting of Kitchener, Lloyd George, Balfour, Churchill, Sir James Wolfe-Murray, Callwell, and Hankey met at 4:30 P.M. as a subcommittee of the CID. It was the task of this group to comply with the fourth conclusion of the January 13 meeting to explore alternative theaters and objectives in the advent of a stalemate in Europe. A final session of the War Council convened at 6:30 in the evening.

One of the first issues for discussion at the 11:30 A.M. session was Sir John French's coastal operation. Ongoing French resistance to the proposal, coupled with plans to send military support to Serbia, had made this an increasingly unlikely and unpopular prospect. Churchill alone expressed any interest in pursuing the operation, remarking that "he felt bound to point out that, if the Zeebrugge project was not feasible, both the Navy and the communications of the Army across the channel were exposed to great risk."[1]

The meeting soon moved to the Dardanelles. Churchill informed the War Council he had communicated with the grand duke and the French Admiralty. The grand duke had responded with enthusiasm and the French had promised cooperation. Undoubtedly mindful of Fisher's continued resistance to the project, he asked carefully "if the War Council attached importance to this operation, which undoubtedly involved some risks?"[2] At this point, Fisher got up and left the room and was persuaded to return to the War Council only through the intervention of Kitchener, although thereafter he maintained "an obstinate and ominous silence."[3]

Fisher's obvious dissatisfaction apart, Churchill's Dardanelles plan was received enthusiastically. Kitchener considered "its effect would be equivalent to that of a successful campaign fought with the new armies. One merit of the scheme was that, if satisfactory progress was not made, the attack could be broken off."[4] Sadly, we have no further explanation from Kitchener as to why he thought so highly of the scheme.

With equal enthusiasm, Balfour declared that a successful attack on the Dardanelles would achieve the following results:

> It would cut the Turkish army in two.
>
> It would put Constantinople under our control.
>
> It would give us the advantage of having the Russia wheat, and enable Russia to resume exports. This would restore Russian exchanges, which were falling owing to her inability to export, and causing great embarrassment.
>
> It would also open a passage to the Danube.[5]

Grey believed it would "finally settle the attitude of Bulgaria and the whole of the Balkans" and considered the "Turks would be paralysed with fear when they heard that the forts were being destroyed one by one."[6]

Having received the unqualified support of his colleagues, Churchill informed them that the naval commander in chief had "expressed his belief that it could be done. He required from three weeks to a month to accomplish it."[7]

Despite this enthusiasm, no decision was made to proceed with the Dardanelles operation at this meeting. Instead, the War Council adjourned for lunch. Before doing so, however, Churchill spoke one last time. His topic was the future direction of the naval campaign. "The ultimate object of the Navy," he declared, "was to obtain access to the Baltic." He went on:

> First, however, as had been explained at a previous meeting, it was necessary to seal up the enemy so far as the North Sea was concerned, and for this purpose, an island was required. The attack on a German island, however, would have to be postponed until some of the new monitors were ready. These vessels would be practically unsinkable by mines, and would be able to operate in shallow water where submarines could not operate. Six would be ready by May and fourteen by July. Once we had secured possession of an island, we could proceed to lock the enemy in with mines, submarines and wire nets. When that was complete we could proceed to the Baltic. To sum up, the naval campaign, he said, consisted of three

stages—1st Phase: The clearing of the outer seas, which was practically complete; 2nd Phase: The clearing of the North Sea; 3rd Phase: The Clearing of the Baltic.[8]

Despite the progress and development of his Dardanelles proposal—and in sharp contradiction to historical assessments to the contrary—Churchill's strategic priorities remained as they had been at the beginning of the war.

PART II: THE SUBCOMMITTEE OF THE CID

After the adjournment for lunch, the subcommittee of the CID (all of whom were members of the War Council) convened to discuss the dispatch of "British troops to another theatre and objective"[9] as per the recommendations of the January 13 meeting. Notably absent from this important meeting was Fisher who, still chaffed by the earlier discussions of the Dardanelles, thereby denied himself a vital opportunity to influence the subsequent direction of offensive operations.

Kitchener nominated three alternative offensive proposals for discussion, all of which had undergone a general staff assessment. These were, an attack on Austria from the Adriatic, assuming Italy to be an ally; an attack on Austria in cooperation with the Serbian Army, using Salonica as a base; and an attack on Turkey. Interestingly, this latter topic—an attack on Turkey—received no apparent attention at this forum, presumably because it had been so successfully supplanted by Churchill's naval-only operation, which had received enthusiastic support in the earlier War Council meeting.

If we are to judge from the rest of Hankey's minutes, the Adriatic proposal was rapidly dismissed. Churchill declared it would be exposed to intervention by Austrian submarines, unless Pola had been reduced, and this would be an operation of the first magnitude, which Italy would not undertake.

Operations against Austria via Salonika—essentially Lloyd George's January 1 proposal—received much more serious attention. Discussions of this particular operation, however, were now complicated by two developments that had occurred during January. The first was the emergence of rumors that Germany would soon send an army to finish off Serbia once and for all.

The second development was the renewed offer from Greece to join the Allies. Almost from the outbreak of war, the Greek prime minister, Venizelos, had held out the prospect of Greek intervention, but negotiations had failed repeatedly. Venizelos's enthusiasm aside, the sympathies of the king and army were not necessarily with the Allies, and neither diplomacy nor the ineffectual Allied guarantee made in early December to protect Greece from Bulgaria had succeeded in drawing her in.

As a result of Venizelos' renewed overtures, however, there were diplomatic moves aplenty throughout January to finally bring Greece into the Allied fold. Before considering this element of the CID's discussions, it is desirable to provide an overview of the Serbian crisis and the diplomatic negotiations with Greece.

PART III: SERBIA AND SALONIKA

Venizelos had made known to the British government on January 7 that, although Greece was reluctant to become involved in war against Austria, war against Turkey would be popular. This fact had coincided with the earliest discussions of Churchill's plans to force the Dardanelles by ships alone and had led, briefly, to the prospect of Greek assistance on the peninsula.

Grey was keen to pursue this new offer of aid and was now willing to offer Greece compensation in Asia Minor (a slice of the Anatolian coast) and Cyprus for an immediate commitment to the war.[10] The Russian foreign minister, Sazanov, was sounded regarding the Greek offer. He was receptive but, anticipating the most likely use of Greek troops in a war against Turkey, warned that Greece would not be allowed to extend her sovereignty over the Straits and Gallipoli. This apart, he was otherwise sufficiently positive regarding the idea to suggest offering Smyrna to Greece as well.

We can pick up events from this point and note that while these discussions were taking place, Prime Minister Asquith suddenly became anxious over Serbia. He wrote to Venetia Stanley on January 18 that the Serbs would be "overwhelmed by the new attack which Austria is preparing unless someone comes at once to their assistance; Roumania for preference, next Greece."[11]

Although the extant writing on the subject is vague on this issue, it appears that from this point, officially at least, Grey gave up the idea of Greek assistance against Turkey and returned to the idea of Greece going to the aid of Serbia. One policy shift had been made, however. Although Greece would be expected to fight Austrians alongside the Serbian Army, she would now be rewarded with Turkish and not Austrian land at the end of the war.

By January 20, the British government's anxiety over Serbia had escalated considerably. The Cabinet had a long talk about the

Balkans and Greece and how to bring them in. While Grey pursued various territorial solutions, including his offer to Cyprus, Asquith and Lloyd George argued strongly in favor of a British supporting force. Lord Kitchener promised to examine the situation carefully from the military point of view.[12]

After this meeting, Asquith urged Grey to "put the strongest possible pressure upon Roumania and Greece without delay, and to promise that if they will form a real Balkan *bloc* we will send troops of our own to join them and save the situation." He believed that all "our side shows—Zeebrugge, Alexandretta, even Gallipoli—ought to be postponed for this."[13]

As for the issue of troops and their availability, Asquith had concluded that "they must come either from those which we already have in France, or from those which we were going to send there."[14] It was this decision and its implications for Zeebrugge that had so frustrated Fisher.

Despite Asquith's instructions to Grey to offer Greece immediate military aid to assist Serbia, he appears to have done nothing. Undoubtedly, this had much to do with the imminent arrival of Millerand, the French minister of war. There was no doubt in anyone's mind that the visit was intended to establish the future use of British troops in France. Rather than Grey, it was Lloyd George who was the most proactive in seeking an expeditionary force for the Mediterranean. On January 21, he took the extraordinary liberty of making an unsanctioned and private contact with the Greek foreign minister in London, M. J. Gennadius. Lloyd George told Gennadius that, should Venizelos ask for it, the cooperation of a British corps of approximately 40,000 men and full financial support would be given if Greece would come immediately to Serbia's support.[15] Lloyd George took the further liberty of suggesting that if Venizelos "requested more that one army corps the English Government would not refuse it."

He made clear that his communication should be kept secret and full pretence made that the request for troops came from the Greeks themselves. Furthermore, he asked that any request for troops be received by no later than 8:00 P.M. on January 22, when Millerand the "French Minister of War would be dining with all the English Ministers."[16] Thus Lloyd George attempted to reinvigorate his Salonika plan by ensuring the preconditions for Greek assistance were established before the critical meeting between Millerand and the key members of the War Council.

Although Asquith kept the southern offensive ball rolling on January 22 with ongoing meetings with Lloyd George, Grey, and

Hankey to "talk over the Servian business" and to discuss the sending of a corps (50,000 or 60,000 men [Asquith's estimation of corps strength]), Lloyd George's machinations failed to bear fruit. Venizelos declined to send a request for troops preferring first to know what Greece was to be offered by way of territorial concessions. Thus disarmed, the meeting with Millerand failed to go to plan. Despite individual pleas from Asquith, Lloyd George, and Grey, Millerand agreed only to "have the question studied but that action at the present time was out of the question, if it comes at all it might come later." For the time being he remained "firm and was adamant on the necessity of reinforcing the French Army."[17]

Thus, briefly, was the question of an expeditionary army placed in abeyance. Asquith was not at all happy with the French attitude, while Lloyd George continued to agitate for immediate assistance to Serbia. Asquith wrote to Venetia Stanley of rather stormy conversations between the "violent pro-Serb" Lloyd George and Millerand and expressed his opinion that the French demand for more troops was a "trifle greedy."[18]

Asquith anticipated the Serbian issue would be resolved at the next War Council meeting when "matters ought to be ripe for a decision." The decision, however, had already been made and the prospects for the Serbian operation were bleaker than even Asquith imagined. Kitchener apparently had caved in completely to Millerand. Esher had recorded in his diary that day that Kitchener had "told Millerand he would not push the Serbian scheme just now."[19]

Meanwhile, unable or unwilling to offer the additional "carrot" of military assistance as Lloyd George might have hoped, Grey resumed negotiations with the Greeks over territorial compensation. No mention, however, was made of military assistance. On January 24, he offered Venizelos "very important territorial compensation for Greece on coast of Asia Minor . . . if Greece will side with Serbia as an ally and participate in the war."[20]

Undoubtedly frustrated by the unsuccessful negotiations with Millerand, Grey would have been pleasantly surprised to learn of Venizelos' response to this offer. Venizelos had steadily come to the conclusion that Greece must come into the war or gain nothing at the peace and was excited at the news. Such an offer was the fulfillment of his dreams for a Greater Hellenic Empire and represented a considerable improvement on offers previously made by the Allied governments.

Venizelos wrote to his king the same day to persuade him to accept the British proposal. The next day, he wrote to the various

Allied governments of the conditions for Greece's participation in the war. The offer of great territories in Asia Minor finally had gained Greece's full attention, but the eternal bugbear of the military threat from Bulgaria persisted.

Gennadius gave Grey a copy of the conditions on January 27. The conditions were as follows:

> 1. Bulgaria's active cooperation. 2. If Bulgaria declined to become involved, then Roumania's participation was essential. 3. If Bulgaria did not offer even "benevolent neutrality," then the Allied Powers must supply a military force which would offer a "strong guarantee against Bulgaria." 4. Allies must provide financial support and military provisions.[21]

Thus for the first time was the idea of sending an Allied force to Greece officially broached by the Greeks as a solution to the Bulgarian problem.

Venizelos had not indicated the size of the force required to secure Greek intervention but Gennadius had suggested that "even 5,000 men would be sufficient to begin with" and pressed Grey "to hold out hopes to Roumania that we would send some force to Salonica."[22] Grey had replied that he "could not hold out hopes of such a thing, or say anything except in consultation and agreement with Lord Kitchener, and when I was authorised to say it would be done."[23]

Why Gennadius had promoted the idea of a small force, when Lloyd George had intimated that so many more troops might be available, is unclear. The most probable answer is that Gennadius had learned of Millerand's resistance to any troops going southward and was amending expectations accordingly. Another possibility is that, because the precondition of Romanian intervention still stood, a smaller number of troops might have been sufficient to draw in Greece.

In reality, Gennadius' suggestion of 5,000 troops was a mere chimera. Elliot immediately telegraphed Grey of conversations with Venizelos that made clear Venizelos wanted real military assistance and not a mere demonstration. As a result of these conversations, Venizelos modified his terms for Greece's involvement in the war. He would withdraw the condition of Romania's immediate intervention on two conditions: (1) Britain and France must offer to send one corps each; and (2) an agreement must be reached between Greece and Romania that "if Greece, having come to Serbia's support, were attacked by Bulgaria, Roumania should intervene against Bulgaria."[24]

Such were the circumstances preceding the War Council of January 28. Almost unanimous support existed within the British Cabinet for military assistance to prevent the defeat of Serbia at the hands of Germany and Austria, although throughout much of events describe above, Churchill contributed remarkably little. Simultaneously, moves were afoot to buy the intervention of Greece and, perhaps, Romania, by the offer of troops to ensure the neutrality of Bulgaria. Lloyd George had informed the Greeks they might expect one or more corps, but discussions with Millerand—and, in particular, Kitchener's undertaking not to press the Serbian operation—made the prospect of military aid highly unlikely. Gennadius' suggestion remained that even a brigade might do the job. This offer appeared to be countered immediately by Venizelos's request of two Allied corps. With such facts in mind, one can now return to the CID deliberations of January 28.

PART IV: THE CID MEETING, LATE AFTERNOON, JANUARY 28

Hankey's record of the CID's discussion of Serbia began with General Callwell's estimation that the Greeks could put 200,000 men into the field to help Serbia. Kitchener then suggested that Britain might send mounted troops to assist the Greeks as they were short of these and it was a deficiency "which would not be very difficult to make up."[25] At this point, Lloyd George suggested—rather whimsically given the status of Bulgaria—that a British Army could land at Dedeagath and cooperate with Bulgaria in an attack on Adrianople.

Incidental discussion followed. Much of this discussion undoubtedly pertained to the war staff's appreciation of possible offensive options which had been requested at the end of the War Council meeting of January 13 in anticipation of major military operations in Southern Europe. Unfortunately, scholars do not appear to have unearthed this document so we do not know, as yet, precisely what these discussions were about. Balfour concluded from this and a previous discussion that "the Adriatic should be ignored; that the naval bombardment of the Dardanelles should be attempted; and that in any case a force should be landed at Salonica."[26] Balfour was surely getting ahead of the discussion as far as Salonica was concerned, but Lloyd George was keen to see such a decision made. He declared "he was very anxious to send an army to the Balkans in order to bring all the Balkan States into the war on our side and settle Austria."[27] He noted rather inaccurately that "M. Venizelos had recently offered to come into the war without conditions, provided that Roumania did likewise."[28]

Kitchener agreed it was desirable to send troops to the Balkans to determine the attitude of the Balkan States. Obviously mindful of his commitment to Millerand, he remarked that he did not think the right moment had arrived. "It was very difficult to get British troops out of France," he added, "and he was sending his last man to France."[29] He observed that "we might send an army of 500,000 men to Serbia, and if the Dardanelles were open we could maintain them there." Thus, in one sentence did Kitchener set the full weight of a southern offensive on the back of a successful operation at the Dardanelles.

This was a quite remarkable assertion by Kitchener and serves to illustrate further the southern inclinations of the War Council, but it hardly addressed the immediacy of the problem set before them. Lloyd George wanted to know "how soon an army corps could be sent to Salonika?" Seemingly oblivious to important diplomatic issues at stake, Kitchener declared there was no pressing necessity, as an Austro-German invasion was impossible owing to the snow.

At this point, Churchill suggested a dispatch of a brigade to Salonica be made as "an earnest of our intention to send more. They need not go further than Salonica, and would be sent solely on political grounds."[30] Lloyd George agreed, but he wanted an army corps *offered* to Serbia at once, and a declaration of the probable date of arrival. Kitchener was reluctant to agree to either suggestion. He argued that "if troops were sent at all, they ought to be followed up shortly by other troops,"[31] and such a commitment could not be made for about a month when the "French difficulty had been cleared up and the German attack over."[32]

Here the discussion of Serbia ended. Prompted by a suggestion from Churchill, who believed reinforcements ought not be sent to France now that the Zeebrugge was not to take place, the subcommittee agreed to recommend to the prime minister that one of the divisions promised to Sir John French for his coastal attack now be withheld. Although it was not stated, the obvious implication was that this force might soon be sent to Salonica in exchange for Greek intervention against Serbia.

PART V: THE WAR COUNCIL MEETING, EVENING, JANUARY 28

The subcommittee then recessed and reconvened at 6:30 P.M. with the full War Council—this time with Fisher in attendance—to explain its deliberations and reach final conclusions regarding the Zeebrugge operation and French's reinforcements. Kitchener spoke first, summarizing the proceedings of the subcommittee. He noted the general agreement with the CID that Salonica was the best place of disembarkation for troops intended to cooperate with Serbia, but the question was when to send them. "There was danger in undue delay, as if we did not move in time, Serbia might be crushed, and we might fail to draw in the other Balkan States."[33] However, he considered that Serbia was not in immediate threat of invasion, owing to snow. Moreover, he noted, "we had at present no troops to spare."[34] He informed the War Council that the subcommittee had decided that the best way to secure troops for other operations was to withhold from Sir John French the reinforcements promised him for his coastal operation. It would, Kitchener said, "be sufficient to send only the Canadians."[35]

Churchill gave his immediate support to this proposal. He explained away his willingness to now give up French's offensive by declaring that "by the middle of March the new monitors would be ready, and the Navy might be able to deal with Zeebrugge."[36] When Kitchener pointed out that the French still expected reinforcements, Churchill suggested that Joffre be reminded Britain had already given more military assistance than they had ever promised. "General Joffre, he declared, "was not our master and could not dispose of our troops."[37]

Although Churchill's point of view received considerable sympathy, the War Council recognized they had to tread carefully with the French. Kitchener finally suggested two possible plans: to send the troops on the expressed understanding that they might be withdrawn in a month or to keep them as a reserve in Britain to be rushed across in case of emergency.

A potential source of a small southern army having now been established, the War Council returned to the prospect of sending troops to fight in Serbia. Kitchener believed useful operations could not start before the middle of March, and some weeks would be required to move up an army from Salonica to Serbia.

The size and nature of the force were then discussed. Balfour reminded the council of Kitchener's idea that cavalry might be sent. Although he warned this would require a great deal of transport, Kitchener thought this might be "a clever solution," presumably because the French would be more receptive to the diversion of the rarely used cavalry divisions rather than a desperately sought infantry.

Churchill was not interested in the proposal and declared that such a discussion was "mixing up a strategical and a political move."[38] He viewed the object of sending a force—even a token one—as a warning to Bulgaria that more British troops would come should they attack Greece while it was fighting in support of Serbia. He repeated his preference for sending a brigade to Salonica immediately.

Whether or not Churchill's idea of sending a brigade to Greece had been inspired by Gennadius is uncertain, but it was only after this observation that Grey pointed out that the Greek minister had expressed the view that 5,000 men sent to Salonica would so influence Bulgarian opinion, that "oppositions of the bands would be checked."[39] Kitchener was reluctant to make such an offer. Once again he expressed his concern that if a brigade were sent before it was certain it could be followed by a larger force, "it would soon become a ridiculous object."[40]

The War Council finally resolved to give Churchill the prickly task of informing French that now the Zeebrugge operation was postponed, and that it had been decided to send him only one division immediately. Churchill was given another task. This was to explain to French "the importance of a diversion in the Balkans designed to draw the various Balkan states into the war."[41]

In the meantime, Sir Edward Grey was "inclined to ascertain whether M. Venizelos agreed with the French Ambassador that 5000 men would be of value."[42] Recognizing the War Council was tinkering at the edges of the problem, Lloyd George suggested that it would "be better to ask him how many men were required to be of any value," but his proposal was ignored.

Grey's position in these discussions is a curious one. He knew from his communications with Elliot that, short of active Bulgarian and Romanian intervention, Venizelos would not move unless the two corps were available. This mystery becomes more extraordinary over the next two weeks during which time a decision is made to offer the Greeks a single corps of French and British troops. No evidence suggests that Grey informed his colleagues that such an offer already had been deemed inadequate by the Greeks and almost certainly would be rejected.

This may have represented a unilateral decision by Grey not to press for more forces to go southward for fear of upsetting the French. It also is evident in his statements to the War Council, however, that Grey's policies had come to rely heavily on success at the Dardanelles. He anticipated the commencement of the Dardanelles operation would more than make up for the extra corps sought by the Greeks for their intervention. He was to be mistaken and disappointed.

For the time being, all decisions regarding a Salonika expedition and military aid must await Churchill's discussions with Sir John French. The deliberations of the War Council to this point suggested its members were uncertain what the purpose of sending a force to the Mediterranean was to be. Was it to fight Austrians and Germans in Serbia, or to entice the Balkan States—in particular Greece and Romania—into the war to do this job for them? This confusion is understandable because Venizelos's request for military assistance in exchange for Greek support for Serbia unexpectedly had superimposed itself onto the CID's broader investigations of alternative theaters of war.

The confusion is best illustrated by the attitudes of Churchill and Lloyd George. Churchill's interest in withholding reinforcements from Sir John French manifested itself primarily in a desire to deny the French more military aid for wasteful offensive operations. This contrasted with Lloyd George and others who spoke in terms of using these troops to help Serbia or to pull in the Balkan States. Churchill supported sending a force to Salonica, but spoke only of a brigade of the best troops and consistently argued that its purpose was entirely political and not military. Other interpretations, perhaps, can be offered to explain his attitude, but this ambivalence to a *major* commitment to the southern theater is entirely consistent with his desire (repeatedly expressed in early January) to minimize any military commitment in the southern theater. If an offer of a brigade would do the job, he wanted it done now. Such an attitude stood in marked contrast to Lloyd George who, as we have seen, was pushing strongly for the Salonika option he had mooted at the beginning of January and was prepared to offer whatever it would take to bring in the Greeks and Romanians.

We can now move to the final two matters for discussion by the War Council. These were the attack on Zeebrugge and the Dardanelles. As we have seen, Churchill had flagged a decision on Zeebrugge during the discussion over the Salonica alternative. Now he declared that the "Admiralty had decided to abandon for the present the suggested naval attack on Zeebrugge, and pending the completion of monitors, to limit our activities to aerial attacks. It might, however, be necessary to reconsider this."[43]

Churchill's took this decision reluctantly, but it was part of the price to pay for securing Fisher's support for the Dardanelles bombardment. During the break between the first and second session of the War Council, he had prevailed on Fisher to give up his opposition to the Dardanelles in exchange for the surrender of his own proposed bombardment of Zeebrugge. As a result of this discussion, the War Council was finally able to gain Fisher's "lingering and reluctant consent to the Dardanelles bombardment as a great diplomatic and political necessity," which, Churchill declared, the "Admiralty had decided to push on with."[44]

Fisher also may have been a little more malleable during this meeting because Churchill had requested funds to construct the two 15-inch, high-speed shallow draught battle cruisers Fisher had been talking up for most of January. Churchill had supported the construction of these vessels at the first session of the War Council by arguing their importance for an attack on Germany from the Baltic. Fisher wrote to Jellicoe triumphantly the following day:

> They are a "flabby" lot! However, a calm has resulted and I go on pegging away. I got two more "light cruisers" carrying 15inch guns yesterday, of 33 knots speed and 22 feet draught of water, and oil for 11,000 miles, and 24 more monitors, so we are getting on![45]

This episode has been used as evidence of Churchill's newly found obsession with the Dardanelles. He acquiesced in Fisher's demands, it is argued, to silence Fisher's criticism of the Dardanelles operation, although he had given up the Baltic operation. Just as conventionally, it has been argued that this episode confirmed Fisher's relentless determination to pursue his Baltic operation.

More recently, it has been contended that, by playing the Baltic card at this time, it was not Churchill who was manipulating Fisher but the other way round.[46] These writers contend Fisher no longer believed in the viability of the Baltic operation but instead used Churchill's interest in such an operation to secure these fast, big-gunned vessels to catch and destroy the German raiding forces that had twice attacked the English coast.

Whether or not Fisher had given up on the Baltic, and this remains a moot point, what is important for the purposes of this work is Fisher's conviction that Churchill had not. On January 25, Fisher wrote to Churchill regarding his new battle cruisers, taking special care to emphasize their value in the Baltic: "but chiefly it is this type of vessel imperatively demanded for the Baltic," he informed him.[47] Mindful of Churchill's hopes for decisive naval action at the earliest possible juncture, and his embargo on all construction that could not be completed in 1915, Fisher ludicrously asserted that these new ships could be completed within eleven months. Evidently Fisher understood that the best way to get his new vessels was to sell Churchill on the Baltic scheme (even though these vessels would be completed well outside Churchill's own time frame for the operation).

As a result of the three important meetings on January 28, several vital decisions were made and rifts temporarily healed. French's coastal operation had been derailed, Churchill's naval bombardment of Zeebrugge postponed, and, with Fisher's lone voice temporarily silenced, the naval-only attempt to force the Dardanelles given an enthusiastic green light. Plans to send troops to aid Serbia were in abeyance pending Churchill's return from France to see Sir John French.

It has been argued in this work that Churchill had originally promoted the naval-only operation to short-circuit Lloyd George's efforts to turn the Mediterranean into a new and major theater of war for the New Armies and keep alive his own northern aspirations. By the end of January, Churchill's naval-only scheme had successfully worked its magic—but in circumstances not anticipated by Churchill. It would be wrong to view the War Council's decision to suspend or delay plans to send troops to aid Serbia solely as a result of French pressure and the shortage of troops. The fact that the British government—and, in particular, Grey and Kitchener—wilted so quickly before French intransigence and did not come out more forcefully in favor of immediate assistance to Serbia was undoubtedly because Churchill had offered a solution to the pressing strategic and diplomatic necessities of the region that did not need troops.

The most serious impediment to a southern strategy was not, therefore, the availability of troops but the existence of the naval-only plan. Despite fears for Serbia and a strong desire within the War Council to bring in the Balkan States, all efforts to secure Balkan intervention between the end of January and the middle of February were—with the single exception of the efforts made by Lloyd George—half-hearted. Despite Grey's knowledge of Greek expectations, he was prepared to sit back and await the outcome of the Dardanelles operation.

The challenge now facing Churchill was the fact that the government's entire southern strategy had become intimately linked to the success of the Dardanelles operation. Aid to Serbia, aid to Russia, Greek and Romanian intervention, and even Kitchener's rather eccentric plan to attack Hungary all now rested on the plan. In early January, when the War Council began general discussions on a southern strategy, no such pressure existed. Now Churchill's naval-only operation hardly dare fail.

Churchill should not be considered entirely responsible for the high expectations the War Council now held for the Dardanelles operation. Chapter 13 will show that this was partly a product of his colleague's own prejudices and unreasonable optimism. First among those who placed unreasonable expectations on the Dardanelles operation was Lord Kitchener, who, as was stated earlier, must bear a burden of responsibility equal to Churchill's for future developments. He understood that it was the command of the Straits that was the linchpin to any plan to apply moral pressure to the Turks and not a breakthrough by the fleet, but he had his own reasons for letting the naval-only operation run its course.

Nevertheless, Churchill could not escape the fact that it was his pronouncements, combined with a profound tardiness in addressing the limitations of his plan, that kept the naval-only operation alive. He knew his plan could not guarantee the one factor most likely to secure the expectations of the War Council: *command* of the Marmora. This required the capture of the peninsula—and probably the occupation of both sides of the Straits—by an armed force.

Churchill eventually would accept troops, even call for them to add a moral weight to the naval operations, but he would decline to alter his naval-only strategy. Although this severely compromised the War Council's southern strategies, he could not have done otherwise lest delay and a shattered credibility destroy his northern schemes.

With neither Churchill nor Kitchener prepared to address the limitations of a naval-only strategy, this battle would be fought by secretary to the War Council, Hankey, with the complicit Fisher always in the wings.

NOTES

1. Churchill Papers 2/86 (also extracts found in Gilbert, *CVIII*, 463–465). Minutes of War Council Meeting, January 28, 1915, 11.30 A.M. session.

2. Ibid. This particular quotation comes from Gilbert, *CVIII*, 463.

3. Asquith to Stanley, Gilbert, *CVIII*, 462.

4. Churchill Papers 2/86 (also extracts found in Gilbert, *CVIII*, 463–465). Minutes of War Council Meeting, January 28, 1915, 11.30 A.M. session. 463.

5. Churchill Papers 2/86 (also extracts found in Gilbert, *CVIII*, 463–465). Minutes of War Council Meeting, January 28, 1915, 11.30 A.M. session. Many

of these advantages were identified by Kitchener and Hankey at the War Council meeting of January 8. See *CVIII*, 393.

6. Gilbert, *CVIII*, 464. Minutes of War Council Meeting, January 28, 1915, 11.30 a.m. session.

7. Ibid.

8. Ibid.

9. Gilbert, *CVIII*, 465. Minutes of Sub-Committee of War Council Meeting, January 28, 1915.

10. The idea of compensation in Asia Minor had been hinted at during Eliot's conversation with Venizelos on January 7. The suggestion of offering Cyprus had emanated from Lancelot Oliphant in the Balkan Department of the Foreign Office. See Leon, *Greece and the Great Powers, 1914–1917* (Thessalonika, 1974), 90. However, Churchill claimed he made such a recommendation very early in the War.

11. Gilbert, *CVIII*, 427. Asquith to Venetia Stanley, January 18, 1915. The news came from historian George Trevelyan who was in Serbia at the time.

12. Asquith to King George, CAB 41/36/2.

13. Asquith to Venetia Stanley, January 21, 1915; Gilbert, *CVIII*, 437.

14. Ibid.

15. Gennadius's telegram noted, "In your official reply your Excellency is begged not to mention this dispatch, but to say only (if such is the case) that Greece is ready to assist Serbia provided England will send the army corps mentioned." Leon, *Greece and the Great Powers, 1914–1917*, 105.

16. Ibid., 106.

17. Reginald Brett Esher, *The Tragedy of Lord Kitchener* (London: John Murray, 1922), 209.

18. Brock and Brock, *H. H. Asquith's Letters*, 393.

19. Esher, *Lord Kitchener*, 210.

20. Leon, *Greece and the Great Powers, 1914–1917*, 92.

21. Ibid., 109.

22. Ibid., 95. This was all recalled in a telegram on January 27 to Elliot from Grey, who at the same time was forwarding the text of Venizelos's telegram to the French.

23. In the concluding paragraph of this telegram, Grey noted the following, in an unknowing reference to Lloyd George's earlier subterfuge: "Incidentally I found that the Greek Minister was fully aware that discussions had taken place here respecting the sending of an army corps to Salonica, though the subject of sending troops there at all had never been mentioned to him at any time by me. I therefore made no secret of the fact that we were considering it." Theodoulou, Christos, *Greece and the Entente, August 1, 1914-September 25, 1916*, 95.

24. Leon, *Greece and the Great Powers, 1914–1917*, 108–109. Also Christos, *Greece and the Entente, August 1, 1914-September 25, 1916*, 96.

25. Minutes of the CID Meeting, late afternoon, January 28, 1915.

26. Ibid.

27. Ibid.

28. Ibid.
29. Ibid.
30. Ibid.
31. Ibid.
32. Ibid.
33. Gilbert, *CVIII*, 468–470 (excerpts only); also Churchill Papers 2/86. Minutes of the War Council Meeting, early evening, January 28, 1915.
34. Ibid.
35. Ibid.
36. Ibid.
37. Ibid.
38. Ibid.
39. It is probable that they are connected. Note Grey's reference to "the bands." This clearly implies prior discussion. Such evidence of discussion not covered in the minutes is a noteworthy reminder just how much of importance is not available to the historian.
40. Ibid.
41. Conclusion of War Council Meeting, January 28, 1915, Gilbert, *CVIII*, 470.
42. Gilbert, *CVIII*, 468–470. Minutes of the War Council Meeting, early evening, January 28, 1915. See also Churchill Papers 2/86.
43. Gilbert, *CVIII*, 469. Minutes of the War Council Meeting, early evening, January 28, 1915.
44. Esher's journal entry January 29, 1915, Marder, *From the Dreadnought to Scapa Flow*, vol. 2, 211.
45. Marder, *Fear God and Dreadnought* vol. 2, 148. Letter, Fisher to Jellicoe, January 29, 1915.
46. Mackay, *Fisher of Kilverstone*, and John Tetsuro Sumida, *In Defence of Naval Supremacy: Finance, Technology, and British Naval Policy 1889–1914* (Boston, MA: Unwin Hyman, 1989), 292, are two examples.
47. Marder, *Fear God and Dreadnought*, vol. 2, 145.

CHAPTER 13

Three Perspectives on the Naval-Only Operation: Callwell, Balfour, and Hankey

During the first days of February, while responding to entirely separate duties, the director of military operations and intelligence (DMO), Charles Callwell; Arthur Balfour; and Lt. Col. Maurice Hankey coincidentally produced appreciations of Churchill's naval-only operation. All are valuable documents, providing much greater insight into the deliberations of the War Council than is available in the minutes taken by Hankey and each add to our understanding of the evolution of the Dardanelles operation.

CALLWELL

As part of his regular duties, Charles Callwell maintained a correspondence with chief of staff, BEF, Gen. William Robertson. In a letter of January 30, Callwell summarized the decisions made at the War Council of January 28. He noted the War Council's determination to send a corps of troops to Salonika in the hope this might draw Bulgaria, Romania, and Greece to the Allied side and ensure that Serbia was not crushed, and he explained how this plan had temporarily fallen foul of Millerand.

Callwell also wrote of Kitchener's plan, broached at the War Council, to undertake a southern offensive through Hungary, noting that "this might be sound and effective . . . if we can secure the

Dardanelles."[1] He then gave his views on the Dardanelles operation, which he "did not like."[2] He continued:

> The forcing of the Dardanelles is to my mind an amphibious business with a large military force operating against the Gallipoli Peninsula; but the naval attack <u>may</u> succeed, and if it does, it will be a tremendous coup.[3]

Callwell did not explain here why it would be a "tremendous coup," but this will become evident later. Critically, Callwell then touched on the key flaw in Churchill's naval-only operation when he once again addressed Kitchener's "grandiose plans" for a southern offensive through Hungary: *"without the run of the Straits and the Black Sea,* I do not see the way to a big campaign in Hungary even if it were strategically sound from other points of view, and of that I am more than doubtful" (emphasis added).[4] Callwell's comments make clear he did not anticipate that the operation on which they were about to embark would give the Allies the control of the Straits or the Black Sea.

Here is evidence that, like Churchill's Admiralty advisers, Callwell's key concern over the operation was the value of the fleet inside the Marmora with unsecured lines of communication. He made these concerns more explicit four days later in another letter to Robertson. He informed Robertson that opinion within the War Office was "hardening in favour of a move in the Near East." Mirroring—or perhaps parroting—the hopes of Grey, Kitchener, and Balfour he noted that:

> of course, if the naval attack upon the Dardanelles succeeds, and if the advance of the fleet to Constantinople brings the Turks to their knees, all will be well. We get the Bosphorus, open the roads for ammunition to reach Russia, let out our grain ships, restore our wheat prices in this country. . . . Moreover we secure Bulgaria and rope in Roumania and Greeks. The effect in Italy would also be very great.[5]

These were now well-rehearsed hopes for the operation. However, Callwell went on to provide the critical rider that seems not to have been understood by the civilian members of the War Council:

> But then the attack on the Dardanelles without military assistance may fail, and even if it succeeds it does not guarantee

> passage for colliers, merchant shipping, and so on, which can be held up by field guns and maxims from the banks. The definite securing of the water-way will, if the operation be purely naval, *depend entirely on the political effect which the preliminary success may exert at Constantinople. . . . With military assistance I think the success of the attack ought to be assured, and it would mean that we got the Straits for good and our fleet with its communications secure could if necessary go on and knock the Bosphorus defences to pieces. As you know, they are not nearly as formidable as the others but quite formidable enough to give pause to a fleet which was en l'air in the Sea of Marmora and unable to get up coal or ammunition.* (emphasis added)[6]

Callwell's letter was an acknowledgment that the success of the naval operation rested almost entirely on the moral impact of the bombardment process

Four days later on February 8, he wrote to Robertson, "the navy are confident of gradually forcing the Dardanelles but they realize that after forcing the Dardanelles their communications will be doubtful without military aid."[7]

It is evident Callwell understood completely the critical importance of communications, especially to any plans to successfully attack the Bosporus forts and open the way for trade and the support of a Russian Army. Over the forthcoming weeks, Kitchener and Churchill would ignore such apprehensions. Instead each would contend that the gradual destruction of the forts would create circumstances that would not only admit a fleet to the Marmora but also secure the peninsula. Thus, the question of providing an army sufficient to take the peninsula by force never arose and the naval-only operation remained on course. When the idea of troops was belatedly mooted, each argued they would only be needed to "occupy" rather than "capture" the peninsula and the naval-only operation remained fundamentally unaltered.

BALFOUR

If the military representatives on the War Council understood the critical limitation of Churchill's plans, did its civilian members? Were they well-informed participants in this great gamble or misguided bystanders. We can gain some insight into this question through Balfour's appreciation of the naval-only operation. This took the form of comments on Lord Fisher's January 26 memorandum, which Fisher had sent him secretly him after the War Council meeting on January 28.

Balfour believed that operations of secondary importance, such as the Dardanelles, should be attempted only if they did not compromise the overwhelming strength of the Grand Fleet or compromise "the duty of check-mating the German advance in France and Flanders."[8] Presumably because it did not threaten Britain's naval dominance, nor require troops withdrawn from France, he considered the bombardment of the Dardanelles an offensive plan that could be begun immediately. He identified the advantages of the operation precisely as he had done at the War Council meeting and deemed the risk negligible. The absence of a submarine threat meant the crew of any ship sunk could be rescued. He was particularly enthusiastic about the Admiralty's description of the potential of naval bombardment:

> I understand the Admiralty view to be that with our 12 and 15 inch guns all the Turkish heavy artillery could be silenced, and that, when silenced, such light field guns as the enemy possessed would be insufficient effectually to obstruct the passage of an armoured Fleet. If this be so (and it is purely a technical question) the co-operation of a military force is not absolutely necessary; and the Fleet may for this operation may be regarded as self-sufficing. I do not remember any close parallel in naval history; but it has rarely, if ever, happened before that guns mounted in ships have markedly outranged guns mounted in fortresses.[9]

This profoundly optimistic assessment of the Dardanelles operation was corroborated by Balfour's testimony to the Dardanelles Committee. Balfour contended that the key distinction between an attempt to "rush" the Straits and the Carden gradual bombardment was that the former, apart from causing heavy losses, would not have secured the lines of communication for the fleet inside the Marmora. He did not view Carden's plan as formidable because

> the idea was at that time the force of troops on the Gallipoli Peninsula was not very formidable and above all they had not what they had later, high angle howitzers and guns above the calibre of a field gun. The idea was that if you destroyed the forts completely you would not be cut off but could go in and

> out of the Sea of Marmora and coal your ships and all the rest of it.[10]

The composite picture provided by Balfour's comments on Fisher's memorandum and his evidence to the Dardanelles Commission is that Churchill not only had spoken with considerable optimism of the capacity of the fleet to break into the Marmora but also had minimized the threat to the fleet's lines of communication thereafter. Balfour's support for the operation—and his evident enthusiasm for it—appears to have been based on the questionable assumption that Churchill's operation would give the Allied fleet *command* of the Marmora and not merely temporary access to it. He was clearly much less aware than Callwell that this was not likely to be the case.

Other evidence suggests that Churchill might have led the War Council to believe that, with the permanent guns in the forts silenced, and with only rifles and field guns to threaten them thereafter, armored ships could come and go through the Marmora. In other words, unlike Carden's plan, in which all supplies would follow the fleet into the Marmora after *all* guns had been destroyed on both sides of the Straits and in which this status would be maintained by further action of the fleet, Churchill imagined individual ships would leave the Marmora as required to recoal, revictual, and rearm. Alternatively, the War Council might have been led to believe that other battleships could bring supplies through the Straits to the fleet in the Marmora.

When the issue of communication was put to Oliver at the Dardanelles Commission, he stated that it had been considered that a battleship might be sent down to collect more ammunition if it were needed and that supplies might be brought through the Straits in other battleships. Oliver's testimony on this point was unconvincing and suggested such ideas were quickly dismissed. The commissioners, not surprisingly, ridiculed the proposition.

Even a layman can imagine the difficulties of a lone battleship—possibly filled to the gunwales with ammunition—attempting to run the full length of the Dardanelles with every field gun and howitzer on either side of the Straits pointed at it. The idea of battleships carrying sufficient ammunition or supplies for an entire fleet would seem unlikely and the difficulties of transferring such supplies at sea were not to be ignored. In any event, the problem of recoaling remained. Oliver reluctantly conceded these points, but it seems Churchill was less open with the War Council on January 13. Unlike Carden, he had dismissed very early on in the debate the importance of secure lines of communication and was prepared to risk success on the moral impact of the fleet's entrance into the Marmora.

That Balfour's overall appreciation was based largely on what Churchill had said—or had failed to say—to his War Council colleagues is corroborated by other evidence. His comments on the submarine threat reflect Churchill's comments at the War Council on January 28. As early as January 13, Churchill had used the submarine threat to dismiss plans to operate in the Adriatic, while the counterargument—the absence of a submarine threat—helped secure the Dardanelles operation. This would prove quite an extraordinary assertion, for even before the naval operation had begun, Fisher was panicking about the imminent threat from submarines and both he and Churchill would use the threat of submarines to hurry the operation to a conclusion. Moreover, strong evidence supports that the assertion was a deliberate untruth.[11]

There is also the issue of his ongoing tardiness, deliberate or otherwise, in addressing the threat of mobile guns and howitzers. An example of this evidence is Jackson's appreciation of January 15 discussed earlier. Jackson made clear that there were more than 200 guns of 6-inch and above to be silenced—a fairly accurate estimate as it turned out—many of which would be concealed and probably protected from direct gunfire. That some of these might be formidable high-trajectory howitzers capable of seriously damaging armored ships and devastating unarmored ones had been indicated in Carden's plan of January 11 when he noted that "[t]erms defences includes permanent, semi-permanent and field works also guns or howitzers whose positions are not yet known."[12]

A study of the documents and discussions within the War Council of January 1915 indicates the absence of any reference to "howitzers." Churchill mentions only field guns on January 13. Balfour's February 1 note, as we have just seen, refers only to field guns, as indeed do Callwell's letters to Robinson. This suggests the idea that more formidable howitzers had not been discussed or, worse, had been dismissed. These examples, by themselves, would not be remarkable but for the fact this coyness regarding howitzers—especially on behalf of Churchill—continued and that, thereby, the War Council was never fully apprised of the risks a fleet would face forcing the Straits or securing its lines of communication.

At the Dardanelles Commission, Vice Admiral Oliver stated that the Admiralty was able to acquire little information about the mobile gun and howitzer and threat on the peninsula.[13] This claim does not withstand analysis. As early as September, Rear Adm. Arthur Limpus had warned of the positioning of a number of mobile guns, many of which were howitzers. Before the attack began on February 19, dozens of howitzers and heavy mortars were lining the peninsula, and by Churchill's own reckoning, the Turks would have from three to four weeks to bring in more. For Churchill to treat the threat of these weapons so lightly before the War Council was a serious act of folly—or omission. Not only were there numerous six-inch howitzers on either side of the Strait, there were many eight-inch howitzers as well. Although the former were unlikely to sink an armored vessel, the eight-inch howitzers were a much more formidable threat. Both, of course, were capable of inflicting serious damage to any vessel and could sink unarmored vessels with ease.

It ought to be noted that the issue of howitzers and mobile guns always represented a concern to Carden. Although pitiably inadequate for the task, on January 15, Carden requested two four-inch to six-inch howitzers for each of three old battleships for use inside the Straits against concealed guns.[14] At least some of these were supplied and conveyed to the Mediterranean atop the turrets of the *Majestic*.

There are other examples of the manner in which Churchill generally was prepared to enhance the prospects for the operation through exaggeration. Churchill informed the War Council on January 28 that Carden had said the operation would take from three weeks to a month to complete. What Carden had in fact said was that he "might do it all in a month about" and had warned that the time required for the operation "depended greatly on morale of enemy under bombardment, garrison largely stiffened by the Germans, also on weather conditions. Gales now frequent."[15] The most charitable assessment of Churchill's time frame would be to describe it as optimistic.

Finally, one other matter must be addressed that surely must have affected the War Council's appreciation of Churchill's naval-only scheme. Balfour referred to the "silencing" of the forts. As will be seen subsequently, this expression was not used carefully or consistently, especially by Churchill. When a fort was "silenced," it meant its guns ceased to fire. It did not necessarily mean they had been destroyed and could never fire again. It was generally impossible—even with the aid of aerial reconnaissance—to tell whether the "silence" was feigned, temporary, or permanent until one placed a ship within range, and this Carden's plan expected the ships would have to do.

It is probable that these subtleties were not grasped by or conveyed to the War Council by Churchill and that, for some time at least, the War Council understood "silencing" to imply the permanent destruction of the guns. The difference between a gun that could not be repaired and one that might be repaired was fundamental to the issue of "communications" and, therefore, to the efficacy and desirability of the entire operation. Balfour's comments suggest that he assumed the forts could be dealt with in a manner that ensured that they could no longer pose a threat to an armored fleet.

It is worth remembering the message conveyed to the War Council by Churchill on January 13. The destruction of the forts was to be completed by ships operating outside the range of their large guns. Moreover, the interceding minefield would have to be swept only *after* the fleet had silenced the forts.[16]

Yet, if Churchill was saying these things to his War Council colleagues, he was doing so with precious little support from his advisers. Fisher had repeatedly expressed concern over the impermanent effects of bombardment and Richmond wanted a force of 4,000 marines sent to the Dardanelles for the expressed purpose of destroying the guns in the forts.[17] Jackson had made clear in his January 5 memorandum that military assistance was needed to put guns permanently out of action, although he had subsequently compromised himself by his comments on January 15.

With little doubt, therefore, the picture painted by Churchill for his naval-only operation was excessively sanguine. The bombardments could destroy the forts without coming into the range of their guns. The minefields need be only swept after this had been achieved. The bombarding ships would be in waters free of submarines. Mobile guns were a minor issue and howitzers, apparently, were not even worth mentioning. With such information provided to the War Council by Churchill, it is not surprising that Balfour could make the kind of optimistic appraisal for the operation that he did.

This, however, represents only half of any assessment intended to explain the War Council's enthusiasm for Churchill's operation and the level of Churchill's culpability. The other issue was who had said what about what might happen once the fleet had broken through.

Remarkably little can be found on Churchill's pronouncements in this regard. Five documents offer a guide. The first is his telegram to Carden on January 3 in which he wrote, "Importance of results would justify severe losses."[18] The second is his memorandum to Fisher of January 11 in which he declared that "[t]he forcing of the Dardanelles . . . and the arrival of a squadron strong enough to defeat the Turkish Fleet in the Sea of Marmora, would be a victory of importance, and change to our advantage the whole situation of the war in the East."[19] Third, he wrote a letter immediately after the War Council meeting of January 13: "If the attack opens prosperously it will very soon attract to itself the whole attention of the Eastern theatre, and if it succeeds, it will produce results which will undoubtedly influence every Mediterranean power."[20] Fourth, his response to the Cattaro plan, provides precious little to go on but implies strongly that he believed a breakthrough into the Marmora would secure the Balkan Armies to finish the job begun by the navy or precipitate revolution in Constantinople.

Fifth, to these documents can be added, with caution, the testimony of Victor Augageneur, the former French minister for marine, to the Marine Commission in 1917. Churchill discussed the plan with Augaganeur in late January 1915. Augaganeur claimed Churchill spoke confidently of the capacity of the fleet to break through into the Marmora, rating highly the potentialities of a ship like the *Queen Elizabeth*. Of what might be achieved thereafter, Augageneur declared Churchill felt certain that "once the forts at the entrance of the Straits were demolished the Turks would abandon the struggle."[21] Churchill would repeat a similar sentiment to Augageneur in a memorandum on February 2.[22]

Clearly, Churchill expected great consequences from a breakthrough into the Marmora, and judging by his brash comments to Augageneur, these results might occur even as soon as the forts at the entrance had been destroyed. Generally, he was remarkably vague as to what exactly these were. Cumulatively, however, with the exception of the destruction of the Turko-German Fleet, his comments in these documents suggest that his hopes rested on the moral impact of the operation rather than on anything that might be achieved militarily by the fleet, beyond, perhaps, the destruction of the Turko-German Fleet. In an unguarded moment at the Dardanelles Commission, Churchill acknowledged the relative impotence of the fleet inside the Marmora when he declared, "but of course, we could do nothing without an army except arrive there, destroy the enemy's fleet and negotiate."[23]

Notably absent from this final comment is any plan to *bombard* Constantinople. Although most histories assume that this was an option open to the fleet, it was not. International treaties precluded the bombardment of cities.[24] As late as March 4, Churchill had informed his staff that "[i]t is not intended to bombard Constantinople."[25]

It is difficult to tell whether the War Council understood this final point, although, at the very least, it must be expected that Grey and Asquith knew this. However, this made it all the more important that the War Council understood the limitations of Churchill's plan and, in particular, the problems the fleet would have in securing its own line of communication. On this point, Churchill is utterly culpable. Although, Balfour's expectations, like those of his colleagues, were undoubtedly influenced by their own closely held perceptions and prejudices, it is evident they were buoyed by the belief the fleet, having once destroyed the forts, could operate indefinitely inside the Marmora. It is difficult otherwise to understand their extraordinary hopes for the operation, in particular plans to open the Bosporus.

Over the coming weeks, even when success became imperative and the issue of communications became essential to that success, Churchill did precious little to disabuse Balfour and the War Council members on this critical issue. The facts were that the need to secure the fleet's line of communication was never a *sine qua non* of Churchill's original plan. He made the following admission before the Dardanelles Commission: "I think that could be faced, I think the advantages of going into the Sea of Marmora and sinking the Turko-German Fleet, and the political possibilities in the Balkans and Constantinople arising there from were not dependent upon keeping open our communications."[26]

The first person singular is important here because the decision to ignore the matter of communication was undoubtedly a unilateral one. Churchill took this risk on behalf of the War Council but never in consultation with it. Had it been otherwise, the story of the Dardanelles operation might have been different. Had they been alive to the potential problems of a fleet in the Marmora, while the Turks continued to command the Straits with mobile forces and including the certainty of mobile howitzers, the operation surely would have been placed under serious review.

Kitchener and the War Office must share equal responsibility for this situation, however. They understood fully the nature of the operation and acquiesced in it.

Of all the members of the War Council, it was Hankey who first addressed the shortcomings of the plan to admit fully armoured vessels only into the Marmora. In doing so, he took up the cudgel so recently surrendered by Fisher at the War Council meeting of January 28 and began pressing vigorously for military support for the Dardanelles operation.

HANKEY

The day after Balfour composed his response to Fisher's memorandum on February 1, Hankey completed a memorandum to the prime minister summarizing what he perceived to be the War Council's expectations for the forthcoming Dardanelles operation. It is an important memorandum if one is to understand fully the origins of the Dardanelles campaign. Yet it was neither produced at the Dardanelles Commission Inquiry nor quoted by Hankey in his book *The Supreme Command 1914–1918*. The essential object of the memorandum was to secure military support for the Dardanelles operation. "I have been immensely impressed," he declared, "with the cumulative effect of the arguments in favour of military action in the Dardanelles at the earliest possible date."[27] Overlooking the fact that there were precious few supplies from any source to give to the Russians, he emphasized the need to open a supply line to Russia:

> Unless the Dardanelles and Bosphorus can be opened up very soon, Russia will not receive the supplies indispensable to an offensive campaign, and the spring and summer may pass by without a decisive blow being struck at Germany or Austria. *Hence the opening of a line of communications through the Dardanelles and Bosphorus is an indispensable military requirement in order to enable the Allies to take the offensive.* (emphasis added)[28]

Of secondary importance was the influence the operation might have on the Balkan nations and the opportunity it offered for operations against Austria by a British army via the Danube River. Repeating Balfour's assertions at the War Council meeting, he identified the freeing of shipping locked in the Black Sea and the opportunity to access Russian wheat as further reasons for pursuing the Dardanelles operation.

His critical plea for the conversion of the operation into an amphibious operation came in the final two paragraphs:

> *The reason why a military expedition is mentioned is that, as pointed out by the First Lord at the Sub-Committee, the navy can perhaps open the Dardanelles and Bosphorus to warships, which are more or*

> *less impervious to field gun and rifle fire, but they cannot open these channels to merchant ships so long as the enemy is in possession of the shores. . . .*
>
> It is suggested that the Russians . . . should be asked to put pressure both on the French and on ourselves to release the comparatively moderate forces required for this operation, which should be cloaked by apparent, but really sham, attacks through Serbia and at Alexandretta or Haifa. (emphasis added)[29]

Hankey's assessment of the advantages to be gained through an attack on the Dardanelles is an accurate reflection of the contributions made at the War Council on January 28 by a number of the War Council members, including Balfour, Lloyd George, Asquith, and Grey, although undoubtedly a lot more of his own thinking appears in this assessment than he has revealed.

The key point of interest is that Churchill had made clear to the other members of the subcommittee of the War Council on January 28 that his naval-only operation was designed to open the Dardanelles (and perhaps the Bosporus) for armored vessels only.

That Churchill offered this information to the gathering of the subcommittee suggests he might have been attempting to rein in his colleague's expectations for the operation, in particular Balfour's talk of establishing a trade route through to the Black Sea. That the War Council continued to hold such expectations after this declaration was made seems only to be explained by one of two possibilities. Either the War Council recognized the threat to the fleet's communications but, like Churchill, was prepared to risk everything on the moral impact of the fleet breaking into the Marmora or, despite Churchill's concession, they remained ignorant of the implications for the fleet of an operation that could not also secure the movement of unarmored supply ships into the Marmora.

It is impossible to give a definitive answer to which proposition is correct. Given our earlier assessments, however, the latter seems the most likely alternative. One might have reasonably expected the members of the subcommittee to understand the implication of an operation designed to admit armored vessels *only* into the Marmora. Such vessels as were able to get through could sustain themselves only by supplies brought through the Straits in unarmored merchant ships. If unarmored merchant vessels could not get through the Marmora, the fleet would soon be forced back through the Narrows. Balfour's evidence suggests this concept was not grasped by at least some members of the War Council and that Churchill did not reveal such possibilities to the War Council. Without doubt, Churchill's flagrant disregard of the mobile gun threat to armored vessels and his failure to address the issue of howitzers would have contributed to the impression within the War Council that the fleet could come and go as it pleased. It might be noted once again that Hankey's memorandum made no reference to a howitzer threat. The assumption therefore remained that such a threat did not exist.

Incidentally, Hankey's memorandum ignores any apprehensions over the likely collapse of Russian forces or the urgent need to aid the Russians in the Caucasus. The issue of aid to Russia is not borne of fear that Russia was facing collapse or defeat. Rather, the aid was to be given so that Russia could go on the offensive against Germany or Austria at the earliest opportunity. Hankey bundled the idea of freeing Russian troops from the Caucasus (presumably for offensive work elsewhere) with several other "minor advantages," which he considered "scarcely of sufficient moment to influence the decision."[30]

Hankey's memorandum was not in touch with reality in a number of respects. How it was imagined Britain could spare supplies during a time of rapid military expansion before spring is difficult to understand. The advantages of freeing merchant shipping generally was overstated, and the notion implicit in the opening paragraphs of his memorandum that the Russians would throw away millions of men fighting the Germans while her allies remained on the defensive in the west seems questionable.

Nevertheless, given that these largely represented the cumulative views of the War Council, his suggestion that the peninsula must be occupied to secure these opportunities ought to have had a considerable impact on Asquith. It did not.

The discussions outlined in Hankey's memorandum would seem to have represented perfect opportunities for Churchill to have sought military assistance for his operation—had he wanted it. He could have readily argued, just as Hankey had now concluded, that his rather speculative operation could not ensure the burgeoning expectations of the War Council unless the peninsula was occupied. If the War Council considered the strategic, political, and economic advantages of the operation of vital importance, then military assistance on a large scale must be forthcoming to seize at least one side of the peninsula. Churchill could have shot home his point by adding that, although the fleet might break into the Marmora, it was the most earnest concern of his advisers that the fleet, with unsecured lines of communication, would be largely ineffectual thereafter. Although he spoke of difficulties of trade, he was apparently silent on this vastly more weighty issue.

Hankey's memorandum is also important because it represented the first step in the political process that finally secured troops for the Dardanelles operation. As the last paragraph of Hankey's memorandum shows, he was the first member of the War Council to grasp the efficacy of shelving the Salonika operation so recently mooted within the War Council and instead sending whatever troops were available to support the Dardanelles operation.

NOTES

1. Callwell to Robertson, January 30, 1915, Papers of FM Sir William (Robert) Robertson, King's College, London.
2. Ibid.
3. Ibid.
4. Ibid.
5. Callwell to Robertson, February 4, 1915, Robertson Papers.
6. Callwell to Robertson, February 4, 1915, Robertson Papers.
7. Callwell to Robertson, February 8, 1915, Robertson Papers.
8. See Miller, *Straits*, 400–401. Balfour's "Notes on Fisher's Memorandum." Also elements cited in Marder, *From Dreadnought to Scapa Flow*, vol. 2, 216.
9. Ibid.
10. CAB 19/33, Dardanelles Commission, Question 4276–4278.
11. George Cassar, *The French and the Dardanelles* (London: George Allen and Unwin, 1971), 53.
12. Gilbert, *CVIII*, 405–406. Secret and Personal Telegram, Carden to Churchill, January 11, 1915.
13. CAB 19/33, Dardanelles Commission, Question 1783.
14. CHAR 13/65. Telegram, Carden to Admiralty, January 15, 1945.
15. Gilbert, *CVIII*, 406. Carden's memorandum of January 12.
16. See Ibid., 478–479. Oliver's February 2 memorandum circulated to Asquith, Grey, Kitchener, and Balfour would have done little to alert any of these people to the dangers of the naval assault. Oliver described the assault on the outer forts in the following way: "When each fort in turn at the entrance has been subjected to this slow, deliberate bombardment, and the forts are considered to be out of action, a squadron of older battleships will be sent closer to draw the fire of the forts. If the fire is serious, the ships will withdraw out of range and the long range bombardment from ships at anchor will be resumed. When the ships can approach to within range of the forts without drawing heavy fire, the forts will be subjected to fire from the secondary armament at a suitable range for accurate shooting and all

range finding positions. Searchlights and other accessories will be destroyed."

This quotation leaves one with the clear impression that the guns in the forts were to be destroyed at long range. Close range was only ever intended to be used to destroy such things as searchlights and other accessories. This ignored entirely the advice given by Jackson in early January, that men would have to be landed to put guns permanently out of action and does not reflect at all what Carden said he would do and what he actually did at the Dardanelles. He used a three-tiered assault, which he intended to repeat inside the Straits. The forts were to be attacked at a long, medium, and, finally, close or decisive range. It was intended to silence the forts at long and medium range, but it was expected the forts could be only permanently damaged at a decisive range (as close as four kilometers). Indeed, Carden went one step further, and contrary to Churchill's and Oliver's expectations and pronouncements regarding the use of the marines, he would, from the very beginning, take every opportunity to land men to destroy guns. He learned very early on that this would be the only way the guns in the forts could be permanently put out of action.

17. See Richmond's diary entry for February 9, Marder, *Portrait of an Admiral*, 140.

18. Gilbert, *CVIII*, 367, Telegram, Churchill to Carden, January 3, 1915.

19. *The World Crisis*, 541, Memorandum, Churchill to Fisher.

20. Gilbert, *CVIII*, 414–415. Churchill to Asquith, Grey and Kitchener.

21. Cassar, *The French and the Dardanelles*, 57.

22. Churchill told Augageneur that the appearance of the Fleet in the Marmora would provoke an uprising at Constantinople. Ibid., 66.

23. CAB 19/33, Dardanelles Commission, Question 1350.

24. Cassar, in the first of his works on Kitchener, pointed out that this was not an option. See George Cassar, *Kitchener: Architect of Victory* (London: Kimber, 1977).

25. ADMIRALTY PAPERS (hereafter ADM) (Public Records Office, London) 137/1089.

26. CAB 19/33, Dardanelles Commission, Question 1450.

27. CAB 42/1/30: Hankey to Prime Minister Asquith, Memorandum: *The War: Attack On Dardanelles*, February 2, 1915.

28. Ibid.

29. Ibid.

30. Ibid.

CHAPTER 14

The Search for Troops I: Salonika versus Gallipoli

However naïve his hopes for the Dardanelles operation might have been, Hankey's appreciation that troops would be better used to capitalize on any advantage gained by the navy rather than as a political tool to secure Greek or Romanian aid to Serbia was probably a sound one. His suggestion that Russia be encouraged to put pressure on Britain and France to send forces to the Dardanelles was entirely at odds with the plans mooted in the War Council for Britain to put pressure on France and Russia to send forces to Salonika.

We left our discussion of the Salonika operation with the War Council decision to send Churchill to France to inform Sir John French that some of his anticipated reinforcements might instead be diverted to Salonika to secure Greek and, perhaps, Romanian support for Serbia. Churchill returned from France on January 31. He immediately informed Kitchener of his discussions with French. The upshot was that French wanted all reserves promised him but had agreed to make two divisions available, subject to emergencies, from the middle of March onward.[1]

Churchill's report on his visit was quite matter of fact and showed no disquiet at all over French's decision. There is some evidence that Churchill's advocacy apparently had not been quite as intense as his colleagues might have hoped. After the meeting, a rather self-satisfied French recorded in his diary that he felt that "On the whole, I rather brought him [Churchill] around."[2] If

Churchill had been successfully persuaded not to press his case too strongly, then why? Had Churchill felt the need to remain on good terms with French and, if so, why did he consider this particular friendship so important? There is no doubt French was entirely familiar with Churchill's northern plans. He had discussed them with him in the past and he would do so in the future. Churchill would be reluctant to put his relationship at risk so long as French remained central to the execution of one or other of these plans.

Churchill's summary of his discussions with French displayed none of the apprehensions that beset Hankey over the absence of troops to support the naval-only operation, nor even concern over the possibility, according to French's proposal, that experienced troops might not be available in the Mediterranean before the beginning of April.

Nevertheless, like his War Council colleagues, he continued to see merit in using a modest number of troops as a political tool to secure the intervention of the Balkan States. On February 2, he sent French a pile of Balkan telegrams remarking that "[t]hey will show you why a sabre stroke is needed to cut the tangle." As for the Dardanelles, he merely remarked that the "Dardanelles goes forward steadily and all the ships are sailing."[3] This is clearly not a man dwelling on the absence of troops at the Dardanelles.

Not surprisingly, it would be Lloyd George, rather than Churchill, who would be the catalyst for further movement on the Salonika plan. Shortly after the events described above, Lloyd George visited France and discovered Millerand had failed to mention to his colleagues the British government's desire to divert troops to the Mediterranean to draw in the Balkan States. He quickly discovered that like-minded politicians in the French government were prepared to send troops to Salonika and he was determined to press the issue again within the War Council.

Unfortunately, at this very time, the likelihood of Greek assistance was reaching a new low ebb. While the Allies had been mulling over the possibility of neutralizing the Bulgarian factor by sending a token force to Salonika, Venizelos had sought a commitment from Romania. Romania, however, would not agree to "anything in the nature of a threat to Bulgaria."[4]

Next, Venizelos had attempted to buy Bulgarian support through a deal by which King Constantine would offer Bulgaria the rich Macedonian province of Cavalla. Venizelos expected Greece to be compensated by the Allies with significant concessions in Asia Minor, and he discussed this with Elliot.[5] Unfortunately for Venizelos, he considerably overestimated Grey's largesse. Grey's offer was so far below Venizelos's expectations that Elliot refused to forward the proposal to him and here the discussions stalled.[6]

On February 2, just about the time of Lloyd George's venture to France, Venizelos learned that Bulgaria had obtained a loan from Germany and all discussions on Greek intervention became entirely academic. From this point onward, it was evident no agreement could be reached with Bulgaria, and thereafter any thoughts of territorial concessions ended.[7]

The only inducement left now to draw in Greece was the offer of military support. On February 9, the War Council sat to discuss the matter again. Lloyd George announced that his trip to France had secured one French Division, should the British send the same, and a small Russian contingent.

There was general support for this modest expedition. The War Council members all rather naively concluded that the offer almost certainly would bring in Greece and possibly Romania. After all, as Churchill had remarked, the expedition could not be landed without involving Greece. Additionally, Bulgaria would be paralyzed. Militarily, the Graeco-Serbian army would be protected, more particularly if Russia was able to send troops.

In addition to these advantages, Kitchener pointed out that it "might be very useful to the Navy in their attack on the Dardanelles to have some good troops at Salonika."[8] When conversation turned briefly to the Dardanelles later in the meeting, he again remarked, "that if the Navy required the assistance of the land forces at a later stage, that assistance would be forthcoming."[9]

Only Sir John French, who had come from France to discuss the matter, expressed any real reservations about the proposal. He was concerned the offer might draw in Greece but not Romania and considered that "it would not be good strategy to detach a British, a French, and perhaps a Russian division to Salonica merely in order to bring Greece into the War."[10]

The most ardent opponent of the operation, Hankey, remained silent throughout the entire meeting. He had not remained passive, however, and continued to press for the diversion of troops to the Dardanelles instead of Salonika. Since writing his memorandum to Asquith on February 2, he had obtained from the naval historian, Julian Corbett, a rather salutary assessment of the Duckworth expedition of 1807. He circulated this to all members of the War Council in a not entirely successful attempt to promote discussion on the naval-only operation.[11]

On February 10, Hankey wrote to Balfour of his strong opposition to the "Serbian proposition" and expressed his belief that the Dardanelles was "the only extraneous operation worth trying."[12] He noted that, in contrast to the first lord, every officer from Lord Fisher down did not believe the Dardanelles position could be taken without troops. He believed that a mere reserve of 12,000 Turkish troops was in the Gallipoli Peninsula, and therefore it could be taken with a relatively small force. He concluded:

> Nevertheless I am quite reconciled to the Salonica proposal, because I am convinced that, if only we can get troops out to the Levant on any excuse they will, if the Navy achieve any considerable measure of success, be landed at Gallipoli! I misread Lord K altogether, if this is not so.[13]

Three days later, he again assailed Asquith in another attempt to secure troops for the Dardanelles operation. Asquith wrote to Venetia Stanley on February 13 of his discussions with Hankey:

> He thinks very strongly that the naval operation . . . should be supported by landing a fairly strong military force. I have been for some time coming to the same opinion, and I think we ought to be able without denuding French to scrape together from Egypt, Malta and elsewhere a sufficiently large contingent.[14]

Was Churchill moved by this growing interest in sending an army to the Dardanelles instead of Salonika? At the Dardanelles Commission, Churchill claimed that "at all times, in all discussions" he supported everything that would "promote and expedite" the concentration of an army in the Mediterranean.[15]

Although this might be said, with considerable qualification and reservation, of the period after the middle of February, it could not be said of any time before. Moreover, whatever efforts he did make continued to be geared toward securing Balkan intervention and not to securing support for his naval-only operation. This is not made at all clear in his comments.

When the idea of withholding reinforcements from the Western Front arose on January 28, Churchill had rather surprisingly failed to suggest these might be used to support his naval operation. Churchill's assertion is also critically at odds with an entry in Richmond's diary of February 9. Richmond, who was assistant director of the operations division (A.D.O.D.), wrote of Churchill's reluctance to send either marines or his Naval Division—the only military forces over which Churchill did have control—to the Dardanelles. Richmond recorded that he wanted to have 4,000 marines for "operations of landing and destroying forts which have been knocked out by ships. . . . Winston refused to send more than 2000." He noted that Oliver thought it was "about time the Naval Division earned its keep" and be sent out "*en masse* for the business . . . but no, not one of them would the 1st Lord allow to go."[16] Instead:

> Winston proposes mad things and hangs on to his silly Naval Division . . . he proposes archaic plans of bombardments, which would lead to nothing but opposes combined operations which would lead to something. Winston very, very, ignorant, believes he can capture Dardanelles without troops and that Borkum can be destroyed by bombardment. Strange fallacies.[17]

This quotation is of interest for other reasons. First, it draws to our attention the belated decision to send 2,000 marines to support the Dardanelles attack. This decision appears to have been made on January 29[18] and seems to represent a limited victory of the Admiralty war staff over Churchill's naval only operation. This issue will be addressed in more detail subsequently, but the point is that Churchill had to be induced to send even 2,000 marines to support his operation.

The second point is the evidence of Churchill's ongoing interest in Borkum. The third point is that this interest demonstrates Churchill's determination to maintain the naval-only element of the operation. The fourth point is what it tells us further of the nature of Churchill's operation and the fears of the Admiralty staff for it.

Richmond's diary, like Jackson's memorandum of January 5, made clear that yet another of Churchill's advisers believed that, while the forts' guns might be "silenced" by the ships, they could not be "destroyed" by them. The final destruction of the guns must be achieved by troops. Despite an apparent awareness of these concerns at the Admiralty—and their grave implications for the security of the fleet once inside the Marmora—Churchill failed to demand the troops needed to deal with this problem.

Instead, the official Admiralty documents produced by Vice Admiral Oliver at this time scrupulously maintained the fiction that the fortification could be made innocuous by the fleet alone.[19] In particular, they avoided any suggestion that the marines belatedly committed to the operation might be required to complete the destruction of the guns in the forts. How could this be otherwise when the key premise of the entire operation was that the fleet could do this without aid? In the end, it was soldiers (and not ships) who destroyed the vast majority of guns at the Dardanelles.

Oliver's February 2 memorandum—forwarded by Churchill to Asquith, Grey, Kitchener, and Balfour—briefly and vaguely outlined the expected progress of the bombardment and the nominated the ships to be employed. This memorandum accepted absolutely the capacity of the bombarding ships to "silence," "reduce," and "destroy" the forts as per Carden's plan. The Churchill ingredient was added when he noted that:

> It is expected that the slow, irresistible destruction of the forts by vessels which cannot be reached effectively by their fire will have a great effect on the morale of the garrisons of those forts which have yet to be attacked, and will go far to shake the confidence of the Turks in their German advisers, and it may possibly result in an overthrow of the German rule in Constantinople.[20]

In such a scenario, marines would hardly be needed at all. Thus, despite Richmond's advice to him, Oliver's memorandum indicated that the two battalions of Royal Marines were to be available for "any small landing operations which can be carried out under the fire of the ships' guns, such as destroying mining stations and fire-observation stations."[21] Mobile guns were to be dealt with by the howitzers to be provided and the smaller guns of the fleet.[22] Thus the naval-only plan—and the assumption that the fleet could destroy the large guns commanding the Dardanelles Straits—remained essentially intact and unchallenged.

Three days later, the Admiralty sent Carden a more detailed and lengthy memorandum.[23] It has been said that Churchill had no input into the instructions given to Carden, but this telegram has many of the hallmarks of Churchill about it. The role of the Marines was again mentioned:

> They will be of service as a garrison for the base or for any small landing operation of a temporary nature in circumstances where they can be efficiently protected by the guns of the fleet against superior Turkish forces. They should not be landed against superior forces or entrenched positions where they

cannot be efficiently supported by the ships' guns without first obtaining Admiralty sanction.[24]

Earlier this memorandum had identified "torpedo tubes" as a possible target for the marines if they could not be destroyed by gunfire. "It may be necessary to land men," it was noted, "if the enemy's infantry can be kept at a sufficient distance by shell and machine-gun fire." It was further noted, however, that "[i]f there is any doubt as to the torpedo tubes being destroyed, it may be possible to take ships past them by securing colliers or other merchant vessels along-side." This latter comment is of interest for two reasons. First, this unlikely proposition bears the mark of Churchill's active imagination. It seems unimaginable that the fleet would venture past these tubes with merchant vessels strapped to their sides and continue up the channel thus encumbered to meet the Turko-German Fleet. One might wonder from where the large numbers of merchant vessels needed were to come. Second, these instructions are a powerful example of the writer's willingness to force the fleet through the Marmora with communication unsecured.

The most glaring example of the obfuscation surrounding the likely use of the marines on the peninsula was perpetrated by Churchill at the February 9 War Council meeting when he explained that "two battalions of marines (were being sent) to capture some torpedo tubes close to the water's edge of the Dardanelles."[25] Given Richmond's suggestion discussed earlier that Churchill had been pressured into sending marines because of the War Groups desire to secure the permanent destruction of the guns in the forts, this pronouncement represented omission of a serious order.

The obfuscation surrounding the mobile guns and howitzer also continued unabated. In neither of the papers discussed above was the word "howitzer" mentioned, save for reference to the howitzers it was intended the navy would use to silence the enemy's field guns on the peninsula. Indeed, the last time this word was spoken or written was in Carden's telegram of January 11.

Despite, or perhaps, because of the evident apathy of Churchill and Oliver over military support, the pressure to use troops to secure the fleet's lines of communication continued to grow throughout February. On February 13, Jackson completed a memorandum entitled "Attack on Constantinople."[26] This detailed the manner in which the forts were to be reduced and minefields swept.

In this memorandum, Jackson viewed the role of the Marine Brigade quite differently to the papers prepared by Oliver (and perhaps

Churchill). If the marines were not prevented from doing so by Turkish forces, they were to complete the demolition of forts and guns and establish lookout stations. This represents a repetition of the advice given in his January 5 memorandum and is fundamentally at odds with the Oliver and Churchill memoranda, which continued uncritically to accept Carden's proposition that the forts and their guns might be neutralized by the fleet alone. It is also entirely at odds with Churchill's pronouncement to the War Council on February 9.

The import of Jackson's memorandum was that, should the enemy strength be great and the marines unable to land, the destruction of the forts and guns could not be "thoroughly completed." A passage into the Marmora could not be undertaken with communications secured and the fleet might be seriously threatened on its return. Jackson's closing paragraphs, therefore, included a plea for troops:

> the provision of the necessary military forces to enable the fruits of this heavy undertaking to be gathered must never be lost sight of; the transports carrying them should be in readiness to enter the straits as soon as it is seen the forts at the Narrows will be silenced.
>
> To complete their destruction, strong military landing parties with strong covering forces would be necessary. The full advantage of the undertaking, however, would be obtained only by the occupation of the peninsula by a military force acting in conjunction with the naval operation. The pressure of a strong field army of the enemy on the peninsula not only would greatly harass the operations, but also would render the passage of the Straits impracticable by any but powerfully armed vessels, even though all of the permanent defenses had been silenced.[27]

Jackson concluded, "The naval bombardment is not recommended as a sound military operation unless a strong military force is ready to assist in the operation, or, at least, follow it up immediately [after] the forts are silenced."

Jackson clearly wanted, as a bare minimum, to land troops to secure the destruction of guns in the forts. If these and other guns were not destroyed, he did not consider it a sound military action.

Churchill has claimed that Jackson's final comment was an example of mixed thinking. He has argued that Jackson's reference to gathering the "fruits of this heavy naval undertaking" and his suggestion that troops follow up the operation "immediately the forts are silenced" implied that troops could enter the Marmora via the Straits. This is a deliberate misrepresentation. Jackson meant only that the troops be used to complete the destruction of the forts after they had been silenced. This is made quite clear by his statement that Turkish control of the peninsula would "render the passage of the Straits impracticable by any but powerfully-armed vessels." Churchill knew that any significant body of troops entering the Marmora would have to do so in unarmored and unarmed merchant vessels.

Jackson's concerns were corroborated the following day by A.D.O.D. Richmond, who completed a paper entitled "Remarks on Present Strategy" in which he strongly supported an attack on Turkey. Richmond criticized the naval-only attack because it would forfeit the numerous advantages to be gained by a joint attack. He warned that without an army in the Gallipoli Peninsula, the Straits could never provide a safe thoroughfare for trade. He also cast doubt on the ability of the fleet to destroy fortifications and allowed no possibility whatsoever that the ships could destroy field and other guns "entrenched on the heights." He believed that the most recent experiences, corresponding with the past, had shown that ships alone could not capture the forts. "An army," he wrote, "is indispensable."[28]

Richmond forwarded a copy of his paper to Hankey who declared it "A1." Hankey passed it on to Fisher who considered it "excellent." In the meantime, Fisher had been doing some lobbying of his own. Five days earlier, he had written to Lloyd George with the observation that "to bombard the Gallipoli Peninsula without military co-operation on the Peninsula is most deplorable!"[29]

Richmond's paper, like Jackson's paper and Hankey's memorandum to Asquith, was a plea for secure lines of communication. Perhaps more significant, his closing paragraph also cast serious doubt on the key assumption of the Carden plan—that the fleet alone could *destroy* the forts—even given the opportunity of bombardment at decisive range.

Leaving aside their very real doubt about the capacity of ships' guns to destroy the guns in the forts, it is quite evident that Churchill's plan to admit an armored fleet only was entirely at odds with a least three of his key advisers—Fisher, Jackson, and Richmond. It already has been demonstrated the degree to which Churchill's plan was completely at odds with Carden's original proposal.

Moreover, it was now increasingly at odds with the new focus of the War Council, championed first by Hankey and then Asquith, to open up *immediate* access to Russia via the Dardanelles and Bosporus.

Despite the serious and evident limitations of his plan, Churchill was reluctant to alter in any fundamental way his attitude to the use of troops in his operation. It is evident that Churchill was fully aware of the concerns of his advisers but that he was choosing to ignore them. The evidence suggests he was prepared to risk breaking into the Marmora with the Straits lined with fully operational howitzers and field guns, and with the guns in the forts damaged but not destroyed. In so doing, he was prepared to risk the subsequent limitations this would place on the fleet and its ability to achieve the moral and military successes expected of it. Although Oliver's plan allowed for neutralizing hidden guns and howitzers by the fleet, it does not appear that Fisher, Richmond, Jackson, or even Churchill himself believed these dealt with the issue satisfactorily.

The great difficulty Jackson or Richmond or anyone else faced in telling Churchill that his plan would admit only fully armored vessels into the Marmora—and then only temporarily—was that Churchill already knew this. After all, *that* was his plan and he was determined to stick to it.

NOTES

1. Gilbert, *CVIII*, 475–476. Letter, Churchill to Kitchener, January 31, 1915.

2. French, *Sir John French*, 275.

3. Gilbert, *CVIII*, 477–478. Letter, Churchill to Sir John French, February 2, 1915.

4. Elliot to Grey, January 31, 1915, Christos Theodoulou, *Greece and the Entente August 1 1914–September 25, 1916* (Thessalonika: Institute for Balkan Studies, 1971), 101.

5. Ibid.

6. Grey proposed to offer Greece "Smyrna and a substantial portion of the hinterland to be hereafter defined." Theodoulou, *Greece and the Entente*, 101. A plan to add Cyprus to the offer was declined by Kitchener.

7. Lord Percy's memorandum, Public Records Office, FO 371, no. 2264. Cited in Theodoulou, *Greece and the Entente*, 102. Apparently the British government became aware of this on February 3. See Hankey, *The Supreme Command*, 276.

8. CAB 42/1/36, Secretary's Notes of War Council meeting, February 9, 1915.

9. Ibid.

10. Ibid.

11. CAB 42/1/15, Letter from Julian Corbett to Colonel Hankey entitled, *The War: The Dardanelles*, dated February 5, 1915.

12. Gilbert, *CVIII*, 500. Hankey to Balfour. Also cited in Miller, *Straits*, 411.

13. Hankey to Balfour, cited in Miller, *Straits*, 411.

14. Gilbert, *CVIII*, 512. Private Letter, Asquith to Venetia Stanley, February 13, 1915.

15. See Douglas Jerrold, *The Royal Naval Division* (London: Hutchison and Co., 1923), 58.

16. Marder, *Portrait of an Admiral*, 140. Diary entry by Richmond, February 9, 1915.

17. Ibid.

18. Most accounts indicate the decision to send out marines was made on February 6. This is not the case. This decision must have been made earlier as the subsequent memorandum, which mentions marines makes clear.

19. Oliver to Churchill (subsequently circulated to Asquith, Grey, Kitchener, and Balfour), paper, February 2, and Oliver to Carden, paper, February 5, Gilbert, *CVIII*, 487–489.

20. Oliver's memorandum, Gilbert, *CVIII*, 479–482, February 2, 1915.

21. Ibid. Hankey's minutes of the War Council meeting of February 9 record Churchill stating only that "[t]wo battalions of marines had been sent out. Their object was to capture some torpedo tubes close to the water's edge in the Dardanelles."

22. Oliver's memorandum, Gilbert, *CVIII*, 479–482. In early January, Carden requested two howitzers for each of three battleships that would be used in the bombardment.

23. Gilbert, *GCIII*, 485–490. *Dardanelles Operation Orders*. The greater part of this was apparently prepared by Oliver.

24. Ibid.

25. CAB 42/1/33. Secretary's Notes of the War Council Meeting, Febraury 9, 1915.

26. Gilbert, *CVIII*, 506–512. Memorandum by Jackson, February 13, 1915.

27. Ibid., 512.

28. Marder, *Portrait of an Admiral*, 142–145.

29. CHAR 4/11/5. Letter, Fisher to Lloyd George, 10/2/15.

Sir John Fisher,
First Sea Lord
(Courtesy Library of Congress)

David Lloyd George
Chancellor of Exchequer
(Courtesy Library of Congress)

Lord Kitchener
Secretary of State for War
(Courtesy Library of Congress)

Winston Churchill
First Lord of the Admiralty
(Courtesy Library of Congress)

Maurice Hankey
Secretary to the War Council
(Courtesy Library of Congress)

Field Marshal John French
Commander in Chief, BEF.
(Courtesy Library of Congress)

John Jellicoe
Commander-in-Chief,
Grand Fleet
(Courtesy Library of Congress)

The Protagonists

The Kiel Canal (aka the Kaiser Wilhelm Canal) under construction. The picture left shows the giant lock gates at Holtenau under construction, circa 1890. The picture at right shows Kaiser Wilhelm II laying the foundation stone for the high bridge near Levensau, June 21, 1893. (#HU 68385. Photograph courtesy of the Imperial War Museum, London.)

(#HU 68387. Photograph courtesy of the Imperial War Museum, London.)

The Problem

From the opening days of the war, Churchill sought, at the earliest opportunity, to apply the might of the British Fleet in decisive, war-winning offensive operations. He first thought of an amphibious assault by a vast Russian Army against Germany's Baltic coast. Unfortunately for the British, the building of the Kiel Canal (formerly known as the Prince Wilhelm and Kaiser Wilhelm Canal) made this impossible. The German Fleet could move between the Baltic and North Sea with considerable rapidity and launch offensive operations against the portion of the British Fleet inside the Baltic or that left behind in the North Sea. The High Sea Fleet must be either defeated in battle or prevented from entering the North Sea by blocking or blockading the canal and the North Sea debouches. Much pre-war study had gone into these problems and had concluded that the threat of the mine and torpedo made such operations impossible. Churchill continued to believe that these same weapons could be used against the Germans to achieve an effective close blockade which would force the High Seas Fleet to sea and defeat. First, however, an island base nearer the German coast must be captured. But, again, how to make this possible? In November, 1914, Churchill ordered the first four of his big-gunned monitors, the start of his unsinkable fleet. Perhaps here was the answer to this problem.

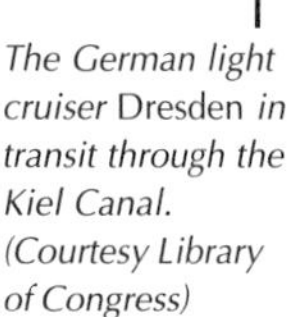

The German light cruiser Dresden *in transit through the Kiel Canal. (Courtesy Library of Congress)*

The island base of Heligoland. (Australian War Memorial, Negative Number H12338.)

HMS Abercrombie, *a 14inch gunned monitor.*
(Australian War Memorial, Negative Number G01082.)

The Solution

Churchill hoped his fleet of monitors could overcome many of the impediments to close blockade and amphibious operations against Germany's coastline. The monitors' shallow draft would allow them to negotiate the shoal-infested waters surrounding their objectives and protect against submarines and mines; their large guns would allow them to bombard the enemy's defenses beyond range and dominate them sufficiently to allow the storming of the island by a divison of troops landed from specially built landing craft. Once captured, the monitors would form the core of the island defenses. Churchill's final plans envisaged the monitors operating from this base to blockade Germany's North Sea debouches, effectively denying egress to the High Sea Fleet. Just as hopefully, Churchill anticipated the activities of these vessels would precipitate a decisive naval battle which would give Britain command of the North Sea. There after, Germany could be assailed from the Sea and victory achieved.

The Marshal Ney, *a 15inch gunned monitor. (# SP 123. Photograph courtesy of the Imperial War Museum, London.)*

(#H2681, Courtesy of Ulster Folk and Transport Museum, N.I.) This series of pictures highlight the extraordinary 'bulging' of the monitors, in this case, that of HMS Abercrombie. *The bulging was designed to make the vessel proof against the torpedo and the mine. This feature, combined with its exceptionally shallow draft, made the vessel ideal for in-shore operations. However, the bulging and other design faults made many of the early monitors unwieldy and exceptionally slow. The monitor did contribute to some useful bombardment operations. However, as a weapon Churchill hoped would make a decisive contribution to his various amphibious plans, it fell woefully short of the mark, in both a practical and tactical sense.*

The Unsinkable Fleet

(#H2228, Courtesy of Ulster Folk and Transport Museum, N.I.)

(#H2230, Courtesy of Ulster Folk and Transport Museum, N.I.)

The 15inch guns of HMS Queen Elizabeth. *(Australian War Memorial, Negative Number G00224.) On January 13th, 1915, Churchill argued before the War Council that the mighty guns of the Queen Elizabeth would make a decisive difference at the Dardanelles. The weaponry was formidable, but the task set for it – the destruction of individual guns in the numerous forts and revetments protecting the Dardanelles – was beyond it. The relative small nature of the targets, insurmountable difficulties with spotting the fall of shot, the need to constantly be on the move against shelling from mobile artillery, the restricted and frequent use of in-appropriate 15 inch shells, and the distance over which most shelling took place within the Straits, ensured that the greater part of the 253 shells fired by the* Queen Elizabeth *between February 19 and late March landed ineffectually. The damage done to fortifications might occasionally look impressive – as in the photograph below – but it did little harm to the Turks.*

The Queen Elizabeth

A 15inch shell being lifted aboard the Queen Elizabeth. *(Australian War Memorial, Negative Number G00195.)*

A photograph taken on April 25 showing damage done to a Turkish fort by a 15inch shell. (Australian War Memorial, Negative Number G00218.)

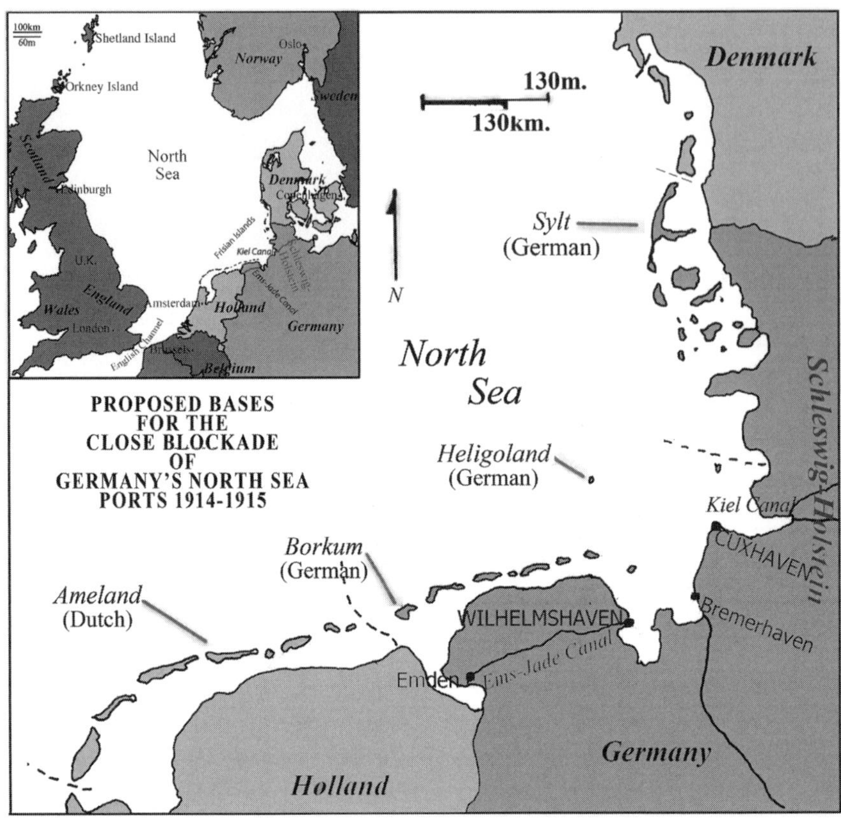

Churchill's Island Bases. At the outbreak of war, the Dutch Island of Ameland was Churchill's first preference for a base for close blockade. This was subsequently replaced by Sylt and, finally, Borkum. Heligoland was preferred by A.K. Wilson but was considered the most challenging of all to capture. Other sites nominated by Churchill were Esbjerg off the west coast of Denmark and the Laeso Channel, off its east coast, the Norwegian port of Ekersund and Kungsbacka Fjord in Sweden. With the exception of Heligoland, Sylt and Borkum, the occupation of all these places assumed either a breech of neutrality by Britain, or the accession to the allied side of one or other of these neutral states. It was the realization that neither option was likely to be fulfilled that hardened Churchill's interest in the German islands and his focus changed permanently from thoughts of blockading the entrance to the Baltic to blockading the debouches of Germany's North Sea ports. By the beginning of 1915, Borkum alone was being mentioned in Churchill's proposals.

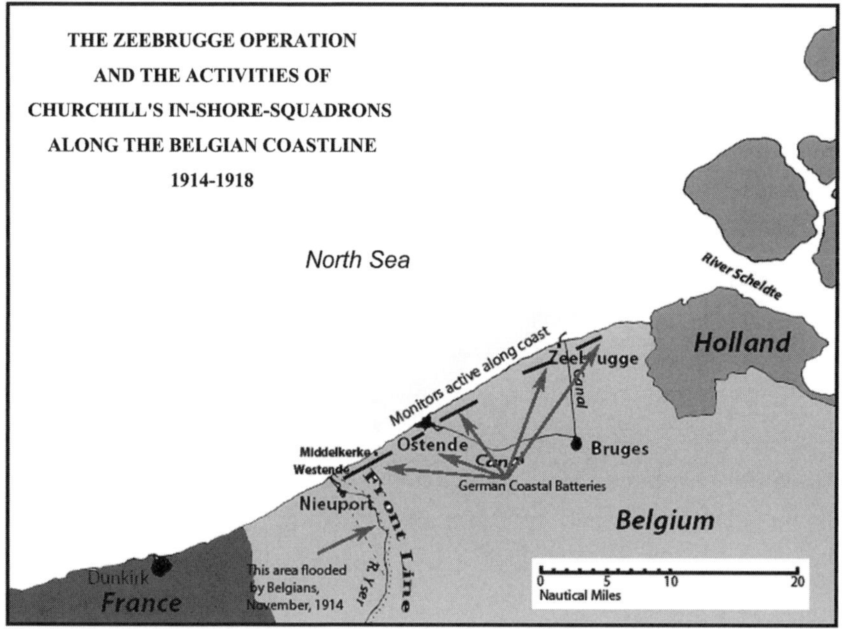

The Zeebrugge Operation. During the latter part of 1914 and into early 1915, Churchill urged Sir John French to launch an attack along the Belgian coast to retake the important ports of Ostende and Zeebrugge. German control of these ports and their linking canals posed a major submarine threat. At Fisher's prompting, Churchill suggested that Zeebrugge "should at the critical moment – and as the thong of your attack – be assailed from the sea; and then kicked back towards Ostende. . ." His faith in his in-shore naval squadron, including at this point, three monitors, was considerable. In October 1914, he had written of the absolutely devastating support his bombarding fleet could offer. "For four or five miles inshore," he informed French, "we could make you perfectly safe and superior. Here, at least, you have their flank, if you care to use it." Neither the coastal operation nor the amphibious assault on Zeebrugge ever took place and the Belgian ports remained in Germany's hands for the duration of the war. As the various monitors reached completion during the latter half of 1915, many were assigned to bombardment and blockade operations against these ports. Although the monitors did resist submarine attack, their bombardment operations achieved only modest results. Their activities became ever more difficult as the Germans added to the range and number of their coastal batteries. In 1918, a daring naval assault was conducted against Zeebrugge, blocking for a time the entrance to the port.

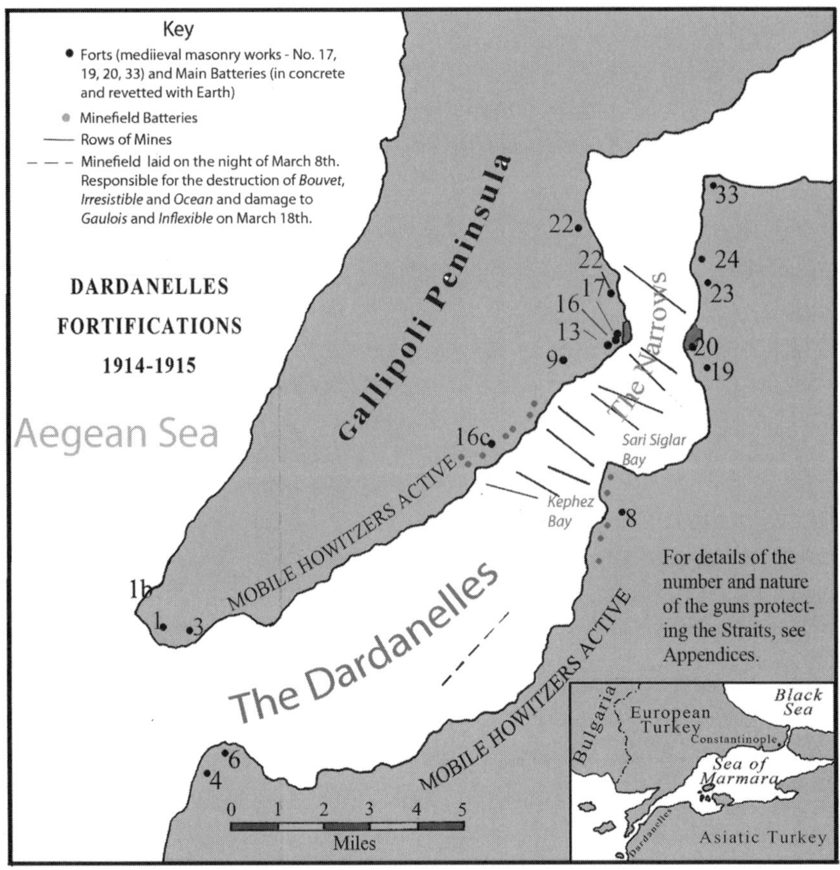

Gallipoli Map. Despite his long-standing interest in the Dardanelles, Churchill was not enamored with plans being mooted by the War Council to send a large Allied army to the Mediterranean to draw in the various Balkan States. Such proposals would have seriously compromised his own aspirations for operations in northern Europe. Instead, Churchill proposed a 'naval only' attempt to force the Dardanelles. This began on February 19, 1915, and continued for a month. The attack on the outer forts was quickly successful, although there were portentous signs to be found for anyone who cared to look. The bombardment had destroyed one or two guns only, the destruction of the rest being achieved by landing parties after the Turkish defenders had withdrawn. The attack on the outer forts would be the only time the fleet was able to bombard outside the range of Turkish guns. Once inside the Straits, the fleet was exposed to constant fire from numerous guns, many of which were almost impossible to detect, let alone destroy. Although many of these guns could only inflict nominal damage on the armored battleships, they forced them to remain constantly on the move or to frequently change berth, with a consequent decline in accuracy. Moreover, these guns presented serious problems for the inexperienced fleet of minesweepers, the task of which was to sweep the two substantial mine-fields protecting the Straits. Following the loss of or damage to a third of his battleships on March 18, de Robeck declined to continue the naval operation, preferring to await an amphibious assault on the peninsula the following month. Despite a commonly held belief to the contrary, de Robeck's decision was not based on a belief the Straits could not be forced but his conviction that a breakthrough would not facilitate the entrance into the Marmora of the large army that was then gathering in the Mediterranean to secure Constantinople.

CHAPTER 15

The Search for Troops II: An Army for the Dardanelles?

It is surprising, given Hankey's agitation and the mounting pressure within the Admiralty for military assistance, that neither influence bore directly on the decision to send troops to the Dardanelles.

The decision was made at an impromptu and informal meeting of the War Council on February 16. It is almost certain this meeting began after the Greek's flat rejection the same day of the Allied *demarche* to send a French and British Division to Salonika if the Greek Army went to the aid of Serbia.[1] Hankey records that the meeting "began as an informal conference between one or two Ministers, others subsequently being called in."[2]

As a result of this "scaled down"[3] War Council meeting, it was decided to make available the 29th Division in England and the Australia and New Zealand Army Corps (ANZACs) in Egypt to "support the attack on the Dardanelles."[4] Thus, in the space of one month, the War Council had traveled full circle: Asquith's sideshow had now become Hankey's "only extraneous operation worth trying."[5]

Hankey was greatly relieved by the decision. He wrote to Balfour, who had not attended the meeting, that all naval officers believed that sooner or later troops would be required. He was immensely relieved by the decision, although he feared it was too little too late.

Churchill was undoubtedly quite receptive to the idea the 29th Division being sent to the Dardanelles. It was obviously desirable to have troops available to capitalize on any success the fleet might have, and the force being discussed did not represent the full-scale commitment to a southern theater mooted by Lloyd George or Hankey in January, nor the substantial British commitment Kitchener had anticipated would be needed to storm the peninsula.

Churchill's attitude around this time seemed to mirror that of Callwell who had written to Robertson on February 4 in the following manner:

> K[itchener] and the Government are rather bitten with the idea of a big British force in Hungary and attacking the Germans from the south. It might come to that if matters remained in a state of impasse, say, in May. We want to get on now and have done with Austria-Hungary and Turkey, and so render any developments in the direction of making the Near East our own main theatre of war, out of the question. If I had my way I should be surely tempted to send the 29th Division and a Territorial division and a brigade of mounted troops with the least possible delay to the Aegean, because I believe that 40,000 British troops out there within a month might exert a very great effect upon the strategical situation as a whole, and I do not believe that the same force planted down in France or Flanders would make any very material difference at the present time.[6]

Churchill had anticipated some form of assistance from Russia and perhaps Greece or Romania. While the Dardanelles plan was developing, there had existed the possibility–prompted by Kitchener's pronouncement within the War Council—that Alexandretta would be attacked at the same time. By mid-February, this and other possibilities had either diminished or disappeared, and Churchill's naval-only plan to force the Straits was now seriously short of the moral or practical support that might be provided by a military force situated near by.

Moreover, in the preceding two days, Churchill had received memoranda from Jackson and Richmond strongly reinforcing the value of troops. If he needed any reminder of his war staff's sentiments, he received a note from Fisher that day: "I hope you were successful with Kitchener in getting a Division sent to Lemnos *tomorrow!* Not a grain of wheat will come from the Black Sea unless there is a military occupation of the Dardanelles!"[7]

Despite this very considerable push from his naval staff and the belated offer of military assistance, the essentials of the naval operation remained unchanged and Churchill did not seem inclined to change them.

Later in the day of February 16, a full sitting of the Cabinet was given the details of the attack, including the decision to support the operation with troops. One member of the Asquith Cabinet, Charles Hobhouse, recorded in his diary:

> The plan for attacking Constantinople was discussed. . . . No risks are to be run, and the operation may take a fortnight or 3 weeks. Meanwhile the Greeks are to evacuate Lemnos and we are to seize the island, station a division of troops there, *and subsequently are to occupy the Gallipoli peninsula. We are promised a military rising and ultimate revolution on the fall of the first fort. W.S.C. said policy was decided at War Council and he would take all responsibility.* (emphasis added)[8]

If this is an accurate reflection of the rather sanguine nature of the Cabinet's discussions and, in particular, Churchill's pronouncements at the meeting, it would appear that the apprehensions conveyed by Richmond and Jackson in their earlier memoranda had little bearing on the decision to send troops or Churchill's keenness to accept them. He intended to use the soldiers to occupy the peninsula only *after* the fleet had broken through. The War Council still anticipated that the moral impact of a successful bombardment and the fleet's entrance into the Marmora would result in the rapid capitulation of the Turks. A letter written to Kitchener by Churchill indicates that it might have been suggested at the Cabinet meeting that the Turks could be expected to evacuate the peninsula if the naval bombardment was successful. Once this had occurred, the peninsula could be occupied by the forces now made available to secure the Straits.

It is possible Churchill was forced down this path because Kitchener had offered him no alternative. Lord Esher recorded in his diary that Kitchener had told Churchill, "You get through! I'll find the men."[9] In other words, Kitchener was prepared to supply troops to occupy the peninsula after the fleet was in the Marmora and not to capture the Straits to help the fleet break through.

Even though this was probably true, Hobhouse's diary suggests that Churchill was entirely content with the situation as it stood and had made no effort to present to the Cabinet the arguments contained within Richmond's and Jackson's memoranda. Churchill's pronouncements reveal no expectation that the peninsula would have to be fought for and no intention to delay the naval operation for the arrival of troops to work in unison with the fleet.

At the Dardanelles Commission Inquiry, Churchill claimed he made Jackson's concerns clear to his colleagues earlier in the day. He asserted that he read parts of Jackson's memorandum at the impromptu War Council meeting, including the last two vital paragraphs, to support any decision to send troops:

> "The necessity of troops to support this heavy naval undertaking should never be lost sight of."
>
> I read that out to emphasize the need of troops. Troops were apparently now in existence, and Lord Fisher and I were pressing for them by every means. So I read out within 24 hours of my receiving it this demand for troops put at the end of Sir Henry Jackson's paper.[10]

To support his argument he quoted elements of the minutes of the meeting in which he had said the words "heavy naval undertaking," which were to be found in Jackson's memorandum.

Churchill's assertions would appear to be incorrect. There is evidence that reference was made to Jackson's memorandum, but this appears in the minutes of the War Council meeting of February 19, and not the meeting of February 16. No minutes of the February 16 meeting were kept. Only a summary exists of the conclusions written on February 17 by Hankey. The words "heavy naval undertaking" form part of the minutes of the meeting on February 19.

Whatever Churchill's assertions, it is extremely unlikely he would have dared to quote *verbatim* the last two vital paragraphs of Jackson's memorandum for, concerned as they were with the fleet's lines of communication, they are in fundamental disagreement with the Churchill plan to admit fully armored vessels into the Marmora, and with any idea of entering the Marmora, only after the peninsula had been secured. Moreover, it would have disclosed the belief of a senior adviser that the guns in the forts would need to be destroyed by soldiers and could not be destroyed by ships.

Despite the offer of a body of troops, the Churchill plan, which could not meet the growing expectations of the War Council, remained unchanged.

With a small force now available to assist the operation, on February 18, Churchill decided to add two extra battalions of Royal Marines and five battalions of the Royal Naval Division to the force to be sent to the Mediterranean. These troops were to go without artillery and were intended to "operate solely under the guns of the fleet."[11] He wrote to Kitchener, "If our operations at the Dardanelles prosper, immense advantages may be offered which cannot be gathered without military aid. The opportunity may come in 3 weeks time. And I think at least 50,000 men should be within reach at 3 days notice."[12]

Churchill's letter defined the support this force would give as "either seiz(ing) the Gallipoli Peninsula when it has been evacuated, or . . . occupy(ing) C'nople if a revolution takes place," although given the unpredictable political circumstances of Turkey and the Balkans—in particular the Greeks—he had not ruled out the possibility that this force's final resting place might be Salonika. "We should never forgive ourselves," he concluded, "if the naval operations succeeded and the 'fruits' were lost through the Army being absent."[13]

It is in this last sentence that one first sees the influence of Jackson's memorandum. It had been Jackson who had referred to securing the "fruits" of a successful naval operation. Churchill and Jackson, however, were defining the fruits of success quite differently. Churchill defined these as securing the peninsula if the Turks evacuated after or during a breakthrough into the Marmora, or occupying Constantinople if a revolution took place, or using the troops at Salonika to draw in Greece.

The fruit Jackson sought as a first preference was for the troops to work "in conjunction" with the fleet to secure a line of communication through the Marmora by the capture of the peninsula. As a second preference, he sought the final destruction of the forts by strong landing parties immediately after they had been silenced by the fleet. He had made clear that he considered the operation would be largely "fruitless" unless the troops destroyed the Turkish forces on the peninsula as well as their mobile guns and howitzers.

Despite Churchill's subsequent obfuscation on this point, the import of Jackson's and Richmond's memoranda was that soldiers would be required to *fight* for the peninsula. Neither Jackson nor Richmond appeared to countenance at all the idea that the Turks would conveniently rush from the peninsula the moment the fleet was through and, thereby, resolve many of the fears regarding communications. They were extremely reluctant to support Churchill's "cart before the horse" plan, which was to get the fleet through and then hope other events took place that secured the fleet's lines of communication.

The idea the Turkish troops on the peninsula would evacuate and allow its effortless occupation appears to have been a comparatively new fact and not at all part of the original Churchill formula. It contrasted with his January 28 observation that his plan was designed to admit fully armored vessels only into the Marmora. This implied the continued occupation of the peninsula by the Turks. It is evident from the foregoing that the source of such a proposition was neither Richmond nor Jackson.

The genesis of the "evacuation" theory is obscure but seems to have occurred at one of the two Cabinet meetings on February 18, although it might well have been earlier. Equally obscure is the origin (and author) of the complementary theory that, once the fleet broke through, it would sever the Turkish supply lines to the peninsula and the garrison would be forced to surrender or be starved into submission. Primarily for this reason, it was expected the Turks would evacuate the peninsula when success was imminent. Unwisely, this argument appeared to take no account at all of the difficulties the fleet would have with its own line of supplies.

It is desirable to address these issue amid our discussion of the February 16 War Council meeting and the Richmond and Jackson memoranda because this new fact slammed the door shut on Jackson's and Richmond's concerns over lines of communication. If the Turks were going to rush from the peninsula immediately after the fleet was through, there really was no problem of communications. British and ANZAC troops could occupy the peninsula at their leisure and, if required, mount mobile guns and howitzers to dominate the field forces on the other side of the Straits, or so it was believed.

Churchill had been thrown a timely lifeline to counter the growing apprehensions of his naval staff, which, if declared fully to his War Council colleagues, possibly would have resulted in the postponement or termination of his naval-only operation. The evacuation theory allowed him to transform an operation designed to admit fully armored ships into the Marmora into an operation that also would give the Gallipoli Peninsula to an Allied army without fighting for it.

Unfortunately for Churchill, there was a serious incompatibility between his call for 50,000 men—including the 29th Division—and the conviction, now beginning to resonate within the War Council, that the primary role of any force at the Dardanelles would be to occupy the Gallipoli Peninsula behind a *fleeing* enemy. This incompatibility became manifest when, against the competing needs of the Western Front, Kitchener reconsidered his decision to send the 29th Division to the Dardanelles. By degrees, this one issue of communication would unravel Churchill's naval-only scheme and complete its transformation to an amphibious attack on April 25, 1915.

NOTES

1. Elliot informed Grey that "co-operation of Greece was out of the question unless Roumania joined, not only by attacking Austria in Transylvania, but in conjunction with the Greek forces. He considered presence of the French and British divisions entirely insufficient to protect Greek flank, and repeated that for Greece to join Serbia under such conditions would be to commit suicide." Theodoulou, *Greece and the Entente,* 106–107.

2. See fn in Gilbert, *CVIII,* 516. The conclusions of the meeting can be found in CAB 22/1, also Gilbert, *CVIII,* 516.

3. The members present were Asquith, Lloyd George, Churchill, Fisher, Grey, and Kitchener. Hankey was informed of the proceedings on February 17 and wrote up the conclusions of the meeting.

4. Gilbert, *CVIII,* 515, Conclusions of War Council Meeting, Feb. 16, 1915.

5. Gilbert, *CVIII.* Letter Hankey to Balfour, February 10, 1915.

6. Callwell to Robertson, February 4, 1915, Robertson Papers.

7. Gilbert, *CVIII,* 471. This letter to Churchill is dated January 29 in the Companion Volume. This is incorrect. The correct date is February 16.

8. Edwards, *Inside Asquith's Cabinet,* 222.

9. 516. Excerpt from Lord Esher's Diary, February 16, 1915.

10. Ibid.

11. Gilbert, *CVIII,* 520. Memorandum, Churchill to Fisher and Oliver, February 18, 1915.

12. Gilbert, *CVIII,* 518–519. Letter, Churchill to Kitchener, February 18, 1915.

13. Ibid.

CHAPTER 16

The Search for Troops III: The 29th Division Withdrawn, War Council, February 19

At the War Council meeting on February 19, Kitchener announced that recent Russian setbacks meant the Germans would soon attempt a decisive victory in the west before the arrival of the New Armies. In the circumstances, he had decided to withhold the 29th Division. If more troops were needed for the Dardanelles, they could be drawn from Egypt.

Churchill, Grey, Lloyd George, and Asquith were all shocked by his decision. None agreed with his appreciation and argued that it would be Serbia that would be threatened by a setback in Russia, not the Western Front. Churchill considered the 29th Division essential to provide a "stiffening" for the ANZAC troops and his inexperienced Naval Division, and he thought it desirable to have a reserve on the spot. Lloyd George wanted even more troops to be sent, while Asquith argued that the best way to help Russia would be "to strike a big blow at the Dardanelles."[1]

Balfour, alone, was sympathetic to Kitchener's cause. He shared Kitchener's conviction that, if the Gallipoli Peninsula was occupied and the passage through the Dardanelles secured, Britain would achieve all that was required. At one point he declared that "if the Navy was successful at Gallipoli, the effect would be almost as great as the occupation of Constantinople."[2] He therefore could not understand Churchill's need for two army corps. Kitchener and Balfour each believed that the troops then on offer would be adequate to occupy the peninsula after the Turks had evacuated. The idea that the Turks would evacuate the peninsula once the fleet was through had now acquired a decisive currency.

Churchill was beginning to become entangled in a web of his own intrigue. His rosy view of his naval-only operation was now militating against even modest military support. He warned the War Council that the fleet could "only open the Straits for armoured ships, and could not guarantee an unmolested passage for merchant ships unless the shores of the Dardanelles were cleared of the enemy."[3] This repeated his January 28 assertion in the CID subcommittee meeting. It appeared to be an invitation to the War Council to consider that, even if the navy succeeded, the peninsula had to be cleared of Turkish troops to achieve this. While identifying an important flaw in his plan, in the hope this might secure troops necessary to reap the fruit of a naval success, Churchill went no further in describing the limitation of the naval-only operation. There was no mention here of the difficulties his fleet would have maintaining its own line of communication. In the circumstances, his comments did not have the desired effect.

The prime minister was led to read some extracts from a 1906 CID paper, on "The Possibility of a Joint Naval and Military Attack upon the Dardanelles," which, he noted, "tend(ed) to show that military co-operation was essential to success."[4] Desultory discussion followed during which the War Council endeavored to establish the relevance of the report to the present conditions. It is not possible to establish who said or argued what, but, according to Hankey's recollections, the sum of the discussions seemed designed to sustain Churchill's naval-only operation. Turkey continued to be perceived as a vulnerable and weak enemy, while modern developments served to enhance the efficacy of naval bombardment.[5] Churchill was caught between a rock and a hard place. To present a truly effective case for military assistance, he would have to compromise his entire naval operation.

The discussion of the CID paper failed entirely to draw the War Council to resolving the issue of military support. Lord Richard Haldane, who had not been present at the impromptu meeting on February 16 during which the decision to send troops had been made, rather pertinently pointed out that the War Council had neither established the number of troops required nor "the precise purpose for which they were to be used" at the Dardanelles.[6]

Kitchener merely repeated that he considered three divisions ample but did not elaborate on how he expected them to be used.

This was not good enough for Churchill, who then recalled the various phases of the Dardanelles:

> The first proposal was to send no troops at all, leaving the Dardanelles to be dealt with by the Navy. The next phase was that the 29th Division only was to be sent to Salonica with the view of thereby involving Greece in the war. Then the situation had again changed by the Russian defeat in the East, and it became desirable to ensure success in the Dardanelles. If this operation was successful, it was possible that the Greeks might change their minds, and that a complete change might be brought about in the Balkans.[7]

This was a reasonable assessment of the development of the Dardanelles operation. The War Council, indeed, had changed its expectations and now increasingly demanded definite results be gained from a successful entrance into the Marmora by the fleet. Meanwhile, as Churchill had asserted earlier in the meeting, the Balkan States he had hoped would be influenced by his operation were now somewhat cooler toward the Allies. The presence of a substantial body of troops could make all the difference.

Be this as it may, it was not only Kitchener's obstructionism regarding the 29th Division that limited the prospect of a adequate force being provided to support the operation, but Churchill's continued refusal to come clean over the issue of the fleet's lines of communication.

For Churchill to have secured the 29th Division, he needed to explain that the occupation of the peninsula was essential for the ultimate success of his armored fleet, which could not remain within the Marmora without coal, ammunition, and other supplies. So long as the Turks knew that their control of the peninsula must cause the fleet to return ignominiously through the Straits within weeks, the moral influence the fleet alone could exert on the Turks would be seriously compromised. Unless there was a substantial body of troops nearby to multiply the moral pressure on the Turkish soldiers on the peninsula and elsewhere, there would be little reason for evacuation, surrender, or revolution in Turkey. The operation would, therefore, remain the highly speculative operation conceived in January.

It would always be much better to have a force ready to exert a moral pressure on the Turks and Balkan States *before* the fleet broke into the Marmora than to bring it together after, especially if this success failed to result in the anticipated Turkish flight from the peninsula. If the Turks did not take flight during or immediately after a successful naval operation, the comparatively impotent status of the fleet inside the Marmora would soon become known.

Had Churchill declared all this, it would have been difficult for Kitchener to resist Churchill's pleas. Such a declaration, however, probably would have resulted in preparations for a full-scale assault on the peninsula in the spring or withdrawal from the operation altogether. Either alternative would have had disastrous results for Churchill's northern plans. Thus hamstrung, Churchill could make little inroads into Kitchener's expectation that the existing supply of troops would be ample to occupy the peninsula and to secure a passage of the Dardanelles after the fall of the forts.

At another point in the discussions, Balfour asked about "the precise political effect of an occupation of the Gallipoli Peninsula combined with naval command of the Sea of Marmora."[8]

Churchill broke in and said it would give the forces control of Turkey, while Kitchener believed "in this event the Turkish Army would evacuate Europe altogether."[9] This confident assertion forestalled any further discussion on how the peninsula was to be captured and the probable consequences of the peninsula remaining in Turkish hands. How were the modest forces available to occupy the peninsula in the face of a large, fully alert Turkish force, with ample time to reinforce, and that subsequently showed a disinclination to withdraw? What would be the consequences for the fleet and, indeed, the entire operation? How was the command of the Marmora to be achieved without the control of the Straits?

Although the meeting was lengthy and the debate hot, Kitchener could not be persuaded that the 29th Division should be sent immediately. The War Council agreed only to prepare transports to send the ANZAC troops to Lemnos and the 29th Division to the Mediterranean if required at a later date.

It was, however, not the end of discussion over the 29th Division or over the broader issue of sending troops. Although Churchill was insistent that a force of 50,000 was desirable to reap the fruits of a naval success, it was Lloyd George who was truly "pushing the envelope" as far as troops were concerned. During the meeting, he had identified 97,000 men available for "Constantinople or, if that operation failed, to support the Serbians."[10]

Lloyd George had reluctantly accepted that Churchill's Dardanelles operation had priority in the Mediterranean, but he had not forgotten his own eastern schemes nor had he lost his conviction that the war might be won in the east with a serious military offensive. Over the next several days, he would lead the fight for a substantial force to support the Dardanelles operation should a British fleet successfully enter the Marmora. Churchill would follow closely on Lloyd George's coattails and continue to pursue the 29th Division. Meanwhile, his inherently flawed naval operation—begun that very day—would proceed unaltered.

NOTES

1. Gilbert, *CVIII*, 527–534. Secretary's Notes of War Council Meeting, February 19, 1915. See also, CAB 42/1/36. This specific quotation, 529.
2. Ibid., 529.
3. Ibid., 531.
4. Ibid., 531–532.
5. Hankey was subsequently to assert a number of issues were considered. These included the following: "the adverse effect on Turkey of the severe defeats in the Balkan wars; the fact that Turkey was at war on three other fronts (the Caucasus, Egypt, and Mesopotamia); the hope that as a result of aircraft reconnaissance the value of naval bombardment would be greatly increased; and the belief that the development of the submarine would greatly harass Turkish communications with Gallipoli."
6. Gilbert, *CVIII*, 531–532. Secretary's Notes of War Council Meeting, February 19, 1915.
7. Ibid., 532.
8. Ibid., 533.
9. Ibid., 544.
10. Ibid. This comment by Lloyd Geoge, 529.

CHAPTER 17

The Search for Troops IV: The Lloyd George Memorandum

By the end of the third week of February, it was evident that most members of the War Council, including Churchill, believed that a substantial force should be made ready to take advantage of any gains achieved by a breakthrough of the fleet into the Marmora. The "advantage" considered most likely was the capture of the peninsula after the Turks had bolted. There was also some appreciation that the presence of troops would encourage the various Balkan States and discourage the Turks.

In the middle of February, Kitchener offered to send the 29th Division to the Mediterranean but reversed his decision on February 19. In its place, he offered to send more troops from Egypt. What has puzzled historians ever since was Churchill's insistence, despite the availability of other forces, that Kitchener should send the 29th Division at the earliest opportunity. This issue occupied much of the debate regarding troops within the War Council during late February, and it was pressed by a man who hitherto had been content with no military assistance at all. Why now such preoccupation with a single division?

It is important to understand that the difference between Kitchener and Churchill was not so much *if* the 29th Division would be sent, but *when*. Kitchener was comfortable with delaying the 29th Division's departure until the Western Front was deemed secure and until the naval operation had made substantial progress. He anticipated that if the fleet were successful, the Turks would evacuate the peninsula and there would be sufficient troops to secure the peninsula thereafter without the assistance of the 29th Division.

Churchill wanted the 29th Division available and ready immediately. Recent histories have noted the inconsistency between Churchill's advocacy of a naval-only operation in January and his repeated demands for this division in February and March. As will be seen, it confused some of his colleagues as well. The difficulty Churchill faced was in explaining why this particular division was immediately important if, in the first part of the operation, they were needed only to occupy the peninsula after the Turks had withdrawn? Surely other soldiers could do this?

Inevitably, the suspicion arose among his colleagues, and this remains the thesis of some historians, that Churchill had lost confidence in his naval-only operation and intended the 29th Division to be part of a force that would take the peninsula. In the following chapters, it will be argued that this was not the case. Despite the pressing need for the 29th Division, Churchill was meticulous in maintaining the naval-only integrity of his operation, despite its serious flaws. Instead, he viewed the 29th Division as a force most likely to expedite the Dardanelles operation, help secure rapid success, and help him maintain a viable timetable for his northern offensives. The 29th Division was intended to secure Balkan support—in particular that of the Greeks—and apply pressure to the Turks. Despite Lloyd George's aspirations, Churchill still hoped to contain any commitment to a southern theater so he could press on with his northern schemes. The 29th Division was a modest price to pay.

* * * * *

Despite Kitchener's *volte face* over the 29th Division on February 19, Churchill drafted instructions the following day requesting the organization of transportation for his Royal Naval Division and the 29th Division in anticipation the latter might be sent at a later date. The Royal Naval Division was to be sent without its usual train of equipment and would go directly to Lemnos where it would wait aboard ship for operations.

Additionally, Churchill informed Kitchener in a minute accompanying these instructions that he wanted transports organized for a force of 8,000 or 10,000 infantry from Egypt to be ready by February 27 should the Dardanelles operation "take a favourable turn."[1] In this case, he informed Kitchener, in an obvious acceptance of the emergent evacuation theory, it would "be vital to have enough men to hold the lines of Bulair."[2] The 2,000 marines then at Lemnos would not be sufficient. If the "operations in the Dardanelles take a leisurely course" this emergency action might not be needed. In such circumstances, the ships collected "would form part of a larger fleet of transports" for a force of approximately 40,000 men.

Kitchener was confused by Churchill's reference to holding the lines of Bulair and asked "Is it to prevent the 75,000 Turks from escaping? I hardly think we should have enough for this at night if they are determined to get through."[3] Churchill replied that it was intended to prevent the peninsula from being reoccupied if the Turks cleared out: "As to cutting off their retreat—that is much more ambitious and only a good General on the spot can judge that. It may be that a part will go and the next might be cut off."[4]

This disconcerting mixture of optimism and arrogance represented the new foundations of the naval-only operation. Churchill's unmodified view of the power of naval bombardment and Kitchener's unshakeable belief in the limited martial prowess of the Turks had combined to sustain an operation that few advisers, naval or military, had the heart or the stomach for. Rather than challenge Kitchener's expectation the Turks would evacuate the peninsula, Churchill merely sought a small force to prevent their return once this unlikely event occurred. The idea of occupying Bulair would soon give birth to an even more bizarre leap of faith designed to sustain the naval-only operation in the face of Kitchener's optimistic expectations.

Kitchener already had telegraphed Maxwell, informing him that a force was being concentrated at Lemnos (presumably Churchill's marines) "to give co-operation that may be required and to occupy any captured forts"[5] and ordering a force of 30,000 ANZACs be prepared for service and transportation to Lemnos any time after March 9. Now, in keeping with Churchill's request, Kitchener instructed Maxwell to get in touch with Admiral Carden and be prepared to send him a considerable force should it be needed before this date.[6]

Churchill's call for military assistance did not alter the naval-only operation in the slightest degree. If it represented a concession to Jackson's concerns, it hardly met his case. If the Turks did not panic, there was no hope this force could achieve anything of value. Anything short of an absolute rout and there was little hope that Bulair, by far the most heavily fortified and entrenched part of the peninsula, would fall to any landing from either outside or inside the Straits. The soldiers were to react to opportunities, not create them. The fleet would do all the hard work on its own. If the fleet did break through, its lines of communication would only be secured with the Turks full cooperation.

While Churchill was ensuring the assistance of his "advanced party" to capitalize on an unexpected success, Lloyd George was readying to do combat with Kitchener for even more troops. On February 22, he circulated a memorandum that took the next logical step for use of troops at the Dardanelles. His memorandum reiterated the concerns he had voiced at the February 19 War Council meeting regarding the Dardanelles adventure. He wanted a force ready not only to occupy Gallipoli but also adequate to "establish our supremacy in that quarter."[7] If this were supplied, he believed "Rumania Greece and . . . probably, Bulgaria would declare for us." Without an army, he argued, the advantages gained from the navy's success would be lost.[8] Unwittingly, Lloyd George was wrapping Churchill ever more deeply in the threads of his dilemma. If it were intended a force would be used to fight the Turks other than on the peninsula, how were they to get there? Surely Churchill's plan designed to admit fully armored vessels only into the Marmora could not provide a solution to this prickly question? Churchill, however, would quickly contrive an answer.

Fisher, for one, was quite taken by the paper. He wrote to Lloyd George on February 23, "I am in complete accord with your phenomenal paper! Yesterday I had to write these following words to a most influential personage. <u>Rashness in War is Prudence—and Prudence in war is Criminal</u> <u>The Dardanelles futile without soldiers!"</u>[9]

Coincidentally, or perhaps inspired by Lloyd George's memorandum and prodded a little by Fisher, Churchill took up the cudgel and began drafting a memorandum of his own before the War Council meeting scheduled for the next day.[10] In it, he identified a force of 109,000 men—including the 29th Division and a Territorial Division from England—he considered were now available to support the Dardanelles operation:

> With proper military and naval co-operation, and with forces which are available, we can make certain of taking Constantinople by the end of March, and capturing or destroying all Turkish forces in Europe (except any that shut themselves up in Adrianople). This blow can be struck before the fate of Serbia is decided. Its effect on the whole of the Balkans will be decisive.[11]

Churchill believed all these were capable of being concentrated within striking distance of the Bulair Isthmus by the end of March if orders were given immediately. As soon as the Dardanelles were open they could "occupy Constantinople, taking the lines of Chataldja in reverse. Operating from the Constantinople peninsula and protected on three sides by the Allied fleet they would be in a position to compel the surrender of any Turkish forces in Europe."

In the closing lines of this memorandum, Churchill observed that "[t]his army is also well placed for future contingencies which cannot now be foreseen."[12] He then nominated a number of southern operations, most of which represented discussion from earlier meetings.

The import of the final lines of this memorandum is that Churchill had at last succumbed to the southern strategy promoted by Lloyd George and Hankey, but had he? Had he finally conceded that his northern plans would be lost in the development of a southern offensive on a grand scale? A clue to the answer lies in his, as yet, uncirculated memorandum: "With proper military and naval co-operation, and with forces which are available, we can make certain of taking Constantinople by the *end of March*" (emphasis added).[13]

Churchill was continuing to work rather earnestly to his own private timetable. He wanted any moral advantage to be gained by the presence of the 29th Division to act on the Turks and Balkan States before and immediately after the fleet had broken through and not at some uncertain point in the future. Kitchener's wait-and-see approach ensured delay and increased the prospect that, although the fleet might break through, all advantage might be lost.

Churchill's draft memorandum spoke to the inclination of members of the War Council (like Lloyd George and Hankey) who hoped a successful naval operation might lead to a British-led southern offensive. He would not have failed to understand that, in the climate prevailing within the War Council at the time, it would be these arguments that would secure the 29th Division at the earliest opportunity. Two regular units (the 29th Division and a Territorial Division) drawn from Europe—perhaps temporarily—still remained well short of Lloyd George's large-scale use of the New Armies mooted in January. These forces, combined with a successful naval attack, might still be sufficient to arrest the southern avalanche.

The other line of argument, always open to Churchill, he still refused to take. Had he been truly committed to a southern offensive, he would have outlined more fully the limitations of his naval-only operation and pressed unreservedly for an amphibious assault. This, however, would have signified failure and caused immeasurable delay. While prospects for success in the Mediterranean would have been improved, it would have been fatal to his northern aspirations, which all the while were progressing with the completion of a large force of monitors, landing barges, and other paraphernalia.

Thus Churchill drafted his memorandum seeking the immediate assistance of the 29th Division while continuing to press on with the naval-only operation. For the time being, it remained only a draft and, although he spoke of it at the meeting the following day, it was not circulated until, after amendment, several days later. Instead, he chose to support Lloyd George who was the most active in calling for troops within the War Council. Despite their efforts, neither he nor Lloyd George had been able to persuade Kitchener that the 29th Division should be added *immediately* to the large body of troops already available to take advantage of the fleet's success. The War Council meeting of February 24, however, would provide each with yet another opportunity to do so.

NOTES

1. Gilbert, *CVIII*, 536. Winston Churchill Minute (no title).

2. Gilbert, *CVIII*, 535, Churchill to Kitchener, February 20, 1915. Bulair was the narrow but heavily fortified neck of the Gallipoli Peninsula. Churchill routinely underestimated the difficulties any force, naval or military, would have in capturing this position.

3. Kitchener to Churchill, Gilbert, *CVIII*, 537.

4. Gilbert, *CVIII*, 535, Churchill to Kitchener, February 20, 1915.

5. Gilbert, *CVIII*, 537–538. Telegram, Kitchener to Maxwell, February 20, 1915.

6. Ibid., 537–538. Somewhat confusingly in the very next sentence Kitchener told Maxwell to gather transports to send troops immediately to Lemnos.

7. Gilbert, *CVIII*, 544–547. Memorandum by Lloyd George, *Some Further Considerations on the Conduct of the War, February 22, 1915.* Also, CAB 42/1/39.

8. Gilbert, *CVIII*, 544–547.

9. Gilbert, *CVIII*, 547, fn. Fisher to Lloyd George, February 23, 1915.

10. Gilbert, *CVIII*, 547–548. Memorandum, Winston S. Churchill, February 23, 1915.

11. Ibid.

12. Ibid. The Chatalja Lines were Turkish defensive lines protecting Constantinople from the west.

13. Ibid.

CHAPTER 18

The Search for Troops V: The War Council Meeting, February 24

The meeting of the War Council on February 24 began with a general discussion of troop movements to support the Dardanelles operation. It was explained by Churchill and Kitchener that 2,000 marines were at Lemnos and an advanced party of 10,000 troops from Egypt was being organized for "unexpected contingencies."

Balfour, not unreasonably, was concerned over how this small "advanced party" of troops was to be used and asked, "if the strength of the garrison of the Gallipoli Peninsula was known?"

Kitchener indicated that although intelligence was not good on this point, the garrison was believed to be about 40,000. At this point, he made the surprising declaration that he wished to learn from Carden as "to the possibilities of landing a force to attack the forts in the rear, and also as to the possibility of holding the Bulair."[1]

Kitchener's inquiry regarding landing a force to attack the forts in the rear was quite remarkable. It suggested that, in addition to preparing a force to hold Bulair should the Turks evacuate the peninsula, he was beginning to consider a full-scale assault on the peninsula if they did not. It is possible this inquiry may have been prompted by the intelligence—apparently gained from Carden—that only 40,000 enemy soldiers were on the peninsula and not the 75,000 Kitchener had suggested to Churchill several days earlier. It certainly represented a sudden change of thought. He had only just completed and circulated a memorandum entitled "Remarks by the

Secretary of State for War on the Chancellor of the Exchequer's Memorandum on the Conduct of the War" in which he had declared there were not enough troops available to capture the Gallipoli Peninsula.[2] Perhaps now Kitchener was beginning to consider it possible that the peninsula might be attacked with a force somewhat smaller than the 150,000 he had thought in early January would be necessary for such an operation.

Unknown to both Kitchener and Churchill at this time, a rather surprised and confused Carden already had expressed to General Birdwood, Commander ANZAC Corp., Egypt, how he might use the advanced party of troops Churchill and Kitchener were organizing for him.[3] Unaware that the offer of these troops was based on the grandiose possibilities of "Turkish evacuations" and the "occupation of Bulair," Carden indicated that he might use them to occupy the tip of the peninsula should they be needed to reduce the threat of mobile guns against the bombarding squadron once inside the Straits.[4] The proposal was not at all what Churchill had had in mind for this advanced force, and he would soon make clear that these troops were to be used to *secure* the success of the fleet and not to achieve it.

Kitchener's evacuation theory received remarkably little critical analysis from the War Council either at this meeting or any other. When Haldane sought to know if the Turks could be driven out of the Gallipoli Peninsula by naval attack alone, his curiosity was immediately struck down by Kitchener who stated, "if the fleet succeeded in silencing the forts, the garrison of Gallipoli would probably be withdrawn. Otherwise they would run the risk of being cut off and starved out."[5] The starvation scenario now formally stood alongside the evacuation scenario as a reason to press on with the naval-only operation rather than seriously consider taking the peninsula first.

When the idea that the Turks might be starved into submission was considered seriously, it was found to be fallacious. The Turks had ample supplies on the peninsula and further supplies were not likely to be cut off absolutely in any circumstance. Meanwhile, the fleet inside the Marmora would face an equal or more serious risk to its own lines of supply.[6] Churchill was entirely mute on such issues within the War Council. Even more culpably, he appears never to have broached such possibilities with Carden or de Robeck, while the one line of inquiry initiated by Kitchener was, as will be seen, short-circuited by Churchill. Although for different reasons, Churchill wished no more than Kitchener to see his naval-only operation transmuted into a full-scale amphibious assault.

The only concession he made was to continue pressing for the 29th Division because its presence in the Mediterranean might just make the difference between sustained Turkish resistance and a Turkish rout and Balkan intervention. He argued that "with a comparatively small number of troops we might be in Constantinople by the end of March. No one could tell how far-reaching the results of such an operation might be. Moreover we were now absolutely committed to seeing through the attack on the Dardanelles."[7] He enumerated the force identified in his memorandum of the day before (but which he had not yet circulated to the War Council) and claimed that all could be in the Levant by March 21.

Kitchener began to tire of Churchill's persistence. Convinced the Turks would run and, therefore, unable to understand Churchill's need for the 29th Division, he finally asked if Churchill was now contemplating a land attack. Churchill replied that he was not, but he thought it quite conceivable that the naval attack might be held up temporarily by mines and some local operation required. Why mines would result in local military operations on the peninsula is obscure, but his reference to "local operations" was fair and accurate.[8] He had already initiated preparations for a substantial force for such operations. It cannot be assumed that Churchill's response to Kitchener's question meant he intended to use the 29th Division for these minor operations, or that Kitchener understood as much. Churchill was simply stating that "local operations" would be required, and this was common knowledge.

Despite Churchill's response, Kitchener pressed his advantage. He wanted to know what this force would do when it reached the Dardanelles. Repeating the lines of his memorandum, Churchill replied:

> [T]hey could be put into Constantinople . . . or European Turkey towards the Bulgarian frontier . . . the allied forces could then be sent up through Bulgaria to Nish . . . another plan would be to send them to Salonika . . . or they might be sent up the Danube.[9]

This prompted Haldane to ask whether there were not 200,000 Turkish troops in Thrace and whether the risk to the British forces would not be very great.

Lloyd George, like Kitchener, was also concerned that Churchill's call for troops meant he was now endeavoring to convert the naval attempt into a joint operation. After all, it had been Churchill's naval-only operation that had torpedoed his Salonika option and his plans for a great southern offensive. He was not about to let Churchill wriggle out of his commitment now. Was it being proposed, he asked, "that the Army should be used to undertake an operation in which the Navy had failed?"

Churchill once again asserted it was not his intention but could conceive "a case where the Navy had almost succeeded, but where a military force would just make a difference between failure and success."

In such circumstances, Kitchener declared, he could not "understand the purpose for which so many troops were to be used" and reiterated his conviction that as soon as the forts were being silenced, one by one, the entire Turkish army (including the Gallipoli garrison) would decamp to Asia. He foresaw little fighting at all and believed that with patience and wise negotiation any forces guarding Constantinople probably would surrender.[10]

Churchill drew his response directly from Lloyd George's memorandum, although the sentiments were not unlike those he had expressed himself on February 19: "troops would be required to support our diplomacy." Churchill was declaring his wish for a moral margin to ensure the success of the naval-only operation and limit the likelihood of it sliding into a full-scale amphibious assault on the peninsula. Kitchener was rather perversely arguing the forces available, none truly efficient, would be adequate for the purpose. He need only have asked himself what might be the consequences if the Turkish army did not decamp to the Asian shore as he prophesied.

After considerably more discussion, Kitchener finally conceded the army's intention "to see the business through," if the fleet could not get through the Straits unaided. This was a somewhat strange thing to do given that most of the discussion had surrounded the use of troops *after* the fleet had broken through. Nevertheless, it was a landmark decision and, had Churchill truly been driven by a surreptitious desire to secure troops for an amphibious assault, from this point he ought to have considered his mission accomplished.

Churchill, however, refused to relent. Kitchener's concession to "see the business through" did not signify his intention to send out the 29th Division *immediately*, and therefore this did not satisfy Churchill. Once again taking a lead from Lloyd George's memorandum, Churchill said the main aim of the operations:

> should be to get the Balkans out. The capture of Constantinople was a means to this end. The presence of 100,000 men would

> have a great moral effect. Up to now our diplomacy had been paralysed because we had nothing to offer. If we could make an offer we might bring out a million men in the Balkans. He would be willing to send a quarter of a million men to effect this result, if we had them.[11]

Without a doubt, Churchill was overstating his willingness to commit troops to the southern theater. It was entirely inconsistent with his previous pronouncements. With his heart, if not his mind at this juncture, firmly with his northern schemes, he would not have wanted a quarter of a million men diverted to the Mediterranean and he would make this clear several days later. What he did want was a rapid resolution to this southern adventure and a result in which the Balkan States carried the bulk of responsibility. If an extra division of troops would make a decisive difference, he wanted them immediately.

Churchill's comments prompted Balfour to observe that the Dardanelles operation had perhaps two objectives: "our immediate objective was Constantinople in order to open the Black Sea, obtain the Russia wheat, and obtain a line of communication with Russia. Our ultimate object might be a much larger operation."[12]

Balfour's declaration identified a fundamental difference between Churchill and other members of the War Council. Despite his most recent assertions, Churchill, first and foremost, saw the attack on Turkey as an operation designed to bring in the Balkan States without a major military commitment. He had conceived the naval-only operation to preempt a larger operation, not to precipitate it. Even had the Balkan States failed to come in, Churchill would have been more than content had the fleet managed to destroy the *Goeben* and *Breslau*.

Balfour was suggesting that bringing in the Balkans and perhaps working alongside them in a major offensive might be a subsequent and *ultimate* object of the operation as originally proposed and that the *immediate* object of the Dardanelles operation was the capture of Constantinople and the defeat of Turkey. Balfour had consistently misunderstood and overstated the prospects of the original scheme. He had failed to grasp that, under Churchill's original, highly speculative, conception, the "immediate" objectives of which he now spoke—that is, the capture of Constantinople and the defeat of Turkey—had never been likely *unless* the actions of the fleet had inspired the assistance of Balkan armies.

Churchill ought to have argued that Balfour's expectations of Russian wheat and secure lines of communications through the

Bosporus for trade with Russia were unlikely under a naval-only operation. He had twice before touched lightly on the fact that the fleet could not secure a safe passage for merchant vessels, but Balfour still appeared not to understand this. Again, to have effectively curtailed Balfour's rather fanciful expectation, he would have drawn too near to explaining the full implications of the fleet entering the Marmora *before* the Straits had been secured. So profound would have been the consequence for his naval-only operation and near-term northern schemes, he remained unwilling to do this. Instead he had allowed the War Council to be swept away by Kitchener's and, to a lesser extent, his own contention that the Turks would rush from the peninsula and, indeed, from European Turkey once the fleet was in the Marmora. In doing so, he was unable to sustain an effective argument against Kitchener and Balfour for the immediate transportation of the 29th Division to the Mediterranean.

Ironically, despite his refusal to send the 29th Division, Kitchener appeared to be moving ever closer to serious amphibious operations on the peninsula. The War Council meeting closed with Churchill promising to put to Carden those questions posed by Kitchener early in the meeting, while Kitchener promised to instruct Birdwood to discuss the prospective use of troops with Carden. What Kitchener did not declare was that he had already telegraphed Maxwell on the morning of February 23 requesting to consult with Carden on a number of issues. He wanted to know the following:

- What were the number and location of Turkish troops?
- Whether Carden considered troops would be needed to take the forts, and how many?
- Would troops be needed to take forts in reverse?
- Would the Bulair lines have to be held?
- Would operations on the Asiatic side of the peninsula be advisable?

Although his profoundly optimistic pronouncements within the War Council would suggest otherwise, these questions indicate Kitchener was harboring serious doubts about the operation and was anticipating an amphibious assault on the peninsula at some point in the future.

Churchill, on the other hand, was not yet ready to surrender his naval-only operation and took an immediate opportunity to make clear to Vice Admiral Carden that the operation would go ahead as planned.

Entirely ignorant of Kitchener's communications with Maxwell, he drafted a telegram to Carden requesting a response to the same set of questions Kitchener had sent Maxwell, and he showed it to him before the War Council meeting dispersed.[13]

Later in the day, Churchill learned of Carden's correspondence with Birdwood in which Carden had outlined a plan to use the advanced party of 10,000 men to occupy the southern end of the peninsula. Concerned that Carden's communications with Birdwood preempted his own questions, Churchill informed Kitchener he had decided not to send his telegram until Carden and Birdwood had had further discussions. Churchill then set about sending two telegrams to Carden designed to keep the essentially naval-only operation firmly on track.[14]

The first was an official telegram signed by Jackson. Carden was informed that the War Office did not consider his suggestion to use the troops on offer to take the tip of the peninsula "an obligatory operation for ensuring success of first main object which is to destroy the permanent batteries."[15] Some troops were to be held in readiness for minor operations such as destroying masked batteries and engaging enemy forces but the "main army" was to remain at Lemnos until the fleet had forced the passage when "holding Bulair lines may be necessary to stop all supplies reaching the peninsula."[16]

Churchill then took the rather curious step of reinforcing this message in a telegram of his own, which he also forwarded to Kitchener: "The operation on which you are engaged consists in forcing the Dardanelles without military assistance, as generally described in your telegram No. 19 of the 11th January and in your instructions from the Admiralty."[17]

He informed Carden that he should use only his small parties of marines to destroy particular guns and torpedo tubes. The other forces were being sent to "reap the fruits" if his operation were successful. The 10,000 men offered, some in Egypt, some in Lemnos, were for "unexpected contingencies, should your operations proceed more rapidly than had been estimated." They were not to be used "in present circumstances to assist the naval operations which are independent and self contained." He advised Carden that the 29th Division might be sent, but they did not affect his immediate operations.

It seems reasonable to assume that these telegrams were motivated to some extent by the concerns expressed by Kitchener and Lloyd George at the War Council meeting that Churchill's call for more troops concealed an intention to have the army undertake a full-scale invasion of the peninsula. The telegrams also were driven by Churchill's own desires to sustain the naval-only integrity of the operation. It is important to observe that, as per the early February Admiralty memoranda, and in notable contrast to Jackson's memorandum of mid-February, neither message includes any intention to use any of the forces near the Dardanelles to complete the destruction of the guns inside the forts.

Carden's recommendation of how the advanced party of 10,000 troops might be used indicated he was of a mind to respond to Kitchener's questions in a way that would propel the operation rapidly toward an attempt to take the forts in the rear by a full-scale military operation. The telegrams were a powerful antidote. From this point forward, Carden and de Robeck clearly understood that it was their job to force the Straits with the minimum assistance from the forces being gathered in the Mediterranean. Nevertheless, over the next few days, they took every opportunity to land forces to complete the destruction of the forts at the entrance of the Dardanelles.

Having successfully reinforced the naval-only operation, Churchill's efforts were now duplicated by Kitchener. After he had read Carden's telegram to Birdwood, the official Admiralty reply composed by Jackson, and Churchill's personal telegram to Carden,[18] Kitchener telegraphed Maxwell that the object of the operation was to gain entrance to the Marmora mainly by naval means, gain possession of the Bosporus, and overawe Constantinople. A successful operation would "doubtless" see the retirement of the Gallipoli garrison and allow a force to occupy the peninsula.[19]

He told Maxwell that "there would be no objection to the employment of a military force to secure hold of forts or positions already gained and dominated by naval fire so as to prevent their re-occupation or repair of damage by the enemy." He instructed that the brigade and equipment be sent immediately to Lemnos and the "rest of the Australian and New Zealand force be in readiness to embark at Alexandria at short notice."

Kitchener's telegram to Maxwell set the parameters for the Birdwood and Carden discussions much in the same manner that Churchill's telegram had done with Carden. Despite the availability of troops, the operation would remain essentially naval only. Unlike Carden and de Robeck, however, Maxwell and Birdwood had been blessed with an insight into why, despite the availability of troops, there was no intention within the War Council to authorize a joint operation to take the peninsula. The first reason, undoubtedly no surprise, was an insufficiency of the troops available to take the peninsula against a determined Turkish opposition. The second reason was Kitchener's conviction the Turks would be unable or unwilling to hold the peninsula once the fleet was through.

Kitchener's advice to Maxwell differed with Churchill's advice to Carden in two other important respects. First, Kitchener had given permission for some and perhaps all of 10,000 troops readied for immediate use in Egypt to be used for minor operations. Churchill had told Carden he could only use his small force of marines. Second, Kitchener wrote of using these forces for operations in and around the forts, including ensuring that the Turkish guns could not be re-used. Churchill wrote only of destroying "particular" guns—presumably mobile ones—with his marines and, should the opportunity arise, occupying Bulair with the additional force. Although Kitchener was apparently some way along this line of thinking, it would be some time yet before Churchill was prepared to address the fiction that the forts could be "destroyed" by the fleet alone and before he conceded that additional forces would be needed to put them *permanently* out of action.

Kitchener's telegram also requested Birdwood inform him how many troops he believed would be needed for operations on the peninsula and how many would be required for further enterprises after the Dardanelles had been forced. He wanted an appreciation of the likely reaction to success at Constantinople, Birdwood's private assessment of the current operations, and, finally, whether he thought success would be achieved without a full-scale operation to take the forts in reverse.

All these questions suggest that, whatever Churchill's actions to the contrary, Kitchener was gearing himself for a possible assault on the peninsula. Churchill, however, continued to resist such a prospect and, two days later at the War Council meeting of February 28, he would formally reaffirm the naval-only nature of the Dardanelles operation.

NOTES

1. CAB 42/1/42, Secretary's Notes of War Council Meeting, Feb. 24, 1915.

2. CAB 42/1/45, *The War: Remarks by the Secretary of State for War on the Chancellor of the Exchequer's memorandum on the Conduct of the War,* February 25, 1915.

3. Prior suggests Carden was informed troops would be forthcoming through a minute written by Churchill on February 20. See Prior, "Churchill's 'World Crisis,'" 281. For a copy of the minute, see Gilbert, *CVIII*, 536. Carden's response to Maxwell at this time was that since there had only been one day's firing he could only reply that there was no immediate need for troops.

4. Gilbert, *CVIII*, 549. Telegram, Vice-Admiral Carden to Lieutenant-General B irdwood, February 25, 1915.

5. CAB 42/1/42, Secretary's Notes of War Council Meeting, Feb. 24, 1915.

6. It appears that it was not until early April that Churchill explored the problems the Turks might have with water on the peninsula. This, too, proved a dead end. See Churchill to de Robeck, April 6, de Robeck to Churchill, April 7, and Balfour to Churchill, April 8, Gilbert, *CVIII*, 774–775, 777, 779.

7. CAB 42/1/42, Secretary's Notes of War Council Meeting, Feb. 24, 1915.

8. A possible explanation is to be found in the memorandum prepared by Oliver and sent to Carden in early February. Oliver wrote of using Royal Marines to destroy "mining stations and fire-observation stations." Prior, on the other hand, believes this concealed Churchill's intention to undertake a land attack: "if the naval attack was held up by mines, the only effective help that could be rendered by the military was the occupation of the peninsula." Thus, Churchill was indeed contemplating a land attack but, because of his constant advocacy of the purely naval operation, could not say so directly." See Prior, "Churchill's 'World Crisis,'" 279.

9. CAB 42/1/42, Secretary's Notes of War Council Meeting, Feb. 24, 1915.

10. Gilbert, *CVIII*, 559.

11. CAB 42/1/42, Secretary's Notes of War Council Meeting, Feb. 24, 1915. Also Gilbert, *CVIII*, 560.

12. Ibid.

13. Ibid., 549. It seems probable that the War Council meeting accepted as occurring in the morning of February 24—and recorded by Hankey as such—actually took place in the evening of February 23. A letter written by Asquith to Venetia Stanley at 3:30 P.M. on February 23 records, "A much more serious thing is coming up at 6, when we have another War Council," Brock and Brock, *H. H. Asquith's Letters*, 445. There is no reference to a War Council meeting on February 24 in his correspondence. However, a letter written on February 25 indicates a Cabinet meeting took place on both of these dates. The next War Council meeting mentioned is the one that occurred February 26. Churchill indicates he showed his draft letter to Kitchener during the Cabinet meeting in the morning of February 24. In the main body of this work, I have assumed that the War Council meeting occurred in the morning of February 24. However, it is my guess, the War Council meeting occurred on the previous night. Churchill most likely drafted his telegram shortly thereafter and showed it to Kitchener during

the Cabinet meeting of February 24. Later in the morning, he became aware of the correspondence between Birdwood and Carden and decided not to send it. However, it is worth noting that, in Gilbert's companion volume, Gilbert has the same letter from Asquith to Stanley dated February 24, thereby assuming the War Council meeting took place at 6:00 P.M. on February 24. This could not have been the case. Gilbert, *CVIII*, part 1, 554–555. If the meeting did take place in the evening, it had to have been the evening of February 23. These are minor matters, but are worthy of correction.

14. Ibid., 550.

15. Gilbert, *CVIII*, 551. Telegram Jackson to Carden, February 24th, 1915.

16. Ibid., 551. At the Dardanelles Inquiry, Churchill claimed that Jackson had come to him with a draft after discussions at the War Office, where it had been made clear that the "advanced party" of 10,000 troops were not to be used in the manner Carden had suggested. However, there is absolutely no hint in Churchill's letter to Kitchener that Churchill was responding to a request from the War Office. Rather, there is a sense that the initiative was entirely Churchill's and that it was his intention to maintain the naval-only integrity of the Dardanelles operation. At the War Council meeting when he spoke of this telegram, he made no mention of the War Office and spoke of it being an Admiralty decision to send it. It is important to note that there is no intention in either message to use forces to complete the destruction of the guns in the forts.

17. Gilbert, *CVIII*, Telegram, Churchill to Carden, February 24, 1915, 10.30 P.M.

18. This is assumed because Kitchener proceeds to mention a figure of 40,000 Turks on the peninsula. This is the number mentioned by Carden in his telegram.

19. Gilbert, *CVIII*, 551–552. Telegram, Kitchener to Maxwell, February 24, 1915.

CHAPTER 19

The Search for Troops VI: The War Council Meeting, February 26: The Balfour Memorandum and Churchill's Reaffirmation of the Naval-Only Operation

The War Council met again on February 26 and, again, the most important agenda item was troops for the Dardanelles. Two memoranda were to be at the center of these discussions. One was Churchill's completed but, as yet, uncirculated memorandum addressed to Asquith, Lloyd George, and Balfour.[1] It was identical to the draft he had written on February 23 save four points.

The first was a new two-paragraph introduction denying Kitchener's argument that the Western Front was threatened by a transfer of troops from the east and that the result could be influenced by the British divisions wanted in the Mediterranean.

The second was that Churchill now calculated 115,000 troops were available for operations against Turkey instead of 109,000 mentioned in the first memorandum. Churchill believed these troops could be concentrated at the Bulair Isthmus by March 21 if orders were given immediately.

The third and most significant point was that, following Kitchener's commitment at the previous War Council that his army would "see things through," Churchill now added to the final paragraph that "if the naval operations have not succeeded by then (March 21), they can be used to attack the Gallipoli Peninsula and make sure that the fleet gets through."

The fourth change was that he had dropped the final line of his draft, which suggested that the various strategic moves into

Bulgaria, Romania, and Serbia could be made "either simultaneously with, or in advance of, the dispatch of a larger force." Evidently, he now thought better of advocating a plan with which he did not agree to secure the two extra divisions he hoped would lead to the rapid defeat of Turkey and the intervention of Bulgaria, Romania, and Greece.

Churchill spoke to the sentiments of his memorandum throughout the meeting. His memorandum was effectively a declaration to persist with the naval-only operation until all the troops then available had been collected in Egypt. If it succeeded, they would be sent over Bulair and on to Constantinople. If it had not succeeded, the troops would be used in an amphibious assault on the peninsula.

The second memorandum discussed at the meeting was prepared by Balfour and entitled *The War*.[2] There was little common ground between this and Churchill's. Balfour's document was a reaction to Kitchener's argument with Churchill over the 29th Division. Kitchener had said there were already troops enough if the navy did its job. Churchill had said the 29th Division was needed immediately but had generally—but not exclusively—spoken of using the 29th Division in operations *after* the navy had been successful. Balfour was trying to address the inconsistency.

Elaborating on his comments at the previous War Council meeting, Balfour argued that "the forcing of the Dardanelles is the preliminary stage of *two* military operations." He called these the Bosporus operation, by which he meant the securing of free communication with Russia, and the Balkan operation, which would include measures to bring in Romania, Greece, and possibly Bulgaria against the Central Powers.

He was certain that the War Council "*must* send as many troops as may be required to make the Bosporus operation, to which we are now committed, a success." He appeared to assume this was about 40,000 men. However, he did not believe any more should be sent until two questions had been answered: "Do we want the Balkan States to join us at once? And (b) Would sending 110,000 men induce them to join us?"

If the answer was yes to both of these questions, then the requisite number should be sent immediately. He, however, believed that the Bosporus operations should be completed first and then negotiations should occur with Balkan States to determine what assistance would be needed to bring them in.

Balfour was proposing the piecemeal approach most feared by Churchill. Should his proposals gain support, serious delay in the operation would be ensured and the door would be left wide open for a full-scale southern offensive.

* * * * *

The War Council meeting of February 26 began on a positive note with Churchill declaring that the outer forts were reduced. When Asquith asked what was meant by "reduced," Churchill declared this meant they were "completely demolished as far as further hostilities were concerned."[3] Within days, this was to be shown to be an entirely false assertion but, for the time being, it was the cause of much optimism. This undoubtedly influenced the subsequent War Council discussions, in particular, Churchill's apprehension that a shortage of troops might prevent Britain from reaping the fruits of a naval victory.

With the outer forts now apparently taken care of, discussion for the first time focused on operations inside the Straits. Churchill explained that minesweeping inside the Straits had commenced and would be followed by an attack on the forts at the Narrows.

Just as he had at the last War Council meeting, Lord Haldane threatened, briefly, to rain on Churchill's parade when he asked whether the Turkish military field force might cut the retreat of ships in the Straits by the use of heavy field artillery.

Churchill remained typically dismissive of this threat and contended that even six-inch guns were not easy to move about. Kitchener then once again declared with confidence that "once the Fleet was through the Straits, the Bulair lines would become untenable, and the Turks would probably evacuate the Peninsula."[4] Unfortunately, again in the face of such optimism, no one thought to ask what might happen if the Turks failed to evacuate the peninsula.

Only Haldane expressed any dissatisfaction with this response. Creeping ever closer to the critical flaw in the Churchill plan, he rather pertinently suggested that the "Turkish guns might be brought up on the south side."[5] He, at least, seemed to have grasped the fact that command of the Straits did not depend solely on the command of the peninsula. Somewhat surprisingly given his stance on the issue of communication, Hankey at this point noted that he believed the roads on the southern side of the peninsula were very bad.

In any event, Churchill declared—now for the third time—that "the navy were only attempting to force the passage for armoured ships, the passage of which could not be interfered with by field artillery."[6] Kitchener then added that "if the forts were reduced the requisite military effect would be gained."[7]

Haldane's question and Churchill's reply could give no clearer indication that Churchill was ignoring absolutely Jackson's warning over the need for troops to secure the fleet's lines of communication. Even more important, Haldane's comments suggest that such an issue had received little attention—if any—in previous discussions and that he did not realize that Churchill was unconcerned by a threat to communications. Kitchener's assertions ensured that this vital issue would receive no greater attention on this occasion and would remain unclarified.

There is a real sense here that Kitchener and Churchill were now speaking of two very different operations. Churchill, in what appeared to be an ineffectual attempt to keep a lid on the War Council's expectation, is promising to get a force of armored ships into the Marmora—nothing more. Mobile guns and howitzers on both sides of the Straits or on the Asian side alone would prevent the use of the Straits by any other vessels. Kitchener on the other hand stubbornly argued that once the fleet was through, the Turks would evacuate the peninsula.

Kitchener's scenario opened up much greater opportunity than did Churchill's. The peninsula could be occupied, the Asian side of the Straits dominated by British howitzers, and a military force could enter the Marmora to capture or occupy Constantinople. Furthermore, Kitchener's scenario suggested the fleet could be supplied as and when it was required.

Evidently, Churchill did not share Kitchener's certainty, but he was again content to be led along by him rather than address why his expectations might not be fulfilled and the probable consequences for the operation if they were not.

It was complete folly for Churchill to remain mute on such vital issues because Kitchener's contention that the fleet could achieve these objectives by itself continued to provide ample grounds for withholding the 29th Division. It also ensured the War Council's expectations for the operation would grow well beyond that which Churchill knew his plan could deliver.

Even more extraordinarily in the circumstances, Churchill now set about reaffirming the naval-only nature of Dardanelles operation. He told the War Council that, upon hearing a military force was to be sent to him, Carden "had proposed to land troops on the Gallipoli Peninsula in order to capture and hold the end of the peninsula."[8]

He did not explain why Carden had considered holding the end of the peninsula as important. Instead, Churchill told the War Council that the *Admiralty* had informed Carden that the "the military forces were not intended to participate in the immediate operations, but to enable him to reap the fruits of those operations when successfully accomplished."[9]

Thus, Churchill reaffirmed before the War Council the essentially naval-only nature of the Dardanelles operation. The Navy would force the Dardanelles with only limited assistance from a small number of soldiers. He had refused to countenance the use of troops to complete the destruction of the guns in the forts as recommended by Jackson and mooted by Kitchener in his correspondence with Maxwell and Birdwood. The peninsula would be occupied only *after* the fleet was inside the Marmora and only *if* the Turks first evacuated the peninsula.

The Turks, it was being argued by Kitchener, would likely evacuate the peninsula because their lines of supply would be severed once the fleet was through. Churchill does not deny this possibility, but the occupation of the peninsula, although desirable, was not essential to his plan. He would enter the Marmora whether or not this facilitated subsequent action against the peninsula. Having Kitchener speak so confidently of a Turkish rout once the fleet was through, however, was not without its advantages. The vital issue of communications and the need to secure the peninsula could continue to be ignored.

Having reaffirmed his naval-only operation, Churchill appealed yet again for the 29th Division. Perhaps mindful of the points made in Balfour's memorandum, he focused his attention on more immediate operations. "In three weeks time Constantinople might be at our mercy. We should avoid the risk of finding ourselves with a force inadequate to our requirements and face to face with a disaster." He repeated the lines of his memorandum, yet unseen by his colleagues, when he stated that the troops were required:

> to occupy Constantinople and to compel a surrender of all Turkish forces remaining in Europe after the fleet had obtained command of the Sea of Marmora . . .
>
> With an army at hand this could be accomplished either by fighting, or by negotiation, or by bribery. The Chatalja lines would be occupied from the reverse side, the flanks being commanded by men-of-war. . . . The actual and definite object of the army would be to reap the fruits of the naval success.[10]

These were not unreasonable arguments, but again Kitchener could not be persuaded that there were not already soldiers enough for such operations. He calculated that, even if every man available were sent, this would number 89,500 men. He wanted to await the clearing up of the situation in Russia and some signs of a probable result in the Dardanelles before sending the 33,000 men of the 29th Division and Territorial Division, whom he believed could not make the difference between success and failure.[11] He reiterated his belief that "the whole situation in Constantinople would change the moment the fleet had secured a passage through the Dardanelles."[12] He wanted to wait until the defenses at the Narrows began to collapse, when he believed they would be in a "better position to judge the situation."[13]

At this point, Balfour tried to resolve the impasse between Kitchener and Churchill by reference to his memorandum. He described his so-called Bosporus operation and suggested that:

> if the purely naval operation were carried out, . . . the command of the Sea of Marmora would be secured; the Turkish troops remaining in Europe would be cut off; the arsenal and dockyard at Constantinople could be destroyed; the conditions of the Turks would become worse every day they held out; the Bosphorus could be opened; a line of supply for war-like stores opened up with Russia; and wheat obtained from the Black Sea.[14]

As we have seen, Balfour had similarly summarized the virtues of the naval operation at the War Council meeting of January 28 when Churchill was seeking the go-ahead.[15] He had again emphasized the importance of Russian wheat and communications with Russia at the War Council on February 24.[16] On these occasions, Churchill had remained silent on the difficulties an operation designed to admit fully armored vessels only to the Marmora would have in achieving such objectives.

This time Churchill, who would not have welcomed such an optimistic assessment of the naval operation amid discussion designed to secure the 29th Division, was a little more forthcoming. He declared:

> that no wheat could be obtained. Merchant ships could not make the passage, as they would be liable to be sunk by field guns and howitzers. The passage would only be open to armoured ships and transports, for which special arrangements and convoy would be required. It might even be necessary to

> land the troops opposite the Bulair lines and march them across to other ships in the Sea of Marmora.[17]

Of all the moments in all the War Council meetings during this time, this remains one of the most extraordinary passages. Balfour's assertion that the Bosporus operation would succeed without any troops was forcing Churchill to identify the shortcomings of his plan to admit fully armored vessels only into the Marmora. It might be noted that he had, for the first time, mentioned the possibility of howitzers. Yet, beyond this, he conceded little. His suggestion that troops *might* be convoyed through the Straits was disingenuous. If merchant ships could not make it through the Straits because of field guns and howitzers, then troops in merchant ships could not either. The Bulair route over the narrow, but heavily fortified, neck of the Peninsula had been his preferred option from the moment troops had become available and from the very first discussions regarding the use of troops inside the Marmora, but there is no evidence to show that the Bulair route was anything other than a figment of Churchill's imagination. His equivocation now over the practicability of the only other route troops could take into the Marmora—the straits themselves—reflected the enormity of the confession, a confession he was still unable or unwilling to make but which now was absolutely essential if he was to catch up with the growing expectations of the War Council.

On January 13 when the operation had been first mooted, there was no intention whatsoever to use troops at the Dardanelles. This, afterall, had been the great selling point of the Carden/Churchill plan. The original plan need not, could not, and, indeed, did not guarantee the movement of troops into the Marmora. All Churchill's and Kitchener's subsequent plans to use troops at Constantinople were built entirely on the slim prospect the Turks would evacuate the peninsula or that a revolution might occur. What was still missing, however, in the calculations and pronouncements of each, was a visible and viable means of getting the troops—now deemed essential by the War Council—into the Marmora to "reap the fruits" of a successful naval operation. The question was simple but never put: If the Turks stayed on the Peninsula with their field guns and howitzers, how were troops going to get into the Marmora to secure the success of the fleet?

Churchill's equivocation over Bulair continued to conceal some very serious flaws in the naval-only operation. It avoided addressing, for example, how the unarmoured merchant vessels required to take the troops from Bulair to Constantinople or elsewhere in the Marmora were to make their way through the Straits still commanded by Turkish howitzers and field guns. Nor, by way of further example, did it explain how precious hospital ships—essential to the care of sick and injured troops—might make the same journey, nor the considerable number of supply ships required to sustain a large army inside the Marmora.

Concealed, also, were the potential problems faced by the fleet itself with unsecured lines of communications. If the Turks did not evacuate the Peninsula as was hoped and expected, and command of the Peninsula could only be secured by starving the Turks into submission through a prolonged seige, was it expected that the fleet inside the Marmora would outlast the Turks on the Peninsula? Moreover, potentially denied all manner of supply, could the fleet satisfactorily conduct sustained bombardment operations elsewhere inside the Marmora—especially against the Bosporus forts? Unless the later took place successfully, could the Russian fleet and Russian army assist in the capture of Constantinople as Kitchener anticipated?

Churchill's very considerable culpability in such matters was further compounded by his obfuscation over the need to use soldiers to complete the destruction of guns in the forts. He had led his War Council colleagues to the understanding that the forts were to be reduced by the fleet at ranges *beyond* the guns of the enemy. Even in mid-February, based on the information Churchill had provided to the War Council, it would have been possible for most of its members to have been entirely ignorant of the fact that Carden expected only to destroy the forts at a "decisive" range, which routinely would put the ships well within the range of any guns that had not been destroyed or seriously damaged by the longer range bombardment. Equally, they would have been ignorant of his War Staff's reservations over the capacity of the fleet to 'destroy' the guns in the forts even at a so called "decisive" range and their belief that soldiers must be used to achieve this. If this was not done, any movement of troops through the straits would likely face not only mobile guns and howitzers but the bigger, large caliber guns in the forts as well.

During the War Council meeting, Edward Grey showed that he at least understood that many of Balfour's hopes for the operation depended on factors outside the navy's control when he stated that "what we really relied on to open the Straits was a *coup d'etat*."[18] What Grey ought to have said, had he really understood the critical issues at stake, was that "[w]hat we really relied on for a *coup d'etat* was military control of the Peninsula." *Only then might it have been possible to apply the full moral weight of the fleet and the soldiers behind it against the Turks.*

Here again was a perfect opportunity for Churchill to put to the War Council a proposal for an immediate joint operation on the peninsula. Rather than accept such limitations inherent in his plan to admit fully armored vessels only into the Marmora, might it not be better to launch an amphibious assault on the peninsula, secure the fleet's lines of communication, and thereby ensure that the fleet could operate effectively once inside the Marmora?

It was Hankey and not Churchill who grasped this nettle. Hankey rarely spoke at War Council meetings and that he did so at this moment reflected the seriousness of what he had to say. He declared that:

> the probable main use of troops at Constantinople was to open the Dardanelles and Bosphorus to all classes of ships. ***First it might be necessary to clear the Gallipoli Peninsula***. *Once this was accomplished, the forces could be withdrawn from there unless it was necessary to defend the Bulair lines. Next it might be necessary to clear out the position south of the Dardanelles.* (emphasis added)[19]

Hankey was declaring that, at some point, the peninsula—and for that matter the Asian side of the Straits—must be *captured* and occupied by Allied troops to secure success. If it did not occur before the fleet broke into the Marmora, it would have to occur immediately after. The Gallipoli peninsula must be the first object of full-scale military action and not Constantinople or elsewhere in the Marmora as purported by Kitchener and Churchill.

Neither Kitchener nor Churchill picked up this proposal. Instead, perfunctory discussion continued to anticipate the Turks moving into full retreat the moment it appeared the fleet would get through the Dardanelles. Churchill saw "no risk of a repetition of Admiral Duckworth's expedition to Constantinople, but if we had insufficient troops the Germans would soon discover it and would tell the Turks, and we should accomplish nothing."[20]

This final assertion was a declaration, albeit ambiguously, of two important points. The first was that he did not fear for the fleet inside the Marmora. The second was an implicit admission that the fleet could *guarantee* nothing in the Marmora without the moral or military support of an army. If the Turks refused to be intimidated by the fleet, if they did not panic or capitulate, if the Bulgarians, Romanians, or Greeks failed to act in support of the fleet's actions, the fleet alone could achieve no permanent success.

It was over the sum of these two points that Churchill had always differed from his naval advisers. Churchill believed the fleet could force its way into the Marmora with limited support from the army and limited risk to the fleet. He also believed that it could exit the Marmora with limited loss. The possible destruction of the Turko-German Fleet apart, he knew that what might happen thereafter depended entirely on moral rather than military matters, but he was more than happy to take this calculated gamble. To improve his odds, however, he was keen to have an army on standby to maximize the moral pressure on the enemy and possibly draw in the Balkan States.

On the other hand, his naval advisers were reluctant to risk a fleet—even an old one—in an enterprise, the success of which depended on moral rather than military issues. None of them had ever been able to understand what it was expected the fleet might achieve inside the Marmora without secure lines of communication.

Churchill was not alone in seeking the troops for moral reasons and subsequent discussion within the War Council meeting followed along this line. Lloyd George said that the dispatch of 100,000 men, following close on the fall of the Dardanelles, ought to produce a great effect on the Balkans.

Despite Churchill's pleas, and those of Lloyd George, Kitchener again declined to send more men from Europe. An angry Churchill wanted placed on record that "he dissented altogether from the retention of the 29th division in this country. If a disaster occurred in Turkey owing to insufficiency of troops, he must disclaim all responsibility."[21]

It has been pointed out that some historians believe Churchill's persistent call for the 29th Division concealed a growing doubt over his naval-only operation and an intention to use the troops to see the fleet through.[22] One can note six points in response to this. The first is Churchill's reluctance to the use any troops at all for his operation—even marines—which is evident in our earlier discussions, and the degree to which this put him at odds with his naval advisers.

Second is the great length to which he went to reaffirm the naval-only nature of the operation in his telegram to Carden and through his declaration at the War Council meeting.

A third point is that the peak of Churchill's insistence on the 29th Division coincided with a period of high optimism for the naval-only operation. This does not suggest his insistence on the 29th Division was based on any anxiety over the ability of the fleet to get through to the Marmora. It might, however, reasonably reflect a fear that opportunities might be lost through the absence of troops, thereafter, and the diminishing likelihood of Balkan intervention.

Fourth, the manner in which his Royal Naval Division was sent to the Dardanelles, unencumbered by its heavy equipment and directed straight to Lemnos to operate under the guns of the fleet, indicated he did not expect it would participate in a major land battle.

Fifth, it was Kitchener and not Churchill who took the initiative in committing the army to seeing the navy through with military assistance. Intentionally or otherwise, Churchill had taken action that would retard this eventuality, and he had avoided addressing fully the issue of mobile guns and howitzers and the fleet's lines of communication once inside the Marmora. This was the strongest card in his hand, if he truly wished to secure immediate military support for an attack on the Gallipoli Peninsula. Yet he refused to use it.

Sixth, as will be seen subsequently, Churchill would persist with his naval attempt long after he had secured all the military assistance he had sought, including the 29th Division. He did so against the ever-increasing conviction of his naval advisers, as well as Carden and de Robeck, that a joint operation was the only likely means by which to secure the political and military objectives of the enterprise.

Although Churchill was confident at this time that his fleet would find a way through to the Marmora, he knew the only certain way the fleet would secure all that was hoped for was if the peninsula was taken *before* the fleet entered the Marmora. This scheme would remain an absolute last resort for him because such a campaign almost certainly would mean the end of his northern schemes. Instead, he spoke, like Kitchener, of the Turks evacuating the peninsula and he spoke of sending troops, now recognized as essential to success, across Bulair, and he fought vigorously for the extra division he hoped would help make this happen. Then suddenly, in the last days of February, it looked as though all the pieces of the puzzle were about to fall into place. The Turks looked set to run, and Greece was ready to go to war without any further commitment of Allied troops. Lloyd George's great southern offensive might yet be avoided and Churchill's northern dreams could live on.

NOTES

1. Gilbert, *CVIII*, 563–564. To compare this with his original draft, see 547–548.

2. Gilbert, *CVIII*, 561–563. Memorandum by A. J. Balfour entitled *The War.*

3. See Ibid., 565. Indeed most of the guns in the forts could still be used. Most of those destroyed were demolished by landing parties on February 26 at Sedd el Bahr and on February 27 at Kum Kale.

4. Gilbert, *CVIII*, 568. *Secretary's Notes of War Council Meeting*, Feb. 26, 1915 (567–577).

5. Ibid.
6. Gilbert, *CVIII*, 568.
7. Ibid.
8. Ibid.
9. Ibid., 568.
10. Ibid., 569.
11. Ibid., 569.
12. Ibid.
13. Ibid.
14. Ibid., 569–570.
15. Gilbert, *CVIII*, 463–464.
16. Gilbert, *CVIII*, 560.
17. Ibid., 570.
18. Ibid., 570.
19. Ibid.
20. Ibid., 571.
21. Ibid., 574.
22. Prior and Ben-Moshe are two examples.

CHAPTER 20

Ascendancy Assumed

Just as had occurred after the previous three War Council meeting, Kitchener briefed Maxwell and Birdwood immediately after the explosive War Council Meeting on February 26. Unfortunately, reacting precipitately as he always did to the vagaries of War Council deliberations, his communications displayed little consistency with earlier decisions. The absence of consistency in this on-the-run high-level policy was increased by Kitchener's failure to keep Churchill and the Admiralty—or his own war staff—abreast of these communications.

In a communication with Birdwood, he outlined his latest appreciation of the operations Birdwood's forces were intended to support. Troops were to be used only for minor operations such as the final destruction of batteries after they had been silenced by the fleet. Presumably prompted by comments made by Churchill and Hankey at the War Council meeting, Kitchener took pains to identify mobile howitzer batteries concealed inland as potential targets for military operation.[1]

Kitchener went on in his telegram to make another significant step toward the commitment of troops when he told Birdwood he could "apply for and obtain any additional forces from your corps in Egypt that you may require up to the total of its strength."[2]

Thus was Birdwood given permission to use all 40,000 men to assist Carden in his operations. Kitchener was now way ahead of Churchill who had only recently instructed Carden that the marines were available for minor operations on the peninsula, while the advanced party supplied by Kitchener was to be used to take advantage of any success achieved by the fleet, including the occupation of the lines at Bulair.

Kitchener was sending a confusing message. He was giving Birdwood permission to use large numbers of troops, but he had not lifted his instruction that all action be limited to minor operations. This would lead to some confusion in Egypt.

Kitchener went on:

> *It is anticipated that when the forcing of the Narrows is practically assured the Turks will probably evacuate the Gallipoli peninsula,* and a small force at Bulair will then be able to hold it. . . . *I anticipate that the gradual overpowering of the batteries by naval fire will exert great moral effect upon the Turks, and the more gradual and certain the naval operations, the greater will be the effect produced.* (emphasis added)[3]

This paragraph illustrates the degree to which the Dardanelles operation and, more particularly, the idea of sending troops into the Marmora were continuing to be sustained by Kitchener's belief in the "moral" impact of the operation rather than any "military" elements. Although the War Council's hopes for the operation had increased markedly over the preceding five weeks, the means by which to achieve them were no less speculative. Wishful thinking abounded.

Kitchener's expectations were now being shared uncritically by one of his key advisers, Callwell. The man, who a few days before had noted the vital issue of the fleet's "communications" and had acknowledged the relative ease of any attack on the outer forts in comparison to those inside the Straits, now had succumbed entirely to Kitchener's wishful thinking. He wrote to Robertson that "the Dardanelles affair is getting on very nicely and, *if the Navy will only go very cannily and not rush things,* I believe the Turks will drift off out of the Gallipoli Peninsula and its occupation will be a fairly simple matter" (emphasis added).[4] From the military perspective, the strength of the entire operation now rested on the belief that the gradual destruction of the Turkish forts and a threat in their rear would cause the Turks on the peninsula to evacuate. Once this was achieved, guns could be landed to dominate the Asian coastline, thereby facilitating the admission of an armed force into the Marmora.

In a rather obvious response to his disagreement with Churchill in the War Council meeting over the 29th Division, Kitchener asked Birdwood whether he thought more than 64,000 troops would be required for operations at Constantinople after the channel had been forced and suggested he get in touch with local sources to determine what would be likely to happen after the fleet was through. This brief glimpse of self-doubt was in marked contrast to his confident assertions within the War Council over the previous several days. His otherwise stubborn optimism would have received a further dent later that day when Maxwell conveyed to him the opinion of Colonel Maucorp, former French military attaché. Maucorp considered "[a] military expedition is essential for opening the Dardanelles passage for the Allied fleet, and it would be extremely hazardous to land on the Gallipoli peninsula as the peninsula is very strongly organised for defence."[5]

Nevertheless, the last days of February continued to develop as a period of high optimism. Operations inside the Straits began on February 27, and Carden's telegrams did little to dilute a pervasive sense of satisfaction over the progress being made. It is certain that Carden's telegrams failed to convey one vital fact. The gradual bombardment of the forts had left serviceable all the guns. His use of the word "reduced" in his telegram of February 25 was careless in the extreme, and Churchill's explanation that this meant they were completely demolished so far as further hostilities were concerned was unhelpful also. They were silenced on the 25th because the Turks had evacuated the forts. They were "reduced" on the 26th because marines were landed and they were destroyed by hand. Unfortunately, Carden's brief telegrams were unclear on these points. If Churchill recognized the distinction—and it is possible at this stage that he did not—he was not letting on.

Carden's telegrams of February 27 summarized a good day's work, but he included a number of lessons for those who cared to look: that mobile guns had the potential to seriously disrupt naval operations inside the Straits; that these guns could be destroyed only by landing parties; and that these parties could only be assured of success as long as the 40,000 Turkish troops believed to be on the peninsula continued to run away.[6] As a fourth lesson, even if the fleet broke through into the Marmora, no soldiers would follow. A more ominous warning came the following day when Carden informed the Admiralty on February 28 that the guns in the forts had not been destroyed by the bombardment. This seems to have been ignored.[7]

It would be fair to say, however, that up to but not including February 28, the Admiralty might have gained from Carden an overly sanguine view of the operations against the outer forts. Nevertheless, from February 28 onward, Churchill's considerable optimism for his operation could not have been based on a belief that his ships were destroying the guns in the forts or that they were effective against the mobile weaponry. It can only have been based on the ease with which his marines had secured the complete destruction of the forts and the fact that his operation now appeared to be securing the allies he had always hoped it would.

In either event, Churchill gleaned only the positive from these results. He excitedly telegraphed the Grand Duke to request the Russian Black Sea Fleet to ready itself at Sebastopol to come to the entrance of the Bosporus at the right moment and that troops be ready for rapid embarkation.[8]

He also directed Vice Admiral Oliver to request an entire French Division, which had been offered for the operation only in the previous two days, be sent to Lemnos without delay.[9]

Excited that events might go as quickly as he had hoped, Churchill was gearing the forces available for the next stage of the operation. If the peninsula were evacuated, a force could move through the Dardanelles or, more likely, across Bulair and on to Constantinople. Alternatively, military assistance from one or other of the Balkan States might still be expected.

Such at least were Churchill's ever more confident expectations. Within the Admiralty, things were not quite so sanguine. Fisher wanted reassurance that such expectations were reasonable and sought advice—rather belatedly one might have thought—from Julian Corbett on the possibility of gaining control of the peninsula with little or no use of troops.

In a brief note sent to Fisher (following earlier conversations) Corbett argued that "should a landing be required at the extremity of the Gallipoli Peninsula, the real operation should be disguised by an effective threat against the rear of the Bulair neck." Based on the example of the Battle of Nanshan during the Russo-Japanese War, he believed such an action offered "the promise of an evacuation and unopposed landing."[10]

His casual willingness to draw parallels between Nanshan and Bulair was questionable in the extreme and seem, in retrospect, quite irresponsible. The Turks at Bulair, unlike the Russians at Nanshan, were never in any real threat of being cut off. They had made Bulair virtually impregnable against any amphibious assault and had large reinforcements available to defend against such an attack. Amphibious landings in the vicinity of Bulair were problematic if not impossible. There was, therefore, very little reason to believe that Russian anxiety—so heavily emphasized by Corbett in his analysis of Nanshan—would be duplicated within the Turkish forces.[11] On the contrary, they had anticipated such a problem and had prepared effectively against it and this knowledge was commonplace. Fisher, however, found some virtue in Corbett's advice and began to encourage Churchill to, at the very least, feign an amphibious assault at both ends of the peninsula to accompany further naval operation

A diversion at Bulair designed to panic the Turks on the Peninsula was attempted on April 25 and failed dismally, although it did cause a brief delay in the commitment of forces to the attack at Helles.

In all this discussion of Turkish evacuation and the movements of allied troops thereafter, one other extraordinary state of affairs must be kept in mind. To this point, neither Carden nor de Robeck had been informed that troops were to be moved into the Sea of Marmora in large numbers for operations either through the Straits or across Bulair and that this was likely to occur as a result of a Turkish rout as a result of the naval-only assault. Had their guidance been sought rather than that of Corbett, it is quite certain they would have provided a different perspective regarding such prospects.

Carden and de Robeck were ignorant at this time of another critical fact. Not only were they required to break into the Marmora, but the War Council was now expecting a break through the Bosporus as well. Disturbingly, neither plans nor guidelines had been drawn up for a naval assault on the Bosporus and, as late as the War Council meeting of February 24, the Prime Minister had wanted to know whether "the question of opening the Bosporus had been considered?"[12] Still playing catch-up with the expectations of the War Council, it was not until the end of February that Churchill instructed Jackson to prepare a paper on the Bosporus attack.

Although the Bosporus was considered a lesser challenge than the Dardanelles, it would require another extensive bombardment from Carden's forces. Without success here, however, the support of Russian forces—naval and military—would not be possible and all the hopes for the operation as outlined by Balfour could not be fulfilled. Not the least of these was the assumption that the control of the Bosporus and, therefore, the Black Sea would prevent European Turkey being reinforced from Asia. If we are to judge from Callwell's correspondence with Robertson, all the professional members of the War Council understood that any attempt at further large-scale bombardment inside the Marmora significantly increased the importance of secure lines of communication and, therefore, the command of the peninsula. Churchill's failure to satisfactorily address this issue within the War Council must be recognized as a monumental omission. Nevertheless, Kitchener ought to be held no less accountable.

Such matters were, for the time being, unimportant to Churchill. With the prospect of a Turkish rout apparently before him, Churchill's frustration at not having the requisite force to secure the fruits of success began to show. He finally circulated his memorandum of February 25 to the members of the War Council, adding the following:

> I must now put on record my opinion that the military force provided . . . is not large enough for the work it may have to do; and that the absence of any regular troops will, if fighting occurs, expose the naval battalions and the Australians to undue risk.[13]

The timing of this exhortation is relevant to the suggestion that Churchill wanted these extra troops to take the peninsula in a full-scale amphibious operation. This plea, undoubtedly the strongest by Churchill, was made at a time of high optimism over the progress of the operation and does not appear to be based on any apprehensions over the progress of the naval operation.

Churchill's optimism increased over the next few days. The following day he received word from Grey that the Greeks now believed that "the capture of Constantinople ought not to take place without Greek co-operation."[14] When Churchill learned that the Greeks had offered three divisions to Gallipoli, Asquith described him as "breast high about the Dardanelles."[15] His excitement was not surprising. It appeared, briefly, that his original gamble was about to pay off. The Greeks were about to come in on the possibilities of the naval operation alone.

On February 28, Churchill wrote to Carden asking him to estimate the number of days "excluding bad weather" that would be required before it might be possible to enter the Marmora.[16]

He also began to consider Turkish surrender and wrote to Grey that "should we get through the Dardanelles, as is now likely, we cannot be content with anything less than the surrender of everything Turkish in Europe."[17]

Moreover, he even began anticipating the withdrawal of his Royal Naval Division, which was on "temporary" loan to Kitchener. He wrote to Kitchener on March 1 that he proposed "to place the Royal Naval Division under the orders of General Birdwood or whoever you appoint for these operations: *but I must have liberty to withdraw them by the middle of April in order that they may complete at home for other duties*" (emphasis added).[18] This does not suggest Churchill was anticipating using them for hard fighting on the peninsula. It stands in marked contrast to his exhortation a mere two days earlier that he would not be responsible for failure at the Dardanelles if there was an insufficiency of troops. That Churchill hoped his Royal Naval Division might soon return home to participate in one or other of his northern schemes will be the focus of subsequent discussions.

NOTES

1. Gilbert, *CVIII*, 579–580, Telegram, Kitchener to Birdwood, February 26, 1915.
2. Ibid.
3. Ibid.
4. Callwell to Robertson, Gooch, *The Plans of War*, 312.
5. Gilbert, *CVIII*, 578–579. Maxwell to Kitchener.
6. Ibid., 584.
7. Prior, "Churchill's 'World Crisis,'" 281.
8. Gilbert, *CVIII*, 584. Churchill to Grand Duke Nicholas.
9. Ibid., 585.
10. Gilbert, *CVIII*, 605. Corbett to Fisher, note, March 1, 1915.
11. See Julian Corbett, *Maritime Operations in the Russo-Japanese War 1904–1905,* vol. 1 (Annapolis, MD: Naval Institute Press/Newport, RI: Naval War College Press, 1994), 249–262. Corbett directed Fisher to this analysis in his brief note.
12. Gilbert, *CVIII*, 560.
13. Ibid., 587. Gilbert footnotes his volume on page 587 with the following: "The memorandum of 23rd February Churchill wrote on his note 'Tell Hankey to circulate to War Council only.' But later he added 'Put Up' and 'Hold.'" The memorandum was circulated, as there is a copy of it in the Public Record Office, CAB 37/124, and Churchill later referred to it in his statement to the Dardanelles Commission, 1571. It is this writer's guess, Gilbert does not realize two versions of this memorandum were written, despite both being in his book, and it was the second, amended version, which was subsequently circulated.
14. Gilbert, *CVIII*, 590.
15. Gilbert, *CVIII*, 604. Asquith to Venetia Stanley, March 1, 1915.
16. Gilbert *CVIII*, 591, Telegram, Churchill to Caren, February 28, 1915.
17. Gilbert, *CVIII*, 591–592. Churchill to Grey, Gilbert.
18. Ibid., 593.

CHAPTER 21

After the Dardanelles: The Great Southern Offensive or Borkum/Baltic?

So pervasive was the optimism over the imminent success of the Dardanelles operation that, on March 1, Hankey circulated an extensive memorandum entitled "After the Dardanelles. The Next Step."[1] This, we are told by Hankey, had been prepared in consultation with military and naval staffs and was prompted by his concern that no one really knew what should occur once the fleet entered the Marmora.

Just as he had done in his February 2 memorandum to Asquith, Hankey's memorandum drew together the threads of discussions at past War Council meetings.

He generally accepted Balfour's thesis that the operation had two parts. The primary and immediate objective of the operation was to seek out and destroy the Turko-German Fleet and, more particularly, the "*Goeben*," while the ultimate object was to open "the way for military operations against Austria, in which a British army will, it is hoped, co-operate with the armies of Rumania, Servia and perhaps Greece."[2]

The most important information came in the section "Subsidiary Objectives" in which he discussed "a number of military operations which, *though secondary in importance to the destruction of the Turco-German Fleet, are nevertheless of vital importance to the ultimate goal—the bringing in of the Balkan states* (emphasis added)."[3] Hankey was making a technical distinction between an operation that might admit the fleet into the Marmora to sink the Turkish Fleet, and a fleet that would be needed to achieve anything more. Thus, he was making a distinction between the proposal originally put to the War Council by Churchill, and a proposal that would secure the new, heightened expectations of the War Council.

The first expectation among these was

> *The clearance of the Gallipoli Peninsula and of the defences on the Asiatic side of the Dardanelles.* . . . It is desirable, as soon as possible, to effect this, in order, whatever may be the result of the negotiations at Constantinople, to have a safe and uninterrupted line of water communications to Constantinople.

Hankey italicized the opening sentence of this section. It was one of three points italicized in the entire memorandum and repeated his assessment of the operational priorities made at the last War Council meeting but which largely were ignored by Churchill and Kitchener. He clearly wished to reduce the speculative component of the operation by ensuring that the fleet could remain in the Sea of Marmora should the Turks not surrender immediately. There was now, however, one major difference from his earlier attitude. While he considered this move imperative, he was now accepting, pragmatically, that the peninsula would be secured only *after* the fleet was in the Marmora.

This memorandum, written by one of the most conservative and aware members of the War Council illustrates the level of optimism that existed at this time. He underestimated many things, including the number of troops on or near the peninsula and overstated others, including the capacity of the fleet to cut off Turkish communications and the level of assistance that might be given by the Russians.[4] Nevertheless, he made clear that all the great things he hoped would come to pass, including the opening of the Bosporus, were best preceded by the capture and occupation of the peninsula.

Hankey's memorandum was a *de facto* summary of all the concerns hitherto expressed to Churchill by his staff but which Churchill had scrupulously avoided addressing since he conceived the plan in early January.

Although he gave some support to Churchill's and Kitchener's contention that the Dardanelles defenses would become ineffectual once the fleet broke through, he understood that the Dardanelles and Asiatic side of the Straits must be secured by force as soon as possible to secure the full potential of the operation. Both Churchill and Kitchener, of course, were entirely at odds with this proposition. Kitchener had assumed the Turks would evacuate the peninsula and that it would become militarily irrelevant once the fleet was in the Marmora. Churchill was pushing a similar argument in late February, although his original plan to admit fully armored vessels only into the Marmora had offered no solution to the problem of communications, and he generally had been indifferent to it.

Hankey was also at odds with Churchill and Kitchener on two other issues. He did not attach any credibility to the use of troops inside the Marmora until *after* the peninsula had been taken. Second, he did not consider it possible that trade or transport could proceed through the Bosporus until it had been occupied—possibly by extended military operations—on *both* sides. Kitchener and Churchill had assumed a mere bombardment by the fleet would suffice to admit the Russian Fleet and the Russian Corp.

Despite Hankey's comments over the need to occupy both sides of the Straits, Churchill would glean only what was useful to him from the memorandum and apply it at the next War Council meeting where he would refer to only one aspect of the paper. This aspect was Hankey's assertion that the *ultimate* object of the operation was to have a British army fighting in the south alongside the armies of the united Balkan States.

Churchill knew this was the present thinking of the War Council and undoubtedly realized that his own belated call for troops to assist in achieving the *immediate* objectives of the operation had increased the likelihood of a serious southern offensive. He would soon make clear that he hoped to limit any British commitment to a southern offensive and, having once drawn the Balkan States into the war, direct future energies to his northern schemes.

* * * * *

Not surprising given the aforementioned, the War Council meeting on March 3 was characterized by discussion anticipating the imminent success in the naval operation.[5] Churchill read two telegrams from Carden. He said, "the net result" was "that forts 8 and 9 were in the process of being destroyed, and the forts at the entrance had been practically demolished."[6]

Churchill's assertions were careless and his optimism hardly justified. The first telegram summarized operations on March 1. Landing parties had destroyed most of the material mentioned. The second telegram told of attacks on *Canopus, Swiftsure,* and *Cornwallis* by forts eight and nine and also by field batteries and howitzers. The telegram stated that the "ships withdrew at 5.30 P.M. after inflicting damage on fort nine which ceased firing at 4.50 P.M. All three ships were hit several occasions one man slightly wounded."[7] In fact, the telegram did not indicate at all that fort nine was "in the process of being destroyed"[8] and made no mention of the impact of the ships' firing on fort eight as claimed by Churchill.

After Churchill's optimistic appraisal of the telegrams, discussion turned to "The Future of Constantinople" and then "After the Dardanelles. The Next Step."[9] Churchill informed the War Council that, as a result of a successful bombardment of the outer forts, "Russia was preparing to embark an army corps at Batoum."

Churchill went on to enumerate the forces that could now be disposed for the operations in the Marmora. These now included a Russian army corps and three Greek divisions. He now appeared much more relaxed about the 29th Division and showed little concern when Kitchener indicated he wished to keep the question of the deployment of the 29th "open" until he had heard from General Birdwood regarding the number of troops needed in the Mediterranean.

The rest of the meeting revolved around many of the issues addressed in Hankey's March 1 memorandum. Churchill's summary of events "if and when the Dardanelles were forced" was a loose summary of Hankey's memorandum.[10]

It is notable, however, that for all the recent discussion of troops and the role Hankey anticipated these would play at the Dardanelles, Churchill described a largely "maritime" operation which, apart from the additional duty of destroying the Bosporus defenses, retained almost intact the integrity of the original naval-only operation. He did not elaborate on the use of troops or address the issue of the peninsula, in particular the importance of clearing it and the southern side of the Straits as soon as possible. Nor did he mention his plans to transport troops via Bulair or Kitchener's plans to send them through the Straits.

Other elements of Hankey's paper were discussed. Balfour "hoped that the railways running along the shore of the Sea of Marmora on both the European side and the Asiatic side would be cut." Later he suggested:

> that the road on the Asiatic shore of the Dardanelles be broken up directly the ships effected a passage. This would prevent the possibility of field guns and howitzers being brought in to embarrass us after the Straits had been forced. The road round

> the head of the Gulf of Xeros ought also to be broken up so that nothing could pass in or out of the Gallipoli Peninsula.[11]

He asked whether the Admiralty anticipated opposition from howitzers.

I am was struck by the incongruity of this question at this point in the operation. The telegrams quoted at the beginning of this meeting indicated that Carden's operations were being interrupted by "mobile guns and *howitzers*."[12] This suggests that Churchill was not reading the entire telegram to his colleagues and generally had continued to make light of these obstacles. Churchill's coyness regarding howitzers has been noted. He had mentioned the greater number of "howitzers" only once since January 13, although field guns had been referred to regularly. Balfour's question suggested that even at this late juncture the War Council perceived the howitzer as a "potential" problem rather than one that already existed. It seemed to assume that the naval operation would destroy all such weapons then protecting the Straits.

On this occasion, Churchill did little to clarify these issues, although he was at last more open regarding the howitzers. He responded to Balfour by stating only "that the longer the delay the greater was the chance of such interruptions." He went on to add that "he had obtained six howitzers, which had been mounted on board some of the ships, for the special purpose of dealing with the shore howitzers."[13] It was perhaps not the right time to point out that, in what is surely one of the more bizarre elements of the operation, these guns sitting atop the turrets of the bombarding ships were supposed to deal with the numerous howitzers on both sides of the Straits. It was a forlorn hope.

Kitchener's contribution to Hankey's and Churchill's summary of events was to repeat his expectation that "when the forts began to fall, the garrison would either surrender or slip out over the Bulair lines in small parties by night."[14]

Again Kitchener and Churchill were explaining how the operation would take place before either had received any appreciation from the Mediterranean. The assumption that lines of communication could be severed at Bulair had yet to be discussed with, or confirmed by, anyone in the Mediterranean. It is extraordinary that no one pointed out that, if frightened, Turks could slip out over the Bulair lines under the cover of night with the fleet on both sides, then determined Turks might bring supplies in the opposite direction also under the cover of night.

Such critical thought was beyond everyone on March 3. Victory had been assumed and Churchill followed his summary of events with the enthusiastic observation that Britain:

> ought to be content with nothing less than the surrender of Turkey in Europe. Everything in Turkey in Europe comes from Asia and we should cut them off from there. Now that the Greeks had expressed their intention of joining we should have plenty of men available. Everything in Europe, arsenals, arms and even the fortress of Adrianople, ought to fall into our hands. Constantinople was only a step towards the Balkans.[15]

Inevitably, with Constantinople almost captured and Greece's intervention assumed, discussion now turned to the *ultimate* object of the operation: the marching of the Balkan States and a British army against Austria. When the final point of Hankey's paper—a proposal for operations up the Danube after the defeat of Turkey—was discussed, Churchill made his reluctance to support this operation quite clear:

> [W]e ought not to make the main line of advance up the Danube. *We ought not to employ more troops in this theatre of war than are absolutely essential in order to induce the Balkan States to march. He was still of opinion that our proper line of strategy was an advance in the north through Holland and the Baltic. This might become feasible later on when our new monitors were completed.* ***The operation in the East should be regarded merely as an interlude.*** (emphasis added)[16]

This declaration by Churchill for a preferred line of strategy through Holland and the Baltic and a limited British commitment to any southern offensive represented a frank summary of his real strategic priorities. Despite his Dardanelles "interlude," these priorities had remained unchanged from the early days of January and, indeed, from beginning of the war. Although he had belatedly sought modest military support to "reap the fruits" of a successful naval operation in the Dardanelles—and had at one point supported the idea of ongoing operations in the south—he remained ardently opposed to the *full-scale* southern offensive that the War Council now saw as the "ultimate" objective of the Dardanelles operation.

Now that his great Dardanelles gamble appeared likely to succeed, Churchill was turning his mind to his northern schemes, which had, throughout the early stages of the Dardanelles, been simmering quietly in the background. Even before Kitchener had decided to send the 29th Division to the Dardanelles, Churchill had written to him on March 1 indicating his intention to withdraw his Naval Division for "other duties" by the middle of April. It is probable that these "other duties" were to include preparations for an assault on Borkum.[17]

Churchill's declaration came a day after he had written to his COS, Oliver suggesting that, after the Dardanelles operations were finished, a squadron of "*Queen Elizabeths*" should go into the Baltic.[18] Richmond completed a memorandum on March 6 deprecating the idea, but this did not prevent Churchill from including the proposal in a letter to Sir John Jellicoe two days later.[19] The letter first revisited his proposed attack on Borkum and his plan to use some of his "unsinkable" monitors to take the island:

> The First Sea Lord is making extraordinary exertions to complete 6 Monitors by May 1st, 3-14inch, 2-15inch and 1-12inch. Allowing a fortnight to veer and haul on, the attack on Borkum should take place on or about the 15th of May. I hope you have reflected on my long letter to you of the (   ) [*sic*]. Besides Monitors we shall have a bombarding squadron of 8 or 10 older battleships now being fitted with booms to carry double torpedo nets. Oil-ships converted into unsinkable transports will be ready to carry 12000 men.[20]

Evidently, in composing this letter, Churchill had taken the effort to establish precisely which monitors might possibly be ready by his mid-May date for the Borkum operation: three of four 14-inch gun monitors, both 15-inch gun vessels, and one of eight 12-inch gun vessels. That the date for the operation (perhaps linked to tides and moonlight) was apparently much more important to him than awaiting the completion of more of his monitors, hints at a tight timetable for the Borkum operation, and highlights the degree to which his aspirations for this project had the real potential to press on the needs of the naval-only operation at the Dardanelles. Perhaps uppermost among these needs—if the operation was to have any chance of success at all—was time and patience. Each was at a premium as far a Churchill was concerned.

In the second paragraph of his letter, Churchill introduced Jellicoe to his bold new proposal broached with Oliver several days earlier. Somewhere between the fifth and seventh day of the operation, he declared, a fast division of *Warspite, Queen Elizabeth, Tiger, Queen Mary,* six *Arethusa* class cruisers, and the M Flotilla, which would be preceded by six E-boats would enter the Baltic and, supported by the Russian Fleet and its new super dreadnoughts, blockade Germany's northern ports and destroy its political influence in Scandinavia. The Germans, he anticipated, could then be kept continually on the run defending against attacks by monitors against Cuxhaven in the North Sea or against raids by his fast fleet in the Baltic. He concluded:

> Our affairs in the Dardanelles are prospering though we have not yet cracked the nut. They are involving profound political reactions. Constantinople is only a means to an end, and that end is the marching against Austria of the five united Balkan states.
>
> Similarly here in the North strategy and politics move together, and it should be possible by a proper use of our fleets and armies in that combination which sea-power renders possible to bring both Holland and Denmark into the fighting line.[21]

Churchill wrote here only of the five united Balkan States marching against Austria. There is no suggestion, in contrast to the aspirations of other members of the War Council that this be alongside a large British army.

The import of this communication suggests strongly that all the decisions being made by Churchill at the Dardanelles continued to be tempered by a timetable for his northern offensives to which he remained strongly wedded. The anticipated use of the *Queen Elizabeth,* which remained an important part of the bombardment operation at the Dardanelles, quite obviously required that this operation be completed first.

Whatever its potential shortcomings, the naval operation must continue unabated to a successful and rapid conclusion if Churchill were to maintain his northern time frame and retain the credibility necessary to pull off his northern ambitions. Troops were a welcomed adjunct to the naval operation. They might provide the impetus required to draw in the wavering Balkan States, or they might secure any success achieved by the fleet. Nevertheless, he had no intention of modifying or delaying his naval operation to accommodate them. Only as a last resort would a full-scale amphibious assault be launched to capture the peninsula and see the fleet through to the Marmora.

In the heady days of early March, Churchill believed himself on the verge of vindication and he had reenergized his Borkum/Baltic scheme in view of imminent success at the Dardanelles. Unfortunately, unbeknown to him, his hopes for the Dardanelles had already received the first of a series of terminal blows that would prematurely end his naval-only scheme, transform it into a full-scale amphibious operation, and destroy forever his northern dreams.

NOTES

1. Gilbert, *CVIII,* 593–602. Hankey's Memorandum *"After The Dardanelles: The Next Steps."*
2. Ibid., 594.
3. Ibid., 598.
4. Much later, de Robeck took issue with the idea that the Turks on the peninsula could have been isolated from the mainland by the fleet alone. He pointed out that only one road along the Bulair Isthmus could be controlled by the navy and then only by day. Another road could not be seen from the sea and could be bombarded only with continual aerial reconnaissance. This was impossible because of the distance to Bulair from the nearest island airfield. It seems probable, that had he been asked, de Robeck would have proffered similar advice in March 1915. This said, the Admiralty ought not to have needed to be told.
5. Gilbert, *CVIII,* 610–617. Extracts from Secretary's notes of Meeting of War Council, March 3, 1915.
6. Ibid., 610.
7. Gilbert, *CVIII,* 609. Telegram, Carden to Churchill, March 3, 1915, 12.45 A.M.
8. Gilbert, *CVIII,* 610. Extracts from Secretary's notes of Meeting of War Council, March 3, 1915.
9. Gilbert, *CVIII,* Extracts from Secretary's notes of Meeting of War Council, March 3, 1915. The discussion of these matters took up the greater part of the meeting.
10. Ibid., 614.
11. Ibid., 614.
12. Gilbert, *CVIII,* 609. Carden to Churchill, telegram.
13. Ibid., 615.
14. Ibid., 615.
15. Ibid., 616–617.
16. Ibid., 617.
17. It is possible that Churchill intended to use them in French's coastal scheme. See letter from Gilbert, *CVIII,* 444–445. French to Churchill, January 23, 1915. Gilbert, *CVIII,* 444–445.

18. Marder, *Portrait of an Admiral,* 145. It may have been that Churchill only spoke to Oliver on the matter. Marder writes only that Churchill "advocated" the idea. By whatever method the message was conveyed, it resulted in Richmond's assessment, *"Considerations Affecting the Dispatch of 'Queen Elizabeth' Class to the Baltic,"* 145–147.

19. Gilbert, *CVIII,* 656–658. Letter, Churchill to Jellicoe, March 9, 1915.

20. Ibid., 656.

21. Ibid., 658.

CHAPTER 22

The Dardanelles in Decline: Reality Check, Birdwood to Kitchener

Amid the intense optimism that prevailed in the very early days of March, Churchill had begun to redirect his strategic sights northward. Almost as soon as he had done so, however, news began to emanate from the Mediterranean that very soon would shatter the illusion of imminent success at the Dardanelles.

The first of this news, not at this stage known to Churchill, was received by Kitchener from Birdwood in the evening of March 3. In this, the first of several communiqués, Birdwood belatedly disabused Kitchener of one of his more cherished assumptions. If the army were required by the navy to land to take concealed guns or howitzers it would not be possible "to restrict movements to minor operations."[1]

Following Kitchener's somewhat confused message to Birdwood that he should conduct only small operations but could call on all his troops up to one corps, Birdwood went on to inform Kitchener that, with the exception of two mounted brigades, he planned an operation with his whole corps to take the tip of the peninsula. From there he hoped it would be possible to dominate the Asiatic side of the Straits.

Other parts of his letter addressed the questions that had been posed by Kitchener. He had not been able to gain any local information regarding the need for troops at Constantinople but offered a personal opinion that "when the Fleet arrives before Constantinople and threatens the bombardment of the city, opposition will collapse." However, he went on to note that he was not in a "position to know whether this would result in laying down of arms by Turkish Army." He highlighted the amateurish approach to the whole Dardanelles affair when he declared he had "no information to guide me in advising as to operations after the Gallipoli Peninsula has been taken, and I have as yet no maps of the country."[2]

The most serious import of Birdwood's communication with Kitchener is Birdwood's assumption—not unreasonable given Kitchener's earlier communications—that Kitchener had given him permission to take the peninsula. He simply had put two and two together, something Kitchener was having great trouble doing. Soldiers were to assist the fleet in the destruction of mobile guns and howitzers. By his reckoning, this could not be done with a small force and Kitchener had given him permission to call on his whole corps, if required. Thus, he would invade from the tip of the peninsula and gradually overrun it from there, destroying all gun emplacements along the way.

Birdwood followed his telegram with another telegram nine hours later in which he elaborated his plans.[3] He had since spoken with Carden and had undertaken a reconnaissance some way up the Straits. He estimated the strength on the peninsula to be approximately 40,000 men, but this was undoubtedly Carden's figure.

Birdwood noted Carden's determination to force the Straits as per his instructions from the Admiralty. Should it not be possible to silence the guns in hidden positions, Carden would either ignore the damage inflicted or cooperate with the army in their destruction. He believed that urgency would determine whether there would be time to wait for the latter alternative, because his troops could not be ready before March 18 at the earliest. He recommended an operation in which the navy made a demonstration at Bulair with transports not needed for a main attack at Cape Helles. Troops would move up to a point at which forts at the Narrows could be taken in reverse and concealed batteries could be dealt with, although he warned that the peninsula was "heavily entrenched . . . and is supported by howitzers."[4] He then anticipated having to move a "good part" of his force to the Asiatic side to deal with the guns there.

Birdwood observed that the action of his force would depend on the progress made by the navy up to March 18:

> but, in any case, troops will be moving in the right direction, and would probably keep a strong force entrenched in covered

> position from Kephez Bay to Nagara, on the Asiatic side to protect the Narrows. With the command this secured of the lines across the Narrows, there may not be much further opposition until the Bulair lines are reached.[5]

After the Narrows, he would attack Bulair, which he rather confidently asserted could be taken with the assistance of the fleet working from both sides of the peninsula.

Birdwood's telegram would be followed by another several hours later. It was even more bleak regarding the naval-only prospects, but little of what he said could have been of any real surprise to Kitchener. Birdwood's news, however, carried special weight because it came from the officer in the field and ought to have been sufficient to demand a fundamental reassessment of the naval-only operation. Unfortunately at this critical moment, by fate or design, Churchill would once again intervene and ensure that the naval-only operation remained firmly on track.

Three hours before the first of Birdwood's communiqués with Kitchener, Carden had updated Churchill on naval proceedings.[6] It was mixed news. Operations, he told him, had once again been slowed by weather. Reconnaissance had been possible on only one day since February 19 and the search still continued for concealed guns. Then, in reply to Churchill's question of late February 28, Carden informed him that it would take 14 days of good weather to break through into the Marmora, but in the same sentence he rather significantly requested permission "to take QUEEN ELIZABETH into the Straits when desirable."[7] Portentous signs here.

Many historians contend that Churchill was excited at Carden's reply that it would only take 14 days to break into the Marmora. Those who do are sometimes careless of the fact that it was 14 days of *good weather,* which was essential for reconnaissance, spotting, and bombardment. Given the considerable number of days since February 19 during which full operations had been impossible, all that could reasonably be assumed by Carden's reply was that operations easily could have taken another month or longer.[8] The same telegram noted that seaplanes had "been able to fly on one day since 19th owing to rough weather." Perhaps, at least, Churchill could at this stage still attribute some of the delay to the inclement weather rather than to any inherent flaws in the naval operation.

Certainly, Churchill seemed determined to draw only the positive from Carden's telegram, and he sent a Secret and Personal Telegram to Carden at 4:35 P.M. on March 4 outlining the action to be taken once the fleet broke into the Marmora.[9] His first task was to destroy the Turko-German Fleet, wherever it was. Thereafter all lines of communications with Constantinople were to be cut, and he hoped that as much as possible of the Turkish Army would be cut off on the European shore and be forced to surrender later.

Then, for the first time, Churchill informed Carden that it would also be his task to force the Bosporus. He was advised to contact the Russian Black Sea Fleet when he was within four days of entering the Marmora so they could blockade the Black Sea mouth of the Bosporus and bombard the outer forts with long-range fire to increase the moral effect of his own bombardment. This instruction ignored the Russian's expressed belief that the guns in these forts were stronger and more numerous than those of their fleet—and it completely overlooked the possibility that the *Goeben* and/or *Breslau* might retreat to the Black Sea and prevent this bombardment from happening.[10]

Despite the considerable angst that had developed over the 29th Division in the preceding 10 days, Churchill's telegram left Carden none the wiser as to the intended use of the troops then being gathered. Indeed, just as had his summary to the War Council on March 3, Churchill's telegram maintained the naval-only integrity of the naval plan to a remarkable degree. It was as if he had almost forgotten the previous week's arguments over the 29th Division and was determined, regardless of the consequences, to do as much as possible without involving troops. Thus, Carden remained entirely ignorant of the fact that both Churchill and Kitchener expected that the operation then in progress would facilitate the entrance into the Marmora of a vast army.

Was this oversight—albeit on a monumental scale—on behalf of Churchill or was his inaction more calculated? What response might Churchill have expected from Carden had he informed him of these facts? With little doubt, Carden would have deemed absolutely essential the capture of the peninsula—and probably the southern side of the Straits as well—before troops could enter the Marmora. In the event, it was left to his successor, John de Robeck, some weeks later to recommend this course, thereby terminating the naval-only operation.

In the meantime, Carden was kept very much in the dark. Even his most recent discussions with Birdwood would not have helped his understanding. As Birdwood's telegram to Kitchener has just shown, Carden evidently understood he must continue to force the Straits unassisted, although, given Birdwood's flawed appreciation of Kitchener's communique, he might now have had some hope the army would assist by occupying the peninsula, should the fleet fail.

After writing to Carden, Churchill wrote to Kitchener[11] informing him that Carden considered "it will take 14 days on which firing is practicable to enter the Sea of Marmora, counting from the 2nd of March. Of course bad weather would prolong and a collapse of the Turkish resistance at the later forts would shorten this period."[12] In the circumstances, Churchill thought it was time to "fix a date for the military concentration so that the arrival of troops can be timed to fit in with the normal fruition of the naval operation."

He informed Kitchener that the transports for the Australian Corps less those troops already at Lemnos would arrive at Alexandria between March 8 and March 15 and that these troops could be landed at "Bulair, or alternatively, if practicable, taken through the Straits to Constantinople, about the 18th instant." He pointed out that the Naval Division could also reach these same points by these dates. Keeping in mind the 4,000 Australians and 2,000 marines already at Lemnos, Churchill suggested "that we fix in our own minds the 20th March as the date on which 40,000 British troops will certainly be available for operations on Turkish soil" and recommended the French, Greeks, and Russian be informed as such.

Churchill went on to inform Kitchener that he wished to make it clear "that the naval operations in the Dardanelles cannot be delayed for troop movements, as we must get into the Marmora as soon as possible in the normal course."

He closed by informing Kitchener that transport would be available for either the 29th Division or the Yeomanry Division by the March 15 and that it would not be necessary to decide which would be sent until March 10. He wrote, "[t]he need of one good division of regular infantry in an army composed of so many different elements and containing only British and Australian troops raised since the war, still appears to me to be grave and urgent."

Thus, by coincidence, Churchill and Birdwood had set deadlines for the large-scale use of troops almost to the same day (March 18), although for quite different purposes. Birdwood, confused by Kitchener's instructions, expected to use troops to invade and capture the peninsula after this date should the naval operations fail. Churchill anticipated success by this time and expected troops would enter the Marmora via Bulair or through the Straits to "reap the fruits" of a naval victory. Although he had declared in his February memorandum that, by this time, operations might be undertaken to see the fleet through, little evidence suggests this is how he expected to use them at this time.

Churchill's timetable for combined naval and military operations was absurdly optimistic and presumptuous in the extreme. It is quite jarring when juxtaposed with Birdwood's correspondence with Kitchener. At this very moment, the first lord of the Admiralty knew much less than the secretary of state for war about the real nature of the naval operations at the Dardanelles.

That Carden considered the naval operation might be over by March 18 was nonsense. Only three or four days of firing had been successful in the previous fortnight and opportunities for aerial reconnaissance had been even lower. Churchill could just as likely have expected the operation to take another six weeks rather than a mere two.

Unfortunately, Churchill's news fell on receptive ears. Kitchener needed no encouragement to continue the naval-only operation, nor did he need encouragement to continue ignoring Birdwood's plans for the use of troops. Kitchener immediately informed the general that "from the Admiral's estimate I understand that by 20th March he will probably have accomplished the forcing of the Dardanelles."[13] Thus, as a result of Churchill's ludicrous assertion, March 20, 1915, was anticipated as the culmination of the naval operations against the Dardanelles. Such news undoubtedly would have been a surprise to Carden.

Following Churchill's recommendation, Kitchener went on to propose to Birdwood that the Australian, French, and Naval force of 65,000 men be concentrated at Lemnos from March 12 after which time he anticipated another and clearer estimate of the navy's likely passage of the Straits.

Having established the forces available for operations, Kitchener outlined the tasks to be undertaken by them. Deflected by Churchill's optimistic forecasts of a naval breakthrough, he took the opportunity to disabuse Birdwood regarding his intention to take the Helles position with the ANZACs:

> Unless the Navy are convinced that they cannot silence the guns in the Straits without military co-operation on a large scale, in which case further orders will be issued, there is no intention of using troops enumerated above to take the Gallipoli peninsula.

Thus was Birdwood told to forget all his plans—for the time being at least—to capture and occupy the peninsula to assist the fleet's breakthrough into the Marmora and to secure the destruction of the mobile guns and howitzers. Should the fleet fail, and the peninsula need be taken, Kitchener expected more troops would be required. Birdwood, therefore, would have to await reinforcements from England. He anticipated being able to make a decision on this matter by March 10. Such had been the date proposed by Churchill.

In the meantime, Kitchener declared only "small bodies of troops will be required for subsidiary operations while the fleet are successfully silencing the forts." These were to be made available to the admiral from the brigade then at Lemnos.

Still anticipating the abandonment of the peninsula, Kitchener told Birdwood that, should it appear by about March 18 that naval success was imminent, transports carrying the whole force for operations should follow the fleet "at close intervals" through the Straits and land "at or near Constantinople or on the mainland on the European side . . . which ever place . . . may be found advisable. Because it was anticipated the Turks would evacuate the Peninsula, only a small force would be necessary to hold the Bulair Lines." Therefore, Kitchener declared, "the concentration of the troops at the entrance to the Dardanelles is not so much for operations on the Gallipoli peninsula as for operations subsequently to be undertaken in the neighbourhood of Constantinople." This was just as Churchill had requested.

As to Russian cooperation, Kitchener, instructed that:

> After sinking the Turkish Navy on their arrival at Constantinople, the first duty of the Fleet will be to open up the Bosphorus for the entrance of the Russian Fleet, which will be accompanied by a corps of Russian troops, probably numbering 40,000 men, and the operations on land will take place in co-operation with these forces.

For so many reasons, this is a shamefully inept and arrogant piece of work from Kitchener. He had expressed his expectation that the attacks on Constantinople would take place in cooperation with the Russian corps. This could not occur until the Turkish navy had been sunk and Bosporus forts destroyed. The Turkish Fleet might retreat to the Black Sea and prove inaccessible and there was no time frame for the completion of the attack on the Bosporus. It was certain to require a number of days and perhaps weeks, if it were at all possible. What would happen if it proved impracticable to land the 65,000 soldiers? Would it be possible to keep these men safely aboard ship? A far larger question was how these men were to get into the Marmora in the first place. Although the Gallipoli Peninsula might be evacuated and, thereby, no longer present a threat to unarmored ships, how were troop ships to be protected from mobile guns and howitzers on the Asian shoreline during the long passage through the Straits? A similar question might be asked regarding the Russian troop ships it was anticipated would come through the Bosporus and which would face a threat from both sides.

At the heart of Kitchener's ludicrous optimism was his conviction the Turks would run from the peninsula and that this would be enough to allow the forces through to the Marmora. Even this expectation, however, does not seem sufficient to explain his assessment of what would happen once the fleet was through. This blindness to reality must surely have been supported by Churchill's ongoing refusal to address the issue of mobile guns and howitzers and the difficulties the fleet would have in eradicating this menace whatever it might achieve against the forts. Churchill had not announced that these weapons must prohibit the movement of troops into the Marmora. Churchill could not do so and keep his naval-only operation alive and on time.

Birdwood, by contrast, had no reason for coyness. At 12:55 P.M. on March 5, he expressed to Kitchener his doubt that the "Navy can force the passage unassisted."[14] He continued:

> In any event the forcing of the passage must take a considerable time; the forts that have been taken up to the present have been visible and very easy, as the ships could stand off and shoot from anywhere, but inside the Straits the ships are bothered by unknown fire. The weather at present is very bad, only one out of several days being fine, and operations are much delayed in consequence.

It was an appropriate rejection of the nonsense perpetrated by Churchill and Kitchener that the operations might be completed by March 18. It was undoubtedly an opinion with which Carden would have concurred.

Instead of preparing for minor operations to assist the fleet as Kitchener had instructed, Birdwood again wrote of full-scale amphibious assaults and the best way to conduct these. He rejected Bulair and Besika Bay on the Asian shoreline and proposed, as the best line of action, "a cautious advance from Helles Point."

The following day, Birdwood telegraphed Kitchener with even more disturbing news, this time from Cairo where he had returned to make the necessary arrangements with Maxwell regarding his Australian Corps.[15] He repeated his concern that the naval operation would not succeed. He went on to say that he:

> had no intention of wishing to rush blindly into Gallipoli peninsula, and quite realise that my movements must entirely depend on the progress made by the Navy . . . but if my anticipation is fulfilled and military co-operation is needed I should propose to make my first and definite objective the line Kilid Bahr-Gabatepe. When this is attained, the Fleet would be enabled to get through to the Sea of Marmora. The Bulair Lines would then be reduced *en route* by bombardment from both sides, and for the time being my role would have been accomplished.[16]

The most important element of the telegram was his assertion that:

> Once the Fleet is through the Dardanelles, I agree that the Turks might evacuate the peninsula, and that my transports should therefore follow the Fleets, if such a course should be safe. *I fear, however, that the transports would be liable to loss from guns, with which the Navy might not have been able to deal, elsewhere than in the forts* (emphasis added).

Here was the news that Churchill had been so reluctant to make clear to Kitchener and the War Council. Churchill had been unwilling to make clear to anyone that his plan, designed to admit fully armored vessels only in to the Marmora, was unlikely to provide the conditions under which a military force could enter the Marmora. Even more culpably he had suggested that troops could enter the Marmora via Bulair. Thus, the naval-only operation could continue unabated.

Nevertheless, Kitchener cannot be forgiven for what was really a self-imposed blindness to the reality Birdwood had described in his telegram. His refusal to seriously address any possibility other than that the Turks would evacuate the peninsula had repeatedly short-circuited any discussions of this prospect not happening and had aided and abetted Churchill's refusal to come clean on the critical issue of communications.

NOTES

1. Gilbert, *CVIII*, 625–626. Lieutenant-General Birdwood to Kitchener, March 3, 1915, 6:15 A.M.

2. Ibid., 625.

3. Gilbert, *CVIII*, 625–626. Birdwood to Kitchener, telegram, 3:20 A.M., March 4.

4. Ibid., 626.

5. Ibid.

6. Gilbert, *CVIII*, 625. Carden to Churchill, telegram, 12:05 A.M., March 4.

7. Ibid.

8. Marder is an example of this. He states that "[o]n March 2nd, he (Carden) reported that, given fine weather, he hoped to be off Constantinople in about two weeks." Marder, *From Dreadnought to Scapa Flow*, vol. 2, 241. This puts the emphasis entirely in the wrong place.

9. Gilbert, *CVIII*, 627–628.

10. It also ignored the difficulty Carden would have in knowing when he was within four days of entering the Marmora. Churchill had been told in January that this was critical for Russian assistance. Their ships carried coal for four days steaming and they could not recoal on the Black Sea in bad weather. If events were not timed precisely, they would be steaming away to recoal just as the Straits were forced.

11. Gilbert, *CVIII*, 628–629. Letter, Churchill to Kitchener, March 4, 1915.

12. It is unclear why he said, "from the 2nd of March." Carden's telegram makes no mention of this date. Churchill's request for this information was made on February 28 and his reply was received on March 4 at 12:05 A.M. However, March 2 might have been the day on which Carden had penned his reply.

13. Gilbert, *CVIII*, 632–633. Kitchener to Birdwood, telegram, 11:30 P.M., March 4.

14. Gilbert, *CVIII*, 637–638. Telegram, Birdwood to Kitchener, March 5, 1915, 12.15 A.M.

15. Gilbert, *CVIII*, 643. Telegram, Birdwood to Kitchener, March 6, 1915.

16. Ibid.

CHAPTER 23

The Dardanelles in Decline: Reality Check, Carden to Churchill

[G]un fire alone will not render forts innocuous.
—Vice Admiral Carden to Winston S. Churchill, March 6, 1915

Despite its serious import, Churchill appears not to have been kept abreast of any of Kitchener's correspondence with Birdwood or its implications. He was, therefore, not aware of just how bleak the military perspective on the Dardanelles naval operation had become, or how far down the road to a full-scale amphibious operation Kitchener was being driven. He was, however, at this time, beginning to receive a reality check of his own. Most immediate of all, the Greek intervention that looked so promising after the fall of the outer forts was rapidly disappearing in face of Russian intransigence over a Greek force at Constantinople.

In the early days of March, the Greeks had fallen silent on the Dardanelles and then the Russian government refused to accept the proposal for Greek cooperation in any expedition to Constantinople. Churchill was furious with the Russians and he wrote a desperate letter to Grey on March 6 beseeching him to remove the Russian impediment to Greek assistance.[1]

Churchill was in the process of losing his dream of a united Balkan Front and the best means by which to minimize the British military commitment to the Mediterranean. He had repeatedly made it plain that the taking of Constantinople was but a means to this end. Now Russia seemed set to dash all these hopes.

Meanwhile, such word as came from Carden was not encouraging. His summary of operations on March 4 carried no good news.[2] Demolition parties, with marines in support, had been landed at Kum Kali and Seddulbahr, but they were engaged by the enemy and were forced to withdraw. Covering fire of the ships was only partially successful because the seaplanes were unable to locate the enemy.

In other words, the troops being landed to destroy guns were now being routed and the navy had been ineffectual in support.

Churchill was impatient to know more and at 9:12 A.M. he sent a telegram asking Carden to report "to what point mine-sweeping had progressed within the Straits up to the evening of 4th March." He also wanted to know whether shellfire had yet destroyed Forts 8 and 9. These were the forts he had reported to War Council on March 3 that were in the process of being destroyed.

Carden gave his Admiralty update for March 5 operations on March 6.[3] Attacks on the Narrows had begun by indirect fire of *Queen Elizabeth* supported by *Prince George* (carrying the six-inch howitzers requested by Carden in January) and *Inflexible,* which endeavored to destroy howitzers. Forts 13, 16, and 17 were attacked and the magazine in 16 was blown up. Spotting by ships inside the Straits was ineffectual because of the heavy fire from concealed guns. Seaplanes were equally ineffectual because of the wounding of one pilot, the death of another, and the destruction of a plane.

Later in the day, in a personal telegram of his own, Carden replied to Churchill's Secret and Personal telegram.[4] The telegram summarized minesweeping operations and addressed the difficulties planes were having in spotting for the ships. Three points were of particular significance, however, and fundamental to the efficacy of a naval-only operation. The first was Carden's references to opposition experienced by the Royal Marine. The second was the inability of the fleet to adequately protect the landing parties from enemy fire. The third, and most important, was Carden's assertion that "*experience has shown that in order to render a fort innocuous, it is absolutely necessary to land and destroy each gun. With few exceptions the guns in forts at the entrance was found serviceable*" (emphasis added).[5]

This telegram ought to have had a profound impact on Churchill. The great experiment of the naval-only operation was a failure. The attack on the outer forts—by far the easiest part of the entire operation and one that had employed both distant and *close* bombardment—had failed to destroy the main armaments. This operation had succeeded because the Turks had fled and allowed marines to do what Jackson had warned in early January would be necessary—place charges down the barrels of the guns and blow them up individually. The problem was the Turks were now no longer running away and the navy was having great difficulty supporting landing parties.

The import of this private telegram to Churchill—almost entirely ignored by studies on this subject—and very possibly unseen by anyone other than Churchill[6]—was of sufficient gravity to precipitate a fundamental reassessment of the naval-only operation. The fact that the naval operation had been repeatedly restricted by all sorts of problems and had not, therefore, been able to prove itself inside the Straits was irrelevant to any decision to continue the naval-only operation. The operation had failed at its first hurdle. The deliberate bombardment of the fleet—even at decisive range—had not destroyed the guns of the forts. From this point, the operation could only get more difficult. Moreover, although the fleet might still temporarily silence the forts and succeed in breaking into the Marmora, it would leave behind not only considerable numbers of mobile guns and howitzers but repairable large caliber guns in the forts as well. Where was the moral pressure expected from the gradual and relentless destruction of the guns in the forts?

Churchill now had even more cause to reassess the operation than Kitchener had given by Birdwood. Extraordinarily, he maintained a perverse sense of optimism over the operation, although the degree to which this optimism was real or feigned, calculated or careless, is a moot point. He had, it will be recalled from the last chapter, only several days earlier reenergized his Borkum/Baltic scheme (and he had yet to pen his letter to Jellicoe in which he was to write so enthusiastically that the operations at the Dardanelles was "involving profound political reactions"[7]). It was, he might have rationalized, therefore premature to surrender his naval-only assault even if it proved impossible for an army to follow it through the Dardanelles. It was, he might have argued to himself, not the time to cast any doubts at all over the efficacy of his naval-only operation and its capacity to fulfill the expectations of the War Council. The success to this point might yet draw the cooperation of Russia and bring in the Greeks and all would be well for the Dardanelles—and for Borkum/Baltic.

Churchill telegraphed the grand duke the same day that "[p]rogress was good on the 5th and 3 principal forts at Kilid Bahr were damaged especially Fort Toprak with 2–35cm guns. We should like to know by what date Russian Fleet will be ready to co-operate and when Russian Army corps will be ready to embark."[8] Later, in a letter to Kitchener he wrote, "An analysis of the forts mentioned in Carden's telegram shows that the progress is more important than I first supposed. Fort No. 16 whose magazine was blown up, contains two 14 inch guns, and is regarded as a very important factor in the defences." The optimism was unwarranted. This one piece of good news was incorrect. The main magazine for these guns had not been destroyed.[9]

Carden's reports to the Admiralty on the 7th, 8th, and 9th of March gave Churchill no further cause for optimism.[10] Bombardment activities were being restricted by fire from howitzers, which forced ships to continually shift berth. The use of seaplanes was hindered by rough seas. Although there were comments on the silencing of some forts and hits and explosions in and around others, progress evidently was not being made on the permanent destruction of the forts. Even the use of the *Queen Elizabeth* inside the Straits had not produced incontrovertible results.

Despite the damning implications of Carden's private telegram and the rather indifferent news in the Admiralty telegrams, Churchill took it upon himself to inform the Cabinet that day that "steady progress was being made in the bombardment and reduction of the Dardanelles forts."[11] There had, in fact, been no reduction of forts save those at the entrance demolished by landing parties and Carden already had conveyed there was no real prospect of such "reductions" in the future except through further landing operations, which were increasingly impracticable.

Carden promised to send a summary of up-to-date operations the following day. Perhaps here Churchill would find cause to seriously rethink the naval-only operation.

Undoubtedly mindful that it was on this day he had recommended Kitchener decide the fate of the 29th Division, Churchill sent Carden an urgent telegram some hours before the commencement of the March 10 War Council meeting: "It is important that your appreciation of the situation should reach me as soon as possible. When can I expect it?"[12]

Neither Carden's reply to this telegram, nor the important appreciation requested by Churchill, reached him in time, and he entered the War Council armed only with the latest Admiralty telegrams. In any event, Kitchener had a surprise in store. Even before Churchill gave the War Council his summary of operations, Kitchener declared "that the situation was now sufficiently secure to justify the dispatch of the 29th Division." Here, rather belatedly, was the answer to all Churchill's prayers. Kitchener took one step further and proposed sending the Territorial Mounted Division to Egypt as a reserve. In round numbers the grand total (of forces available) "might be regarded as 120,000 men and 250 guns." Kitchener estimated that this force would be opposed by 60,000 men in and about the Dardanelles and possibly another 120,000 men for the defense of Constantinople. That Kitchener so casually contemplated an operation against substantially superior numbers—which might quickly be reinforced—was quite extraordinary.

It is often said that Kitchener made his decision to finally send these forces as a result of an improved situation on the Eastern Front—his own explanation here. It is more likely, however, that it was the weight of information that had come from the Mediterranean via Birdwood that forced his hand.

After Kitchener's pronouncements, Churchill gave his appreciation of naval operations. He said there was not much news from the Dardanelles as the bombardment had been interrupted by thick weather. He then gave a cursory summary of recent operations. He highlighted the *Queen Elizabeth's* attack on fort 13, noting that eight rounds had been fired and three had struck the fort. However, he made no mention of the ongoing difficulties of reconnaissance and spotting, no mention of Carden's assertion that the forts could be silenced only by landing parties, nor the fact that these landing parties were now meeting heavy opposition, and he made no mention of the difficulties posed by field guns and mobile howitzers. Choosing his words carefully, he concluded his assessment by stating that "[t]he Admiralty still believed that they could effect the passage through the Straits by naval means alone, but they were glad to know that military support was available, if required."[13]

Churchill's assertion that the Admiralty still believed the fleet could break through into the Marmora by naval means alone was in fact far from the truth if the "destruction" as opposed to the temporary "silencing" of the fortifications were a prerequisite to the fleet entering the Marmora. Only if the importance of the fleet's communications now counted for naught among his Admiralty advisers could Churchill's assertion be seen as fair and reasonable. Additionally, the word emanating from the Mediterranean was now quite clearly in opposition to a continuation of the naval-only operation.

The warning contained in Carden's telegram to Churchill of March 6, was corroborated by Carden's second in command, John de Robeck on March 9 in his "Appreciation of present position in Dardanelles and proposals for future operations," in which he expressed the belief that forts could be "dominated" but not "destroyed" and that in this case even if warships passed into the Marmora, the passage would be barred to the unarmored supply ships necessary to maintain them there.[14] He noted, "The situation is therefore reduced to the point at which military cooperation is considered essential in order to clear at least one side of the straits of the enemy and their mobile batteries."

De Robeck was formally declaring what had been implicit in Carden's March 6 telegram. The gradual bombardment might admit a fleet to the Marmora but the forts, mobile guns, and howitzers would continue to pose a threat thereafter.

The latter portion of this quotation once again demonstrates the significant gap between the Carden plan and the Churchill plan. De Robeck believed the threat to the fleet's lines of communication were grounds for a military operation on the peninsula. He obviously was unaware that the plan presented by Churchill to the War Council had never anticipated that supply vessels would accompany the fleet and that Churchill, at least, was unlikely to be moved by such concerns.

De Robeck's appraisal also indicates that, like Carden, he is unaware that the War Council intended to send a large military force through the Straits after it had broken through. If he had known this, he surely would have nominated it as another reason for a military attack on the peninsula.

The Admiralty received more negative news from Admiral Limpus on March 10, although it is unclear whether this telegram, like de Robeck's assessment, was known to Churchill at the time. He stated plainly that "he considered a landing in force on the peninsula essential."[15] Limpus believed that the point of the operation

> *is to get free passage in to the Marmora*. If this is accomplished, successful action can be taken against Constantinople, and then, if necessary against the Bosporus. It is quite possible that when the Dardanelles are forced, all serious resistance by the Turks would cease. Anyhow the first thing is to win the passage of the Dardanelles (emphasis added).[16]

Like de Robeck and Carden, he believed the forts at the Narrows and the howitzers could not be dealt with effectively. He believed, therefore, that even after the minefields had been swept, this gauntlet still would have to be run by armored ships. Even if the armored ships succeeded in breaking through, supply ships would not be able to. Limpus wrote, "Without supplies and colliers it is little use going into the Marmora."

He concluded, "The question then is one of landing, fighting for and holding the Gallipoli Peninsula."[17]

Whether or not Churchill had read these communications, Carden's summary when it came ought to have held few surprises for anyone capable of a sober assessment of his telegrams of the previous week:

> The methodical reduction of the forts is not feasible without expenditure of ammunition out of all proportion to that available . . . ships inside Straits constantly exposed to fire from concealed guns with which it has been found impossible to deal effectively their plunging fire is very destructive but up to the present its accuracy has been poor though it is improving . . . we for the present are checked by absence of efficient air reconnaissance, necessity of clearing mine fields and presence of large numbers of movable howitzers.[18]

He repeated his warning to Churchill on March 6 when he concluded: "*Our experience shows gun fire alone will not render forts innocuous most of the guns must be destroyed individually by demolition*" (emphasis added).

Individually and cumulatively, these assessments were a damning indictment on the further progress of a naval-only operation. De Robeck and Limpus and Carden really left little hope that that the fleet's guns could destroy the guns in the forts at any range. Moreover, none believed the fleet would achieve anything of significance once in the Marmora unless its lines of communication were first secured.

Nevertheless, Carden recommended that "indirect fire from *Queen Elizabeth* from outside the Straits and *Lord Nelson* or *Agamemnon* from inside the Straits with old battleships ready to close and take advantage of results of long range fire" be attempted. This would push the attack more vigorously. He also suggested, however, that "until it is considered advantageous to commence bombardment on large scale it is not advisable to send Battleships far inside by day as it only affords practice to the enemy's howitzers."

As a result of Carden's telegram, Sir Henry Jackson concluded, as surely Churchill ought to have done four days earlier, that troops were now required to capture the peninsula. In a memorandum to Oliver, he noted Carden's concerns over howitzers and the guns in the forts and his belief that "demolition parties are essential to render the guns useless."[19] He pointed out that these problems had all been foreseen and small forces supplied to deal with them, but hitherto Carden had been instructed "not to risk the force on shore in positions where they could not be covered by ship's guns without further reference to the Admiralty." He also pointed out that Turkish forces had prevented landing parties from completing demolition at the entrance and would be even more successful inside the Straits. Jackson said there were "now ample military forces ready at short notice for co-operation with him, if necessary; and I suggest the time has arrived to make use of them."[20]

Jackson considered Carden's proposal to use the *Queen Elizabeth, Lord Nelson*, and *Agamemnon*'s covering fire to allow old battleships to close in and take advantage of long-range fire as a dangerous break from Carden's original plan, even though this tactic had been used on the forts at the entrance. Armed now with the knowledge that few of the guns at the entrance had been destroyed by the naval bombardment and aware of the vigorous resistance the Turks were now putting up, he evidently saw danger in ships placing themselves within range of forts inside the Straits. His most compelling argument for immediate military assistance, however, was the need to ensure safe passage for the troops now being prepared for operations inside the Marmora. He declared that the Gallipoli Peninsula must be cleared of the enemy's artillery and:

> *Its occupation is a practical necessity before the Straits are safe for the passage of troops as far as the Sea of Marmora.*
>
> *I suggest the Vice Admiral be asked if he considers the time has now arrived to make use of military forces to occupy the Gallipoli peninsula, and clear away the enemy artillery on that side*—an operation he would support with his squadrons. (emphasis added)

In light of the discussions at the recent War Council meeting, which now considered a military force operating inside the Marmora as indispensable to the complete success of the Dardanelles operation, and given Jackson's comments regarding the necessity of occupying the peninsula *before* troops could be admitted to the Marmora, Churchill ought now to have considered his operation incapable of achieving the desired results. Although the fleet might force its way into the Marmora, the troops deemed essential for success could not follow. Perhaps more important, Jackson was now formally supporting Carden's conviction that the fleet might temporarily silence the forts but would not and could not destroy them and that, although the fleet might break into the Marmora, it would face a serious threat from the forts should it be forced to return.

Remarkably, Churchill was unswayed. Rather than press for the immediate conversion of the enterprise to a joint amphibious operation, he sought merely to escalate the intensity of the naval operation. Despite having read Jackson's memorandum, he sent Carden a telegram he had begun drafting the day before. His instructions discarded the cautious and deliberate approach hitherto considered essential to maximize the moral pressure on the Turks. Loss of ships and men were now to be ignored. The expectation that naval losses would boost Turkish morale was forgotten. Carden was told to "overwhelm the forts at the Narrows at decisive range by the fire of the largest number of guns great and small. . . . Under cover of this fire the guns at the forts might be destroyed by landing parties and much of the minefield swept up."[21] This was to be repeated until all guns at the forts were destroyed and mines cleared.[22]

Churchill asserted in *The World Crisis* that his entire War Group—even Jackson—acquiesced in the telegram. This seems extremely unlikely given Jackson's memorandum. If the War Group did support the telegram—and there is evidence it was signed by Fisher and Oliver—they were responsible for a truly bizarre communication. Decisive range required the fleet to get through the minefields first. Decisive range also meant coming into the effective range of the forts, something it had always been intended to avoid. Moreover, the sequence of events described would suggest that landing parties would have to journey extraordinary distances along the peninsula to complete the destruction of the guns in the forts. That such a proposition was possible is inconceivable.

The reference to landing parties was a landmark concession from Churchill. He appeared now to be acknowledging that the permanent disablement of the guns demanded military intervention, albeit on a small scale. Hitherto, he had failed repeatedly to acknowledge this. His determination to press the naval operation ignored the fact that the landing of small demolition parties would prove fruitless in the face of Turkish opposition and that the landing of large-scale parties inside the Straits was an invitation to disaster. Thus had Jackson recommended an amphibious assault on the peninsula.

His telegram failed to address the problems the mobile guns and howitzer were posing for effective bombardment operation, nor did it address the now-vital issue of troop movements after the fleet was through should these weapons remain operational. Jackson had made plain that the occupation of the peninsula was essential if troops were to be used in the Marmora. Churchill was now unilaterally making a decision to proceed with an operation that could not admit a military force into the Marmora as per the expectations of Kitchener.

Technical difficulties of a more intense bombardment were overlooked as well. This would make the study of the fall of shot almost impossible, not the least because of the clouds of dirt and dust. The destruction of forts at "decisive" range was really only practicable on or near the shorelines. Forts higher up could not be attacked and destroyed because the elevation of the fleet's guns would not permit it. Churchill's telegram was a message from a desperate man determined to cling to his plan and his timetable regardless of consequence.

We now come to something of an historical muddle, which requires some attention if we are to attempt to understand how Churchill now stood on the issue of military assistance at this critical juncture. Having instructed Carden to attack more aggressively and, thereby, ignoring Jackson's assessment of the operation, Churchill belatedly addressed the matter of military support with his prime minister.

At midnight on March 11, Churchill wrote to Asquith, "The 1 Sea Lord and I attach the greatest importance to Ian Hamilton [recently appointed by Kitchener over Birdwood to command the expeditionary forces in the Mediterranean] getting to Lemnos at the earliest possible moment." Ignoring altogether that the imminent need for military assistance about which he wrote was entirely a result of his own decision to escalate the naval operation, he added:

> The naval operations may at any moment become intimately dependent on military assistance. In view of the exertions we are making we are entitled to a good military opinion as to the use of whatever forces may be available. The enclosed telegrams will show you what the position is. I trust you will be able to represent this to Kitchener.[23]

One of the telegrams to which he referred was Carden's summary of events.[24]

Asquith read Churchill's note later that morning. He wrote to Venetia Stanley that he had:

> just been reading the Admiralty secret report of the operations so far; they are making progress but it is slow, and there are a

> large number of howitzers and concealed guns (not in the forts) on both shores which give them a good deal of trouble, and have made a lot of holes in the ships, though so far the damage is not serious. I think the Admiral is quite right to proceed very cautiously; Winston is rather for spurring him on.[25]

It is presumed Asquith approached Kitchener regarding the matter because he wrote to Churchill later that day that "Hamilton cannot leave until we have thoroughly studied the situation with which we may be confronted. I hope we will get him off Saturday night . . . 'more haste and less speed.'"

A day later on March 13, Kitchener wrote again to Churchill:

> In answer to your question, unless it is found that our estimate of the Ottoman strength on the Gallipoli Peninsula is exaggerated and the position on the Kilid Bahr Plateau less strong than anticipated, no operation on a large scale should be attempted until the 29th Division has arrived and is ready to take part in what is likely to prove a difficult undertaking in which severe fighting must be anticipated.

In *The World Crisis,* Churchill claimed that this note from Kitchener was a response to a request he made for a formal statement from the War Office on Sir Henry Jackson's minute. Similar assertions were made at the Dardanelles Inquiry.

The nature of the military assistance being sought by Churchill at this time is further confused by evidence from Hankey's diary. He recorded on March 12 that:

> Sir Ian told me he is in an embarrassing position as Churchill wants him to try to rush the Straits by a *coup de main* with such troops as are available in the Levant (30,000 Australasians and 10,000 Naval Division). Kitchener on the other hand wants him to go slow, to make the Navy continue pounding the Straits, and to wait for the 29 Division.[26]

What is apparent from this evidence is that Churchill is now desperate for decisive intervention from both Carden and Hamilton. This sudden enthusiasm on Churchill's behalf for some precipitate action contrasts markedly with his declaration at the War Council on March 10 that "[i]t was . . . evident that Admiral Carden did not expect to get through the Straits for a week or two. The forts must first be thoroughly broken up; there was no hurry; and some time might still be necessary, particularly if thick weather was encountered."[27]

This declaration, one might be reminded, had been made in full knowledge of Carden's belief that the forts could not be destroyed by ships alone.

What had caused the change?

At the Dardanelles Inquiry, Churchill asserted that his March 11 telegram and a second on March 15, which recommended more aggressive action by Carden, were based on intelligence received regarding shortages of ammunition in the Turkish forts and German and Austrian intentions to send submarines to the Dardanelles. As far as the March 11 telegram is concerned, this is untrue.[28] The intelligence was received on March 12, the day after the above telegram was sent, and Churchill and Fisher were not aware of it until March 13.[29] This, therefore, cannot stand as an explanation for Churchill's request for more aggressive operations

A more compelling explanation remains—that is, Churchill's desire to meet a deadline for his northern operations, which Churchill still hoped might begin at the beginning of May. Carden's telegram made evident the naval attempt was going to take some time longer than the one month he tentatively had suggested would be required for the completion of the operation and that Churchill seemed determined to hold him to.

Moreover, Churchill's expectation that military support would be available on March 20, should the navy need assistance, had been dashed by Kitchener's unexpected decision to prohibit any *large-scale* military operations until the 29th Division had arrived, and this would not be until some time in April.

So, one finds Churchill, despite the reservations of Jackson, Limpus, de Robeck, and Carden himself, prescribing a more aggressive and risky naval operation while simultaneously priming Hamilton for military assistance at the earliest opportunity.

It is not clear just what kind of military assistance Churchill wanted. One of the difficulties we have in understanding this is that Churchill's directions to Carden anticipated landings to destroy the guns in the forts only. Hankey's rather eccentric expression "rush the Straits" does not help the historian. This would suggest he wanted troops to assist the naval operation according to his telegram to Carden on March 11. That is, to capture and destroy forts that had been silenced from *inside* the Straits.

In view of his telegram to Carden, it is almost certain that Churchill was not inviting Hamilton to attempt to take the forts in reverse in a major land operation. Hamilton's expression "rush the Straits" does not fit the bill.[30] Also, Churchill must have known that such a plan would require naval operations to cease while the fleet supported the landings. Such had been recommended in Jackson's letter to Oliver. It is also surprising that if Churchill was now hoping the army would occupy the peninsula, he did not indicate this to Carden or seek his guidance on this matter as recommended by Jackson.

What is clear, however, is that, having spent the previous three weeks arguing the indispensability of the 29th Division, he now was prepared to force the Dardanelles without them at the very moment when his wish had been granted. It was, in short, a strange time to encourage a more aggressive naval attack at the very time a substantial force had been provided to enhance the prospect of success.

Additionally, Churchill's new instructions to Carden offered a naïve solution to fortifications but ignored entirely the issue of mobile guns and howitzers. Leaving aside the impact these were having on the effectiveness of the operations, he refused to address the problems mobile guns and howitzers would pose for the movement of troops into the Marmora and the supply of the fleet, which now preoccupied naval and military advisers alike.

In summary, the evidence shows Churchill directing Carden to undertake a more dangerous and aggressive naval operation in an attempt to force the Straits. The army would provide only forces, in addition to the marines, to destroy fortifications silenced by the fleet. He made this decision against the advice of Carden, Jackson, de Robeck, and Limpus—all of whom had declared that neither the guns in the forts nor the mobile guns and howitzers could be *destroyed*. All these men believed that no purpose would be served by a fleet in the Marmora until all major armaments had been put permanently out of action. All these men now believed this could be achieved only by a full-scale invasion and occupation of the peninsula.

Churchill's determination to see through his naval-only operation has been noted many times in this paper. To this extent, his preparedness to ignore his advisers would be unremarkable except for two new critical developments. The first development, of course, was that the War Council now expected the naval operation to facilitate the entrance into the Marmora of a substantial body of men to "reap the fruits" of the naval operation. Despite Kitchener's insistence to the contrary, Churchill knew—and he was certainly being told as much by his naval advisers—these men would never enter the Marmora through the Straits. This left only Churchill's contention that they would enter the Marmora via Bulair, and nothing supports the efficacy of such a proposition. Certainly Churchill never asked Carden's opinion on the matter. Quite extraordinarily, even at this late juncture, neither Carden nor de Robeck had any idea that a large body of troops would be used in the Marmora. Thus, by continuing his naval-only agenda, Churchill risked denying his fleet and the operation the support of the substantial body of men he had spent the last several weeks gathering to ensure the success of the Dardanelles operation.

The second development was Kitchener's decision to send the 29th Division. This coincided almost to the day with Churchill's telegram to Carden. The inconsistency between Churchill's decision to hurry on the naval operation and the fact that such a decision would necessarily forego the support of this newly won prize—hitherto considered essential by Churchill to "reap the fruits" of naval success—has been noted. Why in the name of haste was Churchill determined to press on with such a fundamentally flawed naval operation in the face of such strong opposition, particularly when he now had within his grasp the military forces believed necessary to ensure success?

This book returns to the contention that Churchill was being driven by a personal agenda, present from the beginning, which viewed the Dardanelles operation as little more than a prelude to his war-winning northern schemes. Both time and prestige were of the essence if he were to see such dreams fulfilled. Delay at the Dardanelles would see his May deadline slip by, while failure would end his dreams altogether. Success, on the other hand, would provide the prestige deemed essential to force his northern schemes on its reluctant participants. In such circumstances, Churchill remained determined on a naval-only success to the bitter end, even if the subsequent political and strategic successes were not achieved.

NOTES

1. Gilbert, *CVIII*, 645. Draft letter, Churchill to Grey, March 6, 1915. Churchill thought better of the aggressive hyperbole and chose not to send it.
2. Ibid., Telegram, Carden to Admiralty, March 5, 1915, 4:30 A.M, 636–637.
3. Ibid., Telegram, Corden to Admiralty, March 6, 1915, 643–644.

4. Gilbert, *CVIII*, 646. Secret and Personal Telegram, Carden to Churchill, March 6, 1915.

5. Ibid.

6. The typed copy of this telegram to Churchill in the Churchill Archives does not have a circulation list, nor does it have Oliver's or Fisher's telltale initials. It is not mentioned in *The World Crisis* and I have not seen its import considered in any text.

7. Op cit., Gilbert, *CVIII*, 656–658.

8. Gilbert, *CVIII*, 647.

9. Ibid., 651. See Corbett, *Naval Operations*, vol. 2, footnote, 196.

10. Reports March 7 and 8, Gilbert, *CVIII*, 652–653.

11. See Asquith to George V, Gilbert, *CVIII*, 659.

12. The following is drawn from War Council minutes, March 10, Gilbert, *CVIII*, 663–673.

13. Ibid., 665.

14. Prior, "Churchill's 'World Crisis,'" 292. Memorandum by de Robeck, "Appreciation of present position in Dardanelles and proposals for future operations," March 9, 1915.

15. CAB 19/30, Memorandum Limpus, March 10, 1915.

16. Ibid.

17. Ibid.

18. Gilbert, *CVIII*, 661–662. Telegram, Carden to Admiralty, March 10, 1915, 2.55 P.M.

19. Gilbert, *CVIII*, 676–677. Jackson to Oliver, March 11, 1915.

20. Ibid.

21. Gilbert, *CVIII*, 677–678, Secret and Personal Telegram, Churchill to Carden, March 11, 1.35 P.M.

22. Ibid. It is an entirely plausible argument that Jackson's memorandum was written *after* he had seen Churchill's reply to Carden and in particular Churchill's suggestion that the fleet, "choosing favourable weather conditions . . . overwhelm the forts at the Narrows at decisive range by the fire of the largest number of guns great and small that can be brought to bear upon them." This does seem to imply something of a rush at the Straits.

23. Ibid., 679. Letter, Churchill to Asquith, March 11, 1915.

24. Gilbert, *CVIII*, op cit., 661–662, Telegram, Carden to Admiralty.

25. Gilbert, *CVIII*, 682–683. Letter, Asquith to Stanley, March 12, 1915.

26. Gilbert, *CVIII*, 681, excerpt, Hankey's Diaries, March 12, 1915.

27. Gilbert *CVIII*, 643, Minutes of War Council Meeting, March 10, 1915.

28. See Churchill's introductory arguments at Dardanelles Commission, 89.

29. Martin Gilbert in volume 3 of his Churchill volumes writes that DNI, Captain Hall, rushed the telegram declaring this news to Churchill and Fisher on March 19, the day after the naval attack and it had immediate impact on them both. See Gilbert, *CVIII*, 356. Marder has correctly pointed out the error regarding the date. See Arthur J. Marder, *From the Dardanelles to Oran: Studies of the Royal Navy in War and Peace 1915–1940* (London:

Oxford University Press, 1974), footnote 22. The fact that the information was received on March 12 but not made known to Churchill and Fisher on March 13 is recorded in Patrick Beesly, *Room 40: British Naval Intelligence 1914–1918* (London: Hamish Hamilton, 1982), 80–82. Confusion continues to live on, however. See Geoffrey Penn, *Fisher, Churchill and the Dardanelles* (South Yorkshire: Leo Cooper, 1999), 153. He notes the error in the date but continues to assume that Fisher and Churchill were not aware of the intelligence until March 19.

30. A small clue can be found in a brief note from Fisher to Churchill on March 12 in which he wrote, "Carden to press on! . . . and Kitchener to occupy the deserted forts at extremity of Gallipoli and mount howitzers there!"

CHAPTER 24

Hamilton Departs

Although Churchill was determined to press on with his naval operation, he was now very much alive to the reality that the large-scale use of troops would be needed to help the fleet through. Churchill had wanted troops ready by March 18, to be taken through the Straits or across Bulair for operations on Turkish soil beginning on March 20. This date had been nominated after Churchill's excessively sanguine assessment of Carden's March 4 telegram indicating it would take 14 days of fine weather for the fleet to break into the Marmora. He also had written in his memorandum of February 26 that, had the naval operation not succeeded by March 21 (the date he had at this time hoped the 29th Division and another Territorial Division would arrive in the Mediterranean), the army might be used to attack the Gallipoli Peninsula and see the fleet through.

It is apparent that one way or another, Churchill was determined to see March 19 to March 21 mark the period of naval success or the beginning of large-scale military assistance for the Dardanelles operation. It was surely more than a coincidence that these dates were within a day or two of the one-month period it was originally thought the operation might take.

Kitchener's belief that it was reasonable to enter the Marmora with 60,000 men or more but impossible to take the peninsula with the same number had, as Churchill discovered on March 11 to his considerable chagrin, thrown a spanner in his works. No large-scale operations on the peninsula to assist the fleet—from either inside or outside the Straits—were to occur until the reinforcements from England had arrived.

Churchill hoped Hamilton might be able to persuade Kitchener otherwise and would have been dismayed to learn the contents of the secret instructions given to Hamilton by Kitchener before he left.[1] He informed Hamilton that the

> employment of military force on any large scale for land operations at this juncture is only contemplated in the event of the Fleet failing to get through after every effort has been exhausted. Before a serious undertaking is carried out in the Gallipoli Peninsula all the British forces detailed for the expedition should be assembled, so their full weight can be thrown in.[2]

Kitchener's instructions to Hamilton did not preclude "minor operations to clear areas occupied by Turks with mobile guns or for the demolition of forts already silenced by the Fleet," but he wanted most of the force reserved for the advance on Constantinople. He thereby ignored Birdwood's and Jackson's warnings that small-scale operations were no longer practicable.

Kitchener's subsequent guidelines were naïve and fraught with difficulty. Once the fleet was through and the Turkish Fleet destroyed, Kitchener anticipated the opening of the Bosporus for the passage of Russian forces. He appeared to assume this would not be a difficult task. He wrote casually of forces being landed on the east side of the Bosporus to sever east-west communications. This would be achieved by British and French forces, which would "probably have been brought up to the neighbourhood of Constantinople." This was as close as he came in this letter to explaining how troops were to get into the Marmora.

At another point, he wrote of occupying Bulair with support of the fleet on both sides of the Straits. This must have assumed that a substantial force had occupied Bulair from inside the Straits because Hamilton and Birdwood had explained to him the difficulties of attacking Bulair from the Gulf of Xeros.[3] The value of a fleet at Bulair probably was overrated. Although the isthmus was at its narrowest at this point, a spine of hills would prevent the fleet enfilading across the width of the Bulair Isthmus, and the fleet's difficulty with entrenched or concealed troops already had been demonstrated. Moreover, it is doubtful the fleet had any intention of pausing to reduce Bulair on the way to fighting the Turkish Fleet.

Additionally, bombarding ships would have been exposed to field guns and howitzers on both sides of the Straits and could not have remained safely near shore.

Carden still had no idea that, should he break into the Marmora, one of his tasks would be to transport and protect an army to Constantinople. Churchill had not yet bothered to inform anyone in the Mediterranean that troops were gathering to do other than "reap the fruits of victory."[4] Again, was it an oversight by Churchill or a judgment based on the apprehension that Carden would declare the intention to transport troops through the Straits as impossible?

Whatever Churchill's motives might have been, he made no effort to officially inform Carden that this would be one of his responsibilities. Instead, he continued to press Carden to be more aggressive. On March 13, he chastised Carden for his ineffectual minesweeping operations: "Two or three hundred casualties would be a moderate price to pay for sweeping as far as the Narrows."[5]

It was in this telegram that Churchill also informed Carden that the Turks on the peninsula were running short of ammunition and that Germany and Austria were seriously contemplating sending a submarine:

> All this makes it clear that the operations should now be pressed forward methodically and resolutely by night and day the unavoidable losses being accepted. The enemy is harassed and anxious now. Time is precious as interference of submarines would be [a] very serious complication.

He concluded by informing him that General Hamilton was on his way, but added, "Do not delay your own operations on his account."

The following day (March 14) Carden replied to Churchill's telegram of March 11. He fully concurred that the "stage is reached when vigorous sustained action necessary for success." However, in the next paragraph, he wrote: "In my opinion *military operations on large scale should be commenced immediately in order to ensure my communication line immediately Fleet enters Sea of Marmora*"[6] (emphasis added).

He anticipated "the losses in passing through the Narrows may be great" and asked that more ships be "in readiness at short notice and additional ammunition be despatched as soon as possible." He went on to explain the problem of breaking through the minefields:

> In order to immediately follow up silencing efforts at the Narrows with close range bombardment, it is necessary to clear

> the minefields at Kephez. So as to economise ammunition the attempt being made to clear at night; this so far has been unsuccessful.[7]

He indicated a final attempt to achieve this would be made that night and, if that failed, also that:

> it will be necessary to destroy fixed and movable light guns defending minefields before continuing sweeping, destroying all these guns will bring ships under fire of forts at Narrows and will therefore entail silencing the latter which must now go on irrespective of air reconnaissances. . . .
>
> This accomplished, sweeping will be carried out working day and night but as minefield is extensive operations may occupy some time and expenditure of ammunition will be very great as forts will require repeatedly silencing.[8]

Such was the circularity of the problem facing Carden. Which link to destroy first? He had finally concluded that, should the minesweeping fail, the only possible solution was to attack everything at once.

Churchill forwarded Carden's telegram to Kitchener and wrote: "Fisher is very insistent, and I agree with him, in asking you to have the troops in Egypt which are available sent to rendezvous at Mudros Bay with the French who arrive on the 18th and the 16,000 men who are already there." He did not wish (he spoke also on behalf of Fisher) in any way "to prejudice any decision which you may take as to the use of the troops after Hamilton has studied the situation with Carden." He thought, however, that it was "only asking for a reasonable precaution that the forces now available be concentrated there."[9]

Carden's telegram urgently requested the *immediate* commencement of large-scale operations on the peninsula to protect his communications, but *still* Churchill held back from making any suggestion that large-scale operations were needed simultaneously with the naval operations. Rather he concluded, "the naval operations of engaging the forts and sweeping the approaches to the Narrows will proceed steadily. They cannot be delayed, because of the increasing danger of submarines arriving and of heavy howitzers being mounted."[10]

At 1:40 A.M. on March 14, Churchill wrote to Carden approving his plan for a more aggressive bombardment and informing him that efforts were being made to ready 59,000 men for large-scale operations any time after March 18. His telegram assumed that he was not, at this stage, contemplating a "rush" without having first cleared the mines and destroyed "all the primary armaments of the forts." He requested that the Admiralty be consulted before he attempted such an operation because it "might then be found that decisive Military action to take the Kilid Bahr plateau would be less costly than a naval rush."[11]

Despite all the talk of troops, the operation remained almost exclusively naval in character. The only significant change was that the naval operations were about to become much more aggressive. This ignored Jackson's and Carden's warnings about the impossibility of destroying the guns of the forts—even at so-called decisive range—and it ignored Carden's, Jackson's, and Birdwood's fears regarding the fleet's communications.

What is of particular interest is Churchill's apparent willingness to contemplate a naval rush through the peninsula before finally succumbing to a military attack on the peninsula. The day before he wrote this telegram to Carden, he had written to the naval secretary and others that a number of tramps and old steamers should be collected at Malta to be used as "barrier breakers . . . if anything like a rush is required at the critical moment."[12]

At this late juncture with two extra divisions now on the way to the Mediterranean, the question of the relative cost of a naval rush versus military action surely missed the point. The critical issue in determining whether or not to proceed with a full-scale military operation on the peninsula ought to have been a sober assessment of the value of the fleet inside the Marmora, while the Turks continued to hold the peninsula and the likelihood of capturing the peninsula once the fleet had forced its way through. This assessment must now consider the capacity of the naval operations to ensure the safe passage of an army through the Straits. Yet, as always, Churchill was prepared to ignore these critical issues.

Fisher, however, continued to badger Churchill on the use of troops. The same day, he wrote to Churchill requesting an immediate meeting of the War Council (with Landsdowne and Bonar Law in attendance). He attached a copy of Julian Corbett's letter of March 1, which explored the value of a feint against Bulair. Fisher suggested that military cooperation be ordered with "all speed and make the demonstration with all possible dispatch at *both* extremities of the *Gallipoli Peninsula*—and telegraph at once for Egyptian Transports to leave with all dispatch."[13]

Churchill evidently was being hurried—indeed pushed—by Fisher to demand the immediate use of troops, although it is interesting Fisher spoke only of a "demonstration." Churchill did not want "a lot of ignorant people to meddle in our business." He expected that Kitchener "will do what we want about the troops being concentrated at Mudros" if he and Fisher saw him together. He continued that "if not there is nothing for it but to wait for Hamilton's report which should reach us Wednesday. Meanwhile the naval operations are proceeding within safe and sure limits. P.S. I am counting much on Hamilton."[14]

The renewed attack was supposed to take place on March 17, but the day before Carden went on to the sick list and was replaced by de Robeck. The attack was therefore delayed a day. Churchill telegraphed de Robeck and asked him to execute the operation "without delay if he thought them wise and practicable."[15] De Robeck consulted with Hamilton where he learned, per Kitchener's requirements, that "no joint Naval and Military action can be decided on . . . pending results of our attack on the Narrows."[16] Whether or not de Robeck was enamored with the plan, he was compelled to proceed with it before Hamilton would commit his troops. He informed Churchill he would attempt the operation.

Around this time Hamilton had telegraphed Kitchener with news that should have come as no surprise. He explained that the Admiralty had been overly sanguine as to what could be done by ships alone and that the Turks were repairing damage to their fortifications, that the coasts were bristling with howitzers and field guns in concealed emplacements, and that the channel was sown with "complicated and constantly renewed minefields."[17]

Despite this sobering news all remained set for the great attack of March 18. The fleet would go in the following day with all guns blazing. The idea of a gradual bombardment and precision shooting had been substituted with weight of explosive and number of shells. Risks were now to be taken and the loss of ships—even considerable losses—accepted. In *The World Crisis,* Churchill played down this change in the operation, but it was significant and entirely contrived by Churchill. Privy to Kitchener's instructions to Hamilton, and limited by strictures placed on him by Churchill, de Robeck reluctantly acquiesced and knew that he had no choice but to continue despite his grave reservations over his fleet's lines of communications.

Even Kitchener, who expected the fleet to exhaust every effort before resorting to a full-scale military landing, had counseled Hamilton that the attempt to force the Straits would "require time, patience and methodical plans of co-operation."[18] It is doubtful he wished to see the loss of large numbers of ships if the fleet might subsequently be needed to support an amphibious landing.

Churchill continued to demonstrate all the signs of a man in a hurry. March 18 was the culmination of the naval attack *only* because Churchill had made it so. Despite his claims of unanimity within the Admiralty War Group, he was clearly the one who continued to push hardest for a naval-only attempt. He was determined to press on with his naval-only operation because the only realistic alternative was an amphibious assault on the peninsula, and this he had no time for.

NOTES

1. Gilbert, *CVIII*, 684–686. Letter, Kitchener to Sir Ian Hamilton, March 13, 1915 entitled *Instructions for the General Officer Commanding-in-Chief the Mediterranean Expeditionary Force.*

2. Ibid.

3. Kitchener informed the War Council on June 12 that he had discussed the idea of an attack on Bulair with Hamilton before his departure. The problem with such a plan was that troops would have to be landed 30 miles from Bulair and this force could be attacked from two sides. Birdwood had said almost precisely the same. See also Birdwood to Kitchener Gilbert, *CVIII*, 638.

4. See Carden's testimony to Dardanelles Commission.

5. Gilbert, *CVIII*, 687–88. Telegram Secret and Personal, Churchill to Carden, March 13, 1915.

6. Ibid., 693. Telegram, Vice-Admiral Carden to Admiralty, Noon, March 14, 1915.

7. Ibid.

8. Ibid.

9. Ibid., 694. Note, Churchill to Kitchener, March 14, 1915.

10. Ibid.

11. Ibid., Secret and Personal Telegram, Churchill to Vice-Admiral Carden, 1.40 A.M., March 14, 1915.

12. See memorandum, Churchill, *The World Crisis*, vol. 2, 546.

13. Gilbert, *CVIII*, 698.

14. Ibid., 699.

15. Ibid., 706. Personal and Secret Telegram, Churchill to Vice-Admiral de Robeck, March 17, 1915.

16. Ibid., Telegram Vice-Admiral de Robeck to Admiralty, 2.10 A.M., March 18, 1915.

17. All this as reported by Asquith to Venetia Stanley in a letter of March 18. See Gilbert, *CVIII*, 707.

18. Ibid., 684. Letter, Kitchener to Sir Ian Hamilton, March 13, 1915 entitled *Instructions For The General Officer Commanding-in-Chief the Mediterranean Expeditionary Force.*

CHAPTER 25

The Fleet Attacks: March 18 and the Aftermath

The attack on the defenses of the Narrows commenced at 10:45 A.M. on March 18. By the end of the day, the battleships, *Bouvet, Irresistible,* and *Ocean* had been sunk with the loss of more than 600 lives, the *Gaulois* had been run ashore, and the *Inflexible* (the only ship capable of chasing and single-handedly destroying the *Goeben*) had been seriously damaged. Despite this, de Robeck informed the Admiralty by telegram on March 19 that "[w]ith the exception of ships lost and damaged Squadron is ready for immediate action."[1]

Hamilton, however, had concluded that the army must help the navy get through and he informed Kitchener that its role would be more "than mere landings of parties to destroy forts, it must be deliberate and progressive military operation carried out at full strength."[2]

At that day's War Council meeting, Churchill was unperturbed by the losses. He sought and gained the War Council permission to continue. This was, no doubt, influenced by Kitchener's announcement that troops at Lemnos would need to return to Alexandria (and the French to Port Said) before they would be ready for operations on the peninsula. This would cause considerable delay to any amphibious operation.

Fisher, on the other hand, now thought increasingly in terms of some kind of land attack at the earliest opportunity and wrote:

> I have only one anxiety the German and Austrian submarines—*when they appear the game will be up!* That's why I wish to

> press on the military co-operation and get a base at Cape Helles anyhow. It will be 3 weeks before the military can do anything according to present arrangements.[3]

On March 21, de Robeck informed the Admiralty that he believed the forts could be dominated sufficiently to enable minesweepers to clear the Kephez minefields. The howitzer and gunfire would have to be faced because "it was impossible for the ships to deal with it."

Later in the day, however, Hamilton and de Robeck again met aboard the *Queen Elizabeth*. They discussed the various options available, and it was apparently here that de Robeck learned for the first time that it was expected troops would be transported through the Straits as or after the fleet broke through. At this point, it was decided that operations would be suspended until a large-scale assault on the peninsula could be undertaken.

On March 23, de Robeck explained his decision to Churchill. He feared that if all the guns were not destroyed any success of the fleet "may be nullified by Straits closing up."[4] He did not believe it possible in the face of the Turkish defenses to land a force inside the Straits of sufficient size to undertake such an operation and concluded that it appeared "better to prepare a decisive effort about the middle of April rather than risk a great deal for what may possibly be a partial solution."[5] In a letter to Kitchener on March 23, Birdwood confirmed that both Carden and de Robeck thought they could break through, albeit with further heavy losses, but that they believed they would arrive with little ammunition and with "no object as regards getting transports through."[6]

One of the great myths of the Dardanelles, which continues in the 21st century, is the belief Churchill's naval-only scheme was discarded because it was concluded the Dardanelles could not be forced by ships alone. De Robeck's telegram and comments to Birdwood make it clear that the naval-only operation was discarded not because it was believed the fleet would not get through but because of fears for its line of communications once the operation had succeeded and because, whatever success was achieved by the fleet, it would not allow the movement of troops into the Marmora.

It is one of the unexplored ironies of the Dardanelles operation that Churchill's belated insistence on troops to *follow up* his fleet's success led directly to the demise of his much-cherished desire to force the Dardanelles by ships alone.[7] This was, of course, the last thing Churchill had wanted to happen. He belatedly sought troops to increase the moral pressure of a successful naval-only operation and then to "reap the fruits" of this success. This was the least he could do to satisfy the expectations of the War Council and still maintain the integrity of his operation. At some point, however, it was inevitable that someone who counted would declare that a naval-only operation designed to admit fully armored vessels into only the Marmora was most unlikely to provide the conditions under which an army could be taken through the full lengths of the Straits to Constantinople. It was inevitable that once the soldiers stormed the peninsula, they would recommend doing so with all the men available and with the full support of the navy.

De Robeck's recommendations were, in their essentials, identical to those made by Carden, Jackson, Richmond, Fisher, and Hankey before him and, predictably, they met the same resistance. Churchill drafted a telegram ordering a renewal of the attack "at the first favourable opportunity."[8] He was doing so now in the full knowledge that military assistance was no longer immediately available, and in effect, he was reverting entirely to his January 13 proposal to force the Dardanelles unaided by troops. Moreover, he was accepting, if de Robeck was correct, that no army would assist the fleet inside the Marmora.[9] Churchill warned of submarine attack and the heavy cost of an army operation and expressed his belief that "the entry into the Marmora of a fleet strong enough to beat Turkish Fleet would produce decisive results on the whole situation, and you need not be anxious about your subsequent line of communications. We know the forts are short of ammunition and supply of mines is limited."[10]

Fisher was not at all happy with the draft. He told de Bartolome he fully supported the idea in Churchill's telegram that he go to the Dardanelles and explain the Admiralty's concerns:

> *but the rest of the telegram I am dead against*. . . . You cannot override the authorities on the spot after having been so specially selected without sending out an envoy like yourself to explain more than is possible in any telegram—all the complexities of the case and the need for urgency—you'll get there in eighty hours.[11]

Fisher drafted a much more benign telegram to de Robeck that encouraged him to be active while awaiting the military intervention he now considered essential.[12]

Faced with the opposition of his War Group, Churchill substantially redrafted his telegram. It was longer than the original and much more carefully considered, and its recommendations less forcefully made, but it nevertheless took every opportunity to deflect de Robeck from his decision.[13] He asked, "whether the time has come to abandon the naval plan of forcing the Dardanelles without the aid of a large army?"[14] Again he warned de Robeck that delay would increase the threat of submarines, that the military operations would cost at least 5,000 casualties and still might yet be checked, and that operations on the peninsula would not overcome the mine danger or neutralize the Asiatic forts.

Against this, Churchill balanced the "risks and hopes of a purely naval undertaking" and proceeded to belatedly enlighten de Robeck on the wishful thinking that had helped sustain the naval-only operation over the preceding two months. The Gallipoli Peninsula would be completely cut off if the navy's ships were on both sides of the Bulair Isthmus. Furthermore, he considered it probable that a general evacuation of the peninsula would take place as soon as it was obvious the Narrows' forts would not stop the fleet. All troops remaining on the isthmus would be doomed to starvation or surrender. Finally, the political effect of the arrival of the fleet before Constantinople might be decisive.

Churchill then addressed the "minimum good results" that would follow a successful passage of the fleet into the Marmora: "Namely, that the Turkish army on Gallipoli continues to hold out and with forts and field guns closes up the Straits, and that no revolution occurs at Constantinople."[15]

In these circumstances, he argued, the army would have to storm Kilid Bahr plateau and secure a permanent reopening of the Straits. He believed ships left behind at the entrance along with those left in Egypt would be enough to support a military operation. He noted that:

> While on the other hand the probability is that your getting through would decide everything in our favour. Further, once through the Dardanelles, the current would be with you in any return attack on the forts, and the mining danger would be practically over. Therefore danger to your lines of communications is not serious or incurable.[16]

While Churchill awaited de Robeck's reply, he maintained steady pressure on Fisher. On March 25, he told him that:

> The Prime Minister seemed disappointed last night that we had not sent de Robeck a definite order to go on with his attack

> at the first opportunity, and he expressed his agreement with the telegram to that effect which I drafted yesterday morning. . . . The arrival of 4 or 5 ships in the Marmora decides the issue.[17]

Asquith had indeed expressed support for another push, but it does not appear he had taken the time to acquaint himself with the concerns of naval experts.[18] Kitchener also wanted the fleet to continue its attempt to force the Narrows. "Once ships are through the Gallipoli military position ceases to be of importance,"[19] he informed Hamilton on March 23. Ignoring every piece of information he had acquired that showed that such operations were now impossible, Kitchener said de Robeck "should call upon the army authorities to provide landing parties of considerable force whenever necessary for the purpose" of destroying guns and demolishing forts.[20] Hamilton, of course, wanted all troops immediately returned to Egypt to prepare for his deliberate and progressive military operation.[21] Kitchener's offer of landing parties of "considerable force" was too little too late.

Despite Churchill's avowed conviction that all would be decided once four or five ships had passed the Straits, it is impossible to believe he was as sanguine as he would have us believe. The fleet was now facing an enemy buoyed by an immense moral victory. More enemy successes had to be expected while the *Inflexible,* the one ship capable of dealing decisively with the *Goeben*, was already out of action.[22] In face of this success, the fear and panic Churchill hoped would contribute to an evacuation of the peninsula or revolt in Constantinople had diminished markedly. The latter had always been a slim prospect: the Turks would demand they retain Constantinople and the Straits in exchange for capitulation, but the British government could offer neither. Nor could the threat of force be used against Constantinople. Despite a general belief to the contrary, the fleet did not intend to bombard the city.

In the circumstances, negotiations with the Turks were likely to be protracted, if ultimately fruitless, and this made good naval communications essential. Yet the operation Churchill proposed ensured that both sides of the Straits would continue to bristle with mobile guns and howitzers and probably repairable high-caliber guns as well. It seemed hardly likely, therefore, that plans to cut Bulair and starve the Turks into submission could work. Most important of all, there seemed no prospect at all that the troops—declared essential by Churchill to reap the fruits of naval success—would ever enter the Marmora, whether this be over Bulair or through the Straits.

Many of these simple truths were spelled out clearly and succinctly to Churchill by de Robeck on the March 27.[23] The result of naval action alone, he declared, might be a brilliant success or quite indecisive. This depended, however, on the effect the appearance of the fleet off Constantinople would have on the Turkish Army, which, dominated by Germans, appeared in control of Turkey. If the Turks were undismayed by the arrival of the fleet in the Marmora and the Straits were closed behind the fleet:

> the length of time which ships can operate as indicated in your 86 and 88 and maintain themselves in the Sea depends almost entirely on the number of colliers and ammunition ships which can accompany the fleet and as the passage will be contested . . . the percentage of large unprotected ships which can be expected to get through is small.[24]

Telegram 86 was Churchill's March 4 instructions to Carden on operations to be undertaken inside the Marmora. Telegram 88 was a copy of Jackson's five-stage plan for the attack on the Bosporus forts. De Robeck was declaring what Churchill had always known: his naval-only operation could not facilitate any form of extended military or naval operations. Thus was Churchill finally caught in a web of his own obfuscation.

Churchill would not have been surprised by de Robeck's assertion that "[t]he passage of supply ships for the fleet through the Dardanelles with the forts still intact is a problem to which I see no practical solution."[25] The only solution was to occupy the peninsula and such an operation would require the assistance of all naval forces available. De Robeck did not accept Churchill's proposition that "a landing at Bulair would . . . cause Turks to abandon Peninsula" and added that "there could be no two opinions that a fleet intact outside the Dardanelles can do this better than the remains of a Fleet inside with little ammunition."[26]

If one doubts that Churchill retained faith in his naval-only operations ability to elicit Turkish surrender, what was driving him to press on with an operation so clearly fraught with difficulty and so clearly unable to fulfill the expectations of the War Council? Hankey, who was close to the scene, offered the explanation that Churchill feared another Antwerp and the damage this could do to him. Esher recorded in his diary that Churchill feared he would "be ruined if the attack fails."[27] Churchill subsequently argued he feared delay because of submarines. Also, he believed the Turks were short of ammunition, and he was worried that 5,000 men would be lost in a full-scale assault on the peninsula. I suggest another explanation: his ongoing interest in Borkum.

NOTES

1. de Robeck to Admiralty, Gilbert, *CVIII*, 709.

2. Ibid., 710.

3. Gilbert, *CVIII*, 717. Telegram, Fisher to Churchill, March 21, 1915.

4. Gilbert, *CVIII*, 724. Telegram, de Robeck to Churchill, 5.35 A.M., March 23, 1915.

5. Ibid., 724. There is an element of mystery surrounding this telegram. Marder quotes what appears to be a paraphrase of this telegram from the Dardanelles Commission in *From Dreadnought to Scapa Flow*, vol. 2, 253–254. Unfortunately, he provides no other details, and I have been unable to locate the reference. What is unusual is that his quotation includes as part of the March 23 telegram the last paragraph of a telegram sent to Churchill from de Robeck five days later, March 28. This was: "In my opinion Gallipoli Peninsula will have to be taken and held by land before Dardanelles can be passed with certainty by capital ships fitted to deal with Goeben and by colliers and other vessels without which utility of capital ships is very limited." See Gilbert, *CVIII*, 757.

6. Magnus, *Kitchener*, 327.

7. Churchill does touch on this in *The World Crisis*, second impression October 1923, 243–244. He laments, "The Army had in fact arrived too late and too ill-organised to deliver its own surprise attack, but in plenty of time by its very presence to tempt the Navy to desist from theirs." Leaving for the moment the fact a surprise attack was never an option at this late stage, this observation ignores the enormous short-comings of the continuation of a scheme designed only to admit fully armored vessels into the Marmora. Had the Fleet been guaranteed secure lines of communications once it had entered the Marmora, de Robeck would not have hesitated to try again.

8. Facsimile reprinted in *The World Crisis*, vol. 2, second impression, 234–235.

9. It had been declared by Kitchener at the War Council meeting of March 19 that the marines, the French contingent, and the brigade of Australians then at Lemnos would return to Egypt to be prepared for an opposed landing.

10. Admiralty to Carden, telegram 109, March 15.

11. Marder, *Fear God and Dreadnought*, 143.

12. This telegram was, presumably, sent. A telegram from De Robeck on March 25 addresses many of the issues raised in Fisher's telegram

13. Churchill to de Robeck, telegram, Gilbert, *CVIII*, 728–730. Gilbert's volume has led some historians to assume only two drafts were written. There were at least three. The first is shown in *The World Crisis*, as noted

above. Two drafts were written on March 23. One is printed in *CVIII*, 724–726. Fisher was not happy with any draft and wrote to Churchill on March 24 that "[a]lthough the telegram goes from you personally, the fact of my remaining at the Admiralty sanctions my connection with it, so if it goes I do not see how I can stay." See Marder, *Fear God and Dreadnought*, 169; Letter, Fisher to Churchill, March 15, 1915.

14. Ibid.

15. Ibid.

16. Ibid.

17. This was the first of two drafts rejected by Fisher and the War Group discussed above.

18. Asquith to Venetia Stanley, March 24: "Winston came to talk about the Dardanelles. The weather is infamous there, and the Naval experts seem to be suffering from a fit of nerves. They are now disposed to wait till the troops can assist them in force, which ought to be not later than (about) April 10th. Winston thinks & I agree with him, that the ships, as soon as the weather clears, & the aeroplanes can detect the condition of the forts and the position of the concealed guns ought to make another push & I hope this will be done." Gilbert, *CVIII*, 731. One might wonder about Asquith's degree of awareness of the operation to this point if he still believed it possible that airplanes would be effective in finding concealed guns, and that the navy would be effective in dealing with them thereafter.

19. Gilbert, *CVIII,* Telegram, Kitchener to Hamilton, March 23, 1915.

20. Gilbert, *CVIII*. 727. Hamilton replied the same day that he and de Robeck were "equally convinced that, to enable the Fleet effectively to force the passage, the co-operation of the whole military force will be necessary."

21. Hamilton also rather pertinently pointed out that "[t]he unsettled weather prevailing in March introduces a dangerous incalculable factor into the operation of landing a force in the face of certain opposition, but the weather next month should be more settled." Ibid.

22. Carden's original plan had recommended at least two battle cruisers enter the Marmora. There were no battle cruisers available after March 18.

23. Gilbert, *CVIII*, 751–753. Much discussion surrounds de Robeck's change of mind. de Robeck makes it clear in this telegram that he was led to believe by Sir Henry Jackson's telegram of February 24 in which he was informed, "the War Office consider the occupation of the southern end of the peninsula to the line Suandere-Chana Ovasi is not an obligatory operation for ensuring success of first main object which is to destroy the permanent batteries." That he, "did not anticipate the possibility of Military co-operation in the forcing of the Straits." He believed that this opinion, "if persisted in would in no wise assist the Navy in their task," and therefore had not pursued military assistance. However, General Hamilton on March 22 had informed him that "co-operation of the Army and Navy was considered by him a sound operation of war and that he was fully prepared to work with the Navy in the forcing of the Dardanelles."

24. Ibid.

25. Ibid.

26. Ibid. de Robeck had preceded the telegram by another in which he had written, "I do not hold check on the 18th March decisive but having met General Hamilton on the 22nd March and heard his proposals I now consider a combined operation essential to obtain great results and object of campaign. . . . To attack Narrows now with Fleet would be a mistake as it would jeopardise the execution of a better and bigger scheme." See Gilbert, *CVIII*, 747, de Robeck to Admiralty, March 22, 1915.

27. Gilbert, *CVIII*, 719. Esher Diary entry.

CHAPTER 26

The Borkum/Baltic Imperative

In early March, Churchill resumed his correspondence with Jellicoe over the capture of Borkum, noting that great efforts were being made to prepare the monitors for the attempt. Several days earlier, he had sought guidance from Oliver on sending a fast fleet of battle cruisers into the Baltic. On March 3, he had attempted to deflect the War Council from a large-scale military commitment in the southern theater by expressing his preference for operations through Holland and the Baltic, noting these might become possible once his monitors were completed. These events indicated clearly that, as far as Churchill was concerned, the imminent success in the Dardanelles was to be the catalyst for attempting one or other of his northern schemes.

Jellicoe responded to Churchill's letter on March 14 in a typically equivocal manner. He assumed from Churchill's letter that he wished him to come southward to discuss the idea of a Borkum/Baltic operation. He suggested that, before doing so, it would be desirable to get some understanding of the plans upon which the operations would be based. He expressed his opinion, based on his own limited information, that the idea of passing vessels into the Baltic seemed impracticable unless Denmark joined in and a regular advanced base was established. He explained he was similarly in the dark regarding Borkum: "The more I look at it (with my present information) the harder seems to be the problems. If I knew all that you know, I might alter my opinion, therefore I ask to have this information and given time to digest it." He suggested he could go to Rosyth after the first week of April to discuss the matter or "could risk the moon and come earlier."[1]

Churchill drafted a reply two days later:

> My Dear Jellicoe,
>
> The ideas I put before you in general outline have not reached a point where definite staff plans can be completed. In the meanwhile I hope you will give them your consideration with a view not to stating the difficulties and risks wh [sic] always can be urged against any of the initiatives, but to means and methods to overcome the difficulties. Your past experience and skill would be invaluable in this, and of course if other alternatives and variations of positive action occur to you—if you have any plans for a naval offensive I should be glad indeed to receive them.[2]

It is evident he remained determined to see his fleet take on a more proactive role in war at the earliest opportunity and at the heart of these were his various plans for operations in Northern Europe.

For an unknown reason, Churchill decided not to send this letter to one of the two men whose support he recognized as critical for his northern schemes. Instead, with Carden's renewed attack on the Dardanelles imminent, he took the surprising step of setting off to France for a visit with the *other* man who could make or break his northern schemes, Sir John French. Portentously, at the bottom of a brief letter written the same day, Fisher warned Churchill of the very thing Churchill was now desperately working to avoid: "The decisive theatre remains and ever will be the North Sea—our attention is being distracted—Schleswig Holstein, the Baltic, Borkum are not living with us now! Your big idea of 3 British armies in Holland in May obliterated by Bulair."[3]

We have an insight into Churchill's discussions with French from French's diary. It makes plain that one of the important topics discussed was an attack through Holland. On March 25, French recorded "[i]n my conversation with K(itchener) . . . on Wednesday night he referred to a possible landing in Holland and *appeared to be rather in sympathy with certain ideas of W. Churchill which the latter communicated to me when he was here the other day*" (emphasis added).[4] The pressure Churchill had brought to bear on Carden over the previous five days ensured that Churchill would be able to say to

French that a full-scale attempt to force the Dardanelles was imminent and that this operation might soon be over.

The meeting between Kitchener and French had been organized by Churchill and took place aboard HMS *Attention.* A variety of other matters were discussed—including ammunition supply and the Dardanelles[5]—but the import here is twofold: First, an important matter for discussion during Churchill's visit to French on March 16 and 17 was Churchill's very strong and ongoing desire to fight the Germans through amphibious operations in the north. Second, Kitchener was "in sympathy" with such an operation. As early as January 8, Kitchener had described operations through Holland as potentially "decisive." If Churchill did, indeed, organize this meeting, it must be seriously considered that a primary motive was to promote or secure support from Kitchener and French for his northern aspirations.

French wrote to Churchill on March 24 of a most successful liaison with Kitchener. It is perhaps more than coincidence, therefore, that on the same day he telegraphed de Robeck to reconsider his decision to halt the naval attack, Churchill drafted (or had drafted) a lengthy and extraordinarily detailed memorandum on his northern strategy and then thrashed out the strategy with Fisher for more than two hours.[6]

The memorandum was of four parts. Part one was entitled the "Capture of Borkum" in which he outlined an extensive plan for the capture of this island.[7] Churchill noted in his opening sentence: "The attack on Borkum should take place as soon as the weather is favourable after May 15th."[8] Part two was entitled "The Closing of the River Mouths." This section assumed that the German High Seas Fleet had failed to come out to challenge the Grand Fleet. In such circumstances and during the month of June, "when more monitors would be available and others liberated by the completion of the Borkum defences" these vessels, with the aid of submarines, destroyers, light cruisers, and aircraft would advance toward and blockade the Jade and Elbe estuaries.

This would facilitate the third part of the memorandum, "The Entry of the Baltic," summarized much as it had been in his letter to Jellicoe.[9] The fourth part was entitled "The Decisive Military Stroke":

> [T]he landing of a British army of invasion not less than 500,000 strong, at Emden, to establish itself on the 30 mile broad neck of the East Friesland Peninsula, and to invest

> Wilhelmshaven in conjunction with the sea-attack, wd be an operation of the highest advantage; & from this broad base an advance cd be made subsequently either through Hanover or Berlin, or into Westphalia. *The effect of such a movement, & indeed of the whole Borkum operation, upon Holland may well at any moment be decisive in determining that country to join the Allies* (emphasis added).[10]

That Churchill was and had been for some time working to his own personal timetable is hinted at by Fisher in a letter to Churchill on April 2: "Let us hope that the Dardanelles will be passed over and *by the desired date* to your honour & glory . . ." (emphasis added).[11]

In this letter is perhaps the most compelling explanation for Churchill's insistence that de Robeck make another immediate effort to force the Dardanelles, yet historians have entirely ignored it: a May attempt on Borkum, an attempt in June to block the Germans North Sea debouches, an entrance into the Baltic of a select fleet of fast battle cruisers and battleships, and finally and climactically, a landing in Northern Europe of 500,000 men of Kitchener's New Armies.

All this, however, as Fisher noted later, must "necessarily await the trend of events in the Dardanelles—we must know what forces remain before embarking on a new undertaking."[12] De Robeck's decision would delay for some three weeks the attack on the Dardanelles and guarantee a serious escalation of the Dardanelles operation. Moreover, the fleet must remain with the soldiers for the duration. It could not desert them.

It was evident that Fisher would decline any new initiatives while the Dardanelles continued. He already had shown great anxiety over the drain of resources to the Mediterranean, writing to Churchill on April 2, "*We can't send another rope yarn to de Robeck!* WE HAVE GONE TO THE VERY LIMIT."[13]

Churchill's great gamble was now all but lost. De Robeck's decision ensured delay and offered the prospect of steady flow of troops southward. Should it go well, it would be much more difficult to avoid the great southern offensive that Lloyd George for so long sought and that Churchill had so hoped to avoid. He also was seeing the moral advantage of a significant naval success slip through his fingers. Should a full-scale attack on the Gallipoli Peninsula go badly, and casualties be great and gains small, the likelihood of the War Council sanctioning the storming of a heavily fortified island held by the Germans and surrounded by submarines was reduced almost to zero.

Nor would the war in Europe stand still for Churchill. While he awaited an opportunity to take Borkum, other plans would be prepared and other directions taken. The campaigning season might come and go and with it any hope the war would be won in 1915. It remained Churchill's conviction—probably shared by few others—that the war could be won in that year. It was not until May that he formerly lifted the embargo on any shipbuilding that could not be completed in 1915.

In view of these significance consequences, Churchill conceded defeat with profound reluctance. After receiving de Robeck's telegram, and in the face of Fisher's obvious intransigence,[14] he wrote, "*I hoped it would have been possible to achieve the result according to the original plan without involving the army* but the reasons you give make it clear that a combined operation is now indispensable" (emphasis added).[15] Of course, none of the reasons given by de Robeck were new to Churchill. All that had changed was that Churchill had lost the power to resist them.

NOTES

1. CHAR 13/49.
2. CHAR 13/49.
3. Gilbert, *CVIII*, 791–92. Note, Fisher to Churchill, 3 A.M., March 16, 1915.
4. Gerald French, *Some War Diaries, Addresses and Correspondence of Field Marshal The Right Honourable The Earl of Ypres Sir John French* (London: Herbert Jenkins, 1937), 187–188. By March 31, Kitchener's interest apparently was waning. French recorded that he "is much weakening on Holland." The issue remains, however, that for a time, Kitchener, and possibly French, shared Churchill's aspirations for some kind of northern offensive.
5. See Gilbert, *CVIII*, footnote 728.
6. Martin Gilbert, *The Challenge of War: 1914–1916* (Egmore, UK: Minerva, 1990), 373. A note from Fisher, quoted by Gilbert, indicates that Churchill undertook this work while quite unwell with "influenza," but more likely a bad head cold.
7. Written immediately after this memorandum was a letter from Churchill to Kitchener regarding the use of a squadron of his armored cars with the army in France. "I know that Sir Douglas Haig would be glad to have it with his Corps; and if they are found to be useful, the value of these cars can be tested." Of interest is the fact that, until this point, Churchill had been keen to see two squadrons to work with the army. Kitchener had

indicated in a letter of March 19 that it was his intention to ask for two squadrons. Now, Churchill indicated that he would be "quite content" for one to serve. The other, it is clear, Churchill had marked for his Borkum operation as the following extract from his March 24 memorandum indicates: "The extensive sands between Borkum, Juist, Memert & the mainland at low water are it is believed vy favourable to the operations of amoured motorcars with maxims. This shd be verified, & experiments made with armoured cars on sandy beaches. A defense of this character wd be most effective against any but the most serious attacks, and a serious attack in great force is most dangerous—almost impossible—to launch in the short time available between the tides. Further acquaintances with these sands wd possibly open out a great role for armoured cars."

8. Gilbert, *CVIII*, 732.

9. One of the force nominated to enter the Baltic was the *Queen Elizabeth*, then at the Dardanelles.

10. Gilbert, *CVIII*, 737.

11. Ibid., 764. Letter, Fisher to Churchill, April 2, 1915.

12. Gilbert, *CVIII*, 763, Fisher to Churchill, March 31 1915. This was in response to Churchill's request for A. K. Wilson to begin concerted investigation on Borkum. By coincidence, on March 26, the British government had learned of news that portended a German attack on Holland. Fisher added in his note, "We are now committed to the Dardanelles at all costs so must anyhow wait till middle of May by which time events in Holland may quite change the position and indicate Terschelling as our base."

Churchill wanted to be able to tell Holland that "if she were attacked or goes to war, we will put immediately (say) half Sir John French's army plus whatever Ld. Kitchener can assign from England at her disposal, and that they can arrive at certain points by certain dates. The vital point to realise is this—that if the Germans can overrun Holland very quickly they will have gained a great advantage; whereas if they are held up at or near the frontiers, they will be ruined." Churchill to Grey and Kitchener, Gilbert, *CVIII*, 748. This letter demonstrates the degree to which Churchill had continued to believe a northern offensive would contribute decisively to the defeat of Germany.

13. Gilbert, *CVIII*, 764. Letter, Fisher to Churchill, April 2, 1915.

14. See Fisher Memorandum, Gilbert, *CVIII*, 754, March 27, 1915. Ibid., 764. See, also, Fisher to Churchill, March 28, 1915 as an indication of Fisher's frame of mind at this time.

15. Not only was Fisher concerned to end the naval only assault, he was now questioning the efficacy of any subsequent amphibious operation. Undoubtedly inspired by Hankey, who was making the same point to Asquith, Fisher's March 27 memorandum insisted that serious investigation be undertaken into the prospects for an amphibious operation before an irreversible commitment be made: "With reference to Private and Personal telegram sent this forenoon (March 27th) by the First Lord to Vice Admiral

de Robeck . . . stating that an official telegram from the Admiralty would be sent him approving his proposed action as conveyed in his private telegram to the First Lord . . . , my opinion is that before any such action, together with the remarks there on of the War Office as to the likelihood of the proposed military operation (in co-operation with the Fleet) being so favourable as to justify the very considerable losses that may ensue.'' Ibid., 754–55.

CHAPTER 27

Conclusion

A primary conclusion of this book is that, to understand the origins and progress of Churchill's naval-only Dardanelles operation, one must understand his consuming interest in the northern theater. To ignore the latter, as most studies have done,[1] is to fail to understand the origins of the Dardanelles operation and the true nature of the fatal slide toward a full-scale amphibious operation.

So monumental was the failure at the Dardanelles and so substantial was Churchill's involvement in it, it was easy for early histories to view this operation as Churchill's failed obsession. In more recent times, historians have recognized that his real interest lay in amphibious operations in Northern Europe and not at the Dardanelles. These historians have contended that, in January 1915, he reluctantly surrendered his northern aspirations for the promise and prospects of Carden's naval-only assault on the Dardanelles. Once this decision had been made, however, his northern schemes were all but forgotten as he directed his energy and resource into the Dardanelles.

This study has demonstrated that such a perspective is incorrect. Churchill never surrendered his northern aspirations. They remained his consuming passion, borne of an interest in and understanding of traditional naval policy that went back to his earliest days as first lord of the Admiralty and before. He nurtured the Carden plan because it offered a viable alternative to the various southern schemes then starting to take shape. These, he feared, would deflect the War Council from his own plans to use the full weight of the navy in combination with Kitchener's New Armies to win the war against Germany in Northern Europe. Had the southern plans—especially those of Lloyd George—been adopted, his own dreams would have been seriously compromised, if not dashed altogether. The naval-only assault also offered the prospect of a decisive naval victory and clear evidence that ships could fight forts. Churchill recognized very clearly that the prestige and experience gained at the Dardanelles would be important in any effort to secure his northern operations.

It is in matters such as these that the real origins of the Dardanelles operation lie and not with the Russian call for aid and Kitchener's declaration that he had no troops to send anywhere. It is in the context of Churchill's preoccupation with decisive operations in northern Europe that this work contemplated First Lord Churchill's wartime activities and, in particular, the events and circumstances of January to April 1915.

* * * * *

This book began with a study of certain events in the opening decade of the 20th century that provide an essential background to Churchill's interest in and commitment to various northern amphibious operations as first lord of the Admiralty in 1914 and 1915. Our starting point was Britain's rather sluggish performance in the Boer War, which precipitated an investigation into the necessity or otherwise of a full-time professional army, in addition to her vast navy, to secure her national interests and her overseas possessions. Soon thereafter, Germany's growing industrial muscle, combined with the ever more belligerent activities of its bellicose monarch, began to stamp Germany as a likely and powerful threat to Britain and her Empire.

These issues, combined with recent technological developments such as the mine and torpedo, posed serious challenges for traditional defense policy and for the central and essential tool of this policy—the Royal Navy. Britain hitherto had contained or dealt with threats from the continent through a policy of blockade and the capture of, or a threat to, the overseas possessions of the offending continental power. This, for more than a century had, of course, been France. When the need arose, an expeditionary force would be raised to assist the much larger armies of her continental allies to provide the *coup de grace* to the rogue state.

Could such an approach to defense be successful in the new century? The reformers concluded that some change was necessary. To fulfill the needs of Empire, a standing army was deemed essential. The idea, however, of committing this army to a continental war was left in abeyance. The navy, through Lord Fisher, eschewed such a proposition and promoted instead a traditional maritime policy to deal with a continental threat. Naval planners were given the task of finding the ways and means of ensuring the success of a naval policy in the face of the new German threat and the technological challenges of the mine and submarine.

So partisan was Fisher and so desperate was he to protect the interests of the navy that he never came to grips with the fundamental questions of the era. Could Britain afford to allow Germany hegemony in Europe? Would a maritime strategy prevent this from happening? Despite evidence of his own serious doubts over naval policy, he never satisfactorily addressed the issue. His future first lord, however, had no such problems.

When Churchill became the first lord of the Admiralty in 1911, he was fully committed to the concept of a continental commitment. He understood fully that to allow Germany to dominate Europe ultimately would weigh heavily on Britain's capacity to maintain her empire. To this end, he was quite scathing toward Fisher's successor, A. K. Wilson, and his determination to maintain a largely maritime strategy in the event of war with Germany. He came to the Admiralty determined to ensure that a British Expeditionary Force would arrive in France in a timely manner to fight alongside the French Army.

Churchill, however, was never about to let the vast power of the Royal Navy be subsumed by the growing influence and power of the British Army. Although an observer at the infamous August 1911 meeting might have concluded that Churchill had accepted that modern developments now precluded the traditional naval policy of blockade and military descents, this was not the case. Having done what was needed to ensure that troops would get to France in a timely manner, he set about finding how these obstacles to aggressive and potentially war-winning operations of his vast Navy might be overcome.

Not long after becoming the first lord in October 1911, Churchill began revisiting Fisher's and Wilson's old plans to occupy an island near the German North Sea debouches to act as a base for blockading vessels. Before the outbreak of war, such a plan was presented as having a number of purposes: aggressive action would introduce an offensive vigor to the activities of the fleet; an attempt at such an operation would force the German High Seas Fleet to come out; and early warning would be provided of any fleet action. This latter advantage, it was argued, would make Britain more secure against a sudden amphibious assault and would provide vital protection to the British Expeditionary Force in the early weeks of war.

With two or three exceptions, Churchill's advisers could find little virtue in such plans, but they would continue to command Churchill's attention. One reason for his ongoing interest in the various island schemes was his conviction that, in the event of war with Germany, Dutch neutrality would seriously undermine the British war effort. He believed, therefore, that Holland would be forced either to fight alongside Britain or to join Germany. In either situation, Dutch ports or Dutch islands would be available for close blockade.

In July 1914, with war imminent, Churchill ordered the various island schemes be dusted off again. Dutch territory was at the top of the list, although there were others. Initially he sang the old tune: instilling a lively vigor into activities of the fleet, the protection of the British Expeditionary Force, enhanced surveillance, and the possibility of precipitating a decisive naval engagement. However, his proposals quickly developed into much larger operations designed to gain control of the Baltic and to land, first, Russian, and later, British, forces on Germany's northern flank.

These larger plans were constrained by two rather significant problems: in 1914, Churchill had no mighty army to land anywhere and no northern adventure could be undertaken until Britain had command of the North Sea. To solve his military problem, Churchill approached the Russians for some of their surplus manpower and even contemplated using a Greek force—but to no avail. However, such matters only blighted his dreams temporarily. All would be well with the arrival of Kitchener's armies in early 1915.

Command of the North Sea was more problematic, and Churchill spent much time contemplating how this might be achieved. The best possibility, of course, was that the High Seas Fleet would be destroyed in a decisive naval battle. Churchill, however, despaired at this prospect. It might not happen for years, if at all.

A second prospect explored by Churchill was the possibility that Britain might be able to develop two modern fleets equal in strength to the German Fleet. Churchill hoped a decisive battle in the Mediterranean, which would free up French forces, might make this possible. The destruction of Germany's commerce raiders would free up more British vessels. Alternatively or additionally, Japan and

Italy might join Britain and put their fleets at Britain's disposal. More desperately, he explored the virtues of Russia's Baltic Fleet.

Should any of these possibilities eventuate, he hoped a large British force could then enter the Baltic free from the fear that those ships left behind would be destroyed by the High Seas Fleet, which had, through the facility of the Kiel Canal, the option of entering the Baltic or North Sea at any time of its choosing.

The third means by which command of the North Sea might be achieved was the blocking of Germany's North Sea debouches. Fisher proposed a major mining program while A. K. Wilson searched for other solutions, including the use of block ships.

None of these prospects bore fruit. The High Seas Fleet stayed home. There was no accretion in strength of British Naval Forces sufficient to provide two fleets equal to the High Seas Fleet, and Churchill's various island schemes continued to be rejected by his naval staff. Wilson's plans were deemed too extreme while Fisher's mining proposals were compromised by a severe shortage of mines and Churchill's repeated assertions that mining was useless unless sweeping could be prevented. This required a secure base near the minefield. Although Wilson would continue to explore other offensive operations, Churchill became ever more convinced that an island base nearer Germany's shores was the essential precursor to offensive operations.

By the end of 1914, Churchill began to believe he had finally hit on the means to overcome the ongoing resistance of his naval staff to what certainly would be a most serious naval and military undertaking: the formation of a big-gunned, unsinkable, and largely expendable fleet of monitors. It would be this force, accompanied by other expendable vessels of his inshore squadrons that would help secure command of the North Sea in the spring of 1915, and it would be this force that would be the central platform of his strategic thinking.

While Churchill pursued such ideas with persistence and vigor, two other fields of opportunity emerged for decisive offensive operations. The first was an amphibious assault along the Belgian coastline in support of Sir John French's armies. Strongly supported by Fisher, this was received with some interest by Churchill, not the least because he viewed it as complementing his northern ambitions. The nearer the British Army could draw to Holland, the greater the prospect the Dutch would join the Allied side. The prospects for the operation ebbed and flowed from October 1914 into the new year, but petered out altogether at the end of January.

The other field of opportunity was the Mediterranean. The first prospect, championed by Churchill, was a naval assault on the Dardanelles to assist the Greek Army in the capture of the Gallipoli Peninsula. The Greeks declined the offer, but the southern theater continued to be alive with possibilities, although, always absent, was an army with which to fight. Churchill would revisit the idea of forcing the Dardanelles several times in 1914, the last in November amid fears of the imminent demise of Serbia. Included in his plans was a proposal to force the Dardanelles with a naval force alone.

Then, in January 1915, the stalemate in Europe and ongoing concerns for Serbia prompted proposals from within the War Council to open a third front in the Mediterranean with the assistance of the Balkan States. Hankey and Lloyd George proposed operations in which a British Army would be sent to the Mediterranean to draw the hesitant Balkan States to the side of the Allies and go to the assistance of Serbia.

In contrast to the traditional perspectives on this subject, this work has argued that Churchill viewed with alarm Lloyd George's suggestion that a large British army should fight in the Mediterranean, because this would have condemned his own northern aspirations, which remained at the heart of his strategic thinking.

The Russian call for assistance at the beginning of January added a new twist to the deliberations of the War Council. Churchill's immediate response to this call was to revisit the idea of a British naval force attempting to force the Dardanelles. Within days, the need for such an extreme action disappeared. Churchill, however, clung to the idea. Although at this juncture no troops were available to send anywhere, the War Council was keen to develop a serious military presence in the Mediterranean. Churchill, on the other hand, repeatedly declared during this time his considerable reluctance to see the New Armies or a portion of them consumed by a southern theater. His late-December memorandum made clear that he believed the war was to be won in the north.

In the second week of January, Carden's novel idea of forcing the Dardanelles by a process of gradual bombardment coalesced with Churchill's need to save his northern schemes and emerged as a formal proposal to take the Dardanelles without troops on January 13. It seemed the perfect solution for the War Council—and for Churchill—and he presented it in a manner that would make it irresistible to his colleagues. The proposal offered immediate action, with limited risk, and would not need troops. If successful, it might precipitate the surrender of Turkey or draw in one or other of the Balkan States. As far as Churchill was concerned, success might mitigate the need to send large numbers of troops southward and, thereby, keep his northern aspirations alive. Moreover, a naval success at the Dardanelles would provide Churchill with the influence and prestige needed to persuade the War Council to seriously consider what were clearly viewed as serious military undertakings.

This version of events stands in marked contrast to the most recent analyses of the origins of the Dardanelles operation, which argue Churchill discarded his northern aspirations in January 1915 in favor of the Dardanelles. Churchill had concluded, it is said, that while the Dardanelles could be achieved, the Borkum/Baltic could not. The evidence produced in this book, however, has shown that Churchill never surrendered his northern ambitions. They remained central to his thinking until the end of March 1915, when he reluctantly conceded that his great gamble had failed. Until then, all his decisions regarding the Dardanelles were influenced by his northern agenda and timetable, and always to the considerable detriment of the Dardanelles operation. It was only with the decision to launch a full-scale amphibious assault on the peninsula that his full energies were committed to ensuring success at the Dardanelles.

Churchill's naval-only plan ended up taking him down a path he had failed to anticipate. The operation rapidly threatened to take him further from and not nearer to his northern ambitions. Promoted, initially, as a largely speculative operation that could be terminated quickly if success was not forthcoming, circumstances quickly contrived to give the operation an irreversible momentum of its own. By the end of January, it was the central platform in the War Council's efforts to knock Turkey out of the war, supply Russia with essential war materiel, draw Greece and Rumania into the war, and save Serbia from a renewed assault from Austrian and German forces.

The question was how these great things were all to be achieved. Some agreement was shared among Churchill's advisers that a fleet, or portions of it, might force its way into the Marmora through a naval-only operation, but it was difficult to find anyone who believed the fleet would achieve anything of lasting value once it had broken through. Although the guns in the forts might be silenced temporarily and the fleet might force its way through, the fleet's lines of communications would close quickly as a result of repair to the forts and the continued existence of numerous mobile forces on either side of the peninsula. Once denied essential supplies, would a fleet, or the remains of one, be able to impose its will on the Turks?

The question was an important one, especially because it seemed likely that the fleet would not be allowed to bombard Constantinople, except for specific military targets. The intention was to intimidate and negotiate, not devastate. But with what and with whom was one to negotiate? Turkey was to have Constantinople taken from it at the end of the war. No Turk would surrender knowing this.

Churchill never satisfactorily addressed these matters with the other members of the War Council. How could he shatter the illusion of the Dardanelles operation without inviting its conversion to a full-scale amphibious operation or to destroy the operation altogether? To take such action would be to simultaneously destroy his ongoing hopes for operations in the north. Churchill claimed at the Dardanelles Inquiry that he did make the shortcomings of the naval-only operation clear to his colleagues. He asserted that he repeatedly informed the War Council that "without an army the results would be imperfect—the Straits would not be open for merchantmen and so on."[2] It is certainly true that by February most members of the War Council ought to have understood that the operation as planned had certain limitations. Churchill, however, never made plain the serious implications for the longer-term operation of the fleet if both shores of the Dardanelles were not first taken by a military force. Balfour, Grey, and Haldane all testified at the Dardanelles Inquiry that Churchill gave them the impression that the fleet would be able to do much as it pleased once inside the Marmora. Communications were not seen as a serious issue in the successful operations of the fleet.

Hankey, Fisher, Jackson, and Richmond all thought better and all, in their own way, agitated for military assistance for the naval operation. Finally, in the middle of February, with plans to send troops to Greece having gone completely awry, the War Council concluded that a military force would be helpful in the execution of the Dardanelles operation. What remained in dispute was how many troops would be sent, when they would be sent, and, most important, what they would do when they got there.

Despite the concerns of his advisers and the inflated expectations of his War Council colleagues, this landmark concession did not prompt Churchill to reassess the naval-only operation in the slightest. As far as he and Kitchener were concerned, joint amphibious assault on the peninsula would not be needed. Churchill argued that once the fleet was through, the pressure of ships on either side of Bulair would force the Turkish troops on the peninsula to withdraw or to capitulate. Kitchener was convinced they would run from the peninsula and, indeed, from all of European Turkey. Thus, the army would be used only to capitalize on the success of the fleet. Troops would be used to occupy an unoccupied peninsula. They would reap the fruits of a naval victory.

This policy became particularly problematic when the War Council, prompted by a memorandum from Balfour, began to accept that the full benefits of a naval success would be achieved only if a large army could subsequently enter the Marmora and occupy Constantinople. This ought to have stopped Churchill and his naval-only operation in its tracks. How was an army to follow the fleet into the Marmora in an operation originally designed to admit fully armoured vessels only? The short answer ought to have been that it could not.

Neither Kitchener nor Churchill, however, considered that even this new expectation justified putting the naval operation under review. Kitchener stubbornly maintained the Turks would rush from the peninsula and therefore an army of 60,000 or more could be convoyed safely through the length of the Dardanelles and into the Marmora.

Although surely not oblivious to the utterly impracticable nature of this proposal, Churchill refused to repudiate Kitchener's wishful thinking. Instead, as has been seen, he spoke of sending troops via Bulair to merchant ships in the Marmora. Once again, precious little shows that such a belief was justified or in any way supported by his advisers. Hankey's rather sanguine memorandum, *After the Dardanelles: The Next Step*, made no mention of such a proposition. He did give credence to the ability of a fleet to sever communications to the peninsula, but his final analysis, like all others, was that the peninsula (and probably the Asian side of the Straits) must be captured to ensure success.

Throughout the latter half of February, Churchill pushed strongly to have the 29th Division sent to the Mediterranean. His efforts to secure the 29th have led many historians to accept that his naval-only operation always had been an alternative forced on him by the circumstances of the time. Other historians have argued that he sought the 29th Division to facilitate its conversion to a full-scale amphibious assault on the peninsula at some point in time. This work has shown that neither perspective is correct. Despite many opportunities and ever growing reasons to do so, Churchill never backed away from his naval operation. His pursuit of the 29th Division was intended to complement the naval-only operation—not replace it. It would be the presence of regular troops that would be most likely to draw in the hesitant Balkan States and thereby mitigate the need to use a much larger British Army in the Mediterranean. British forces, therefore, would remain free for his northern schemes, which he continued to nurture and for which preparations continued to be made.

From March 10 onward, Churchill was fully aware of the extreme difficulty the fleet was having with mobile guns and howitzers. Moreover, on March 6, he had been given unequivocal evidence from Carden that the fleet could not effectively deal with the guns in the forts. Although they might be silenced, they could not be damaged to prohibit further use. The only way to do this was with the support of landing parties, and these no longer could provide support in face of heavy Turkish opposition that the fleet had proved parlous to deal with.

Fortunately, Kitchener had finally declared that he was now prepared to send the 29th Division, which all, save Kitchener, had believed was essential to "reap the fruits of the naval success."

Given this set of circumstances, and the vital need to command the peninsula before troops could move on to Constantinople, Churchill might have been expected to have done one of two things. He might have recommended that when the 29th Division arrived it should be used in conjunction with the other forces available to capture the Gallipoli Peninsula with the support of the fleet. This would help secure lines of communication, possibly allow a military force to enter the Marmora through the Straits, and markedly increase the likelihood of success for the entire operation. Alternatively, he might have maintained a safe but methodical bombardment of the Straits while synchronizing a more concerted effort to force the Straits when the 29th Division arrived.

Instead, as we have seen, on March 11 he telegraphed Carden to consider more aggressive operations within the Straits and began lobbying the prime minister to hold Kitchener to his (Churchill's) understanding that 40,000 troops would be available for operations on the peninsula from March 20 if naval operations had not succeeded by this date. The 29th Division had been all but forgotten.

Despite its inherent shortcomings, Churchill was determined to continue with his naval-only operation until at least March 20. Thereafter, he was prepared to attack the Gallipoli Peninsula with a mere 40,000 to 60,000 men at a time when the weather was still unpredictable and dangerous and before a significant portion of his force had arrived.

This desperate "haste" cannot be explained by recent submarine threats or the belief that the Turks on the peninsula were short of ammunition. This intelligence was not delivered until a day or two later.

Churchill's call for a more aggressive naval assault on the Straits culminated in the full-scale attack of March 18. It was a fundamentally different mode of attack to that originally envisioned in January. The gradual, relentless attack on the forts—which had proven so fruitless over the previous weeks—had given way to a full-scale bombardment designed to subdue the forts sufficiently to allow the effective sweeping of the minefield, which, belatedly, had been recognized as the real impediment to success. The attack on the forts was ineffectual, as was any effort to subdue the mobile guns that constricted all sweeping efforts. Little progress was made on the outer minefield, yet the fleet suffered grievously.

At the War Council meeting of March 19, a decision was made to continue the attack. De Robeck indicated his willingness to do so; however, after consultation with Hamilton, he decided that it was now better to await preparations for a full-scale amphibious assault. Although much has been speculated over this change of heart, with little doubt, de Robeck's decision was based on his discovery that troops, after all, could assist in the attack and based on his belief that troops could not be used inside the Marmora unless and until the peninsula, at least, had been taken. This was never likely to occur as a result of a naval-only operation.

Churchill wanted the full-scale naval assault to continue. This desire was despite the fact that all troops gathered to follow the fleet into the Marmora were returning to Egypt to prepare for a full-scale amphibious landing on the peninsula. In the short term at least, the intent no longer was to land troops—and there were no troops to land—to destroy the fortifications after the fleet had silenced them. If the fleet got through, there was no prospect that troops would follow. Nor would the fleet—now minus two of its battle cruisers—be able to sustain itself beyond a few weeks. Yet, in stark contradiction to his pronouncements in late February, Churchill now maintained in his correspondence with de Robeck that the fleet's entrance into the Marmora would be decisive and nothing more would be needed.

In his own writing, Churchill maintained that he was determined to press on after March 19 because of apprehensions over submarines, his belief that the Turks were seriously short of ammunition (hardly evident in the fleet's recent experience), and fears that an amphibious assault would result in considerable loss of life.

On balance, however, these do not seem reasons enough to try again, particularly when the full weight of the downside inventory is placed on the scales for measure: the evident ineffectiveness of the bombardment; the loss of numerous battleships and the prospect of more losses; the damage to *Inflexible* deemed essential to defeat the *Goeben* should it be repaired in time; the heightened morale of the Turks; the diminished likelihood of Balkan assistance; and the extreme unlikelihood that Constantinople would surrender to any naval force, especially one that did not intend to use bombardment as a weapon.

To this we can add a number of factors that Churchill had thus far chosen to ignore. First, the fleet would not be able to maintain its lines of communications and the knowledge of this would influence Turks and Germans alike. Second, the army then in the Mediterranean would not be able to assist the fleet in the Marmora, nor could the fleet, once in the Marmora, help the army occupy or take the peninsula if such were required. Any plans to break through to the Black Sea would become almost impossible. In such circumstances, little assistance could be expected from the Russians.

Churchill's concerns over submarines and the large military losses that would result from an amphibious assault are not a convincing justification for maintaining the naval-only assault on the peninsula. He did not conceive of the losses a landing eventually would entail. He wrote of 5,000—not 250,000—casualties, and he would argue in April that lodgment on the peninsula would not be a difficult operation. His suggestion to de Robeck that, should the naval-only operation fail, the peninsula could be taken by amphibious assault at a later date does not seem a prudent recommendation if a submarine threat was really at the heart of one's concerns.

In light of the foregoing, more compelling reasons are required to explain Churchill's determination to press on with the naval-only operation. This paper has argued that Churchill understood that, if he lost the naval assault on the Dardanelles, he would also lose the Borkum/Baltic. His correspondence with Jellicoe and his detailed Borkum/Baltic plan of late March coupled with the ongoing preparation of transports, landing craft, and monitors make clear that his hopes for a northern offensive remained very much alive. Unfortunately for Churchill, the Dardanelles would not go as he had hoped, and by the end of March, he had to concede defeat. From this point forward, as his future became consumed by an ever-growing commitment in the south, little would be heard of Borkum/Baltic.

Churchill, however, would make sure that the lost opportunity to win the war in Northern Europe in 1915 was not forgotten.

NOTES

1. Robert Rhodes James, *Churchill: A Study in Failure, 1900*–1939 (London: George Weidenfeld and Nicolson, 1970), and Moorehead, *Gallipoli*, are just two of the authors who make no mention of Churchill's northern schemes in their works and yet have shaped our understanding of this operation.
2. CAB 19/33. Churchill Interview, Dardanelles Commission Inquiry.

CHAPTER 28

Epilogue: Opportunities Lost

An important reason why historians must begin to reconsider the significance of Churchill's "unsinkable fleet" and his commitment to his various northern adventures in 1915 is the extraordinary level of attention he gave them for many years after. As a result of the events of 1915, Churchill was imbued with a profound sense of lost opportunity. This sentiment was clearly evident in the opening chapter of the second volume of *The World Crisis*, and he carried it with him all the way to the outbreak of the World War II when, as first lord for the second time, he found himself with another opportunity to provide his naval solution to a continental war.

Although by the end of March 1915 his plans for a great northern offensive had gone awry, Churchill still had his new and growing fleet of monitors with which to influence the events in the Mediterranean. From May to September, he spruiked these vessels and his bulged cruisers, as the best means by which to force the Straits. The "monitors will go anywhere," he told de Robeck, "and you will be able to use them with freedom. . . . They are the last word in bombarding vessels." When the long anticipated submarine threat finally materialized at the Dardanelles with the sinking of the battleship *Triumph* off Gaba Tepe, Churchill offered the monitors to Balfour, now the new first lord, as vessels "immune from torpedo attack."[1]

On August 21, after results of Hamilton's renewed offensive had become disappointingly clear, Churchill wrote to Asquith and

Balfour citing a number of new factors that now made a successful naval attack more likely. One of these new factors were his monitors, "protected against torpedoes by their structure" and so shallow in draught "that they should be able to pass over the Kephez minefield without danger."[2]

Churchill's agitation only ceased when, in late September, Balfour forwarded comments made on the monitors by de Robeck. De Robeck identified numerous design faults and pointed out that any question of forcing the Narrows with monitors was "for the present not a workable proposition" because most could not navigate the Dardanelles without tugs.[3]

Despite the deflating criticisms of his monitors and their very real limitations, Churchill remained remarkably buoyant regarding the virtue of his inshore fleet and their capacity to act decisively on the outcome of the war. On October 1, in reply to a letter sent him by the famous author, Sir Arthur Conan Doyle, in which he was commended for his contribution to the tank, Churchill wrote in part: "The caterpillars (early model tanks) are the land sisters of the monitors. Both are intended to restore to the stronger power an effective means of the offensive. *The monitor was the beginning of the torpedo-proof fleet*. . . . The caterpillar of the bullet-proof army" (emphasis added). Perhaps reflecting on the monitors' poor showing at Gallipoli, he added, "But surprise was the true setting for both."[4] Here were the first steps in the making of a myth that would emerge more fully in his postwar history of World War I.

In December 1915, Edward Spiers, new friend and confidant, recorded the following conversation with Churchill:

> WC said when we got to sea we shd have understood we had turned G's flank. Clever. Said we sd have forced Holland in at beginning and landed troops there. Said it had been thought of landing at Borkum & making naval & submarine base there to watch G fleet, our short range submarines wd then have come in and 1Div wd have been landed forcing enemy to garrison whole coast and forced g fleet to fight. . . . Said we cd then have put a few big ships in Baltic not to fight a fleet but destroy units & joining hands with Russians.[5]

In 1917, Churchill's island schemes once again emerged at an official level, this time as a solution to the submarine risk that was threatening to bring Britain to her knees. He once again riled openly against the policy of a "distant blockade" and *"still more the policy of distant blockade and nothing else,*" which, in face of the deadly U-boat threat, he no longer believed guaranteed victory or protected Britain from defeat.[6]

The solution to the submarine policy, he proposed, was to return to the policy of close and aggressive blockade. This could be done by the means of "ships which are comparatively immune from the torpedo, and which can therefore operate freely in the enemy's waters to support our flotilla and light craft."[7] Such immunity would be achieved by the building of bulges or "a special construction" round the sides of ships.

Churchill acknowledged that the concept was not new but that it had not been applied previously because this method of protection would have hindered the more modern and more powerful ships in their duties (their top speed would be appreciably reduced). Formerly, the Grand Fleet had not had sufficient preponderance over the High Seas Fleet to risk such adaptations, but with "the accession of the very powerful Navy of the United States"[8] and the completion of many new vessels, such changes could now be made without risk.

To this end, he recommended the establishment of at least two fleets, each capable of meeting the German High Seas Fleet. One, consisting of the fastest and best ships, would be a fast blue water fleet. The other, older vessels fitted with bulges and, therefore, comparatively torpedo proof, would act as an inshore aggressive fleet to beat the enemy into port and force the recall of "his submarines for his own defence."[9] The fleet would be able "[i]n short, to carry out, in spite of the submarine, and by the means of special equipment, the old, well recognised, true war policy of the Royal Navy."[10]

The inshore fleet would capture the long-sought island off the German coast. In most regards, the idea was identical to Churchill's 1915 Borkum schemes. The major difference was the claimed surfeit of large vessels, whereas formerly Churchill had had to make do with his monitors. The scheme now had the rather pressing attraction of appearing to present a solution to the submarine question at a time when the convoy system had yet to prove its worth.

Although making no serious impact, Churchill's paper was analyzed by the then director of the Planning Section, Dudley Pound.[11] Pound would be Churchill's first sea lord during World War II and, again, would have to deal with similar schemes from Churchill. Pound concluded the island could not be held in face of constant bombardment from the mainland and that a protective, although likely ineffective, bombardment from the British Fleet could be maintained only if the High Seas Fleet had first been brought to battle and defeated.

Nevertheless, Pound gave some credence to Churchill's idea of fitting bulges as part of any offensive scheme, if time permitted: "For ships operating in the Bight this would be a great advantage." He also reflected positively on his concept of an inshore fighting force, writing: "The organisation of an efficient inshore fighting force under British leadership should not prove an impossible task and until we have brought the combined resources of the Allies to bear at the decisive point we cannot be said to have done all that is possible to ensure Victory."

The submarine threat was soon overcome by the introduction of an efficient convoy system and the value or otherwise of Churchill's new proposal for an unsinkable inshore fleet, like his unsinkable fleet of monitors of two years before, remained largely untested and unchallenged.

Thus, it was that Churchill went on to make extraordinary claims for his unsinkable fleets at the end of the war in the second volume of his history, *The World Crisis*. The pride of place he gave to his monitors and bulged ships in this history is, perhaps, one of the most profound indications of the degree to which these vessels, and the bold offensive plans he conceived for them, influenced all his strategic thinking during his time as first lord and after.

In a clear and unequivocal lament for the lost opportunities of his time as first lord, he boldly developed the idea, first broached with Sir Arthur Conan Doyle in October 1915, that the "bulged" or "blistered" ship at sea, along with the tank in land warfare, had been the answer to "deadlock" and the secret to a short war. He noted:

> Mechanical not less than strategic conditions had combined to produce at this early stage in the war a deadlock both on sea and land. The strongest fleet was paralysed in its offensive by the menace of the mine and torpedo. . . . The mechanical danger must be overcome by a mechanical remedy. Once this was done, both the stronger fleet and the stronger armies would regain their normal offensive rights. Until this was done, both would be baffled and all would suffer. ***If we master the fact that this was the crux of the war problem***, as it was plainly apparent from the end of 1914 onwards, the next steps in thought will be found equally simple. . . . The remedy when stated appeared to be so simple that it was for months or even years scouted and disregarded by many of the leading

men. . . . *Reduced to its rudiments, it consisted in interposing a thin plate of steel between the side of the ship and the approaching torpedo, or between the body of a man and the approaching bullet.* (emphasis added).[12]

"Here," he declared, "was one of the great secrets of the war and of the world in 1915. But hardly anyone would believe it. . . . The Monitor and the 'bulged' or blistered ship were the beginning of the torpedo-proof fleet."[13]

This passage does not provide the sense that overwhelming and irresolvable difficulties denied the monitor the decisive potential Churchill claimed for it. There is no suggestion here, despite the acknowledgment that they were not used or tested in any real way, that the unsinkability of the monitor or blistered ship was anything more than a figment of Churchill's imagination. There is no recognition that, even had these ships been unsinkable as Churchill claimed, many of the schemes he sought to execute still would have faced immense and probably insurmountable challenges. There is no acknowledgment that even if bulged ships proved unsinkable, they still would be vulnerable to serious disablement from torpedoes, a matter drawn to Churchill's attention by Sir Arthur Wilson in March 1915. In *The World Crisis,* it is not the utility of the blistered ship, but the timidity and lack of resource of those in whose hands this tool was placed, that was to blame for the failure to end the war. A lack of power on his part, and timidity and irresolution on the part of others, had caused four years and millions of lives to be expended in breaking a deadlock, which, but for the adoption of these simple truths, easily might have been avoided.

This conviction would span the beginning of one war to the beginning of another. In 1936, Churchill argued that the growing German menace could be curtailed by a British Fleet in the Baltic. "Its mere arrival in the Baltic . . . would be a severe shock to German opinion and put a stop to further mischief."[14] During March, 1939, Churchill prepared a memorandum on the use of seapower in the event of war with Germany. He believed control of the Mediterranean should be the first goal, and then the "domination of the Baltic."[15] Upon becoming first lord in September, Churchill began immediately to promote another attempt to occupy the Baltic under the codename Operation Catherine.

This is not the place to undertake a study of this period, but to anyone reading the documents of the time, there is a profound sense of *déjà vu.* Churchill retained precisely the mind-set with which he had begun World War I, declaring in December 1940 that he "could never be responsible for a naval strategy which excluded the offensive principle and relegated us to keeping open the lines of communications."[16] He planned for a short war and no ships were to be built that could not be completed by the end of 1940; he sought the development of an inshore squadron, separate from and surplus to the main fleet, that would act decisively on the war; and he retained the conviction that a quick solution could be devised to overcome the new technological barriers preventing offensive action by the fleet.

The old threat of mine and torpedo was to be overcome by the bulging of surplus battleships—unfortunately a scarce commodity in 1939. The new threat from the air would be dealt with by the extensive use of deck armor. In the opening months of the war, he sought to have plated armor then being set aside for tanks and new vessels diverted to his inshore squadron. Following the principle enunciated in *The World Crisis,* this thin piece of steel, along with modern anti-aircraft guns and bulging against torpedoes, would allow his inshore squadron to interpose itself between Germany and her Baltic trade with Sweden and seriously constrain the German war machine. Failing this, he believed other technological advancements, such as his infamous "up-weapons" could be devised to allow capital ships to operate within range of land-based aircraft.

With his strong sense of history, Churchill was not unaware of the parallels with 1914 on the eve of 1940:

> There is a certain similarity between the position now, and at the end of the year 1914. The transition from Peace to War has been accomplished. The outer seas, for the moment at any rate, are clear from enemy craft. The lines in France are static. . . . The great question of 1940, as for 1915, is whether and how the Navy can make its surplus force tell in shortening the war. . . . The supreme strategy is to carry the war where we can bring superior forces to bear, and where a decision can be obtained which rules all other theatres.[17]

First among these was the Baltic.

Once again, in a repeat of 1914, Churchill recruited his own offensive team. This time, instead of Fisher and Wilson, it was admiral of the fleet, the Earl of Cork and Orrery. He tackled the issue of the Baltic with considerable conviction and enthusiasm but, to Churchill's disappointment, the earl was again unable to overcome the objections of his naval staff, this time led by his nemesis of 1917, Sir Dudley Pound. Time and circumstance would overtake the plan, but as late as March 1940, Churchill would view the Baltic as the supreme objective of the naval strategy.

These few examples illustrate the degree to which the Baltic represented the "holy grail" of offensive strategies for Churchill. The Dardanelles operation, which was intended to be a temporary divergence from the main theme in 1915, instead became the defining moment in Churchill's time as first lord in World War I. Instead of one operation begetting the other, it led to the certain failure of both.

NOTES

1. Churchill, *The World Crisis*, vol. 3, 470–471. See also Gilbert, *CVIII*, Pt. 2, 946, Letter, Churchill to Balfour, May 25, 1915. The battleship *Majestic* met a similar fate on May 27.

2. Letter, Churchill to Asquith and Balfour, August 25, 1915, Gilbert, *CVIII*. pt 2, 1151–1155.

3. Gilbert, *Winston S. Churchill*. Vol. 3, 1914–1916 (London: Heinemann, 1971), 542.

4. Ibid., 810.

5. Martin Gilbert, *The Challenge of War: 1914–1916* (Egmore, UK: Minerva, 1990), 600–601.

6. This quotation is to be found in Churchill's memorandum entitled *Naval Policy, 1917*, completed on July 17, 1915. This exceptionally long and detailed document can be found in Gilbert, *CVIV, Part 1—January 1917-June 1919*, 76–99.

7. Ibid.

8. Ibid.

9. Ibid.

10. Ibid.

11. DUPO 5/2, found at Churchill College, Cambridge Collection. The following quotations are from Pound's extensive reply to Churchill's memorandum, *Naval Policy, 1917*.

12. Churchill, *The World Crisis*, vol. 2, 465–466.

13. Ibid.

14. Gilbert, *CVIII*, Vol. V, Part 3. Letter, Sir Maurice Hankey to Sir Thomas Inskip, April 19, 1936. The quotation is a paraphrasing by Hanky of discussion he had had with Churchill.

15. Gilbert, *Churchill*, vol. 5, 1922–1939, 1051. Churchill Memorandum, March 27, 1939.

16. Gilbert, *Churchill, War Papers: At the Admiralty*, vol. 1, 697.

17. Gilbert, *Churchill War Papers: At the Admiralty*, vol. 1, 568–569.

APPENDIX A

Churchill's Unsinkable Fleet

THE HUMBER CLASS MONITORS

These three small river monitors ordered by Brazil and built by Vickers under the name *Solimoes, Javary,* and *Madeira* started sea trials in 1913, but due to the Brazilian Navy being unable to afford them, and to stop others buying them and falling into German hands, the Royal Navy purchased them and they were formally commissioned into the Royal Navy on August 3, 1914. These vessels performed good service along the Belgian coast during October and November, but as they were designed as river vessels, they were entirely unsuited to sustained operations in the North Sea and eventually found their way to the Mediterranean. It was probably the work of these vessels along the Belgian coast under Rear Admiral Hood that prompted Churchill's and Fisher's subsequent substantial monitor building program. Perhaps the most notable success of these vessels was the sinking of the German cruiser *Konigsberg* in the Rufuji River delta in July 1915.

Name	*Formerly*	*Commissioned*
HMS *Humber*	*Javary*	August 8, 1914
HMS *Mersey*	*Madeira*	August 8, 1914
HMS *Severn*	*Solimoes*	August 8, 1914

THE 14-INCH MONITORS

The *Abercrombie* class monitors were built using four 14-inch turrets supplied by the Bethlehem Steel Works in the United States. The guns were originally intended for a Greek battleship, *Salamis*. Upon learning of their availability at the beginning of November 1914, Churchill and Fisher immediately decided to use them for a monitor class. Their shallow draft would make them ideal for heavy in-shore bombardment. Given the origin of the guns for these vessels, they were originally named after four civil war heroes. However, neutral United States did not take kindly to the gesture and, just prior to commissioning, they were renamed. The design process was completed with extraordinary rapidity and it showed in the final product. The vessels were difficult to maneuver and much slower than anticipated. Originally destined for the North Sea, they found their first service at the Dardanelles.

	Name	*Formerly*	*Commissioned*
M1	HMS *Abercrombie*	*Admiral Farragut*	May 12, 1915
M2	HMS *Havelock*	*General Grant*	May 23, 1915
M3	HMS *(Lord)Raglan*	*Robert E. Lee*	May 26, 1915
M4	HMS *(Earl)Roberts*	*Stonewall Jackson*	June 3, 1915

THE 12-INCH MONITORS

These monitors were ordered following Churchill's December 11, 1914, minute to Fisher and the secretary of admiralty requesting more vessels for decisive in-shore operations. They were to be built, said Churchill, "for a definite war operation, and we must look to them in default of a general action for giving us the power of forcing a naval decision at latest in the autumn of 1915." Churchill had sought larger guns but the decision was made to disarm four of the now redundant 12-inch *Majestic* class battleships. Most of these monitors found their first deployment bombarding the major ports, now German occupied, along the Belgian coastline. However, this became increasingly problematic as the Germans installed defensive shore batteries of greater and greater range.

	Name	Guns taken from	Commissioned
M5	HMS *Sir John Moore*	*Hannibal*	July 1, 1915
M6	HMS *Lord Clive*	*Magnificent*	July 4, 1915
M7	HMS *General Crauford*	*Magnificent*	August 19, 1915
M8	HMS *Earl of Peterborough*	*Mars*	September 21, 1915
M12	HMS *Thomas Picton*	*Victorious*	October 27, 1915
M11	HMS *Prince Eugene*	*Victorious*	June 22, 1915
M10	HMS *Prince Rupert*	*Hannibal*	August 21, 1915
M9	HMS *General Wolfe*	*Mars*	October 31, 1915

THE 15-INCH MONITORS

The first two of these vessels quickly followed the eight 12-inch monitors and were born of a mutual need: Churchill wanted more big-gunned monitors and Fisher wished to convert two planned eight-gunned battleships into six-gunned battlescruisers (*Renown* and *Repulse*) ostensibly, he argued, for operations in the Baltic. Thus were to be made available four 15-inch guns for *Marshal Ney* and *Marshal Soult.* However, while the guns were immediately available, the turrets were not. To ensure the Monitors could be completed about the middle of 1915, the turrets were supplied from battleships of the 1913 *Ramillies* class. In May 1915, with the challenges of the Dardanelles now abundantly clear, a decision was made to build two more 15-inch monitors. These were not completed until 1916. They were a considerable improvement on the first two 15-inch vessels. *Ney* had proven such a disappointment that her turret was given to *Terror*, and in its stead, Ney received 9.2-inch guns from the old cruiser, *Terrible*. The greater part of the service of *Soult*, *Terror*, and *Erebus* was in bombardment duties along the Belgian coast, their considerable range being of great assistance to their smaller cousins.

M13	HMS *Marshal Ney*	Completed August 31, 1915	HMS *Terror*	Completed August 6, 1916
M14	HMS *Marshal Soult*	Completed November 2, 1915	HMS *Erebus*	Completed September 2, 1916

THE SMALL MONITORS

At the War Council Meetings of January 28, 1915, it was decided to order 12 gunboats/monitors for operations on the Danube. It was originally proposed they be built in sections, transported to Salonica, and then sent on to Serbia by rail. In February, 14 9.2-inch monitors were ordered using the guns taken from old *Edgar* class cruisers. In March, five 6-inch monitors using excess secondary armament from the new *Queen Elizabeth* class battleships were ordered (in the end most received new 6-inch guns direct from the factory). Following on from the numbering system given to the first 14 monitors, these vessels were numbered M15 to M33 but, unlike the larger monitors, the numbers were retained throughout their service. All ultimately found service in the Mediterranean, although none were used on the Danube.

Source: Buxton, *Big Gun Monitors*, 2008.

APPENDIX B

Dardanelles Defenses

In addition to the formidable array of guns listed below, in March 1915, the straits of the Dardanelles were protected by 10 rows of mines (11 after the line laid down by the *Nusret* on March 8) three 18-inch torpedo tubes, an antisubmarine net, and numerous search lights—some stationary, some mobile—which were virtually impossible to extinguish and which made the nighttime mine-sweeping almost as dangerous as that undertaken during the day.

(Only the major gun emplacements are identified in the map of the Dardanelles Defenses.)

Outer Defences	
Cape Helles	2–24 cm. L/35 Krupp (9.4 in.)
Tekke Burnu	4–12 cm. Howitzers (4.7 in.)
Sedd el Bahr	2–28 cm. L/22 Krupp (11 in.)
	2–26 cm. L/22 Krupp (10.2 in.)
	2–24 cm. L/22 Krupp (9.4 in.)
	4–8.8 cm. quick-firers (3.4 in.)
Orkanie	2–24 cm. L/22 Krupp (9.4 in.)
Kum Kale	2–28 cm. L/22 Krupp (11 in.)
	2–26 cm. L/22 Krupp (10.2 in.)
	2–24 cm. L/22 Krupp (9.4 in.)
	1–21 cm. L/22 Krupp (8.2 in.)
	1–15 cm. L/22 Krupp (5.9 in.) 1/15 cm. L/40 Krupp (5.9 in.)
Intermediate Defences—European Side	
Hanafar	4–12 cm. Seige (4.7 in.)
Kum burnu	6–4.7 cm. Howitzers (1.8 in.)
	4–12 cm. Seige (4.7 in.)
Muii-Zaffer	4–7.5 cm. L/30 Q.F. (2.9 in.)
Suandere (N)	3–10.5 cm. L/45 Q.F. Naval (3.4 in.)
Suandere (W)	4–12 cm. Siege Guns (4.7 in.)
Suandere	4–8.8 cm. L/30 Q.F. Naval (3.4 in.)
	4–7.5 cm. Field Guns (2.9 in.)
Messudieh	3–15 cm. L/45 Q.F. (5.9 in.)
M15 S. side of Suandere	6–15 cm. Mortars (5.9 in.)
M14 N. of Tenkir Dere	4–12 cm. Howitzers (4.7 in.)
M13 S. of Tenkir Dere	6–21 cm. Howitzers (8.2 in.)
M12 Chomak Tenkir Dere	6–15 cm. Howitzers (5.9 in.)
M10 Chomak Dere	4–21 cm. Howitzers (8.2 in.)
M3 Kureves Dere	6–15 cm. Howitzers (5.9 in.)
Intermediate Defences—Asiatic Side	
Dardanos	2–15 cm. L/40 Q.F. (5.9 in.)
	3–15 cm. L/40 Q.F. (5.9 in.)
Kephez Point	3–7.5 cm. L/40 Q.F. Guns (2.9 in.)
	3–5.7 cm. L/40 Q.F. Guns (2.2 in.)
Kephez Light House	4–8.7 cm. Field Guns (3.3 in.)
Messudieh	4–7.5 cm. Q.F. Vickers Guns (2.9 in.)

Ak Tepe	6–5.7 cm. Q.F. Vickers Guns (2.2 in.)
	4–7.5 cm. Field Guns (2.9 in.)
Djevad Pasha	3–15 cm. L/26 Krupp (5.9 in.)
Karantina	4–21 cm. Mortars (8.2 in.)
Karantina	4–15 cm. Howitzers (5.9 in.)
Chamlik	6–15 cm. Howitzers (5.9 in.)
Chamlik	4–21 cm. Howitzers (8.2 in.)
Koja Dere	4–15 cm. Howitzers (5.9 in.)
In Tepe	4–15 cm. Howitzers (5.9 in.)
Inner Defences—European Side	
Derma Burnu	6–24 cm. L/22 Krupp (9.4 in.)
Namazieh	1–28 cm. L/22 Krupp (11 in.)
	1–26 cm. L/22 Krupp (10.2 in.)
	9–24 cm. L/22 Krupp (9.4 in.)
	2–24 cm. L/35 Krupp (9.4 in.)
	3–21 cm. L/22 Krupp (8.2 in.)
	3–15 cm. Howitzers (5.9 in.)
Hamidieh II	2–35 L/35 Krupp (14 in.)
Rumili Medjidieh	2–28 cm. L/22 Krupp (11 in.)
	4–24 cm. L/35 Krupp (9.4 in.)
Yildiz	6–15 cm. L/26 Krupps (5.9 in.)
Inner Defences—Asiatic Side	
Nagara	2–26 cm. L/22 Krupp (10.2 in.)
	5–24 cm. L/22 Krupp (9.4 in.)
	5–15 cm. L/26 Krupp (5.9 in.)
Anodolu	3–28 cm. L/22 Krupp (11 in.)
Medjidieh	4–26 cm. L/22 Krupp (10.2 in.)
	2–24 cm. L/22 Krupp (9.4 in.)
	2–21 cm. L/22 Krupp (8.2 in.)
	3–15 cm. L/22 Krupp (5.9 in.)
Medjidieh Avan	6–21 cm. Mortars (8.2 in.)
Chemenkik	1–35.5 cm. L/35 Krupp (14 in.)
	1–35.5 cm. L/22 Krupp (14 in.)
	1–24 cm. L/35 Krupp (9.4 in.)
	1–21 cm. L/35 Krupp (8.2 in.)
	4–15 cm. Howitzers (5.9 in.)
Hamidieh I	2–35.5 cm. L/35 Krupp (14 in.)
	7–24 cm. L/35 Krupp (9.4 in.)

APPENDIX C

Biographical Notes

Asquith, Herbert Henry (1852–1928). Liberal Member of Parliament, 1886–1918, 1920–1924; Home Secretary, 1892–1895; Chancellor of the Exchequer, 1905–1908; Secretary of State for War, March 30–August 5, 1914; Prime Minister, 1908–1916.

Augagneur, Victor (1855–1931). French Minister of Marine, 1914–1918.

Balfour, Sir Arthur James (later the Earl of Balfour) (1848–1930). Conservative Member of Parliament, 1874–1885, 1885–1906, 1906–1922; First Lord of the Treasury, 1891–1892, 1895–1902; Prime Minister, 1902–1905; First Lord of the Admiralty, 1915–1916; Foreign Secretary, 1916–1919.

Ballard, Rear Admiral George Alexander (1862–1948). Assistant Director of the Operations Division, Admiralty 1911–1914; Admiral of Patrols, East Coast, 1914–1916; Senior Naval Officer, Malta, 1916–1918.

Bartolome, Charles Martin de (1871–1941). Entered Navy, 1885; Commodore, 1914; Churchill's Naval Secretary, October 1914–May 1915; Third Sea Lord, 1918–1919; Knighted, 1919; Rear Admiral, 1919.

Battenberg, Prince Louis Alexander of (later Admiral of the Fleet, Marquess of Milfordhaven) (1854–1921). Director of Naval Intelligence, 1903–1905; commanded 2nd Cruiser Squadron, 1905–1907; Second in Command, Mediterranean, 1908; Commander in Chief, Atlantic Fleet, 1910; Second Sea Lord, 1911; First Sea Lord, 1912–1914.

Bayly, Vice Admiral, Sir Lewis (1857–1938). Commander of the 3rd Battle Squadron, 1913–1914; 1st Battle Squadron, 1914–1915.

Beatty, Admiral David (1871–1936). Naval Secretary to the First Lord, 1912; Commander, 1st Battle Cruiser Squadron from 1914; Commander in Chief, Grand Fleet, 1916–1919; First Sea Lord, 1919–1927.

Bertie, Sir Francis Leveson (1844–1919). British Ambassador at Rome, 1903–1904; British Ambassador at Paris, 1905–1918; First Baron, 1915; First Viscount, 1918.

Buchanan, Sir George William (1854–1924) British Diplomat. 1908–1910 as minister in The Hague, The Netherlands; 1910 appointed British Ambassador in Russia asnd remained in this position until the Russian Revolution in 1917.

Burney, Sir Cecil (1858–1929). Promoted to Rear Admiral of the Plymouth Division of Home Fleet, 1907. Commanded 5th Cruiser Squadron, 1911; commanded Atlantic Fleet as Acting Vice Admiral, 1911; transferred to the 3rd Battle Squadron and confirmed as Vice Admiral, 1912; took command of Second and Third Fleet (subsequently Channel Fleet), 1913; given command of 1st Battle Squadron, December 1914; commanded this squadron at Battle of Jutland, 1916; appointed Second Sea Lord, November 1916; appointed Commander in Chief, Coast of Scotland at Rosyth; commander in chief, Portsmouth, 1919; promoted to Admiral of the Fleet, November 1920; created Baron, 1921.

Buxton, Noel Edward (1869–1948). Liberal Member of Parliament, 1905–1906, 1910–1918; Labor Member of Parliament, 1922–1930; co-founder, the Balkan Committee, 1903.

Callwell, Major General Charles Edward (1859–1928). Intelligence Branch, War Office, 1887–1902; retired from Army in 1909; recalled to Active List, 1914; Director of Military Operations and Intelligence, 1914–1916.

Carden, Vice Admiral Sackville Hamilton (1857–1930). Admiral Superintendent, Malta, 1912–1914; Commander of the Anglo-French Squadrons, Eastern Mediterranean, September 20, 1914–March 16, 1915.

Churchill, Winston Spencer (1874–1965). President, Board of Trade, 1908–1910; Home Secretary, 1910–1911; First Lord of the Admiralty, 1911–1915.

Corbett, Sir Julian (1854–1922). Naval historian; regularly consulted by John Arbuthnot Fisher during his second period as First Sea Lord.

Elliot, Sir Francis Edmund Hugh (1851–1940). British agent and Consul General in Bulgaria, 1895–1903; Minister at Athens, 1903–1917.

Esher, Second Viscount Reginald Baliot Brett (1852–1930). Liberal Member of Parliament, 1880–1885; permanent member of the Committee of Imperial Defence, 1905–1908.

Fisher, John Arbuthnot (1841–1920). Entered Navy, 1854; First Sea Lord, 1904–1910, Admiral of the Fleet, 1905; created Baron, 1909; retired, 1911; head of Royal Commission on Fuel and Englines, 1912–1914; reappointed First Sea Lord, October 1914; resigned, May 1915; Chairman of the Admiralty Inventions Board, 1915–1916.

Fitzgerald, Oswald Arthur Gerald (1875–1916). Lieutenant, Indian Army, 1897; Member of Lord Kitchener's staff, 1904–1916; Lieutenant Colonel, August, 1914; Personal Military Secretary to Kitchener, 1914–1916; drowned with Kitchener in HMS *Hampshire*.

French, Field Marshal, Sir John Denton Pinkstone (1852–1925). Chief of the Imperial General Staff, 1912–1914; Commander in Chief of the British Expeditionary Force, 1914–1915.

Gennadius, M. J. (1844–1932). Greek Minister to London, 1910–1918.

Grey, Sir Edward (1862–1933). Secretary of State for Foreign Affairs, December 11, 1905–December 11, 1916; Viscount, 1916.

Guepratte, Contre Admiral (later Vice Admiral) Emile Paul Aimable (1856–1939). Commanded Division de Complement, August 1914; Escadres de Dardanelles, September 1914–May 1915.

Haldane, Richard Burdon (1856–1928). Liberal Member of Parliament, 1885–1911; Secretary of State for War, 1905–1912; First Viscount, 1911; Lord Chancellor, 1912–1915.

Hamilton, General Ian Standish Monteith (1853–1947). Career soldier; selected by Kitchener to Command the Mediterranean Expeditionary Force, March 1915.

Hankey, Maurice Pascal Alers (later First Baron) Hankey (1877–1963). Entered Royal Marine Artillery, 1895; Captain, 1899; Naval Intelligence Department, 1902–1907; Assistant Secretary of the Committee of Imperial Defence, 1908–1912; Secretary, Committee of Imperial Defence, 1912–1938; Secretary of the War Council, November 1914–May 1915; Secretary of the Dardanelles Committee, May–November, 1915; Secretary of Cabinet War Committee, December 1915–December 1916; Secretary of the War Cabinet, 1916–1918; Lieutenant Colonel, Royal Marines, 1914.

Hobhouse, Sir Charles Edward Henry (1862–1941) British Liberal Politician. Member of the Liberal Cabinet of H. Asquith between 1911–1915.

Hood, Horace Lambert Alexander (1870–1916). Entered Navy, 1883; Rear Admiral, 1913; Churchill's Naval Secretary, 1914; commanded Dover Patrol, 1914–1915; commanded 3rd Battle Cruiser Squadron, 1915–1916; killed at Battle of Jutland.

Jackson, Admiral, Sir Henry Bradwardine (1855–1929). Commander Royal Naval War College, 1911–1913; Chief of Admiralty War Staff, 1913, August 1914–May 1915 special duties; First Sea Lord, May 1915–December 1916; President, RN College, Greenwich, 1916–1919.

Jellicoe, Admiral (later Admiral of the Fleet), Sir John Rushworth (1859–1935). Second Sea Lord, 1912–1914; Commander in Chief, Grand Fleet, 1914–1916; First Sea Lord, 1916–1917; created Viscount, 1918; First Earl, 1925.

Joffre, General Joseph Jacques Casaire (1852–1931). Chief of the French General Staff, 1911; Commander in Chief, French Armies in north and northeast, 1914; Commander in Chief of French Armies in the west, 1915–1916.

Kerr, Rear Admiral (later Admiral) Mark Edward Frederic (1864–1944). Naval Attache, Italy, Austria, Turkey, and Greece, 1903–1904; Head of the British Naval Mission to Greece and Commander in Chief of the Greek Navy, 1913–1915; Commander in Chief of the British Squadrons in the Adriatic, 1916–1917; Major General, Royal Air Force, 1918; Deputy Chief of the Air Staff, 1918.

Kitchener, General, Sir Herbert (later Earl Kitchener) (1850–1916). Sirdar of the Egyptian Army, 1892–1889; Commander in Chief, India, 1902–1909; Agent and Consul General at Cairo, 1911–1914; Secretary of State for War, 1914–1916.

Lambert, Captain (later Admiral), Sir Cecil Foley (1864–1928). Fourth Sea Lord, 1913–1916; commanded 2nd Light Cruiser Squadron, 1916–1918; commanded British Aegean Squadron, 1918.

Lloyd George, David (1863–1945). Liberal Member of Parliament, 1890–1931; Chancellor of the Exchequer, 1908–1915; Minister of Munitions, 1915–1916; Prime Minster and First Lord of the Treasury, 1916–1922.

Limpus, Rear Admiral (later Admiral), Sir Arthur (1862–1931). British Naval Adviser to the Turkish Government, 1912–1914; Admiral Superintendent, Malta, 1914–1916.

McKenna, Reginald (1863–1943). Liberal Member of Parliament, 1895–1918; First Lord of the Admiralty, 1908–1911; Home Secretary, 1911–1915; Chancellor of the Exchequer, 1915–1916.

Millerand, Alexandre (1859–1943). French Minister of War, January 1912–January 1913, January 1914–October, 1915.

Murray, General, Sir James Wolfe (sometimes **Wolfe Murray**) (1853–1919). Chief of the Imperial General Staff, October 1914–September, 1915.

Nicholson, Field Marshal, Sir William Gustavus (1845–1918). Chief of the Imperial General Staff, 1908–1912; First Baron, 1912.

Nicolaevitch, Nicholas (Grand Duke) (1856–1929). Uncle of Tsar Nicholas II; Supreme Commander of the Russian Armies, 1914–1915; Viceroy of the Caucasus, 1916–1917; died in exile.

Oliver, Vice Admiral (later Admiral of the Fleet), Sir Henry Francis (1865–1965). Naval Assistant to Sir John Fisher, 1908–1910; Director of Naval Intelligence, 1913–1914; Chief of Admiralty War Staff, November 1914–1917.

Ottley, Rear Admiral, Sir Charles Langley (1858–1932). Director of Naval Intelligence, 1905–1912; Director of Armstrong, Whitworth and Company, 1912–1917.

Richmond, William Herbert (1871–1946). Entered Navy, 1885; Captain, 1908; commanded HMS *Dreadnought*, 1909–1911; Assistant Director Operations Division, Admiralty 1913–1915; British Liaison Officer, Italian Fleet,

1915; commanded HMS *Commonwealth*, 1915–1916; commanded HMS *Conquerer*, 1917; commanded HMS *Erin*, 1918.

Sazanov, M. Sergei Dmitrievich (1866–1927). Councilor of Russian Embassy at London, 1904–1906; Agent to the Vatican, 1906–1909; Russian Minister for Foreign Affairs, 1910–1916.

Schwab, Charles M. (1862–1939). Steel magnate; Schwab took over the management of the Bethlehem Steel Works in Pennsylvania building it into the largest independent steel works in the world and the second-largest steel works in the United States, 1903.

Souchon, Admiral Wilhelm, (1864–1946), German and Ottoman Admiral during the first world war. His two ships, *Goeben* and *Breslau* eluded the British fleet to arrive at Constantinople on August 12, 1915. Soon, thereafter, his two vessels were transferred to the Ottoman Fleet.

Stanley, Venetia (1887–1948). A cousin of Clementine Churchill and Herbert Asquith's confidante and love interest; Asquith's correspondence with Stanley has provided historians with a rich resource.

Sturdee, Rear Admiral, Sir Frederick Charles Doveton (1859–1925). Assistant Director of Naval Intelligence, 1900–1902; Rear Admiral, Home Fleet, 1909–1910; Chief of the Admiralty War Staff, 1914; Commander in Chief of the 4th Battle Squadron, 1915–1918; Victor of the Falkland Island Battle, 1914.

Tudor, Rear Admiral, C. T. Frederick (1863–1946). Third Sea Lord, August 1914–1917.

Tyrrell, Sir William George (1866–1947). Senior Clerk in the British Foreign Office private secretary to the Permanent Under-Secretary for Foreign Affairs Thomas Sanderson from 1896 to 1903; secretary to the Committee of Imperial Defence from 1903 to 1904; Private Secretary to Sir Edward Grey, 1907–1915.

Wilson, Admiral, Sir Arthur Knyvet (1842–1921). Commander in Chief of the Home Fleet and Channel Fleets, 1901–1907; First Sea Lord, 1910–1911; employed at the Admiralty, initially by Churchill, in an unofficial capacity throughout the war.

Wilson, Brigadier (later Lieutenant) General, Sir Henry Hughes (1864–1922). Director of Military Operations, 1910–1914; Chief Liaison Offer with the French Army, 1915.

References

PRIMARY SOURCES

Churchill, Randolph S. 1969. *Winston S. Churchill. Volume* II, Parts 1, 2. London: Heinemann.

Churchill, Winston. Chartwell Papers. Churchill College, Cambridge.

George, David Lloyd. Lloyd George Papers. National Australian Library, Reel I AJCP MII24.

Gilbert, Martin. 1972. *Winston S. Churchill Companion Volume II Part 3(Heinemann 1969) and Companion Volume III.* Parts 1, 2. London: Heinemann.

Halpern, Paul G., ed. 1984. De Robeck and the Dardanelles campaign. In *The Naval Miscellany 5,* Vol. 125, ed. N. A. M. Rodger. Cheltenham, UK: Navy Records Society.

Papers of Field Marshal Sir William (Robert) Robertson. King's College, London. GB99 KCLMA Robertson W R.

Papers of Field Marshal Lord William Birdwood. Private Records Collection. Research Center, Australian War Memorial. 3DRL/3376.

United Kingdom. Public Records Office. CAB 2.2. 2.3.

———. CAB 19.

———. CAB 29.

———. CAB 31.

———. CAB 42.

———. CAB 63.

SECONDARY SOURCES: ARTICLES

Andrew, Christopher. 1988. Churchill and intelligence. *Intelligence and National Security* 3: 181–193.

Ben-Moshe, Tuvia. March 1989. Churchill's strategic conception during the First World War. *The Journal of Strategic Studies* 12: 5–21.

Dewar, A. C. 1923. Winston Churchill at the Admiralty. *Naval Review* 2.

Ekstein, M. March 1977. Russia, Constantinople and the Straits, 1914–1915. In *British foreign policy under Sir Edward Grey*, ed. F. H. Hinsley. Cambridge: Cambridge University Press.

Erikson, Edward J. September 2001. One more push: Forcing the Dardanelles in March 1915. *Journal of Strategic Studies* 24: 158–176.

———. October 2001. Strength against weakness: Ottoman military effectiveness at Gallipoli, 1915. *Journal of Military History* 65: 981.

French, David. 1983. The origins of the Dardanelles campaign reconsidered. *History* 68.

Gooch, John. 1977. Soldiers, strategy, and war aims in Britain 1914–1918. In *War aims and strategic policy in the Great War*, ed. Barry Dennis Hunt and Adrian W. Preston. London: Croom Helm.

Howard, Michael. 1994. Churchill and the First World War. In *Churchill*, ed. Robert Blake and William Roger Louis. London: Oxford University Press.

Kerner, R. J. 1929. Russia, the straits and constantinople, 1914–1915. *Journal of Modern History* 1.

MacFie, A. L. January 1983. The straits question in the First World War, 1914–1918. *Middle Eastern Studies* 19: 43–74.

Philpott, W. J. September 1993. Kitchener and the 29th Division: A study in Anglo-French strategic relations, 1914–1915. *The Journal of Strategic Studies*: 375–407.

Reguer, Sara. December 1994. Churchill's role in the Dardanelles campaign. *The British Army Review* 108: 71.

Renzi, W. A. 1970. Great Britain, Russia and the Straits, 1914–1915. *Journal of Modern History* 42.

Salmon, Patrick. 1993. 'Between the sea power and the land power:' Scandinavia and the coming of the First World War. *Transactions of the Royal Historical Society* 6: 23–49.

Sweet, D. W. September 1970. The Baltic in British Diplomacy before the First World War. *The Historical Journal* 13: 451–490.

Wilson, Keith. September 1972. The Agadir crisis, the Mansion House speech, and the double-edgedness of agreements. *The Historical Journal* 15: 513–532.

Wilson, Steve L. 2002. The Naval assault on Gallipoli: Going for broke or just broken. Master's thesis, United States Marine Corp Command and Staff College.

SECONDARY SOURCES: BOOKS

Abbott, G. F. 1916. *Turkey, Greece and the great powers: A study in friendship and hate*. London: R. Scott.

Andrew, Christopher, and Noakes, Jeremy, eds. 1987. *Intelligence and international relations 1900–1945*. Exeter: University of Exeter Press.

Arthur, George. 1920. *Life of Lord Kitchener*. Vol. 3. London: Macmillan.

———. 1932. *General Sir John Maxwell*. London: John Murray.

Ashmead-Bartlett, E. 1928. *The Uncensored Dardanelles*. London: Hutchinson.

Aspinall-Oglander, C. F. 1929. *History of the Great War: Military operations, Gallipoli*. Vols. 1, 2. London: Heinemann.

Bacon, Reginald. 1929. *The life of Lord Fisher of Kilverstone*. 2 vols. London: Hodder and Stoughton.

Bayly, Lewis. 1939. *Pull together*. Edinburgh: Chambers Harrap.

Beesly, Patrick. 1982. *Room 40: British Naval Intelligence 1914–1918*. London: Hamish Hamilton.

Ben-Moshe, Tuvia. 1992. *Churchill: Strategy and history*. Boulder, CO: Lynne Rienner.

Blake, Robert, and William Roger Louis, eds. 1994. *Churchill*. London: Oxford University Press.

Bonham-Carter, Violet. 1965. *Winston Churchill as I knew him*. London: Eyre & Spottiswoode and Collins.

Broad, Lewis. 1951. *Winston Churchill: 1864–1951*. London: Hutchison and Co.

Brock, Michael, and Eleanor Brock, eds., 1982. *H.H. Asquith's letters to Venetia Stanley*. London: Oxford University Press.

Buxton, Ian. 2008. *Big gun monitors: Design, construction, and operation 1914–1945*. Annapolis, MD: Naval Institute Press.

———. 1978. *Big gun monitors: Design, construction, and operation 1914–1951*. World Ship Society and Trident Books.

Callwell, Charles E. 1919. *The Dardanelles: Campaigns and their lessons*. London: Constable and Company, Ltd.

Cassar, George H. 1971. *The French and the Dardanelles*. London: George Allen and Unwin.

———. 1977. *Kitchener: Architect of victory*. London: W. Kimber.

———. 1985. *The tragedy of Sir John French*. Cranbury, NJ: Associated University Presses.

———. 1994. *Asquith as war leader*. London: Hambledon Press.

Chasseaud, Peter, and Peter Doyle. 2005. *Grasping Gallipoli: Terrain, maps and failure at the Dardanelles, 1915*. Staplehurst, UK: Spellmont.

Churchill, Winston S. 1923. *The world crisis: 1911–1914*. 2 vols. London: Odhams Press Ltd.

Corbett, Julian. 1994. *Maritime operations in the Russo-Japanese War 1904–1905*. Vol. 1. Annapolis, MD: Naval Institute Press, Annapolis, MD/Newport, RI: Naval War College Press.

Cowley, Robert, ed. 2003. *The Great War: Perspectives on the First World War*. New York: Random House.

Dewar, K. G. B. 1939. *The Navy from within*. London: Gollancz.

Dutton, David. 1998. *The politics of diplomacy Britain and France in the Balkans in the First World War*. London: Tauris Academic Studies.

Edwards, David. 1977. *Inside Asquith's Cabinet: From the diaries of Charles Hobhouse*. London: John Murray.

Ellison, Gerald. 1926. *The perils of amateur strategy: As exemplified by the attack on the Dardanelles fortress in 1915*. London: Longmans, Green and Co. Ltd.

Erikson, Edward J. 2001. *Ordered to die: A history of the Ottoman Army in the First World War*. Westport, CT: Greenwood Press.

Esher, Reginald Brett. 1922. *The tragedy of Lord Kitchener*. London: John Murray.

———. 1934–38. *Journals and Letters*. ed. Oliver Sylvain Baliol Brett Esher and Maurice V. Brett. Vols. 1–4. London: Nicholson and Watson.

Fisher, John Arbuthot. 1919. *Memories*. London: Hodder and Stoughton.

Frame, Tom. 2000. *The shores of Gallipoli*. London: Hale Press.

Fraser, Peter. 1973. *Lord Esher: A political biography*. London: Hart-Davis, MacGibbon.

French, David. 1986. *British strategy and war aims 1914–1916*. London: Allen and Unwin.

French, Gerald. 1937. *Some war diaries, addresses, & correspondence of Field Marshal The Right Honourable The Earl of Ypres Sir John French*. London: Herbert Jenkins.

———. 1931. *The life of Field Marshal Sir John French First Earl of Ypres*. London: Cassell and Company.

French, John. 1919. *1914*. London: Constable.

Gilbert, Martin. 1971–1983. *Winston S. Churchill*. Vols. 3–6. London: Heinemann.

———. 1990. *The challenge of war: 1914–1916*. Egmore, UK: Minerva.

———. 1992. *Churchill: A life*. New York: Henry Hold and Company.

Gooch, John. 1974. *The plans of war: The general staff and British military strategy c1900–1916*. London: Routledge and Kegan Paul.

Gottlieb, W. W. 1957. *Studies in secret diplomacy during the First World War*. London: Allen and Unwin.

Gretton, Peter. 1968. *Former Naval Person: Winston Churchill and the Royal Navy*. London: Cassel.

Grey, Edward. 1925. *Twenty Five Years, 1892–1916*. Vols. 1, 2. London: Hodder and Stoughton.

Grigg, John. 1985. *Lloyd George: From Peace to War 1914–1916*. London.

Guinn, Paul. 1965. *British Strategy and Politics, 1914–1918*. Oxford: Oxford University Press.

Halpern, Paul G., ed. 1972. The Keyes Papers: 1914–1918. Vol. 1. (Cheltenham, UK: Navy Records Society.

———. 1987. *The Naval War in the Mediterranean 1914–1918*. London: Allen and Unwin.

Hamilton, Ian. 1920. *Gallipoli Diary*. Vol. 1. New York: George Doran/Edward Arnold.

Hankey, Maurice. 1961. *The Supreme Command, 1914–1918. Vols.* 1, 2. London: Allen and Unwin.

Hickey, Michael. 1995. *Gallipoli*. London: John Murray.

Higgins, Trumbull. 1963. *Winston Churchill and the Dardanelles*. London: Heinemann.

Hough, Richard. 1985. *Former naval person: Churchill and the wars at sea*. London: Weidenfeld and Nicolson.

Howard, Michael. 1972. *The continental commitment*. London: Temple Smith.

Hoyt, Edwin P. 1976. *Disaster at the Dardanelles, 1915*. London: Barker.

Institute for Balkan Studies, and King's College of London. 1985. *Greece and Great Britain during World War 1: First symposium organized in Thessaloniki (December 15–17, 1983)*. Thessaloniki: Institute for Balkan Studies.

James, Robert Rhodes. 1965. *Gallipoli*. London: B. T. Batsford.

———. 1970. *Churchill: A study in failure, 1900–1939*. London: George Weidenfeld and Nicolson.

———. 1974. *Winston S. Churchill: His complete speeches Vol. 2 1908–1913*. New York: Chelsea House Publishers.

James, William. 1956. *A great seaman: The life of Admiral of the Fleet, Sir Henry Oliver*. London: H. F. & G. Witherby.

Jerrold, Douglas. 1923. *The Royal Naval Division*. London: Hutchison and Co.

Kamps, Charles Tustin. 1982. *Peripheral campaigns and the principles of war: The British experience 1914–1918*. Manhattan, KS: MA/AH Publishing.

Kemp, P. K., ed. 1964. *The papers of Admiral Sir John Fisher*. Vol. 2. Cheltenham, UK: Navy Records Society.

Keyes, Roger. 1934. *Naval Memoirs*. 2 vols. London, Thornton-Butterworth.

Laffin, John. 1985. *Damn the Dardanelles: The agony of Gallipoli*. South Melbourne: Sun Papermac.

Leon, George B. 1974. *Greece and the Great Powers 1914–1917*. Thessalonika: Institute for Balkan Studies.

Lloyd George, David. 1933. *War memoirs of David Lloyd George*. London: Ivor Nicholson and Watson.

Mackay, Ruddock F. 1973. *Fisher of Kilverstone*. Oxford: Clarendon Press.

Magnus, Philip. 1958. *Kitchener: Portrait of an imperialist*. London: John Murray.

Marder, Arthur J. 1952. *Portrait of an admiral: The life and papers of Sir Herbert Richmond*. London: Jonathon Cape.

———, ed. 1959. *Fear God and Dreadnought: The correspondence of Admiral of the Fleet, Lord Fisher of Kilverstone*. London: Jonathon Cape.

———. 1961. *From the Dreadnought to Scapa Flow*. Vols. 1–3. London: Oxford University Press.

———. 1974. *From the Dardanelles to Oran*: *Studies of the Royal Navy in war and peace 1915–1940*. London: Oxford University Press.

Miller, Geoffrey. 1997. *Straits: British policy towards the Ottoman Empire and the origins of the Dardanelles campaign*. Hull, UK: University of Hull Press.

———. 1999. *The Millstone: British Naval policy in the Mediterranean, 1900–1914,* Hull, UK: The University of Hull Press.

Moorehead, Alan. 1956. *Gallipoli.* London: Hamish Hamilton.

Morgan, Ted. 1983. *Churchill: 1874–1915.* London: Jonathon Cape.

Munch-Peterson, Thomas. 1981. *The strategy of phoney war. Britain, Sweden, and the iron ore question 1939–1940.* Stockholm: Militarhistoriska Forlaget.

Padfield, Peter. 1966. *Aim straight: A biography of Sir Percy Scott.* London: Hodder and Stoughton.

———. 1974. *The great naval race: Anglo-German naval rivalry 1900–1914.* London: Hart-Davis, MacGibbon.

———. 2000. *Battleship.* Edinburgh: Birlinn Press.

Patterson, A. Temple, ed. 1966. *The Jellicoe Papers.* Vol. 1. Cheltenham, UK: Navy Records Society.

Penn, Geoffrey. 1999. *Fisher, Churchill, and the Dardanelles.* South Yorkshire: Leo Cooper.

Pollock, John. 1998. *Kitchener: architect of victory, artisan of peace.* New York: Carroll and Graf Publishers.

Prior, Robin. 1979. *Churchill's 'World Crisis' as history.* Vol. 2. Bound thesis, University of Adelaide.

Rose, Norman. 1994. *Churchill: An unruly life.* New York: Simon and Schuster.

Roskill, Stephen. 1977. *Churchill and the Admirals.* London: Collins.

Rutherford, Ward. 1992. *The Tsar's war 1914–1917.* Cambridge: Ian Faulkner.

Scott, Percy. 1919. *Fifty years in the Royal Navy.* London: John Murray.

Siney, Marion C. 1973. *The Allied blockade of Germany 1914–1916.* Westport, CT: Greenwood Press.

Stafford, David. 1991. *Churchill and Secret Service.* New York: Overlook Press.

Steel, Nigel, and Peter Hart. 1995. *Defeat at Gallipoli.* South Melbourne: Sun Papermac.

Sumida, John Tetsuro. 1989. *In defence of naval supremacy: Finance, technology, and British naval policy 1889–1914.* Boston, MA: Unwin Hyman.

Theodoulou, Christos. 1971. *Greece and the Entente August 1st 1914–September 25, 1916.* Thessalonika: Institute for Balkan Studies.

United Kingdom. House of Commons. 1917. *Dardanelles Commission: First report and supplement.* London: H.M. Stationery Office.

———. 1917. *Dardanelles Commission: The Final Report.* Parts 1, 2. London: H.M. Stationery Office.

Van der Vat, Dan. 2009. *The Dardanelles disaster: Winston Churchill's greatest defeat.* London/New York: Duckworth Overlook.

Wallin, Jeffrey. D. 1981. *By ships alone: Churchill and the Dardanelles.* Durham: Carolina Academic Press.

Wester-Wemyss, Rosslyn Erskine. 1924. *The Navy in the Dardanelles campaign.* London: Hodder and Stoughton.

OFFICIAL HISTORIES, DOCUMENTS, AND CORRESPONDENCE

Corbett, Julian S. 1921. *History of the Great War: Naval Operations. Vol.* 2. London: Longmans, Green and Co.

United Kingdom. Foreign Office. 1961. *Official History of the War: The Blockade of the Central Empires 1914–1918.* London: H. M. Stationery Office.

Index

About the Author

GRAHAM T. CLEWS, a secondary school teacher in Canberra, Australia, has had a life-long interest in military history. *Churchill's Dilemma* grew out of a master's degree in history thesis, which was completed under the supervision of Professor Robin Prior at the Australian Defence Force Academy, Canberra. He is now conducting background research for a doctorate on Churchill as First Lord of the Admiralty in World War II.